Learning for Life in the 21st Century

Learning for Life in the 21st Century

Sociocultural Perspectives on the Future of Education

Edited by Gordon Wells and Guy Claxton

Blackwell
Publishing

© 2002 by Blackwell Publishers Ltd
a Blackwell Publishing company
except for editorial arrangement and introduction © 2002 by Gordon Wells and
Guy Claxton

Editorial Offices:
108 Cowley Road, Oxford OX4 1JF, UK
  Tel: +44 (0)1865 791100
350 Main Street, Malden, MA 02148-5018, USA
  Tel: +1 781 388 8250

First published 2002 by the Blackwell Publishers Ltd

Library of Congress Cataloging-in-Publication Data

Learning for life in the 21st century : sociocultural perspectives on
the future of education / edited by Gordon Wells and Guy Claxton.
       p. cm.
Includes bibliographical references and index.
    ISBN 0–631–22330–4 (alk. paper) — ISBN 0–631–22331–2 (pbk.: alk. paper)
    1. Educational anthropology.   2. Learning.   3. Education—Aims and
objectives.   I. Wells, Gordon, 1935–   II. Claxton, Guy.
    LB45.L418 2002
    306.43—dc21
                                                                    2001003978

A catalogue record for this title is available from the British Library.

Set in 10.5 on 13pt Syntax
by Graphicraft Ltd, Hong Kong

For further information on
Blackwell Publishers, visit our website:
www.blackwellpublishers.co.uk

Contents

Contributors

Amelia Álvarez, Department of Sociology and Communication, University of Salamanca, Spain

Igor Arievitch, Department of Education, College of Staten Island of the City University of New York, USA

Katherine Brown, California State University, San Marcos, USA

Margaret Carr, Department of Early Childhood Studies, University of Waikato, New Zealand

Seth Chaiklin, Department of Psychology, University of Aarhus, Denmark

Guy Claxton, Graduate School of Education, University of Bristol, UK

Paul Cobb, Department of Teaching and Learning, Peabody College of Vanderbilt University, USA

Michael Cole, Laboratory of Comparative Human Cognition, University of California, San Diego, USA

Stephanie Stoll Dalton, Office of Educational Research and Improvement, US Department of Education, USA

Pablo del Río, Department of Sociology and Communication, University of Salamanca, Spain

Ritva Engeström, Center for Activity Theory and Developmental Work Research, University of Helsinki, Finland

Yrjö Engeström, Center for Activity Theory and Developmental Work Research, University of Helsinki, Finland, and University of California, San Diego, USA

Caroline Gipps, Kingston University, UK

Ruqaiya Hasan, Macquarie University, New South Wales, Australia

Renée Hayes, School of Education, University of Delaware, USA

Vera John-Steiner, Department of Linguistics, University of New Mexico, USA

Jay L. Lemke, The Graduate Center, City University of New York, USA

Kay McClain, Department of Teaching and Learning, Peabody College of Vanderbilt University, USA

Holbrook Mahn, Language, Literacy and Sociocultural Studies, University of New Mexico, USA

Eugene Matusov, School of Education, University of Delaware, USA

Neil Mercer, Centre for Language and Communications, Open University, UK

Luis C. Moll, Department of Language, Reading and Culture, University of Arizona, USA

Andy Northedge, School of Health and Social Welfare, Open University, UK

Clotilde Pontecorvo, Department of Developmental and Social Psychology, University of Rome 'La Sapienza', Italy

Laura Sterponi, Department of Developmental and Social Psychology, University of Rome 'La Sapienza', Italy, and Department of Applied Linguistics and TESL, University of California, Los Angeles, USA

Anna Stetsenko, Graduate Center of the City University of New York, USA

Arja Suntio, Center for Activity Theory and Developmental Work Research, University of Helsinki, Finland

Roland G. Tharp, Center for Research on Education, Diversity and Excellence, University of California, Santa Cruz, USA

Gordon Wells, Department of Education, University of California, Santa Cruz, USA

1

Introduction: Sociocultural Perspectives on the Future of Education

Gordon Wells and Guy Claxton

What should be the goals of education and by what means can those goals best be achieved? These are questions that need to be regularly reconsidered, particularly in times of rapid social, economic and political change – such as the present. As we enter the twenty-first century, with the new uncertainties and demands created by globalization, the rise of the 'knowledge economy' and the growing recognition of the need for greater ecological responsibility, these questions are more important than ever.

Where are we to look for answers? In stable times they are furnished by tradition. But these are not stable times. Schools may once have done an adequate job of equipping and sifting young people to take their various places in the prevailing society, but that world is gone. In more turbulent times, a radical vision of education may emerge from cultural trauma, as it did in Reggio Emelia in Northern Italy at the conclusion of the Second World War. A whole society pulled together in revulsion at the ease with which they had embraced, or at least tolerated, fascism, and vowed to raise young people who would not make the same mistakes. But many societies today are characterized more by confusion and fragmentation than by such a strong sense of common purpose.

There are two other places we can look for ideas about education. One is the future: what kind of world are today's young people going to inhabit; and what skills and qualities will they need to thrive therein? And the second source of practical inspiration is theory: what are the best ideas available about the potentialities of the human mind and spirit, and about how minds and spirits grow? What do we now know about learning and development that the original architects of school did not; and what fresh perspectives and possibilities are thereby made available? This book starts from these latter two sources of inspiration. Where yesterday is an unreliable guide to tomorrow, and where societies are in complex, heterogeneous flux, we must look to the future, and to the best of current theory, to help us reappraise the means and ends of education.

The contributors to this volume share the view that education is not, at root, about the transmission of specific bodies of knowledge and skills. Rather, it is about the development of understanding and the formation of minds and identities: minds that are robust enough and smart enough to engage with the uncertain demands of the future, whatever they may be, and identities that are attuned to the changing communities of which they are members, and able and willing to participate effectively and responsibly in their activities and thus to contribute to, and benefit from, their transformation. Education, at this point in our history, we would argue, is centrally about the development of a mind to learn.

And we also agree that the way minds grow is not, fundamentally, through didactic instruction and intensive training, but through a more subtle kind of learning in which youngsters pick up useful (or unuseful) habits of mind from those around them and receive guidance in reconstructing these resources in order to meet their own and society's current and future concerns. Thus the minds that young people develop both reflect and modify the habits of mind of their elders, as the latter's ways of acting, feeling and thinking are transformed by the young in the process of appropriating them and making them their own. The idea that education is a process of simultaneous encul- turation and transformation is at the heart of what has come to be called, rather grandly, 'Cultural Historical Activity Theory', or CHAT for short, and it is this perspective that the present writers share. Collectively, we believe that CHAT not only helps to clarify the core questions that confront education at the start of the twenty-first century, but also provides a powerful and coherent basis for developing fresh answers to them.

The diversity in the contributions to this book is indicative of the increasingly widespread recognition of the value of CHAT for addressing educational issues in a variety of contexts. The chapters concern all levels of education from early childhood to professional training, and countries as different as Finland and the United States, Spain and New Zealand, Italy and the United Kingdom. In all these countries a growing number of educators are finding inspiration in the seminal work of CHAT's originator, Russian psychologist and educator, Lev Vygotsky. And the authors of the present chapters are prominent among those who are helping to develop the theory to which Vygotsky's pioneering work has given rise. Though CHAT may at first sight appear complex, its fundamental insights are relatively simple, and they are of profound relevance to educational practitioners and policy-makers. Our aim in this volume is to present them in a way that is at once accessible and practical, both as proposals for action and as suggestions for further investiga- tion and discussion.

An Introductory CHAT

We need to begin by saying a little more about what Cultural Historical Activity Theory actually is. CHAT is a theory of human development that sees human societies and their individual members as mutually constitutive. Cultures play a large role in shaping the development of individual minds; and individuals' thoughts and deeds serve to maintain or to alter the cultural milieu. As people work, play and solve problems together, so their spontaneous ways of thinking, talking and acting – the ideas that come to mind, the words they choose and the tools they make use of – embody an accumulated set of cultural values and beliefs that have been constructed and refined over previous generations. And, as they 'get things done' together, so younger or less experienced people pick up these habits and attitudes from their more experienced friends, relatives, teachers and colleagues. It is through taking part in such joint activities that individual members of a society are inducted into these 'ways of knowing' and take over and make their own the values, skills and knowledge that are enacted in the process. At the same time, since unprecedented problems continually arise, it is through participants' collaborating to find creative solutions that effective new skills and understandings are developed which, in turn, are carried forward to other situations, appropriated by different individuals, and thus pass into the culture at large.

There are two further features that significantly enrich this way of understanding human behaviour and development. The first is the key role of artifacts. Many other animals make use of material tools and resources, and they can learn to do so by watching their elders and betters. Young chimpanzees quickly pick up the art of 'fishing' for termites with a thin stick. Sea otters learn from their mothers how to use stones as 'hammer' and 'anvil' for opening shellfish. But no other species has developed such a diverse and sophisticated array of tools, nor built such an elaborate cultural life around their use, as human beings. Humans find and fashion a wide range of artifacts to extend and mediate their actions, and both the artifacts and the practices involved in making and using them are passed on, and improved upon, from one generation to the next.

For this reason, when looking at both individual and social activity, we need to look beyond solitary actors to the communities to which they belong, and to the inherited resources of artifacts and practices that serve as 'tools' for achieving the goals to which their activities are directed. Wertsch (1998, p. 485) captures this insight when he describes actors as 'agents-acting-with-mediational-means'. In a profound sense, we are so wedded to and constituted by the tools we use that we cannot be understood apart from them. Just as the performance of golfers cannot be understood in the absence of clubs and balls, so too the learning performance of schoolchildren, or the problem-solving processes of a work team, reflect the mental and physical tools to which they have access, and the levels of mastery and senses of occasion which they have acquired. Thus as a group of people engage in an activity together, their ability to carry it out effectively resides not only in their individual knowledge and skills, not just in their ability to collaborate; it is also distributed across the artifacts that are to hand and the 'affordances' (and also the constraints) provided by the environment.

However, the 'tools' that people use, and that shape the ways they think and act, are not only physical and technological objects like cutlery and cars. Just as important are the meaning-making tools that mediate communicative and reflective action, and which have as their outcome such 'semiotic' artifacts as drawings, graphs, theories and works of literature. Books, computer programs and the rules of geometry are tools too. In fact, all joint activity requires such tools in order to coordinate participants' actions and to construct and pass on their understanding of the principles involved. Chief among these 'psychological' tools is, of course, language in all its modes (Vygotsky, 1981), for it is through discourse that shared meaning is made and experience structured and organized as knowledge (Halliday, 1993, p. 48).

This leads to CHAT's second key feature. Since action is mediated by semiotic as well as material tools, participation in the various modes of discourse that organize and interpret action not only provides the context for the learning of language and other semiotic systems, but it also inducts learners into the culture's ways of making sense of experience – its modes of classification, its understanding of means–ends relationships, and its aesthetic and moral values. In other words, it is particularly by learning to use these semiotic tools in discourse with others that humans appropriate the culture's dominant ways of thinking, reasoning and valuing. And in making them their own and in bringing them to bear on new problems and new situations, they may transform them in ways that add to and potentially improve the culture's shared toolkit of meaning-making resources. What distinguishes humans from other species, therefore, is not the small differences in their biological genes, but the ability to develop, pass on and refine a wide variety of material and semiotic tools and practices that are culturally rather than biologically inherited.

In the CHAT view, 'teaching' and 'learning' are not activities that only take place at particular times and in special places. All interactions between people – having meals, bathing the baby, discussing holiday plans – involve using, adapting and mastering cultural tools. Habits of mind are being displayed, conveyed and modified, often without any deliberate intention or conscious awareness. For example, parents and older brothers and sisters typically provide a running commentary, both verbal and non-verbal, on the actions of small children. They create and direct increasingly variegated 'scripts' and coach the child in the part he or she is to play in each. While controlling the overall organization of the scripts to the extent necessary to bring them to a successful conclusion, the elders interact through action, facial expression, gesture and speech, providing assistance, demonstrating and commenting on the actions and objects involved, and explaining their relationship to the goal of the action. They also respond to and comment upon infants' interest in the environment and their attempts to contribute to joint activities and to achieve goals of their own. It is these forms of interaction, Vygotsky argued, that provide the most important opportunities for the 'learning that leads development', not only in the early years but also in the more formal contexts of schooling and the workplace. The 'higher mental functions' do not develop simply as a result of individual learning or intellectual maturation. Rather, they depend upon mastering the use of culturally created semiotic tools such as language, artistic representation and scientific procedures, which principally occur 'interpsychologically' (i.e. interactively) in activities undertaken with other members of the culture.

A corollary of this emphasis on the social origin of individual functions was Vygotsky's argument that learning specific things leads the development of mental tools and attitudes, not vice versa. And this, in turn, led to the concept for which he is generally best known, that of the 'zone of proximal development', or ZPD. Through the support and 'scaffolding' of our joint activities by more experienced others, we can transcend our solo limitations, and expand the range of what we can learn and achieve. In the jointly constructed ZPD, I can engage productively with things that, on my own, would have been beyond my grasp. And in so doing, I come to appropriate and internalize for myself tools that were first provided, modelled or created only in interaction. With the aid of the arm of a chair, or her father's fingers, a 10-month-old, who could not have done it by herself, is enabled to stand and walk a few steps. Through practising walking in this supported fashion, she rapidly develops the ability to walk on her own. The ways we think and learn and know develop in the same way.

Finally, in concluding this brief sketch, it is important to draw attention to two points that were often neglected or glossed over in earlier expositions of CHAT. The first is that, despite the emphasis on collaboration in joint activity, it must be recognized that participants in an activity do not necessarily have identical goals, nor do they necessarily share the same beliefs and values. Clearly, for collaboration to occur, there must be a degree of overlap in goals and a willingness to attempt to understand the perspectives of others. But difference and disagreement are also valuable. Without the contribution of new and even antithetical ideas and suggestions, there would be no way of going beyond ways of acting and thinking repeated from the past; and although well-tried solutions are often a good starting point, they may have to be challenged and transformed if they are to become adequate responses to novel predicaments.

The second point is that CHAT is not concerned only with *cognitive* development. All action, whether practical or theoretical, involves the whole person – body, mind and spirit. Particularly in Western educational contexts, there has been a tendency to ignore the interdependence of feeling, thought and action and to focus almost exclusively on what are seen as purely intellectual activities. But, as Vygotsky emphasized in his last major work, 'Thought has its origins in the motivating sphere of consciousness, a sphere that includes our inclinations and needs, our interests and impulses, and our affect and emotion. . . . A true and complex understanding of another's thought becomes possible only when we discover its real, affective-volitional basis' (Vygotsky, 1987, p. 282).

In the remainder of this introductory chapter, we shall expand on this very condensed summary by considering how the key principles of CHAT throw light on the fundamental concerns of education. We shall also highlight some of the questions and options which the CHAT perspective raises, and which the contributions to this volume serve to explore and illuminate. And we shall conclude with a very brief sketch of each of these chapters.

CHAT Goes to School: Principles and Implications

Cultural relativism

Though the CHAT approach raises questions about the content of education, its implications are most clearly seen in the context of discussions about the 'medium': classroom organization, teaching methods, forms of interaction and assessment, and so on. With the rise of the social sciences since the early twentieth century, and particularly of the discipline of educational psychology, enormous research efforts have been expended on attempting to discover general pedagogical methods that would make education maximally and universally effective. Proven 'scientific' methods have been heralded and applied, only to be succeeded by new methods, equally claiming to be supported by experimental evidence. In the mean time, however, it has become increasingly apparent that such universalizing aims are incompatible with the diverse realities of individual schools and classrooms. No centrally planned pedagogy, or uniformly delivered curriculum, can meet the needs of rural as well as inner-city communities, minority as well as mainstream students, technologically advanced as well as developing countries. Education is not like the motor industry: no one optimal 'technology of teaching', it seems, can be mandated worldwide.

The futile search for a universal, culture-free, 'teacher-proof' approach to education provides a natural point for CHAT to enter the debate about educational means and ends, for perhaps its most fundamental tenet is that all action, including learning, must be understood in its situated complexity and idiosyncrasy. Instead of the curriculum being planned and handed down from a position of lofty omniscience, CHAT suggests that decision-making has to be responsive to the local needs and concerns of students and the communities to which they belong. CHAT does not – and would not attempt to – provide one uniform answer to the questions about the goals of education and how they should be met. Clearly what is selected as appropriate 'content' for education must be related to the present and probable future concerns of the particular students involved, as well as to the canon of knowledge valued by those in immediate authority.

Meaningful, collaborative activity

After the recognition of 'cultural relativism', the next most fundamental educational principle of CHAT is that the kind of learning that leads development takes place through active participation in purposeful, collaborative activity. In the course of working together towards shared goals and of finding solutions to the problems encountered in the process, participants contribute differentially from their existing expertise and take over and transform for their own use the skills, values and dispositions that they find effective in the contributions of others.

Where learning occurs in a systematically organized school setting, the teacher has a special role, as leader of the classroom community, in selecting activities that are appropriately connected to the students' interests, and in advance of their current level of independent performance. These activities must engage students in the kind of present experiences that, as Dewey put it, 'live fruitfully and creatively in future experiences' (Dewey, 1938, p. 28). In other words, in selecting the sequence of activities that make up the curriculum, the teacher should not treat the task as that of 'covering' detached, self-contained topics that, once completed, can be assumed to be finished. Each curricular unit should not only make sense in its own terms, but also encourage the raising of questions for future exploration. So we are bound to ask what kinds of activities do engage different students' learning energies, and at the same time form a coherent part of a longer-term developmental trajectory?

At the same time, however, collaboration should not be equated with agreement and conformity. Although consensus may be an appropriate ultimate aim, the voicing and consideration of alternative ideas, experiences and opinions may be essential if genuine understanding is to be achieved by all participants, and this applies not only to the topic in question but also to the grounds on which people can validly disagree. So CHAT leads us to ask how this balance between collaboration and dissent is to be managed, and by whom. Also, to what extent can the classroom goals be genuinely and appropriately communal, and what place is left for individual enthusiasms – those of both teachers and students? And what does this imply for the planning and carrying out of curricular units and their constituent tasks? In this context we might also ask of what validity is the traditional type of examination, for example, if 'knowing' is to be seen not as an individual possession but a continually evolving communal activity? Are there other types of assessment that honour this 'intersubjectivity' more constructively?

Appropriation and transformation

The next key principle of CHAT is that human development depends on the appropriation and *reconstruction* by each individual of the resources that have been developed within their culture. At the same time as people are absorbing their cultural heritage they are also, through their contributions to collaboratively undertaken activities, transforming, in small or large ways, the situations in which they act and the resources that mediate those activities, thereby opening up possibilities for transforming, even if only slightly, the culture as a whole. Such a view emphasizes the renewal of culture as well as its reproduction and therefore encourages teachers to see students as modifying and improving upon the valued resources from the past as well as simply equipping them with it. At the heart of CHAT there is therefore a tension between education as enculturation and education for autonomy and originality. We must ask how can the concept of individual agency be reconciled with the strong emphasis on socialization/enculturation that is taken to be a central feature of sociocultural theory, as well as of most public education?

We might also note here that traditionally education has tended to ignore social and emotional development, concentrating almost exclusively on intellectual development and, more specifically, on the acquisition of bodies of formalized knowledge. From a CHAT perspective, however, all human activity is inherently social and imbued with emotion. Along with other more humanistic perspectives, which are also challenging the educational status quo, CHAT therefore invites us to inquire how educational activities can be designed to engage the active involvement of the student as a 'whole person' and to contribute positively to identity formation.

Guided participation

Another key principle of CHAT is the need to include less experienced members of a society in the meaningful activities of its more mature members. For CHAT, learning is very definitely 'on-the-job' and occurs primarily through what Lave and Wenger (1991) call 'legitimate peripheral participation'. Since individuals need to internalize and construct for themselves the psychological and linguistic tools of their culture, it is essential that they be included in those activities that rely on such tools, and be given assistance in learning to participate in those activities fully and effectively. The concept of the zone of proximal development, the ZPD, points to the ways in which an individual's engagement can be framed and interpreted by more experienced others. Assistance can take many forms, from the provision of models to be imitated, through the orchestration of tasks and opportunities, to practical 'scaffolding' through feedback and guidance, and explicit explanations of principles and procedures.

However, as the most effective assistance depends on the momentary state of the learner, the ZPD idea is difficult to operationalize in a busy classroom comprising one teacher and 30 or more students. To cope with this problem, CHAT has come to explore, in recent years, the kinds of support that can be offered by peer interactions, and by a whole class working together as a 'community of inquiry'. Simply by pooling their ideas and experiences, a group of children can together create a powerful ZPD. Nevertheless, the class is also a community in which the teacher must combine several roles: organizer of activities and instructor as well as supporter of individual students' development. So CHAT leads us to ask how classroom activities can be organized so that all learners are able to receive assistance that is appropriately pitched in their zones of proximal development. What is the appropriate balance between whole-class, group and individual activity, and between 'hands-on' action, talk, and engagement with texts of various kinds?

Recognizing diversity

In the CHAT view, it is in principle impossible to introduce a learning goal or a learning method into any culturally and historically constituted situation – like a classroom – and expect a common outcome. And this applies *a fortiori* to the multicultural and multi-ethnic classroom which is, in many parts of the world today, the norm. Among their individual members, both students and teachers, there are different identities and values that have their origins in cultural, linguistic, class and gender differences, as well as in individual trajectories of experience and current levels of performance. There are also differences in the futures that students can envisage for themselves and, hence, in the kinds of learning trajectories they wish to follow.

Set against this diversity among learners, however, is the increasing convergence of political and economic organizational structures and the homogenization of global educational provision. With the increasing emphasis on measurable, standardized outcomes, for example, there is a danger that individual aspirations and styles of learning will be ignored and that passive conformity will be valued over individual initiative and creativity. Under these conditions, not only will those who go against the mainstream be disadvantaged but, in the long term, society as a whole will be impoverished, since cultural development requires the interplay of alternative viewpoints and the exploration of alternative solutions to the problems that continually arise.

These considerations lead us to ask: how can such diversity be made a resource in educational activities rather than a problem to be overcome or a basis for divisive practices? To put it another way, how can the situated and variegated nature of learning-and-teaching activities be reconciled with the (understandable) administrative concern for mastery of a standardized, prespecified curriculum and for common outcomes? How can teachers be helped to encourage and be responsive to students' ideas and initiatives while also fulfilling their responsibility to ensure that students master the knowledge and skills that are culturally valued? And we might also wonder how to provide appropriate learning experiences for students with special educational needs or those who, by reason of their cultural and linguistic minority status, are at risk of failure within mainstream educational institutions.

Smart machines and absent others

The final key principle of CHAT we wish to emphasize here is that all learning situations are indelibly social and cultural, even if they involve no face-to-face interaction. A solitary scholar poring over her books is engaging with the voices of the books' authors, and through them with a long tradition of thought. She is also engaging, implicitly or explicitly, with the community that will receive and evaluate her 'essay' or her journal paper – choosing forms of words that have particular resonances in that community, anticipating and addressing counter-arguments, and so on. The recent proliferation of electronic forms of communication, and the opportunities for solitary and distance learning to which these technologies have given rise, have re-emphasized the extent to which CHAT thinking is fundamentally 'cultural' rather than necessarily 'social'.

And these media open up new opportunities and demand the development of new mental competencies and attitudes, or require forms of support, which may differ from those exercised or afforded by traditional education. For example, while educational programmes can now be efficiently delivered in the distance mode, the isolation in which students typically receive these programmes means that they may lack many of the forms of social and emotional support that are, ideally, available in face-to-face learning communities. Rapid-fire video games require and develop lightning sensorimotor reflexes – and appetites for stimulation – that may make sitting still in a classroom increasingly alien and intolerable. Surfing the net affords opportunities to make certain kinds of associations with astonishing ease and rapidity; but may, by the same token, conceal other kinds of connections that are not so easily displayed or unearthed. In written language, school has privileged what have been called the 'essayist' registers of technical–rational exposition, and treated them as the predominant media of learning and assessment. But the semiotic toolkit that contemporary societies both afford and require includes many other forms of meaning-making: oracy, narrative skill and the abilities to 'read' the graphic conventions of film, video, hypertext and the like. Either to ignore these powerful social trends, or simply to bewail them and treat them as subversive of school's 'higher' purposes, is surely not an adequate response. CHAT invites us to explore how education can respond to these demands on the development of young people's minds. We must ask: how should education be responding to the changing relationship between different mental tools and ways of knowing? Is there a better balance to be achieved, and if so how?

Up to now, the application of CHAT to education has focused predominantly on early childhood and the elementary school years. But questions such as these indicate that there may well be much to be gained by taking a sociocultural perspective on adult, distance and higher education, and on professional or work-based learning. CHAT invites us to look at lifelong learning, and the demands of the 'learning society', in terms of a continuing process of absorbing and reconstructing changing cultural milieux. But we do not yet know in any detail how the mechanisms and the objects of cultural appropriation vary across the lifespan. Nor do we fully understand whether there are 'developmental tasks' that require specific kinds of mediation at different ages and stages of life. So CHAT bids us ask what a sociocultural approach to workplace or professional learning would look like. How would the principles explored with respect to schooling need to be modified to provide useful insights, for example, for adult education or the professional development of educators?

Chapter Sketches

These key principles, and the questions to which they have given rise, offer a range of responses to current educational confusion that is different from that suggested by many other frameworks. There are many other questions we could have raised: those we have highlighted above are merely illustrative, as are the hints we have offered about how some of them might begin to be addressed. In the chapters that follow, these issues and hints are explored in much more detail, both conceptually and in practice. They are arranged into three parts that progress from the conceptual to the practical, and from a concern with younger to older age groups. The chapters in the first part, 'Issues and developments in sociocultural theory', build on the introduction by discussing some of the different facets of the CHAT approach in more detail, and in particular, exploring some of the ways in which Vygotsky's original insights and formulations are currently being extended, elaborated and in some cases challenged and reformulated. In the second part, 'Pre-school and school-age learning and development', the focus becomes more explicitly on the kinds of interactions that promote successful development in families, early childhood centres and classrooms. While in the third part, 'Post-compulsory, adult and professional learning', concern shifts to the ways in which CHAT can be used to illuminate the kinds of learning and development that take place in universities, teacher education programmes, school staff rooms and even in distance education.

These broad divisions are rough and ready, at best, and the 'theoretical' chapters both draw on, and prompt speculation about, educational practice just as much as the 'practical' chapters demand and drive the development of theory. This is just as it should be, of course. It will also be clear that the contributors cannot be neatly identified in terms of which of our general themes and questions they set themselves to address, for they are tightly interwoven, and no matter at what specific point you pick up the 'net' of assumptions and priorities that constitute the CHAT perspective, you inevitably find that the rest come with it. Nevertheless, some themes emerge more clearly in some chapters than others, and it is these broad indicators that we describe below, in the hope that doing so will help readers to orientate themselves in the midst of the plethora of ideas and examples that the contributors generate.

Part I begins with Guy Claxton's chapter, which explores CHAT's contribution to 'learning to learn'. He argues that schools should be aiming to prepare young people for a world in which an unpredictable future requires adaptability, initiative and tolerance of ambiguity and uncertainty. What is at issue, he argues, is the development of 'positive learning capabilities and dispositions' rather than domain-specific skills or substantive knowledge. CHAT invites us to consider the social and cultural contexts that support the development of flexible epistemic mentalities and identities, and emphasizes the value of resilience, resourcefulness and reflective open-mindedness. In contrast to explicit attempts to train 'thinking skills', Claxton argues that the sociocultural approach focuses our attention on the kinds of epistemic milieux which teachers create in the classroom, and especially on the affordances of different activities, the nature of the learning commentary, and the qualities that teachers model.

In chapter 3 Jay Lemke explores the tension, for the growing child, between the need to develop a coherent sense of personal value and identity, and the need to understand and accommodate to the diverse and often conflicting points of view of those they respect, or at least need to rub along with. In the process of learning to manage these relationships, Lemke argues, children's minds themselves need to become multiple and contingent. The 'ordered heterogeneity' of any community or organization – Lemke uses the metaphor of a 'village' – demands the ability to master and to juggle different ways of knowing, thinking and valuing. Lemke argues that, from this point of view, school constitutes a curious kind of 'village': one which actually makes it difficult for young people to manage the tension between identity and diversity, and which may fail to prepare them for the complex, modern kinds of 'village' in which they are going to have to live and function as adults.

In chapter 4 Holbrook Mahn and Vera John-Steiner argue that an important aspect of Vygotsky's theory has been largely ignored: the key role of affect in thinking and action. They point out that a core aspect of effective life-long learning is confidence, and the chapter explores ways in which learners' confidence can be built up through supportive interactions. In particular, they stress the importance of caring support from colleagues and mentors in enabling people to be risks-takers in initiating new ideas and pursuing new directions. The authors show that the ZPD cannot be reduced to the kind of narrow cognitive 'scaffolding' that some educators have taken it to be: the *quality* of the relationship is crucial. Mahn and John-Steiner illustrate their argument with examples from well-known 'creative collaborations' and from work on high school and adult students learning a second language.

In chapter 5 Pablo del Río and Amelia Álvarez document the extent of what they call young people's disengagement, which is manifested in many forms, from a lack of concern for public affairs to an absence of commitment to sustained effort in education. This malaise they attribute to the superficial and fragmentary nature of the cultural messages in the media and to similar characteristics in the organization of schooling. As the kind of learning that leads to positive mental development relies crucially on the willing, joint engagement of people in solving meaningful problems, they argue that, in school particularly, students should be challenged to undertake activities that are 'real' and related to their life concerns. Only when learning involves personal commitment does it move beyond accumulation of knowledge and expertise to qualitative mental development. (This is a theme which is taken up in several other chapters.)

In chapter 6 Caroline Gipps explores the implications of sociocultural perspectives on learning for the practice of educational assessment. She asks: if learning is essentially a social process, how can the traditional forms of highly individualized and competitive evaluation be appropriate? Gipps argues for revised methods of assessment that are more 'dynamic', catching something of the learner in action, rather than merely trying to measure summatively how much of a body of knowledge has been transmitted. She discusses assessment methods that are communal, capable of describing how groups of students are developing as social learners And she also points out that the assessment process itself is inherently both a social and a learning situation, in which important power relations between teacher/assessor and learner greatly influence the learners' performance, and in which learners are continually reappraising their relationship to the assessment process, and are learning what is 'required', and how to deliver (or withhold) it.

To round off Part I, Anna Stetsenko and Igor Arievitch (chapter 7) remind us that, from the CHAT point of view, the development of 'higher mental functions' is the result of mastering the tools – material and symbolic – that are used to organize and pursue meaningful activities in the communities in which students are growing up. Much of this process of appropriation, especially in the early years, happens informally, but deliberate teaching becomes one of the most important channels through which cultural tools are transmitted. In the bulk of the chapter the authors describe the seminal contribution of Piotr Gal'perin, one of Vygotsky's students and colleagues, who argued, in essence, that the teacher must organize their work around the most abstract and coherent principles that characterize a particular domain of knowledge. These principles are the core 'conceptual tools', the internalization of which enable students to think powerfully about a whole range of phenomena.

In Part II, 'Pre-school and school-age learning and development', several themes emerge and recur, including the importance of learning dispositions, as these are established at home and in the early years of schooling, and also the importance of students' being encouraged to take initiatives and to engage in activities that are personally meaningful and that bridge the gap between school and the wider communities in which they are also learning and forming their identities. In chapter 8, for example, Margaret Carr demonstrates the ways in which young children's orientations towards (or away from) learning are being moulded through the activities that are offered to them in early education centres, and through the kinds of verbal and non-verbal messages they receive from their teachers and carers, and from each other. Carr argues that, as dispositions begin to develop, so they draw children towards or away from certain kinds of experience, thus narrowing the range of 'learning niches' which the children can inhabit and explore. They thus quickly become self-perpetuating and self-reinforcing, and so making sure that children set off with learning-positive dispositions is of great importance.

In chapter 9 Ruqaiya Hasan emphasizes the role of 'semiotic mediation' in the development of learning dispositions in the young child. It is through conversations of all kinds that the child's developing 'habits of mind' are most powerfully influenced. Drawing on examples from a large longitudinal study, Hasan shows how unremarkable interactions, centring around ordinary, everyday activities, inexorably steer young children's mental and social development, and thereby lay the foundations for further, more specialized forms of study that are either secure and robust, or not. Recorded snatches of such conversations are used to illustrate how the disposition towards curiosity and questioning, for example, can be subtly either cultivated or suppressed. If the former, children enter school eager to learn; if the latter, they are likely to adopt a more passive or receptive attitude.

One of the most useful cultural tools that language affords, especially in the process of grappling with views that differ from or conflict with one's own, is the ability to argue: to probe other people's assertions and to mount public defences of one's own. In chapter 10 Clotilde Pontecorvo and Laura Sterponi use episodes of conversation similar to Hasan's to show children encountering and producing justified interpretations of events which are then corrected or challenged by older children, siblings, parents and teachers. By entering into communal debates and public 'thinking through' of significant issues, pre-school children come to master various rhetorical devices and modes of rational argument. In conclusion, Pontecorvo and Sterponi argue that the opportunity to take part in well-orchestrated 'narrative activities', at home and school, is necessary if children are to be prepared for life in the twenty-first century.

Neil Mercer (chapter 11) argues that 'the prime aim of education ought to be to help children learn how to use language effectively as a tool for thinking collectively' and that, reciprocally, participation in collective thinking stimulates individual cognitive development. For Mercer, genuine dialogue in the context of jointly undertaken activities is the chief means through which children appropriate cultural knowledge and culturally valued strategies of discussion and problem solving. In the second part of his chapter Mercer describes a programme of 'talk lessons' that introduce 8–11-year-old children to the practice of collaborative exploratory talk. Teacher-led, whole-class discussions that make explicit 'the ways we talk' are interwoven with small group tasks that stimulate relevant forms of conversation. Mercer reports data which show that participation in this programme enhances children's ability to carry out problem-solving tasks, both in collaborating groups and alone.

In chapter 12 Paul Cobb and Kay McClain show how Mercer's principles apply equally well to the learning of mathematics in middle-school classrooms. CHAT, they have found, is extremely helpful for the design and interpretation of classroom investigations. Teachers and researchers work as a team to construct, implement, monitor and adjust a range of 'design experiments'. For Cobb and McClain, the collaborative learning of the teachers is as much informed by CHAT as are the activities they construct for the students. They illustrate their approach with data from a group of seventh-graders working collaboratively on a statistical task that involves discovering and exploiting the relevant affordances of some computer-based 'minitools' which enable the group to think in more sophisticated ways. The authors argue that learning is 'distributed' not only across social groups but also across the technological tools that the group can make use of. Through designing teaching on the basis of such principles, students can be encouraged to develop for themselves conceptual tools that will be of real value.

In chapter 13 Seth Chaiklin asks how specific subject-matter teaching can contribute to young people's more general mental and personality development. Some discussions of CHAT seem to focus almost exclusively on the process of learning, as if the content of the activity itself was of only secondary importance. Chaiklin, like Stetsenko and Arievitch, argues that each discipline has at its heart a set of powerful, abstract conceptual tools that, if mastered, give the learner access to valuable forms of more sophisticated thinking. Personality development centres on the acquisition of such powerful mental capabilities, and these can only be developed through working with specific, substantive content. It is a core part of the teachers' role, on such a view, to analyse clearly what the core conceptual tools are in their discipline, and to pose questions and design classroom activities in such a way that learners are drawn into an understanding of these underlying organizing principles.

Part II concludes with a chapter by Stephanie Dalton and Roland Tharp (chapter 14), in which they focus on approaches to learning and teaching that meet the needs of children whose diverse backgrounds put them at risk of educational failure. They put forward five principles or 'standards' for effective pedagogy and illustrate each with examples taken from a diverse array of elementary classrooms. These standards are: that teachers and students should engage together in 'joint productive activity'; that all activities should be designed to develop students' language and literacy; that school activities should make meaningful and timely connections to students' out-of-school lives; that activities should stimulate the development of ever more complex forms of learning and thinking; and that task-focused conversations between students, and from students to teachers, should be encouraged across the board. Though these standards derive from work with students at risk, the authors point out that they are equally appropriate as a basis for planning educational experiences for all students.

In Part III the contributors go beyond school-age students to consider the needs of adult and professional learners. Though this represents less well charted waters for sociocultural approaches to education, these chapters collectively demonstrate how fruitful the CHAT approach can be at this level. For example, in chapter 15 Gordon Wells argues that CHAT must inform the aims and activities of teacher education and professional development, as well as those of the classroom. He begins by proposing that 'inquiry' is the approach to learning and teaching that best enacts CHAT principles and argues that if teachers are to adopt this approach successfully in the classroom, it must also characterize their own learning experiences, both pre-service and in-service. Wells describes attempts to create overlapping 'communities of inquiry' in which school-age students, their teachers and university-based teacher educators collaborate to discover ways of learning and teaching that are empowering for all concerned. In contrast to some similar-sounding projects, Wells argues that it is essential to put the teachers and the students, rather than the academics, firmly in the driving seat.

In chapter 16 Yrjö Engeström, Ritva Engeström and Arja Suntio focus on teacher development within a school community. Describing a partnership between a university research team and a middle school serving a disadvantaged population, they illustrate two ways in which CHAT can serve as a tool for change. First, it was used in the 'Change Laboratory', in which teachers were invited to explore the tensions and problems in the school's current organization. Second, it provided a framework for the analysis of data, collected over a two year period, that recorded teachers' attempts to change that organization. Most significantly, the authors show that the desired change in students' commitment to a learning project, and their ability to bring it to a successful completion, depended on, and was brought about by, a change in the teachers' ways of talking about the students and of evaluating their attitudes and achievements.

Katherine Brown and Michael Cole (chapter 17) also discuss a range of projects in which school pupils, teachers and university staff and students collaborate in the design and running of an after-school club that engages youngsters in a variety of enjoyable but intellectually demanding computer-based activities. The authors contrast two versions of the programme in an attempt to identify the factors that enable some versions to flourish while others fail to surmount similar challenges. While there is no one factor that determines whether such projects thrive or struggle, the importance of the relationship between the programme directors and the local community is significant. If the community holds a model of education, or of how best to interact with children, that is at odds with that of the programme, conflicts, resistances and misunderstandings may emerge that cannot be solved simply on the basis of the project leaders' commitment or enthusiasm.

In chapter 18 Eugene Matusov and Renée Hayes report on their work with education students in the context of a somewhat similar after-school club called La Red Magica. They explore another source of difficulty in such well-intentioned collaborative projects: clashes between the adult students' ideals and expectations, and the challenging behaviour of the school students. To illustrate the value of the CHAT perspective, the authors focus on a critical incident in which one of the young female pre-service teachers was disrespected by a pre-teenage boy. Drawing on records of in-class and on-line discussion of the incident the authors argue that messy, uncomfortable, uncertain questioning, undertaken collaboratively and opportunistically in the midst of challenging situations, results in the development of the intuitions and sensitivities that young teachers will need to manage complex, culturally diverse, teaching situations.

In chapter 19 Andy Northedge from the British Open University tackles what seems to be a difficult, if not paradoxical, question: of what possible relevance can CHAT be, with its central emphasis on the social, situated nature of learning, to adult students grappling with texts in their own homes as part of distance learning courses? With the use of some compelling examples from his own institution, Northedge presents such students not as absorbers of bodies of knowledge, but as self-selected apprentices to a range of scholarly discourse communities. Through their attempts to comprehend the texts they are sent, they are learning what it is to be a member of a particular scholarly 'community of practice'. To do that, they have to be able to connect their own pre-existing perspectives to the technical discourses and worldviews of the discipline, and Northedge argues that whether those connections are successfully made depends critically on the empathy with which the writers of distance learning materials offer the student bridges across which they can walk.

In the final chapter, Luis Moll offers his reflections on the contributions that comprise *Learning for Life in the 21st Century*. He draws out some of the themes that have emerged, and asks to what extent the aims of the book, as set out in the editors' introduction, have been fulfilled.

Part I
Issues and Developments in Sociocultural Theory

2

Education for the Learning Age: A Sociocultural Approach to Learning to Learn

Guy Claxton

People learn in the process of trying to achieve valued goals. We find ourselves in situations in which we wish to attain something, but are not yet sure how to go about it. So we explore and experiment, and if our learning is successful, we gain the knowledge we desire, and develop some skills and 'qualities' along the way. As our tennis serve improves, so we win more points. As we struggle to make sense of difficult material, and to express our understandings better in essays or seminars, so our grades improve. And, as these learnings often take place in the company of others, our social skills, and our intuitive grasp of how other people work and think, develop as well.

But as we learn, we are also changing as learners. 'Learning to learn' is the ever-present shadow of our attempts to gain more obvious kinds of mastery. As we study, so we learn more about what it takes to study and what it means to be a student. If we are successful in pursuing our interests, we have learnt not only how to secure a particular goal, but how to engage more effectively with a kind of uncertainty. Achieving the goal is the 'figure' of any learning activity, if you like, but its 'ground' is the development of our intuitive understanding of, and expertise at, the learning process itself. As we learn what to do, so we change *how* we know, and how we *come* to know. Education is unavoidably concerned with all of these layers and levels of learning.

Most of our learning – whether it be learning to walk as a baby or after a stroke, perfecting a new lab technique, or working through a difficult patch in a relationship – is done with others, and in the context of social partners and material resources that amplify and modify our own accumulated capabilities and dispositions as learners. Even the solitary mathematician, or the school student struggling with her homework, is learning in the context of, and with the aid of, a host of culturally constituted tools – books, symbols,

I am grateful to my co-editor, Gordon Wells, for his meticulous and perceptive comments on an earlier draft of this chapter.

computer graphics – which afford or invite certain approaches to the learning task, and preclude others. The settings in which people find themselves – especially those which they inhabit recurrently – thus channel the growth of their minds.

These recurring contexts constitute the dominant 'cultures' of a person's world. We all belong to a whole variety of 'clubs', each of which binds its 'members' into a shared set of habits, attitudes and judgements about what matters. A family, a school, a group of friends, a profession, a workplace and a nation are all examples of 'cultures', used in this broad sense. As will be obvious from these examples, culture clubs are often 'nested' inside each other, and they can also vary dramatically in the beliefs and values that underpin the ways of speaking, acting and interrelating which they deem 'normal' or 'proper'.

More specifically, in the present context, cultures value different learning achievements, and foreground, or neglect, different layers of learning. For example, one culture may reward intellectual prowess and ignore the development of empathy; another, the reverse. Social groups may privilege different learning methods. One may teach mainly through didactic transmission; another through informal modelling and *in situ* coaching. They may differ in their tacit epistemological beliefs, one assuming that extended periods of rote learning must precede any attempt at creativity, while another views such learning by rote as inherently disrespectful of, and potentially damaging to, the free spirit of the (young) learner. And – perhaps most importantly in the present context – cultures may differ markedly in the extent to which they recognize, value and foster the development of 'learning to learn' as a legitimate, practicable and useful educational objective. The central contention of this chapter is that Western education has, by and large, not seen education in this latter light, as an apprenticeship in the craft of real-life learning, and that it both could, and should.

The Purpose of Education: To Thrive on Uncertainty

Let me start with the 'should'. Education is essentially a moral enterprise. It maps out courses of learning that are designed to give people knowledge, skills, attitudes and qualities that are deemed to be worth having. Educators are in the business of making value judgements about what kinds of minds people need, and are therefore to be cultivated. In adult and professional education these may be quite specific. The doctor needs to have mastered areas of anatomy and pharmacology in order to be able to treat and prescribe. The attorney must know the law and have become skilled in the subtle arts of rhetoric and billing. But the education of the young, being the generic foundation on which all such specialized learning will be built, has to have goals that are both broader and deeper. At root, school exists to equip young people with the knowledge, capabilities and dispositions which they will need to cope well in the world that they are going, as adults, to inhabit (and especially with those facets of mind which cannot be presumed to just develop 'naturally' in the process of growing up). What 'cope well' means, and therefore which facets of mind are valued, varies enormously within and between cultures. Some prize compliance, others creativity; some seek to build a communitarian spirit, others autonomy and individualism. The life-preparation that young people receive depends on their elders' image of 'the good life' and 'the harmonious society'.

But it also depends on whether the elders see their world as stable or changing, and on their image of the future. The goals of education are relative to the future which the 'elders' of a society foresee (Cole, 1996). If that future is imagined accurately, and the curriculum is appropriate, the ensuing education will be empowering. If the methods are ineffective, or if they develop skills that are unequal or inappropriate to the demands of the real world-to-be, then education fails. In a stable society, yesterday's education, if it was well designed originally, will do for the citizens of tomorrow. But if a culture is undergoing radical change, the demands of the future cannot be clearly predicted, and a different kind of preparation is required. If the main thing we know about the future is that we do not know much about it, then the key responsibility of the educator is not to give young people tools that may be out of date before they have even been fully mastered, but to help them become confident and competent designers and makers of their own tools as they go along.

The development of 'learning to learn', the parallel curriculum which, in stable, traditional societies, may not be as visible or highly valued as the handing on of specific, valued knowledge, thus becomes of pre-eminent importance. It can no longer be ignored or left to chance. Though I have already argued that learning to learn necessarily shadows the development of specific domains of understanding and expertise, the kind and the extent of learning to learn depends heavily on how it is viewed and handled. For a culture that is moving rapidly into a period of instability and uncertainty, and of increasing individual opportunity and responsibility for dealing with those demands, an imaginative reappraisal of methods and priorities becomes essential. If this challenge is ducked, the young will flounder (Claxton, 1999).

It seems undeniable that many societies – and not only the 'Western' and 'Northern' – are now in this position. Heads of state regularly pontificate about the need for national work forces that are not only skilful but flexible. Transnational corporations routinely shift vast amounts of capital around the planet in pursuit of the most favourable skills-to-costs ratios, creating widespread vocational insecurity. 'Jobs for life' and the routinization of career that went with them are fast becoming a nostalgic dream (Hutton, 1995; Reich, 1991). Instead, the onus is on individuals, companies and governments to manifest a continual willingness to expand people's 'employability'; to invest in the development of their 'cognitive capital'. In Aaron Beck's 'risk society' (Beck, 1992) everyone needs to be good at learning, and willing to take over for themselves the responsibility for crafting their own working lives.

And it is not just in the workplace that such capabilities and attitudes are needed. Cheap international transportation, multi-ethnic societies, global media and information technology now flood individual lives with a plethora of lifestyle images and options that would have been literally unthinkable a generation ago. The challenge is not just learning to use new programs and machines, nor even developing skills of entrepreneurship; it is managing the explosion of possibilities, and the attendant weakening of a traditionally based sense of identity, that ensues (Gergen, 1991). Thus we can argue that education, if it is to offer an effective preparation for life, should foreground the development of transferable, real-life learning skills and dispositions. But can it do so?

The Sociocultural Approach to Learning: A Tale of Three Discourses

Cultural–historical activity theory (CHAT) provides an ideal perspective from which to see how this challenge is to be met, for, in essence, it asserts the crucial importance of looking at learning in its social, cultural and historical context. There are, if you like, three 'discourses' within which learning and development can be framed. The first is the 'individual–developmental' discourse of psychology, within which the individual person is viewed as a constellation of knowledge structures, skills, habits, attributes, attitudes, beliefs, qualities and dispositions. These are the accumulating residues of experience and inheritance: our tendencies for action, anticipation and interpretation and our orientations towards public issues and private concerns. The talk in this discourse is of hypothetical entities such as 'intelligence', 'short-term memory stores', 'learning strategies', 'personality traits' and such like. Rashid is 'bright' but 'timid'. Heather is 'friendly' but has a 'short attention span'. Psychological terms point to our mental 'default modes' – anyone of which may, in an instant, be overturned or rewritten by circumstances.

In the present context, two such psychologized constructs of particular relevance are what we might call *epistemic mentality* and *epistemic identity*. By 'epistemic' I mean those aspects of a person's make-up that relate to the ways in which they learn and know. Thus 'epistemic mentality' refers to someone's accumulated ways of knowing, learning strategies and styles, and their habits of mind. While 'epistemic identity' refers to the person's view of themselves as a learner and knower: what they are good and bad at learning; what is worth knowing; what say they have in the generation and evaluation of knowledge and expertise; and so on.

The second discourse is the 'social–historical' one (using this phrase, for the moment, in a non-technical sense) of sociology, anthropology, political theory and the other macro-social sciences, which speaks of the changing nature of social structures and institutions, of deliberate policies and implicit cultural practices. The language here too is of abstractions and generalizations cast over time and space: 'power', 'ritual', 'dissident sub-cultures', 'risk society', 'social exclusion' and so on. From this perspective, the individual finds her or himself 'positioned' within structures, practices and 'discourses' that have a cultural, rather than a psychological, reality. Of central interest in what follows will be those aspects of the cultural world that impact most powerfully or directly on the development of epistemic mentality and identity: what I shall refer to as the *epistemic milieu*.

The third discourse, which we might call that of the 'irreducible situated moment', or 'mediated action' (e.g. Wertsch, 1995), asserts that the categories of the first two discourses, being abstractions and tendencies, are in principle never able fully to catch the intricate complexity of the unique moment in which a person interacts with an unprecedented material, social and cultural setting. What the individual does, and how they learn, cannot be predicted on the basis of their psychological attributes, because these are selected, customized and instantiated, in unpredictable ways, on the basis of each shifting context. In the moment, a cloud of possibilities precipitates as a unique way of being, seeded by the perceived demands, opportunities and resources which the setting affords. Likewise, the setting itself manifests as a complex, concrete reality that is dependent on the natures and the perceptions of participating groups and individuals. A student may extend her capability by making intelligent, simultaneous use of the internet and her father: in the moment, she becomes, to use David Perkins's (1993) phrase, 'person-plus'. Her zone of proximal development is expanded; her cognition distributed (Salomon, 1993; Clark, 1997). As Wertsch (1995) says, in any particular instant, the 'person acting with mediational means' is the irreducible unit of analysis, and of intelligence.

As a result of a succession of such momentary encounters, both person and culture are changed. Their structures, processes and *modus operandi* are altered – maybe imperceptibly, maybe quite evidently and significantly. As a father models for his daughter, in conversation, a strategy for thinking about where one might have lost something, she is appropriating and internalizing that strategy for herself (Tharp and Gallimore, 1988). The 'intermental' becomes 'intramental'. While, as a result of an off-the-cuff remark, the family may realize that their familiar old Waring blender affords a startling new possibility – a recognition that changes both the social and the material culture of the home. (I will leave the reader's imagination to fill in what such a possibility might be.)

If we are to take a longer-term view of either personal or cultural development – as education unavoidably must – we have to move back from the intricate particularity of the third discourse into the cumulative abstractions of the other two. Those who are concerned with the dynamics of institutional change (e.g. Fullan, 1991; D. Hargreaves, 1995) return to the second. Those who (like myself in the present context) are concerned with the developing empowerment of the individual, return to the first – but always with the awareness that we are dealing with more-or-less useful fictions and idealizations.

There are those who have used the insights of the third discourse to argue that the other two are in some sense illegitimate, but in doing so they have failed to appreciate the utility of complementary perspectives and languages, none of which is ultimately veridical, but each of which is suited to the pursuit of a particular concern. Thus, to acknowledge that all learning is 'situated' does not mean that we can say nothing about qualities of the person that become increasingly disembedded characteristics of the way they meet uncertainty, for example. To understand the way in which people are enculturated into a view of learning, and of themselves as learners, we need to focus on the situated moment (see, for example, the chapters by Carr, Mercer, and Pontecorvo and Sterponi, in this volume). To describe the progress that is made, as a result of such interactions, towards a set of valued educational goals, we need the language of psychology. Cultural–historical activity theory starts from and works with the insight that these three discourses are simultaneously legitimate and essentially and valuably complementary. It is with the interplay between these different perspectives, in the light of the social context outlined in the first section, that the rest of this chapter is concerned.

The Layers of Culture

One can explore the relationship between culture and learning at any level one chooses, from the global, to the directly interpersonal, to the solo individual trying to make sense of some cultural practice or material artifact. The momentary interaction between a teacher and a student, for instance, is imbued with influences from the classroom culture, from the culture of the subject discipline, from the school, from the community, from the nation and ultimately from the changing nature of international politics and economics – as well as from the home cultures and histories of the individuals concerned. (Lemke, in this volume, explores some of the interactions between these layers, and points out their different time-scales.)

It is unfortunate, therefore, that contemporary sociocultural theorists (in North America and elsewhere) have tended to neglect the wider political and ideological settings in favour of a detailed concentration on the microdynamics of the individual family or classroom, especially the adult–child dyad, and the local characteristics of 'zones of proximal development'. But the values and assumptions of the wider culture necessarily impact on the classroom in multiple ways: through its espoused goals, forms of assessment, social organization, roles and rituals, the language of the teacher's commentary, the materials supplied and the opportunities for learning they afford, and so forth. Whether deliberately or by default, what goes on in the ZPD is channelling students' long-term development of mind in one direction rather than another: a direction that is strongly influenced by the wider cultural values with which the ZPD is imbued (Wells, 1999). If education is to equip young people to live the uncertain life, a concern with the changing nature of society and its corollary demands – with the eventual real-life capabilities and dispositions which will be needed – has to reach down into the micro-structure of the teacher's momentary intentions and interactions.

It is time, in other words, for sociocultural theory to emerge from its historical arguments, its internecine disputes and its sometimes arcane language, and address contemporary issues of major social significance. Wertsch (1995), commenting on this imperative, says: 'The forces of globalization have accelerated in a variety of arenas such as finance, economic production and communication, while simultaneously new forces . . . of nationalism have emerged . . . [with] often brutal consequences'. In this context, he goes on:

> It is disheartening that the human sciences have seemed to contribute so little to understanding, let alone addressing, the issues at hand. . . . This is not solely, or even primarily, the result of some unwillingness or perversity on the part of researchers. . . . We see it as largely resulting from the use of inadequate or inappropriate languages for talking about these problems . . . [that make it] nearly impossible to formulate intelligent integrative pictures of complex phenomena. [Thus] a starting point for making the human sciences more capable of addressing today's major social issues . . . is to find a common language that makes it possible to communicate effectively across artificially drawn academic boundaries. (Ibid., p. 56)

And the problem may also have lain, as I have said, in social scientists' reluctance to look at the social practices and institutions which fascinate them – such as schools – not just as they currently exist, or in terms of minor modifications to classroom practice or school organization, but from the perspective of radical social action, based on an awareness of the past and an imaginative and ethical view of the future of education.

My starting point, then, is the reconceptualization of education as the creation of cultures and contexts within which young people develop the epistemic mentalities and identities characteristic of effective lifelong learners. Schools should become 'communities of practice' where the predominant practice is 'learning' (or 'inquiry', as Wells, this volume, proposes) and where, concomitantly, the 'elders' of the community are themselves exemplary learners, and skilled coaches of the arts and crafts of learning. I shall illustrate my approach with three case studies, showing how certain learning dispositions, appropriate to the 'learning age', can be fostered in the school environment: how, in other words, education can be reframed as an apprenticeship in developing learners' ability to extend their 'zones of proximal development' for themselves. The first two examples relate directly to the development of students as learners. The third looks at cultural factors that affect teachers' openness and responsiveness in the face of imposed educational change. The overall concern, in each case, is to demonstrate how key aspects of learners' epistemic mentalities and identities are shaped by the epistemic milieux in which they find themselves.

Resilience

One of the key qualities of the effective real-life learner is surely the ability to stay intelligently engaged with a complex and unpredictable situation, a property we might call 'resilience'. Resilient individuals will be more inclined to take on learning challenges of which the outcome is uncertain, to persist with learning despite temporary confusion or frustration, and to recover from setbacks and failures, rededicating themselves to the task they have undertaken. The polar opposite of resilience we might call 'fragility' – the tendency to get upset and withdraw at the first sign of difficulty, and to shift from 'learning mode' into a defensive, self-protective stance.

One of the most important influences on the development of resilience is the kind of language which children's parents, teachers and elders use to comment – for the most part informally – on children's learning activities. Particularly critical are the cultural messages that are conveyed through this commentary at crucial moments of difficulty, failure or success. As a child teeters on the brink of frustration or confusion, what kinds of emotional or strategic reactions, and what kinds of attributions and interpretations, are being fed to them through these processes of casual enculturation? Indeed, what kinds of occurrence are deemed worthy of note by their caregivers? Is continuing engagement, despite the lack of immediate success, a cause for an approving smile or a word of encouragement? Or is only success recognized and rewarded? If failure is noted at all, is the child coached to see this as a cause for concern, in need of a kind of emotional cosseting; or as a reflection of lack of ability; or as due to insufficient effort? 'There, there, never mind; let's have a cuddle' may teach the child that frustration will, unless actively soothed and managed, naturally lead on to upset – and such reactions may therefore, paradoxically, make the child more fragile rather than less in the face of future difficulties – especially where external comforting is not available. 'Oh, you stupid girl', or 'You are a clumsy child' encourages the child to take on for herself an internal, constitutional attribution: the idea that she simply doesn't have what it takes. 'Come on, you can do it', or 'Let's think of another way of tackling this' models for the child the idea that success may come as a result of greater persistence or ingenuity, and thus coaches her to appropriate and internalize these interpretations for herself.

Carol Dweck (e.g. 1986, 1999) has investigated some of the core conditions that either support or inhibit the development of resilience. It turns out that the educational culture's 'discourse of ability' is an important influence. She identifies two opposing views of general ability (or 'intelligence') which may infuse the languages of families or teachers. One, the 'entity view', sees ability as a more-or-less fixed, God- or gene-given endowment of general-purpose mental capacity, which effectively sets a ceiling on aspiration and potential performance. The other, the 'incremental view', sees ability more as an acquirable toolkit of learning resources. Dweck has shown that cultures which embody the entity view tend to undermine learners' resilience, making them feel anxious and inadequate in the face of difficulty, leading to avoidance of difficult learning challenges and defensiveness in the face of frustration. Cultures that talk of learning as itself learnable, and which value engagement and tenacity as much as achievement and success, on the other hand, encourage the development of an epistemic mentality that is more robust and an epistemic identity that is more secure. Thus the informal language that teachers and parents use to comment on success, failure and difficulty embodies and conveys a view of learning and knowing which takes up residence in youngsters' minds, channelling the development of their learning dispositions, and influencing how their learning capabilities are expressed and developed (see also Gipps, this volume).

Resourcefulness

My second example is inspired by the growing literature on 'distributed cognition' (e.g. Clark, 1997; Salomon, 1993). Not only, as Vygotsky (e.g. 1978) has long taught us, do individuals internalize the cognitive and linguistic tools they are offered by their epistemic milieux; they also make continual intelligent use of the resources that are afforded by their current environment. They capitalize on found assets, and 'off-load' cognitive effort (both individually and collectively) by exploiting facilities and creating artifacts (such as notebooks, computers and filing cabinets) that shoulder some of the computational or mnemonic load.

Environments 'afford' resources, but these resources do not become functional aids to intelligent learning unless they are perceived as such by the learner. It may well be, as Gibson (1979) argued, that evolution has built into the human perceptual apparatus some of these sensitivities. Even small babies seem to know that a looming shape is probably an approaching object, and therefore affords 'greeting' (if it is a face) or 'ducking' (if it is a ball). But many of our useful 'affordances' have to be discovered. The baby knows that a nipple affords sucking, but not that a restaurant affords eating, too. The affordances that become salient and effective for any individual thus depend critically on the nature of the physical artifacts and social practices which surround them, and on how their attention is directed towards certain uses and interpretations by their human tutors and models. For 'Crocodile Dundee', any encounter with another person affords 'conversation'; for the average New Yorker, it most definitely does not. And functional affordances also depend on other factors such as sub-cultural membership and pre-existing dispositions. For most Londoners, subway trains afford 'travelling' and 'reading'; for others, in addition, they afford 'painting', 'mugging' or 'clowning'.

Thus another of the effective lifelong learner's dispositions is what we might call resourcefulness: the tendency to look out for any utilities and resources that might support current learning. Conventional educational milieux tend to take an individualized, internalized view of human intelligence, rather than this extended, ecological view, and thus fail to provide opportunities to develop (except in particular cases, such as the current infatuation with computers and ICT) the disposition to make intelligent use of the social, technological and material environment. When the 'correct' tools for a particular learning job are neatly laid out – in readiness for a chemistry practical class, or a history investigation, say – an opportunity to develop resourcefulness is missed. Teachers who are involved with the PEEL initiative – the Project for the Enhancement of Effective Learning – in schools in the Australian state of Victoria (Baird and Northfield, 1992), for example, have developed a variety of ways of creating learning situations that are manageably 'messy', with respect to problem-definition as well as the resources needed, thus giving students valuable experience in deciding what resources they are going to make use of, and how.

Educational institutions also differ in the extent to which they provide opportunities for a wide range of epistemic tools to be expressed, exercised and developed. They privilege certain ways of learning and knowing, and marginalize or stigmatize others. For example, the role of intuition in learning tends to be undervalued, and therefore under-exercised, in schools. Certain kinds of complex predicament are best tackled through a rhythmic combination of articulate, purposeful 'hard' thinking, and relaxed, playful reverie – learning through intuition (Claxton, 1997). Yet the predominant culture of Western societies – in their business and judicial systems, for example, as well as in their schools and colleges – is one which disdains intuition, and assumes that hard thinking and articulate clarity are universally to be preferred.

As Fensham and Marton (1992) point out, 'the education of intuition' was one of the four major themes for educational innovation that emerged from the famous 1957 Woods Hole conference (Bruner, 1960); and it was the only one of the four that subsequently sank without trace. If the effective lifelong learner is someone who understands the value of a broad range of ways of knowing, and who is alert to the possibilities and the utilities of each in particular learning situations, then their epistemic cultures have to give them opportunities to practise them. (See Wells, this volume, for a more extended justification and elaboration of a similar view.)

Time and Open-Mindedness

My third and final example of the ways in which epistemic mentality/identity and epistemic milieu interact applies not directly to the world of young learners, but to the ways in which teachers, as learners, relate to educational change. Andy Hargreaves (1994) draws on anthropologist Edward Hall's (1984) distinction between two different cultural approaches to time, the monochronic and the polychronic. In a monochronic culture, tasks are clearly defined and tackled sequentially according to a predetermined timetable. There is a clear sense of the kinds of interactions between people that are 'on task' and those that are not. 'Success' is defined in terms of the production of 'solutions' that (appear to) meet the specification on time. In polychronic cultures, tasks are routinely tackled in a complex, parallel fashion without hard-and-fast deadlines. Social and instrumental interactions are interwoven and informal, often emerging organically and opportunistically. 'Success' is defined in terms of the production of 'solutions' that fulfil the initial intentions, even if not the technical specification, and which also serve to enhance social harmony and cohesion. Hall argues that stereotypically Northern European, North American and 'male' societies are monochronic, while Mediterranean, many 'Southern hemisphere', and 'female' societies tend to be more polychronic.

In terms of educational change, Hargreaves argues that the professional culture of elementary/primary schoolteachers tends to be polychronic, while the professional culture of educational administrators and reformers tends to be monochronic. The latter's natural inclination is to specify changes, and plan their implementation, clearly. Teachers may be given detailed documentation and designated times in which to assemble as teams to discuss the implementation of change, for example. Such an approach frequently leaves classroom teachers, however, feeling pressurized and over-managed, and generates a variety of forms of covert or overt resistance – even when the teachers are broadly amenable to the change itself. Simply through the failure to recognize cultural differences, innovation may come to be subverted or collapse under a rising tide of frustration ('Why are they so slow and fuzzy?' grumble the change promoters) and resentment ('Why are they so pushy and insensitive?' complain the teachers). If adult professional learning is to be supported effectively, managers and curriculum developers who spend their lives far from the chalk-face in a world of logistics, plans and abstractions, may need to become more sensitive to the very different cultures and mentalities that can obtain in staff rooms and classrooms.

A very similar sense of dissonance may accompany children as they move between home and school, or between primary and secondary schools. The culture of the former, for many children, may be significantly more poly-chronic, while the latter, in each case, may be much more monochronic. For children who have grown up in strongly polychronic family cultures, for example, it is not easy to learn to turn engagement with learning on and off according to the dictates of a clock, rather than in response to the delicate ebb and flow of interest, and the shifting pattern of environmental and social affordances. From the sociocultural point of view, it is a major part of the teachers' role to be aware of such cultural transitions, and to build bridges between the different cultures which children from different backgrounds can walk over at a pace that does not exhaust them, or leave some of the stragglers totally behind (Kegan, 1994).

Conclusion

Even a cursory scan of the wider world beyond the familiar box of education suggests that there is a need to shift the focus of attention from the mastery of prescribed bodies of knowledge, skill and understanding towards the cul-tivation of the transferable capabilities and dispositions of effective, real-life lifelong learning (Claxton, 1999). And this is precisely where the sociocultural perspective becomes so important – for these attitudes and abilities cannot be 'taught' or 'trained' directly through programmes of instruction. Lilian Katz (1999), in a recent summary of research on early learning, concludes that 'Dispositions are not learnt through formal instruction or exhortation. Many [of the] dispositions that most adults want children to acquire are learned primarily from being around people who exhibit them; [and] are strengthened by being used effectively and by being appreciated rather than being rewarded'. Children acquire positive learning dispositions, in other words, by being 'apprenticed' to a community within which such dispositions are naturally manifested, modelled, recognized, acknowledged and valued by the 'elders' by whom they are surrounded. The tools and attitudes of learning have to be nurtured within an educational milieu that affords, supports and encourages their expression and their development. This involves not the design of new programmes of study, nor even, in the main, the adoption of new forms of pedagogy, but an attention to the implicit values and assumptions of the culture, and to making sure that its objects, its tasks, its non-verbal signals and so on are consonant with the dispositions that the culture wishes to develop. It is the beliefs and priorities that are dissolved in the micro-'how' of the school that matter; not glitzy new packages of 'what'. (Again, see Wells, this volume, for a similar conclusion.)

Some of the connections between the epistemic milieu and the mentalities and identities that it affords and encourages are not immediately obvious – at least from within the dominant educational culture. It is interesting to discover just how much the development of resilience is influenced by the apparently innocuous discourse of 'ability', for example. It is interesting to see that classrooms that are neatly and tightly scripted may help students achieve, but may unwittingly do so by depriving them of opportunities to develop their own resourcefulness. It is interesting to observe how people's willingness to engage with change – teachers and children alike, maybe – depends on the way in which their culture structures and manages time. There are clearly many more such subtle contingencies between cultures, and the aspects of mind and self which they strengthen or suppress, that are waiting to be made explicit. It is only by adopting a framework within which a view of 'education as enculturation' is itself foregrounded, that such important information can be uncovered, and more empowering educational cultures be created.

3

Becoming the Village: Education Across Lives

Jay L. Lemke

Introduction

An old saying has it that it takes a village to raise a child. As children, we know how much we need to learn about everything and everyone in our communities to live there successfully. As we learn, we gradually become our villages: we internalize the diversity of viewpoints that collectively make sense of all that goes on in the community. At the same time, we develop values and identities: in small tasks and large projects, we discover the ways we like to work, the people we want to be, the accomplishments that make us proud. In all these activities we constantly need to make sense of the ideas and values of others, to integrate differing viewpoints and desires, different ways of talking and doing. As we participate in community life, we inevitably become in part the people that others need us to be, and many of us also find at least some of our efforts unsupported or even strenuously opposed by others.

The challenges of living in a village define fundamental issues for both education and development. In his pioneering work on intellectual development, Lev S. Vygotsky (1934/1963) introduced the basic principle that the contents of our thinking and the habits of our lives originate in our social interactions with others. What we eventually come to feel as something within us begins first as something between us. At about the same time, Mikhail Bakhtin (1935/1981) was beginning to define the broad social diversity in how a community uses language to describe and evaluate the world. This is exactly the diversity we encounter in our dialogues and social interactions with others, and which we must learn to make sense of, and make sense with, in order to live and work successfully in our 'villages'. In this chapter I want to explore what it means for education to take this social–cultural view of learning seriously.

We may prefer one particular way of working, but because we must work together, we also learn how to collaborate. Some of us prefer telling stories, others like to argue; some like to draw, others prefer building things; but we must all learn how our words and their pictures can be combined, and how building gets connected to drawing and to telling. We become individuals who like and prefer, but we always also gradually become in a larger sense the whole village. We learn to take part by learning how parts fit together. Over time we learn that there is nothing worthwhile we can do without a tool someone else has made, without combining ways of working we're comfortable with and ways we're not but others are, without taking into account viewpoints that are unfamiliar or unpleasant, without finding a way through conflict. What we do when we learn is to enter into social activities.

It takes a long lifetime to 'become a village'. Some routines can be learned in minutes, performed in seconds, but they only make sense when integrated into activities that may last for hours and are in turn small links in chains of interdependent projects that keep the village running and changing over the course of our lives and the community's history. We easily sense who we are and what we want in each minute's action, but it takes far more work and wisdom to feel our role and know our will across the longer term of years. In this view of human development, schooling today would seem to be paying too much attention to what we study and not enough to who we become; priding itself on what it brings into the classroom but blinding itself to all it shuts out; teaching isolated literacies but not how to make them work together; and creating many meanings for an hour but few for a day and none for a lifetime.

In this chapter I will focus on how and why we must learn to integrate language, visual literacies, and action itself in order to comprehend the natural world and our human culture: to 'become our village'. I want to pose questions about how our developing personal identities and values interact with our collaborative learning and activity. I want to question easy assumptions about how our efforts in each moment come to add up to the accomplishments of the day. Most of all, I want to ask whether this view of learning as 'becoming a village' can really be accommodated by the present-day institution of the school, or whether we should begin looking at more diverse systems to support not just learning, but getting an education.

Culture, History and the Activities of Learning

Many chapters in this book discuss the basic concepts of culture, history, activity and learning. What matters most to me are the relationships among them: how do we successfully learn through participation in social activities to become members of a culture whose long history is not yet over? When we start from the concept of learning alone, we tend to think only of the person who learns and to forget that *what* we learn is how to live successfully in a world of other people, and *how* we learn is by participating in the activities of our community. When we think of learning as something that happens now, we may forget that that learning only has value if it lasts long enough to be put to use, and that we know much less about changes in behaviour that accumulate over years than we do about what happens in a minute or an hour. I want to explore briefly in this section some important relationships among these notions of learning, activity, culture and history.

I did not choose the term 'village' in the title of this chapter to romanticize the complex, large-scale communities most of us really live in, but because a village is not just a collection of people: it is also a place, filled with culturally meaningful artifacts and with all the elements of a natural ecosystem, to which people also give meanings. The activities that occur in such a real community involve the participation of things as well as people: books, buildings, bacteria, tools, machines, roads and trees. What we gradually learn when we participate in village activities is not just how to collaborate with other people, but also how to make sense of and make use of every part of our communities.

We are always learning how to participate in the activities going on around us – activities that have a history as well as a meaning. The meaning comes from a culture: a particular way of doing, believing and valuing that has evolved over times much longer than any one person lives to see. Each activity connects to others in ways that depend on what is materially necessary and possible, e.g. writing to someone depends on having tools which make marks that last long enough to be read, and on the activities in which those tools were made, as well as those in which the raw materials needed to make the tools were obtained, and even on the activities that physically get what we've written to the people who want to read it. But each of these activities is also connected to others by meanings as well as by material necessities: reader and writer must share a common language or code; we must be able to recognize the meaningful function of an object as a tool-for-writing or an object-for-reading; making the tools and transporting what we write depends on collaborative efforts that are only possible among people who make the same general sort of sense of what each other say and do. Culture-specific meanings help us select from all the materially possible ways of writing or using clay just those that will make enough sense to other people to allow us to get on with life together. What we all need to learn is how to participate in these networks of culturally meaningful social activities: conversations, games, reading and writing, tool-using, productive work.

Participation in socially meaningful activities is not just what we learn, it is also how we learn. Even if we are alone, reading a book, the activity of reading – knowing which end to start at, whether to read a page left-to-right or right-to-left, top-down or bottom-up, and how to turn the pages, not to mention making sense of a language, a writing system, an authorial style, a genre format (e.g. a dictionary vs. a novel) – depends on conducting the activity in a way that is culturally meaningful to us. Even if we are lost in the woods, with no material tools, trying to find our way or just make sense of plants or stars, we are still engaged in making meanings with cultural tools such as language (names of flowers or constellations) or learned genres of visual images (flower drawings or star maps). We extend forms of activity that we have learned by previous social participation to our present lonely situation.

So far this story has been fairly simple. Now it is time to consider the problems and complexity that lie beneath the surface of these ideas about learning, activity, culture and history.

The Strategy of Schooling

We do not in fact learn to participate in every activity just by participating in it. If I walk innocently into an advanced chemistry research laboratory, most of what is going on will make sense to me only as simple actions: moving objects around, mixing and combining, putting things in machines that spin, reading numbers on a computer screen, but I will have very little idea what it all means. I will not know why people are doing what they are doing, or when is the right moment to do what. I will not be able to participate effectively in these activities in the way that chemists do, just by hanging around and observing. I might even become a useful assistant and follow simple instructions, but I would still not know why they were the right instructions. Only if someone patiently began to teach me the basics of chemistry would I eventually be able to learn effectively on my own in this laboratory. But teaching the basics of chemistry is not a normal activity in such labs; everyone who works there is assumed to know all that already, and much more. We live in a community where there are many such specialized activities that are not conducted in such a way that you can learn them just by participating: designing microchips or cancer drugs, auditing investment banks, conducting psychotherapy, diagnosing diseases, writing legal opinions, and so much more.

Our community has arranged itself in such a way that in order to participate in some activities, you must first have participated in others, often in other times and places, disconnected from the primary activity – most obviously in the case of schooling. Chemistry teachers and school chemistry labs are not working chemists or research laboratories; chemistry textbooks are not much like professional scientific writing. The strategy of schooling, in fact, always runs the risk of school becoming too unlike professional practice: a bridge to nowhere. Of course this does not mean that there are not also many activities that can be readily learned just by direct participation, or that there are not also ones in which it is quite normal to teach the basics to newcomers (cf. Lave and Wenger, 1991), but for those activities we have no special need for schooling, and by and large in those activities most people are eventually successful learners, quite unlike the situation in schools today.

Culture and History

We tend to use the word 'history' mainly to refer to very long periods of time: decades, centuries, millennia. In principle, however, everything takes time to happen; every process or activity that goes through distinct changes, stages or phases, has its own history, no matter how brief. For a human life, we tend to speak of a biography, or of the trajectory of human development over the lifespan. Even the speaking of a sentence, or the teaching of a lesson, however, has such a trajectory through time, a micro-history; and we have to pose the question of how these little histories of moments and hours come to add up to the longer history of a life or a community.

The notion of 'a culture' or 'a community' or even 'a language' becomes much more complex (and interesting) when we look at it in this historical perspective. There are no known communities where all the members participate in all the activities (tell all the traditional stories, perform all the traditional rituals, do all the typical daily routines); there is always a 'division of labour' in the sense that some people do some activities and others don't. Men and women play different roles, so do younger and older members, and very often different families, clans or lineages have their own specialized stories, songs, dances, crafts, designs, etc. It is not true that members of a community normally share all their beliefs, values, habits and practices. What is true is that all the different lifeways of groups and categories and individuals somehow fit together, are organized or articulated with one another, so that the community as a whole manages to continue to function. This is not just true of modern multicultural societies; it is true of all human communities. And this state of affairs is itself a product of the community's history.

There was a historical period in the eighteenth and nineteenth centuries when, for political reasons, many governments and those who benefited most from their rule propagandized the idea that 'national cultures' were far more 'pure' and homogeneous than is ever really the case. Culture wars were fought against 'invasions' and 'corruptions' of national cultures and national languages by outside, foreign influences. 'Standard languages' were established by the powerful to pre-empt competition among the wide variety of regional, social-class and ethnic dialects that exist within the artificial boundaries of every nation-state. Among the many myths of that period that we still live with today is the belief that a high degree of linguistic and cultural homogeneity is necessary for effective communication and cooperation within a society. There are simply too many counter-examples from too many times and places in human history to take this assertion seriously. Its primary function today is still to reinforce the artificial advantages of the dominant social groups: those who have unilaterally declared that their own language patterns and activity styles should set the standard for all the rest of us.

In these and many other ways history and culture shape and prescribe what we need to learn and what ways of learning will be available to us. But this is only half the story. What we do now and later, and what others do, makes history and culture. But how? How do the activities in which we learn determine culture and shape history every bit as much as history and culture shape what and how we learn? How do all the moments of all our lives add up to the history of a community? And what does this tell us about how learning could be different from the way it is today?

Across the Scales of Time

How do moments add up to lives? How do the brief activities of an hour add up to the accomplishments of a day, many ordinary hours and days ensure the continuity of social institutions, and the small differences of every action and moment accumulate into the radical changes of history?

Because this is a very large question, let's take it first just for the case of individual development. Imagine that a student in a classroom is engaged in a brief dialogue with a teacher that lasts maybe a minute or less. How can that experience possibly contribute to the formation of the student's personal identity? The notion of identity belongs to a much longer time-scale for characterizing people than the time-scale of short conversations. And yet an identity, a persistent belief or attitude, or even an enduring skill, must have its origins in such shorter-time events.

If we teach something, and the student learns it, does it stick? How do we know? All teachers realize that change in beliefs and identities, and the acquisition of persistent skills, takes time; more time than any one interaction or lesson. There may be 'breakthrough' moments, critical points on the path-way of development, but the pathway itself extends over a longer stretch of time. Each breakthrough has been prepared by many prior experiences, and the effects of that special moment can easily fade, or even be erased or reversed by other later events. It is only over the long haul that serious change happens.

Memory as Re-enactment

What binds one moment, one experience to another? We are accustomed to using the notion of 'memory' as our only answer to this question, but the idea of individual memory treats learning only from the viewpoint of the individual organism, and does not look at the activities in which we participate and all the people, places and things around us that help make memory work. When I return to streets in a distant city I have not visited for years, each new vista evokes memories that I could never have recalled otherwise; indeed contemporary theories of dynamical memory (e.g. Edelman, 1992) suggest that memory is not something stored like a map or picture in my brain, but is a partial recreation of my perceptions and actions, of a prior experience of being in a place and moving through it. Remembering is a process that takes place in a system that includes both me and some parts of my physical environment. Retracing my steps from years ago with recognition of the streets is one aspect of the whole complex activity of 'walking-there', in which my brain, my muscles, my eyes and the streetscape itself are all participants. Memory is not autonomous within the organism; it is an inter-active process of engagement with an environment that re-evokes past similar engagements.

From walking a streetscape to reading the wordscape of a book is a small, if historically crucial, step. As I reread a familiar text, I renew old engagements with it. The marks on the page (like the landmarks on the street) are physically co-participants in the activity of 'reading-there'. If that page is from my student notebook, those marks on paper made in yesterday's lesson, then retracing them with my eyes (or pencil) can re-evoke a whole sequence of thoughts and events from yesterday; indeed I might well start writing again at that point, taking up where I'd left off. Students do this with notes and doodles; professional writers with yesterday's first drafts. Were there no doodle, no draft, some activity would still occur, but it would not be the same one. Meaningful material objects, shaped in one moment's activity, can provide the link to another, related activity in a later moment of time. And the result is the construction of continuity on a longer time-scale than that of each momentary activity.

The human body is itself such a meaningful material object that is shaped by time, and bears the traces of our past activity. Our memories are not just in our brains, but in our muscle tone, in the chemistry of our blood, in every physiological part of us that 'remembers' or persists for times long compared to the time of the events that change them. A string on our finger, a cut on our skin, the twinge of an old injury, a sensitized allergy, just like the writing in our notebook, meet the requirements for binding us across time. Each brief event becomes linked into longer chains of events, into activities and projects, processes that take hours, days or years to unfold. The linkage is formed by every persistent feature of the body and its meaningful physical environment that lasts long enough to bridge from one such event in the chain to another.

How do we link across the scales of time, from the short time-scales of moments, to the longest time-scales of a lifetime, in making and maintaining our personal identities? And what does this have to do with learning?

Identity and its Props

An identity says something about who we are, to ourselves and perhaps to others. It is partly relational: who we are not, among the choices our commun-ity offers us. It is partly uniquely individual: who we have made ourselves be and how we imagine ourselves to be, across many different experiences. At times we are different people: in different activities, in different domains of our lives, with different partners-in-action. But we have also learned the cultural habit of constructing a certain consistency and continuity, a core identity that links all the different people we are into some sort of unity. How do we do this across moments and events, experiences and activities?

We do it by the clothes we wear, the music we play, the books we read, the places we return to, the diaries we write, the people we see again and again, the things we tell ourselves over and over. Above all, by the things we do time and again, renewing our participation in the activities that are typical for us. In all these cases, we are making use of material cues and reminders that tend to keep us in our preferred groove, being the self we want to be.

What about school activities? Which of all the activities that go on in classrooms and schools are the ones through which we are building and maintaining an identity? Is it the rude joke we tell or the smart answer we give that means more for our identity? Does solving equations fit into the 'identity kit' (cf. Gee, 1992; Walkerdine, 1997) we are fashioning for ourselves? Does writing poetry? Analysing maps? Dissecting a frog? Playing basketball?

Identity and Learning

Identities are not phenomena of the moment, or the hour. What matters to the formation of an identity is activity that is reinforced over the long haul, and fairly frequently. An identity that is favourable to science, or to literature, or to sports, is not constructed just in science class, English or physical education. It has to be nurtured, by us and by others, in more parts of the day than a single classroom hour, outside school as well as inside, after school and after schooling. But our curricula are not designed in these terms; we believe we are teaching knowledge, rather than building character. In most education there is no real effort to integrate experiences in school and outside of school; indeed the academic curriculum all but rejects as worthless or irrelevant nearly all that happens to students outside of school.

Our identities are usually also typical of our culture and our historical period. The material artifacts that last over these much longer time-scales, and with which we interact in ways that make our identities reflect our communities and our times, have meaning for us mainly through the media of our culture's representational tools: written language and visual literacies, whether pictorial or diagrammatic. These are the media through which communities bind themselves together across the longest periods of time and with the most specific and detailed meanings, carrying the most information at the least material cost. There are of course also other persistent material media, like architecture and machines, or designed landscapes and cityscapes, that embody less information and require great material cost, but also link the largest numbers of people over the longest times. These may, some day, be joined by today's new media: simulations and computer programs, and the multimedia and hypermedia that our technologies are making it easier and cheaper for more people to create, use and circulate widely.

Learning the Media of Social Collaboration

A lot of education today is still oriented to teaching students to read, write and use various kinds of specialized written materials, their accompanying diagrams, and sometimes mathematics. But we teach the content, not the medium. We teach students scientific and technical vocabulary, but we never point out how science systematically turns verbs into nouns and why it does so. We rarely if ever explicitly teach students how to talk science (Lemke, 1990) or how to write science (Halliday and Martin, 1993) and show them how it's different from (and like) telling a story or writing one. We barely teach students the rudiments of how to draw, considering that skill an expendable luxury, yet the construction and interpretation of complex diagrams lies at the heart of our technical civilization. If few of our students can express themselves by writing fluently in more than one register (scientific, historical, rhetorical, narrative, poetic, etc.), fewer still can express their ideas fluently through drawing either diagrams or pictures. And no attention at all is paid in the curriculum to explaining how complex meanings are expressed by combining words and graphic images.

All media are multimedia. Plain written words are not just language, they also carry meanings that are visually organized: by the choice of font, page layout, headers and footers, typography, paragraphing, etc. Much that we read, we also interpret not just verbally but also by visualizing images. A bare image likewise is interpreted in part through the medium of language. Increasingly, most of our popular and specialized genres of communication are also explicitly multimedia ones: from printed magazines, to textbooks, to webpages, to technical articles and manuals, to business documents, presentations and corporate annual reports. Cheaply printed, unillustrated fiction is one of the last single-medium genres. More obvious still are multimedia such as television, film, and the computerized animation, sound, and video hypermedia that are likely to take over from traditional media for many purposes during the lifetimes of today's students.

Students desperately need to know how to critically interpret combinations of words, pictures, maps, diagrams and specialized symbolic expressions. They need to understand that there are different conventions for doing so in different fields and in different genres. And increasingly they need to know how and when and why to combine these media to express their ideas. It is hard to say to what extent new technologies and methods of teaching will make all students reasonably fluent in multiple media, but I think it likely that individual identities will still fit better with some media or some multimedia genres than with others.

As I said at the beginning: we may prefer one way to work, but because we must work together, we also learn how to collaborate. If we expand the multimedia mix beyond words and images and videos and animations to include the building of structures, the design of machines and the creation of human environments and activities, then the principles of how to combine all our systematic resources for making meanings that last and bind people together across time become fundamental to what education seeks to do. But what kind of educational institutions can be successful at this task?

Beyond Schooling

Students in schools today are deeply alienated from the curriculum. For many students school presents an alternate reality that bears no obvious connection to the rest of their lives. Some take it on faith that obedient conformity will lead to later financial rewards; many are justly sceptical as to whether that promise applies to them. Schools as institutions are isolated from the main-stream of both public and private life. Far from helping students to under-stand the village in which they live, schools become micro-villages in their own right, with their own typical activities that are only distantly related to those outside. The range of activities that occur in schools is narrow and impoverished in its diversity compared to the activities that define the reality of the larger village (see also del Río and Álvarez, this volume).

Consider an example. We have a curriculum for teaching 'science', but by that we only mean teaching students highly simplified accounts of the product of scientific activity: the descriptions and explanations that scientific activity results in. We teach students almost nothing about living, working, profes-sional scientific activity itself. They never meet a real scientist, they never see a real scientific article, they never visit or even see a video of what happens in a real scientific laboratory or field research site. They learn nothing about the dependence of scientific activity on technology or on funding, or about how and why scientists write, calculate and draw diagrams the way they actually do. No connection is made between the science curriculum and the uses of scientific ideas in designing and maintaining the physical plant of the school, the technological infrastructure of the neighbourhood, or the local urban, suburban or rural ecosystem. The real concerns of the students, whether about drugs, sex, disease, food, clothing or music, play no part in the curric-ulum and no connection is made between them and the important scientific issues that underlie each of these legitimate student concerns.

What do students learn in school about the economics and politics of their own local communities? About jobs and employment, about personal finance and legal rights, about crime and its causes? What do they learn about popular culture and its relation to older and longer traditions of fiction, art and music? About the television programmes and films they watch, the music and videos, the games they play? Where does any part of the curriculum, so proud of its 'high intellectual standards', connect in any way with the typical activities and identities of students? (Cobb and McClain and Dalton and Tharp, this volume, show how this can be different.)

If identities must be developed and sustained over time, how can schooling afford to so isolate itself from the mainstream of student identity-formation and still consider itself to have 'educational' value? If the purpose of education is to understand the complexity of the communities we live in and how to participate successfully in collaborative social activities over long time-scales, how can this happen if education continues to be dominated by institutions of schooling that isolate themselves from the rest of social life and organize learning only on time-scales measured in minutes?

Is it wrong to describe schools as buildings consisting of empty rooms where too many children and too few adults talk about or enact pale simulations of the rich and varied activities of the community around them, rather than actually observing or participating in those activities? I have already pointed out that many of the activities of a complex community cannot be learned just by observing and engaging in a 'legitimate peripheral participation' in them (cf. Lave and Wenger, 1991), but that does not justify boycotting all direct contact with life outside school. We do need times and places of retreat and contemplation to review, critique and question activity away from immediate engagement in it. But we need them in order to reflect on direct participatory experiences, not as a substitute for such experiences.

Organizationally, schools minimize the opportunity for long-term intellectual and identity development by severing the bonds between teacher and student every several months, disconnecting the study of each subject from all the others, and even dividing the day into periods defined by a clock rather than by the needs of learning. The whole point of intellectual and identity development is to learn to integrate experience over progressively longer time-scales, but the institutional arrangements of schooling seem deliberately designed to thwart this effort. How often do students get the opportunity to engage in sustained learning projects that stretch their abilities to organize activity across longer time-scales? And what kinds of projects could engage the interest and attention of students on these longer scales?

Schooling is just one, relatively recent educational arrangement. We all know that today many functions of classroom education are becoming technologically obsolete. Students will soon learn how to get information they need on any subject, including explanations and help in understanding them at their own level, from searching for sources on the internet, as they would in any really good library. The teaching of many basic concepts and skills will soon be packaged attractively in combinations of videos, animations, simulations and interactive games that will be easily accessible (if not always cheaply priced). There will be increasing economic pressure, starting with the later grades, to spend taxpayers' money on subsidizing students' access to these packages and only paying for live teachers and classes when they can demonstrate a clear superiority of results.

New technologies can often do the job of simulating and talking about the typical activities of the community far better than the average teacher in the average classroom. Technologies will not, however, be able to substitute for direct participation, nor will they be able to replace thoughtful guidance of students' critical reflection and analysis, nor the emotional encouragement of achievement and creativity that live teachers provide. For these purposes professional teachers will always be needed, especially for younger students. Schools will become places where students and their teachers decide together what comes next: collaborative projects, participatory internships, multimedia study modules, specialized learning activities, places to see and things to do. Students will participate in online peer-discussion groups, in cross-age groups where they can learn from older students and teach younger ones, and they will also have online access to a wide range of part-time mentors who mainly live and work in the world outside schools.

Teachers will not, however, become merely managers of such multi-resource learning systems. They will be concerned with the long term, with who each student is becoming, with how all that learning adds up to an education. They will maintain contact with students over many years. They will take responsibility for posing the difficult questions: about life, about self, about social justice. Again and again, over the very long times it takes to engage seriously with serious matters. A village is not built in a day.

4

The Gift of Confidence: A Vygotskian View of Emotions

Holbrook Mahn and Vera John-Steiner

A significant goal for educational reform and an area of focus for this present volume is helping students to become lifelong learners. An important component in meeting this objective is teachers building on their students' prior experiences, thereby helping them develop the confidence that engenders competence. In this chapter we focus on highly accomplished adult learners and English as a Second Language (ESL) students to explore affective factors that lead to sustained confidence. We look to Vygotsky not only for the theoretical framework through which to examine these affective factors, but also as a model for teachers who instil confidence in their students by offering caring support. His daughter, Ghita Vygotskaya (1999), quotes Elkonin, one of his students, to illustrate the way that his life powerfully exemplified this building of confidence:

> Lev Semonovich possessed an extraordinary ability to give support. I have probably never met a single person who was so little interested in proclaiming his own authorship as Lev Semonovich. It was the extraordinary generosity and scope of ideas of the kind of person who gave everything to everyone. (Ibid., p. 37)

While some aspects of Vygotsky's work are receiving increased attention and appreciation among educators internationally, his writings on the relationship between affect and thought remain largely unknown, although they are central to understanding his work as a whole. Our claim is that an appreciation of his work and particularly of his best-known concept – the Zone of Proximal Development (ZPD) – is deepened through an examination of the role of affective factors in learning. Such an expanded understanding of the ZPD is important in developing pedagogical approaches to meet the needs of all students and especially those of second language learners, who face cognitive and emotional challenges as their learning involves both a new language and a new culture. 'Learning in the ZPD involves all aspects of the learner –

acting, thinking and feeling' (Wells, 1999, p. 331). We use this expanded notion of Vygotsky's concept of the zone of proximal development, as well as some of his unfinished, yet seminal, work on emotions, as a theoretical frame for exploring affective factors in learning. We also hope to illuminate the complexity of learning when thought, emotional experience and practical action are brought together in the analysis.

Vygotsky's Integration of Thought and Affect

At the time of his death at age 37, Vygotsky was working concurrently on two manuscripts: *Thinking and Speech* and *The Teaching about Emotions: Historical–Psychological Studies*. While the former (Vygotsky, 1934/1987) has become a classical psychological work, the latter, a historical analysis of the role of affect based on Descartes' and Spinoza's work, is largely unknown outside Russia, as it only became available in English in 1999 with the publication of volume 6 of Vygotsky's Collected Works. The centrality of emotion, for Vygotsky, is reflected in the concluding pages of *Thinking and Speech*, where he explores the dialectical relationship between thought, affect, language and consciousness.

> [Thought] is not born of other thoughts. Thought has its origins in the motivating sphere of consciousness, a sphere that includes our inclinations and needs, our interests and impulses, and our affect and emotions. The affective and volitional tendency stands behind thought. Only here do we find the answer to the final 'why' in the analysis of thinking. (Vygotsky, 1934/1987, p. 282)

We ourselves were led to an examination of the interrelationship between thought and affect through the directions taken in our respective research projects. We found that exploring the common themes in our work, including the central role played by caring support in facilitating risk-taking in both the learning and creative processes, made the role of affect even more salient. Using Vygotsky's theoretical framework, we draw on Mahn's (1997) research on the role of affect for students learning to write in English as a second language and John-Steiner's (2000) research on creative collaborations among adults.

We examine the ways in which lending support to others can build their confidence and at the same time help promote and sustain lifelong learning and creativity among both accomplished adults who are engaged in sustained creative enterprises and ESL students learning to write in a second language. There is already a rich and diverse literature on cognitive aspects of the zone of proximal development and dialogic, interactive and collaborative learning in the classroom. In this chapter we look at learning through the different theoretical lens provided by Vygotsky's work on emotions and make explicit aspects of the ZPD that have not yet received the same attention. We start with a brief overview of recent developments in the study of emotion.

Emotions and Learning

Although studies of emotion have a long history in the human sciences, there is wide variation in the way emotion is represented. Most authors use what Brothers (1997) calls an 'isolated mind' approach and focus on the physiological basis of feelings not directly related to thought. However, recent research has found affect to be powerfully linked to specific brain structures, and its expression to be determined by situated social interaction. Indeed, Damasio (1999) points out that, in a variety of disciplines, recognition is being given to the importance of the productive synthesis of affect and reason and to the study of their mutually reinforcing roles. Brothers also notes that, in contrast to 'isolated mind' approaches, relational theory focuses on social interaction and conceives of emotion as interactive and shaped by human communicative exchanges (Brothers, 1997). Furthermore, in developmental psychology, Daniel Stern (1985) describes in wonderful detail the way in which infants' arousal, security and attachment are regulated by caregivers through play, naming and the shifting rhythms of their interactions.

This focus on the interpersonal and intrapersonal dynamics in the origins, expression and appropriation of emotion governs our own discussion and helps to expand understanding of the zone of proximal development. Our investigation is guided by the realization that human beings come into existence, attain consciousness and develop throughout their lives in relationship to others. In our discussion of the role of affect in transformative educational practice, we focus on the aspects of social interdependence – human connection and caring support – that foster the development of competence. Of particular concern to us are the ways in which competence is built through dignified, collaborative, caring support, whether between scientists and artists or between teachers and students.

Classroom interactions between students and teachers, on the one hand, and intense creative collaborations among accomplished artists and scientists, on the other, might seem far removed from one another. However, an examination of their underlying commonalities provides insight into the role played by affect in learning and creativity. Joint activities in both are enhanced when the interactions between participants are supported by 'the gift of confidence' (a term borrowed from the philosopher Jean-Paul Sartre). In the reciprocal emotional support offered by partners in collaboration – whether they are novice learners of a new language or individuals engaged in novel, creative endeavours – there is a dynamic interplay between their interactions and the ways in which they appropriate the emotional support. To examine this interplay we use three interrelated concepts developed by Vygotsky in the last years of his life:

1   the zone of proximal development;
2   the relationship between word meaning and word sense;
3   *perezhivanie*, perhaps his least-known concept. *Perezhivanie* describes the ways in which the participants perceive, experience and process the emotional aspects of social interaction.

By expanding the scope of the examination of the ZPD to include affective variables we can both amplify its dynamic character and deepen understanding of this Vygotskian concept. This approach reveals the ZPD as a complex whole, a system of systems in which the interrelated and interdependent elements include the participants, artifacts and environment/context, and the participants' experience of their interactions within it. In addition, we suggest that the complementarity that exists between these elements plays a central role in the construction of the ZPD. When a breach in this complementarity occurs because the cognitive demands are too far beyond the learner's ability or because negative affective factors such as fear or anxiety are present, the zone in which effective teaching/learning occurs is diminished.

In recent years, analyses of the ZPD have emphasized the co-construction of knowledge within a cooperative environment that includes cultural tools, varied forms of social interaction and interpersonal scaffolding (John-Steiner and Mahn, 1996; Wells, 1999). Some authors have referred to these interwoven processes as the 'collective zone of proximal development' (Moll and Whitmore, 1993). Such expanded analyses of the ZPD posit the degree of complementarity as a determining factor in the success of the interaction between the participants, whether the interaction involves adult with child, teacher with student, peer with peer, or whether it occurs among a number of individuals within the ZPD. Aspects of complementarity include a common understanding of the task at hand, an appreciation of one another's cognitive, social and emotional development, and potential contribution.

The Zone of Proximal Development and *Perezhivanie*

The interdependence of these aspects of complementarity is effectively captured by Vygotsky's concept *perezhivanie*, which some equate with 'lived or emotional experience.' *Perezhivanie* describes the affective processes through which interactions in the ZPD are individually perceived, appropriated and represented by the participants. Vygotsky described the central role played by language in an individual becoming aware of, and making meaning from, 'lived experience'. He therefore used the concept of word meaning as the foundation for his investigation of *perezhivanie*. As a prelude to our examination of affective factors in the ZPD we offer an illustration of *perezhivanie*. The African American writer James Baldwin (1976) recalled the powerful influence of a white teacher who provided him with the gift of confidence as well as with a model of resistance. This woman, Bill Miller, taught and mentored the promising 10-year-old Baldwin. 'She had directed my first play and endured my first theatrical tantrums and then decided to escort me into the world' (ibid., p. 22). Baldwin witnessed her personal courage when she fought against racism:

> Bill took us on a picnic downtown once, and there was supposed to be ice-cream waiting for us at a police station. The cops did not like Bill, didn't like the fact that we were colored kids, and did not want to give up the ice-cream. I don't remember anything Bill said. I just remember her face as she stared at the cops, clearly intending to stand there until the ice-cream all over the world melted . . . and she got us our ice-cream, saying, 'Thank you,' I remember as we left. (Ibid.)

Those children who had less connection and emotional rapport with their teacher than this sensitive, future writer were probably affected differently by the scene in the police station than was Baldwin. They had distinctly different *perezhivanija*, as their reactions would have been based on 'the specifics of their past experiences' (Vygotsky, 1934/1987, p. 341). Nevertheless, the courageous actions of their teacher provided an important emotional and intellectual experience for all of these students raised in the isolation of the black ghetto in the 1930s. Baldwin recreates the event by evoking the looks, the paucity of words, and the palpable tension within the police station, all of which contribute to the emotional subtext of this passage.

This example clearly illustrates the emotional aspect of language and the importance of human connection in social interaction, both of which are central to Vygotsky's concept of *perezhivanie*. To explain it, he relied on the dense textures of language as motivated by feelings, enriched by previous experience and focused by volition. As Luria (1934/1987) pointed out in the afterword to *Thinking and Speech*, Vygotsky focused on this affective aspect of learning and made meaning central to his theory:

> Without the exploration of the relationship of the word to motive, emotion, and personality, the analysis of the problem of 'thinking and speech' remains incomplete. The relationship between meaning and sense, and the relationship of intellect to affect, were the focus of much of Vygotsky's work in the last years of his life. (Ibid., p. 369)

In our view, Vygotsky's examination of the ways in which meaning making and the affective aspects of social interaction affect learning in the ZPD needs further development.

Making Meaning

Vygotsky's examination of meaning as central to human consciousness has provided the foundation for its extensive study by sociocultural theorists

(Prawat, 2000; Yaroshevsky and Gurgenidze, 1997). His analysis of meaning, in which he approached the hidden, complex, affective dimensions of thinking and speech by studying the emotional subtext of utterances – what he referred to as 'sense' – is also central to his analysis of *perezhivanie*.

> A word's sense is the aggregate of all psychological facts that arise in our consciousness as a result of the word. Sense is a dynamic, fluid, and complex formation that has several zones that vary in their stability. (Vygotsky, 1934/ 1987, p. 276)

While meaning is often conceptualized as external and sense as internal, there is a social aspect to sense. The individual sense of an utterance includes attributes that are shaped by culture and appropriated through social interaction. The manner in which Vygotsky examined the similarities and distinctions between meaning and sense illustrates his methodological approach – seeking out the integrative, dialectical connections among complex, separate and interdependent processes. He concluded: 'Meaning is only one of the zones of sense, the most stable and precise zone' (idid., p. 245).

Our own recognition of the interdependence of intellect and affect in the making of meaning and co-construction of knowledge remained obscured for a long time, as we shared our colleagues' primary focus on cognition and oral and written language use. During the past few years, however, each of us, in our separate and joint work, has come to recognize the need to examine closely the relationship between emotion and intellect. We believe that Vygotsky's concept of *perezhivanie* can play an important role in understanding the appropriation of social interaction. We have also come to realize that this appropriation in the ZPD plays a crucial role in transformative experiences of all types and is not limited to children and other novice learners. Careful listening, intense dialogue and emotional support sustain the cooperative construction of understanding, of scientific discovery and of artistic forms. This is true in interaction across generations – in parenting, teaching and mentoring – and among creative partners.

We start our examination of these factors by considering affect in the construction of the ZPD outside the classroom, drawing on John-Steiner's (2000) study of intense, creative collaborations. Affective factors play a substantial role in the construction of the ZPD in other than formal school settings, yet this fact is often relegated to the periphery in traditional educational approaches.

Creative Collaboration and Mutual Appropriation

In collaboration, partners create zones of proximal development for each other 'where intellect and affect are fused in a unified whole' (Vygotsky,

1934/1987, p. 373). Emotional scaffolding includes the gift of confidence, the sharing of risks in the presentation of new ideas, constructive criticism and the creation of a safety zone. Partners who have been successful in constructing such a joint system are sensitive to the sense as well as the meaning of each other's language. In producing shared texts, collaborators expand their partner's early drafts; they strive to give shape to their communicative intent by combining precision – or word meaning – with the fluidity of the sense of words. They live, temporarily, in each other's heads. They also draw on their mutuality as well as their differences in knowledge, working styles and temperament.

This sensitivity to the use of language and reliance upon reciprocal emotional support was exemplified by the writers/philosophers Jean-Paul Sartre and Simone de Beauvoir, lifelong partners in their personal and work lives. At times, they produced identical answers to questions. Toward the end of Sartre's life, de Beauvoir interviewed him about his beliefs, friendships, relationships with women, and his writing. At one point he said: 'You did me a great service. You gave me a confidence in myself that I should not have had alone' (de Beauvoir, 1984, p. 168). The profound importance of the 'gift of confidence' is apparent in many long-term partnerships (John-Steiner, 2000). When collaborators challenge long-held assumptions in their domain, they are particularly dependent on their partners' beliefs in the significance of their joint endeavours. Innovative works of literature, drama and science are nourished by sustained support – as are teaching and learning across the lifespan.

One way to look at creative collaboration and cooperative learning is to envision them as dynamic systems between individuals linked by shared objectives. The Cubist painters, Pablo Picasso and Georges Braque, shared a powerful vision; they aimed at revealing 'the interlocking of phenomena . . . of processes instead of static states of being' (Berger, 1965, p. 59). The joy of discovery, the commitment to remain open to one another's ideas, and a temporary erasure of individual egos, were all necessary to their work, which transformed established views of the painterly surface. During their most intensely collaborative years, these two painters chose similar scenes and each incorporated innovations by the other into his own painting. Picasso later recalled: 'Almost every evening I went to Braque's studio or Braque came to mine. Each of us had to see what the other had done during the day. We criticized each other's work. A canvas was not finished until both of us felt it was' (Gilot and Lake, 1964, p. 76).

Complementarities in skills, working methods and temperament can be very productive in collaborative activities. The resulting expansions of self are richly elaborated in John-Steiner's studies of artists and scientists. Interviews with educators and social scientists further support the crucial role, in producing new insights and syntheses, of multiple perspectives from diverse thought and discourse communities. These achievements, however, lack durability without the presence of emotional and cognitive mutuality. Understanding the ways that this mutuality sustains a lifelong expansion of the self can inform teachers who are trying to help their students become lifelong learners.

Collaborative Learning in the Classroom

Teachers are able to collaborate with students in creating environments conducive to transformative teaching/learning if they attempt to understand their lived experiences, knowledge and feelings. Doing so will help reveal the complexities of students' cognitive and emotional development. A teacher's awareness of students' ways of perceiving, processing and reacting to classroom interactions – their *perezhivanija* – contributes significantly to the teacher's ability to engage the students in meaningful, engaging education. Moll and Greenberg (1990) have shown that building on the funds of knowledge and the culturally shaped ways of knowing that children bring to the classroom helps accomplish this goal.

In order both to discover and build upon these funds of knowledge, teachers may find dialogue journals of great value. In these journals teachers and students can carry on a sustained written dialogue and make the kind of human connection that yields insights into the students' lived experiences. To clarify the concept of *perezhivanie* and the ways in which it can contribute to the creation of transformative learning experiences, we look at the students' appropriation of the interactions between themselves and their teacher in these journals. The shared cognitive and emotional interaction in journals facilitates the transformation of experiences from interpersonal to intrapersonal and makes the authors more metacognitively aware of their own writing process – an important aspect of learning to write.

Vygotsky used the distinction between meaning and sense to analyse the process of the individual's appropriation of social interaction. Drawing on the above concepts, Mahn (1997) studied the use of dialogue journals with high school and university ESL students to examine the role of affect in learning. Viewing dialogue journals both as a pedagogical device and as a lens through which to view students' *perezhivanija*, we next explore ways in which students develop emotional and cognitive mutuality in educational settings.

The Value of Dialogue Journals

Journals in which a teacher and students carry on written dialogues have been used by teachers at every level as a means of getting to know their students, engendering trust and lending support (Stanton et al., 1988). Through dialogic interaction in journals, students give salience to experiences that shape their identity and reveal ways that their educational experiences are shaped by affect in relation to ethnicity, culture, gender and class status. As they do this, teachers become more aware of their students' lives and *perezhivanija*. The genuine caring support teachers can offer their students is especially important in high-anxiety activities such as writing in a second language. With a teacher's gift of confidence, students can face their anxiety and take risks with their writing.

Mahn (1997) carried on year-long written dialogues with his high school and university ESL students in journals in which they wrote for 10–15 minutes at the beginning of class on whatever topic they chose. They were encouraged to focus on authentic communication and not to worry about mistakes. They were free to jump from topic to topic and to draw on their own interests and experiences. The relationships that were developed in the journals became an important part of the culture of the classroom, as the confidence that students gained through their journals carried over into the academic writing in Mahn's and other classes. The collaborative aspect of the journal writing and the creation of a relatively risk-free environment also carried over into the course as a whole and contributed to the construction of a collective ZPD.

Students in Mahn's (1997) study of ESL writers revealed their anxiety through frequent reference to their fear of making mistakes. This anxiety inhibited their writing and caused further frustration as they were stymied in their ability to communicate their ideas. In a reflective piece of writing in her journal, one student wrote: 'Because I could not express my feelings completely, I feel heavy pressure in my chest' (Pi Lan). Another student added: 'the grammar ghost was present in every sentence and between the lines' (Jabar). A number of students related that their anxiety was heightened by pedagogical approaches that put the major emphasis on form and mechanics rather than on communicative intent.

By contrast, students gained confidence through dialogue journals, and their writing was transformed as it became a vehicle for self-discovery. The narrative fluency that helped students forge writing identities also helped them to develop ideas more completely in academic writing. 'Writing in journals has built my confidence in writing and lately, I found that writing helps me understand something deeper' (Dat). 'Journals have made writing a lot easier for me. I feel confident when I am supposed to write an essay or something. I am not scared any more when I hear the word "essay"' (Minh).

Key to identity formation was the focus on meaningful communication instead of mechanics. 'For the first time in my life I see English teacher who want his student to be released from the verbs and tenses prison and to wake up from the grammar nightmare. It was a relief' (Jabar). As students became less anxious about their writing, they reported that they became more fluent. They found that when they wrote more rapidly they could get their thoughts down on paper instead of losing each thought as it was edited and re-edited in their minds before committing words to paper. 'The good strategy that really helped was writing without stopping and always having my brain and my hand connected to each other' (Ali). 'My hand and mind work without thinking about it. By learning to write as I'm thinking, the journal makes my thinking flow and helps my idea run smoother' (Jose).

Another student, Trang, provided a metaphor that summarized the experiences of a number of students:

> I realized that journal really help me to write down my idea without any blocking into my elbow. When I have idea in my head and I start to make it go down my arm to the paper, if I think about grammar, structure my idea blocks into my elbow and never goes to the paper.

These comments offer a powerful image of thought imprisoned between mind and hand; Mahn found their thoughts could be released through caring and supportive interaction.

Vygotsky (1934/1987) described the complexity of the move from thought to written utterance/speech in his description of the internal planes of verbal thinking:

> The motive gives birth to thought, to the formation of thought itself, to its mediation in the internal word to the meanings of external words, and finally, to words themselves. (Ibid., p. 283)

He underscored the possibility of a short-circuit occurring at any point along this complex path. However, the complexity of the move from thought to written language is further compounded when a student is writing in a second language. Valuable insights for developing effective pedagogical approaches for teaching linguistically and culturally diverse students can be gleaned by examining students' views on the various obstacles they encounter and attempt to transcend along the paths from thought to written speech. As collaborators we, too, have experienced the silence of uncertainty, relieved by the co-construction of new meaning.

A recurring theme in the students' reflections on the use of dialogue journals was that the responses they received from the teacher played an important role in motivating them and giving them the confidence to take risks with their writing. This confidence, developed through the genuine support in the teacher's responses, helped them to express ideas and emotions that they might not otherwise have attempted. 'I saw a different side of the language. I realized that I could actually write in English. Not only I can write but I get compliments for my writing, and that's very important to me' (Aphrodita). 'Sometimes when I wrote something, I think that people would not understand what I'm trying to say. Every time when I wrote journals and you write little comments on it I feel that I can express what I want to say' (Pancha). The emotional fine-tuning that occurred in dialogue journals thus helped to establish relationships that became the foundation for the collective ZPD of the class as a whole. In the process of creating zones of proximal development through their journals, they also learned about themselves as writers. 'It is probably through the dialoguing with real or imagined others in the process of textual composition that even the most knowledgeable others are able to continue to learn in the ZPD' (Wells, 1999, p. 320). Without understanding the students' *perezhivanija* and the ways that their zones of proximal development are affected by their responses to interactions in the classroom, it is difficult for teachers to offer the support that will motivate their continuing development.

Word Meaning and Sense in a Second Language

In her study of beginning writers and the zone of proximal development, Petrick-Steward (1995) suggests that we think of the ZPD in the activity of learning and teaching as being mutually and actively created by the child and the teacher: not 'as a characteristic, of the child or of teaching, but of the child engaged in collaborative activity within specific social environments' (ibid., p. 13). An important consideration in educational reform is to discover what is necessary to establish classroom environments in which opportunities are created for students to understand their experiences with language and literacy acquisition, their interaction with parents and peers, their value systems and beliefs, and their ways of making meaning of the world. Such understanding can be revealed through dialogue journals and other classroom activities that promote student engagement and awareness of their learning processes.

Through engaging in meaningful communication in their journals, the students developed their own sense of words along with deepening their understanding of word meaning. Students who are acquiring a second language are taught meaning when they are given definitions that they then have to reconcile with their understanding of equivalent forms from their first language. 'The dictionary meaning of a word', wrote Vygotsky (1934/1987, p. 245), 'is no more than a stone in the edifice of sense, no more than a potentiality that finds diverse realization in speech [and writing].'

Second language learners face the challenge of reconciling their developing word sense and word meaning in English with the word sense of the equivalent word in their native language – what that word evokes for them personally. Word meaning in English will predominate over word sense until they develop fluency, until words sound right, until they get a feeling for the language, and until they develop the systematicity and automaticity required to convey profound ideas in English. As has been argued above, all these aspects of fluency are facilitated by their use of dialogue journals. Other methods that can be used to support the acquisition of fluency and the subtle shadings of meaning in a second language include the teacher providing learners with diverse, meaningful models of text, tailored to their needs and concerns, and also creating opportunities for them to write in their native language.

Through interaction in their journals and by shifting the focus from form and structure to meaning, students reflected that they could think better in English, i.e. that they could use inner speech more effectively and draw on word sense to express complex ideas more effectively. They became less concerned with the dictionary meanings of words and began to have confidence that drawing on their sense of the word would not interfere with effective communication. An important part of this process is to instil in students through classroom practice the understanding that it is acceptable for them to take chances in their writing and to develop confidence in their own voices. In a similar vein, creative collaborators are able to take chances in presenting their new work to a doubting and critical audience as they support each other in facing and overcoming their anxieties. It is in this way that creative collaborators and teachers and students construct their joint zones of proximal development.

Conclusion

In an era of increased emphasis on students' scores on standardized achievement tests, the challenge facing those who seek educational reform is to transform teaching practice so that it reflects a greater appreciation of learning. A broad research initiative undertaken by the National Research Council focuses on the advances that have been made in understanding how children learn and how this knowledge can be used to improve student learning. A shift away from 'diligent drill and practice' and toward a 'focus on students' understanding and application of knowledge' is being advocated (NRC, 1999, p. xi). Our contention is that affect plays an important, yet often neglected, role in students' understanding and application of knowledge. Once this is recognized the next challenge is to develop ways in which teachers can gain an appreciation of their students' understandings and experiences of classroom activity and interaction – their *perezhivanija*.

The increasing linguistic and cultural diversity in schools underscores the importance of reform efforts focusing on creating teaching/learning environments that foster 'mutual respect, trust and concern' (Wells, 1999, p. 333). An essential part of students' *perezhivanija* is provided by interpersonal relationships in the classroom. Such relationships are especially important with second language learners, who face additional cultural and linguistic challenges (see Dalton and Tharp, this volume).

While we have described the use of journals as a way of understanding these students' *perezhivanie*, journal writing will not be as effective with some students, such as those who have strengths in areas other than writing.

For these students, oral interviews that probe their responses to particular activities or teachers' observations of students during an activity can also provide glimpses of their *perezhivanija*. What we are suggesting is that part of a dynamic ZPD is providing the metalanguage that relates to the processes of learning, including the affective processes, and not focusing solely on the skills. The teacher needs to pay particular attention to the affective language that students use so that such language can then be more fully incorporated into the dialogic exchange. Students often provide vivid descriptions and powerful metaphors, but these rarely get interpreted as involving both the cognitive and affective aspects of their learning. The relationship between the students and the teacher clearly determines the character of the context for language use and acquisition.

In both of our studies we saw the power of caring support in instilling the confidence with which to meet difficult challenges, to sustain creative endeavours and to attempt something new – all important aspects of sustaining lifelong learning. Vygotsky's caring support described at the beginning of this chapter derived in part from his understanding of the relationship between affect and reason and the importance for education reform of an expanded notion of the ZPD that included emotion.

5

From Activity to Directivity: The Question of Involvement in Education

Pablo del Río and Amelia Álvarez

In a recent survey Spanish teachers were asked what issues were of greatest educational importance to them and what changes they most wished to see. From their responses, it was clear that the factor they considered most important was interest – student motivation. This was also by far what they most wished for. For their part, answering a survey carried out by UNICEF in 20 countries in Latin America and the Iberian peninsula (Portugal and Spain), children and teenagers expressed a deep disaffection with school, despite admitting its importance for their education. Only 9 per cent of respondents in the Iberian peninsula and 8 per cent in Latin America enjoyed going to school. Reports from many governments and international organizations indicate that this malaise affects most countries, not just the most developed ones. Key questions, then, are: What has led to this state of affairs? And what can be done to restore student interest?

The Culture of Gratification and Indifference

Fukuyama (2000) noted two crises in societies in the last third of the twentieth century: loss of meaning and moral collapse. Symptomatic of these crises are a demand for immediate satisfaction, an inability for self-sacrifice, and a dwindling of trust. As a result, parents and educators (and, to a lesser extent, researchers) are faced with a new set of problems in formal and informal education with respect to the young people of today, problems that are paralleled by changes that have taken place more broadly in schools, in community culture and in the media. Although these problems have been addressed by an increasing number of researchers, we would only mention that of the impact on development of the changes in rearing, of schooling and of mass media.

Findings from our own recent research indicate that the ways of perceiving the world that are created by contemporary culture, and the affective and cognitive organization this culture generates in the school, the mass media and the community, are mosaic, episodic and fragmentary, with consequent harmful effects on young people's development (del Río, 1995). In particular, our research is on how the form and content of television influences the development of voluntary attention and the control of action (del Río, 2000), and on how the daily agenda of children's and adolescents' activities has become less productive, and how both school and teachers themselves have lost meaning for children (Álvarez, 1996). The result is that narratives in the media and children's school experiences do not achieve sufficient formative influence to create solidarity, involvement and responsibility. More generally, we have found that boredom and loss of interest in school and in the adult's social world are growing, except in those communities where children are active participants in the productive system of their families (del Río and Álvarez, 1992). As a consequence, young people are finding new ways to give meaning to their lives that are in many ways maladjusted with respect to both school and society. These findings could be further supported and extended by research from related fields and other countries.

In sum, what this research shows is that a marked decrease of involvement is taking place that is most striking in the behaviour of young people. Empirically, the effects of this decrease have been located in three significant sectors: cultural media (for instance, in the content of advertising), social participation (electoral and political participation) and school and university activity. A widespread decline in commitment to cultural, social and school activities has also been detected.

However, rather than seeking to use these findings to create an apocalyptic vision of cultural degeneration, in the remainder of this chapter we shall attempt to identify the root causes of the problem and suggest some ways to re-establish activity, directivity and sense as fundamental orientations that can revive students' motivation and passion for the exciting adventure of education.

Uninvolvement and Educational Indifference

In the early 1960s David McClelland propounded a theory in which involvement was brought about by, and manifested in, narratives of effort and adventure that in some cultures rather than others were matched by higher levels of fulfilment, development and welfare. At the heart of this theory was what, in the universalistic and abstract language of the prevailing models of his time, he called 'achievement motivation' (McClelland, 1961). According to McClelland, the cultures of the Spanish and English empires in the sixteenth century, and that of the United States more recently, fostered that motivation with their expansionist narratives and cultural values. However, if we adopt that way of thinking, it would seem that, by now, the media of the global culture should have handed on those narratives together with the underlying achievement motivation to every Western culture, and even further. Ironically, by contrast, what has actually occurred in a high proportion of countries is an increase in uninvolvement in school, cultures and society.

Again in the 1960s, Krugman (1965) revealed the influence of involvement level on the effects of advertisements. Since then, most advertisers have used a variety of means in order to generate involvement: they all want consumers, especially children and young people, to take full notice of their advertisements and to become committed to their brands and products. But the effect of the avalanche of messages and calls for consumerism that have occurred through-out the last few decades is the opposite of what was intended: the efficiency of advertising in terms of the degree of involvement achieved has actually decreased (Mitchell, 1993). A similar process has also come about with respect to political information: aggressiveness and sensationalism in politics seems to have produced an antipathy to media and political information (McLeod, Kosicki and McLeod, 1994), as well as a reduction in electoral participation in Western democracies.

These facts reveal that a deep confusion exists at present, in which meaning and sense, deep feeling and involvement, are identified with superficial emotion. This is clear in today's mass-media strategies in Western cultures: they seem not to have paid attention to the crucial differences between animal and human ways of feeling and processing. As a result, audio-visual products appeal to primitive reactions in their audiences (for instance, in their ways of catching attention), but ignore the specifically human strategy of using cultural devices for developing higher forms of thinking and feeling. Along similar lines, in research carried out on two types of cartoons on Spanish television, we found that traditional cartoon films, considered by programmers to be less attractive to children, were at least as efficient in catching their attention as the violent and spectacular cartoons that have taken over worldwide television program-ming. Despite this, the traditional cartoons were much more effective in educational and pro-social terms (del Río, 2000; see table 5.1).

At first sight, it might seem that this confusion between superficial and essential is not so endemic in education as it is in the mass media. However, using the same analytic criteria, it can easily be demonstrated. Against the background of fragmented and dazzling information in the public sphere, schools deliver a curriculum which is equally fragmented, although in a dif-ferent manner. Classroom experience is divided into arbitrary units of space and time and based on an endless, unstructured – maybe unstructurable – accumulation of subjects, domains and teachers, each often isolated from the others. However, this fragmentation does seem to differ from the seductive strategies of the mass media, because school culture is based on the supposition that, unlike TV viewers, students are required to pay attention. Involvement can therefore be assumed. But assuming involvement does not ensure its occur-rence. In fact, studies of school performance show a decrease in involvement

Table 5.1   Traits in cartoon series on Spanish television.

Traits	Typology A			Typology B
Narrative structure	High-level hierarchy structures	+	−	Low-level hierarchy structures
Fragmentation	Low	−	+	High
Induced fluency of processing (expository pace)	Easy processing (calm)	+	−	Difficult processing (very fast)
Sensorial attention clinchers	Low frequency	−	+	High frequency
Semantic attention catchers	High frequency	+	−	Low frequency
Pro-social argument	Guide the action	+	−	Subordinate to action

Content analysis applied to most popular television cartoons showed two distinctive typologies according to several traits, named A and B in this table. These typologies were also clearly differentiated by other socio-cultural factors. Most A cartoon series were produced in the 1960s and 1970s, while B series were produced in the 1980s and 1990s. Most A films were either European productions (e.g. *Maja*) or Japanese–European narrative-style productions (*Heidi*), while B were either American (*Captain Planet*) or Japanese new emergent-style productions (*Dragon Ball*).

similar to that noted in the social and media domains: a decrease in voluntary attention, discipline and study skills, and a parallel decrease in learning in subjects such as mathematics, primary language and history, as well as an increase in school failure and student drop-out and exclusion.

However, by contrast, from research concerning significant activities in Castilian-Spanish traditional cultures, Álvarez (1996, 2000) reported that, despite the harshness of their life and its apparent intellectual poverty, people could find happiness and even passion in daily routines and achieve integrated psychic development through the accomplishment of community-shared, meaningful activities. It seems, therefore, that there may be a pointer here towards ways of recovering sense and coherence in contemporary societies and in the educational activities that their schools provide.

Reduction of Meaning

Vygotsky holds that human beings have replaced most of their instincts with culturally created artifacts that mediate both cognitive activity (e.g. traffic lights, a proverb, a law) and emotional behaviour (e.g. a crucifix, a wedding ring, a tragedy such as *West Side Story*). These mediating artifacts enable humans to construct their psyches through participating in activities with others, as postulated by the 'double formation law' for the development of higher psychological functions. Functions such as attention, memory and reasoning are first social and then individual, first external and then internalized. Furthermore, Vygotsky argued that what distinguishes humans from animals more than the power of reason, is feeling: culturally produced artifacts play an even more crucial role in directing our behaviour than in shaping our intelligence if these facets of personality can be considered as things apart.

In the educational models that are the product of modern rationality, such as those influenced by Piaget's logical psychology or those based on the cognitive-science metaphor of humans as computers, this most essential aspect of our culturally developed mind seems to be ignored. Contrary to this metaphor, however, personality is not an inert computer; rather, it is a living functional system which uses knowledge for meaning and action. In many educational practices, it is true, activity is claimed to be important, but it frequently serves as no more than a means of generating motivation to acquire some item of knowledge, rather than being central to the students' lives and providing the goal of actions for which the knowledge is relevant. The reduction of higher feelings to superficial emotion, of sense to information, of activity to tasks, risks causing the disintegration of children's minds. If psychological development requires the dynamic integrity of personality, education should be no less integrated. No wonder, therefore, that the consequence of schooling based on these models is a lack of student involvement, for the development of the whole person through participation in historically situated, jointly undertaken activities that are personally significant and socially meaningful has been reduced to the development of individual cognition that is assumed to be universal, decontextualized and independent of emotion.

Meaningful Activity as the Key Idea of the CHAT Approach

Meaningful activity refers to that real (practical, motor) activity that establishes strong connections with the systems of consciousness developed so far and drives them to new levels of development in their ability to inspire and control real activity. In Vygotsky's view, meaningful activity reorganizes the connections between feelings and thought through mental actions (action + emotion + intellect). A very important aspect of Vygotsky's thought is that he considers an activity to be leading and meaningful only if it produces development – which is the ultimate end of education. Many teachers implicitly assume that the reception of knowledge produces development in and of itself – that any little piece of knowledge taught today will involve great mental changes tomorrow, that micro-tasks will produce macro-results. From a CHAT perspective, however, only knowledge that is embedded in a meaningful activity produces these effects.

Meaningful activities, then, have some typical traits: they serve some purpose and are directed to some goal; they make use of instrumental mediation to produce new things (processes or products); and they usually involve the co-participation of significant others. We shall briefly review these traits, which are so often absent in the fragmented school.

Meaningful Activity is Active

We have already remarked that meaningful activity requires physical action. Basically every activity is movement, and even intellectual activities depend upon real biological movement. However, in contemporary schools most of the time is spent on tasks that are purely intellectual. Elsewhere we have pointed out the disturbing effects this sedentary behaviour has on students, especially male students (Álvarez, 1996). The fact that childhood and schooling have been extended, and that in recent decades young people's development has been divorced from meaningful activity, as we have defined it, multiplies the effects of this physical inactivity.

In meaningful practical activities, the object and purpose of the activity are apparent, the result of the action is contingent and feedback is immediate. When the activities are also productive, the results merge into a product that strengthens the participants' identity and sense of self-efficacy. The produced artifact also becomes an external, stable symbol of the processes involved in producing it.

A. N. Leont'ev (1978) describes a meaningful activity that he designed and carried out in the special education community of Djerzinski at the request of Makarenko, who was concerned because students sitting at their desks did not learn his lessons of vectors and forces in physics; they simply were not interested in the subject. Leont'ev arrived in the community and, after observing the students for a week, suggested turning the method of teaching inside out. He had observed the children's passion for making paper planes and their incessant activity with them during breaks, so he proposed to focus the lessons on the scientific construction of paper planes. In this way, vectors and forces were subordinated to the goal of flying planes, and they became mediating artifacts or tools for guiding the actions and operations – for deciding where to make the cuts and folds necessary to build better planes. As physics became meaningful, it became part of the students' passion for paper planes which, instead of flourishing only outside the classroom, became the energizer of their learning in school.

Meaningful Activity is Emotionally Charged

As the previous sections have made clear, much greater recognition needs to be given to the importance of emotion in learning and understanding. This case is forcibly made by George Steiner (1998), who has argued that, in the educational process, interest in academic subjects is related to a passion for knowledge for its own sake and for the forms in which knowledge is represented. Where this passion is present it would lead to learning, occurring not as an end in itself, but as a necessary means to mastering a topic or field in which the student has a strong and personal interest. One of the authors of this chapter recalls his youthful passion for Greek, aroused in his classmates and himself by a teacher who invited them to be actors in Homer's magical rendering of the epic world of Greeks and Trojans. He still clearly remembers the musicality of the verses, which became tangible as he recited them. Every single student in that heterogeneous group learned Greek and mastered its grammar, unconscious of how special they were in the larger world of Spanish secondary schools. His notebooks, which still make him smile with pleasure, were filled with drawings of resplendently armour-clad Greeks and their gods, killing, dying and crying out. For him, the attraction of that classical (and imaginary) world has withstood the deluge of half a century of contemporary cultural influences. However, this kind of passion is not limited to the arts; it can infuse learning in fields as diverse as basketball and mathematics, biology and philosophy.

In cognitive models of learning and development, by contrast, action and emotion are thought to be independent of the cognitive processing of information. Indeed, feeling is treated as irrelevant, if not as an impediment, to the construction of knowledge. At best, cognizing and feeling are considered to be independent, yielding alternative – or more often, antagonistic – ways of knowing. For example, Petty and Cacciopo (1986) propose two separate ways of processing information: a peripheral way – emotional, superficial – as opposed to a 'central' – or cognitive – way, the latter being superior. Vygotsky (1989), on the other hand, made clear that the various psychological modes of knowing, specifically thinking and feeling, provided they are worthwhile in themselves (as in art), may unite and enhance each other to yield an outcome greater than either of them alone. Together, they weave a web of meaning that is morally, cognitively and aesthetically satisfying, and that also leads to responsible action.

Meaningful Activity is Instrumentally Mediated

It seems legitimate to judge adults in terms of what they are able to do unassisted, which is what conventional achievement tests do. However, Vygotsky insisted that, in assessing a child, it is necessary to go further than measuring unaided 'actual development'; in addition, one must also identify what the child is capable of doing with help, either from other people or from cultural artifacts. He then went on to argue that the space in which education must work is the area between the two levels, in what he called the Zone of Proximal Development (ZPD). Teaching through instrumental mediation, then, is the attempt to assist the learner to master higher mental functions through the provision of scaffolding in the form of external artifacts which, while artificial, in the sense that they do not occur naturally in the external setting, are deliberately introduced into the situation to enable the learner to carry out a task that he or she would not be able to manage unaided. Examples are such cultural artifacts as a ruler, a watch, an abacus, a compass, or a multiplication table on the wall or in the student's notebook.

Every such mediating artifact has certain common attributes with respect to its role in meaningful activity: it is a visible and tangible object; its use gives immediate feedback; and it enables the achievement of the intended outcome. Technical activities are in this sense magic: they turn natural stimuli imposed on animals by evolution and the environment into cultural stimuli that create a new cultural environment which humans impose on themselves in order to free themselves from natural constraints; that is, they condition themselves to do what they want to do (Vygotsky, 1984).

When one of the authors worked on his doctoral dissertation (del Río, 1987), both of us took part in the experimental educational programme on which it was based. The hypothesis to be tested was that educational activities mediated by technological instruments could open new ways for meaningful learning in areas of the curriculum that, from a cognitive viewpoint, could be considered 'tougher' and more challenging. Drawing on Davydov's (1972) experiences in teaching algebra and Zaporozhets' (1970) in pre-school teaching of perceptive forms, we aimed to investigate the possibility of tackling one of the classical problems of 'mathematics shock' in primary school: the confrontation of numerical concepts with spatial concepts, which is introduced at around the age of 8–10 years.

Specifically, we attempted to prove, following Vygotsky and Zaporozhets, that the ability for spatial representation followed a historically and culturally constructable order, rather than the genetically inevitable logical order proposed by Piaget (i.e. topological, projective, then Euclidean space), and that appropriate cultural artifacts could satisfy the need for assistance in the development of spatial abilities and mathematical knowledge. In this way, it was hoped, children who had difficulties with spatial representation could rebuild their spatiality, and would not be assumed to be genetically doomed to become mathematics failures.

Following several iterations in designing the mediating artifacts, we carried out an experimental training programme in a public primary school. To this end we arranged a cognitive–cultural engineering of space in which Norman's mindful design and Vygotsky's 'psychotechnics of the intellect' or cultural engineering were replicated as far as possible. Through this programme and the series of activities that it involved, the students were able, in a meaningful way, to appropriate and gradually internalize a set of external spatial operations mediated by cultural artifacts. These artifacts enabled them to exceed the test scores of 'novice' or inexpert students and eventually to obtain 'expert' scores.

Meaningful Activity is Shared and Socially Mediated

As we have argued, the CHAT model of human activity does not portray human beings as operating on objects directly. Vygotsky said that, initially, the route between the baby and the object goes through another person and the same remains true of learning in school. This interdependent characteristic of activity is what creates structures of distributed meaning and emotional links between meanings: one person is the necessary mediator for another's activity and vice versa (mother for baby, friend for friend). By the same token, a meaningful activity's instrumentally mediated character is what makes that activity explicit, conscious and visible (love is made visible when writing a love letter, and writing becomes meaningful in turn). And this, in turn, is what makes it possible for the novice to appropriate the activity through assisted participation.

In order to point up the complementarity between instrumental and social mediation, we should like to refer again to our educational experiment concerning the development of spatiality. Let us focus now, not on the cultural–historical instrumental engineering, but on the social engineering of the activity's meaning. Our design observed the requirements, discussed above, for an activity to be considered meaningful: it must involve physical activity; it must be motivating, arouse interest and be satisfying; it must restructure intellectual actions, transforming the new intellectual operations and corresponding psychological artifacts into the specific means for achieving the goals of the activity. In our case, these means were the pedagogical product of our educational mindful design. For example, in the programme the means for orienting oneself in such a way that one's movements might be intelligible to others and to machines in objective frames (the change from natural situated space to different Euclidean spaces) was an 'orienting Smurf', a giant analogic–digital compass able to work on the ground, on the desk and on paper; the means for planning, communicating and tracing three-dimensional movements was a three-dimensional abacus; the means to carry something to another place through streets traced in geometrical–Euclidean terms, was a programmable robot capable of moving around and the tools needed to program it.

All the activities were arranged so that the instrumental mediators mentioned above (the compass, the abacus, the robot) were also mediated by social interaction and vice versa: instrumental and conceptual actions went through one or more peers, and interaction with peers went necessarily through instrumental operators. Thus, the intended goals necessitated a double and dialectical mediation for their fulfilment: mediation of social interactions by means of instrumental operations and, conversely, the social mediation of instrumental operations.

This double mediation – the socio-instrumental design and execution of meaningful educational activity – worked very well in the first stages; the group of children with underdeveloped spatial abilities participated enthusiastically and the results eventually evinced an important ontogenetic change: novices became experts and so challenged the pessimistic genetically based argument that such children should be excluded from the learning of mathematics.

The next stage, however, did not turn out so well. Our intention was to enable students to achieve individual mastery of expert cultural actions, so we programmed social mediations so they would eventually give way to personalized external instrumental mediations, such that the child could manage each new operation without assistance from others. The two forms of mediation together were intended to allow the students, with the help of others and cultural tools, to externally control every step of expert activity. Then, having appropriated the external actions, we expected them to internalize these actions; that is to say, the external actions and interactions with tools and people would be transferred to inner gesture and speech, thereby becoming personalized instrumental actions that they could perform 'in their heads'. As an intermediate step, we expected that actions originally carried out collaboratively with peers with the support of double mediation, would next be carried out only with the help of instrumental mediations. For instance, a child with their eyes covered, instead of asking others if a sequential movement or an orientation was correct, would answer that question using cultural artifacts (such as the tactile abacus, or written recording of movements). Many children felt empowered by substituting artifact mediations for help from others. However, a significant number of them refused to make the switch and continued to ask peers and teachers how to do something and to use them to check their progress. It seemed that we had been too successful in our role as experimental teachers, providing assistance in the social zone of proximal development, for we had become the 'meaningful others' on whom these students continued to depend.

At the social level, of course, we had been successful: the students were able to carry out the new activities, thanks to the external, social and instrumental scaffolding we were providing. But at the level of the students' individual development (internalized development) we had been much less successful: instead of the external and socially shared activity being a provisional step, as the Vygotskyan model predicted, it had become the end point of their development.

The complete process, from external, artifact-mediated, intermental activity to internal, intramental activity, was relatively easy for those students who had transferred the action's meaningful and mediating power to the instrumental artifact. However, for many students the shared activity of being socially guided and checked had become a source of satisfaction in itself and we were a part of it. Since they did not want to lose our participation, they refused to replace us with an artifact and, for our part, we felt unable to disengage ourselves.

Since then we have wondered a lot about this turn of events and, in the light of recent developments in cultural–historical theory, we have come to see that the individualistic, rational and cognitive ideal of a unidirectional sequence of development from appropriation to internalization needs to be reconsidered. Human abilities are based on the reconstruction of animal abilities, by extending our social and instrumental biological capacity with the help of social and cultural mediations. In the process, the helplessness that obliges humans to depend on others has turned into an exceptional ability for functional cooperation and distributed intelligence: our abilities are in origin 'shared disabilities' (del Río, 1998). Thus, this extensive need for external mediation, social and instrumental, should not be seen as weakness – only accepted provisionally in children – but as a powerful mechanism of cultural activity and development.

Scaffolding and help in the zone of proximal development are not just a necessary but transient stage in human development. They remain necessary for most activities throughout our lives. We form functional symbioses with our spouses, our parents and children, our friends, and also with social institutions, such as clubs and churches. We also build functional interdependencies with a personal and idiosyncratic array of cultural artifacts – briefcase, car, PC, for example – and with culturally organized locations, such as office, kitchen, local shops, villages, communities. This functional network of persons and objects becomes a kind of external extension of our own unaided abilities and greatly increases our potential for effective action. Put more generally, cultures are systems of distributed and shared functions or abilities that are socially and instrumentally brought into play by the demands of the activities in which we engage and the cultural situations in which they occur.

In some cultures the ideal of personal autonomy and independence plays down this interdependence with people and artifacts and makes it less easy to recognize. However, there are also cultures and individuals that place great value on these social and functional interdependencies, and they should not for that reason be judged to be inferior. If the independent functioning of individuals is more limited, there is greater strength in their collaborative endeavours and, in the activities they value, their achievements can be just as effective. Above all, as the Spanish philosopher Unamuno suggested, these two kinds of functioning should not be considered as opposites, but as two dimensions that generate each other.

It seems to us that, despite the emphasis on collaborative and artifact-mediated activities in cultural–historical approaches to curriculum design (Dalton and Tharp, this volume), there is a lack of debate on what higher capabilities should be seen as desirable to maintain as social–external activities culturally distributed and shared. Nor has sufficient consideration been given yet to what should be individual–external (that is, subject to complete appropriation but not to complete interiorization, using instrumental prostheses such as a dictionary, calculator, diary or word-processing computer program), or, finally, what should be considered to be individual–internal; that is, subject to complete appropriation and total internalization – such as the multiplication table, the conventions of spelling, the ten commandments, or the rules of acceptable classroom behaviour.

The prevalent psychological model (that of a mental individual and an individualistic student) assumes that every human function, ability and activity that has to do with education belongs in the third category; that is, that it should be individual and internal. However, as we have argued above, from a CHAT perspective much greater recognition needs to be given to the distributed, socially and instrumentally mediated nature of action, both mental and physical. In particular, during the years of schooling in which children learn and develop, appropriating and internalizing the socially distributed emotions, identities and capabilities encountered in their families and communities, and in which many actions require assistance in the ZPD, an adequate educational model should give particular emphasis to external and shared sociality, functionality and activity.

Meaningful Activity is Directive

Paying attention, remembering, thinking, reasoning, planning and evaluating are all mental functions that are not self-contained, but processes interdependent with action and emotion. Alexander Luria (1983) defined directivity as the central process that coordinates the different psychological functions and puts them to work towards the leading activity; everything else is subject to that. Human personality is then the product of a cultural and educational process for reconstructing animal behaviour (which is guided by instincts and conditioned by stimuli from the surrounding environment) into human behaviour, which is guided by shared rituals, narratives, artifacts and cultural activities, and governed not so much by stimuli from the environment as by the substitution of direct stimuli by second, third and nth-order sociocultural representations, creating in this way a bio-cultural environment.

Elsewhere (del Río and Álvarez, 1995), we have attempted to give an account of this concept of directivity from a cultural–historical perspective, explaining how directive functions, such as control and self-discipline, decision and will, motives, values and morality, conscience and self-knowledge, become established and are maintained within a culture. Here, however, we wish to reiterate our opening argument that the increasing lack of involvement in society and its educational and political institutions on the part of young people during the last third of the century has seriously weakened their appropriation of the directive functions of their culture, and that there is thus an urgent and vital need to fill the gap. Like the other authors in this volume, we believe that the CHAT perspective provides the best alternative for developing the educational designs and actions that will allow these directive functions once more to be given a central place in the educational activities that make up the school curriculum.

Recovering Meaningful Activities in Education: Some Proposals

There is no possible meaning to activity if it does not lead somewhere – if it does not enable us to achieve something in our lives. However, under the pretext of preparing children for life, the school too frequently imposes activities that actually diminish that life. We believe, therefore, that the time has come to abandon this model of education that extends the duration of schooling but at the same time empties it of the meaning that gives it vitality.

Education is learning for life through learning to live in the here-and-now. Contrary to the mechanistic, externally managed model of education, it is not possible to create a human mind by adding inert pieces – as one might assemble a LEGO structure. Both phylogenetically and over the historical development of particular cultures, human minds and personalities have developed through meaningful action made possible by the interaction of biological potential and cultural activity.

However, in the model of education that has come to prevail in the last decades, the knowledge that was once seen as mediating the achievement of effective participation in life-sustaining activity has been transformed into an end in itself; possessing knowledge has come to be more highly valued than being able to bring knowledge to bear in effective and responsible action. Instead of teachers implementing curricular plans that are imposed on them, top-down, schools should give more responsibility to classroom communities of active teachers and students who, together, select, plan and engage in cultural, meaningful activities (Wells, 1996b; this volume). Here are some suggestions as to how this reform of schooling might be attempted:

- Design educational practices as real activities; not 'in place of' nor even 'as preparation for' real activities.
- Subordinate science and technology to life-sense and knowledge to moral and effective doing. From a CHAT perspective, being more informed is not itself the goal, but the means for becoming wiser, better individuals.
- Give priority to the development of strong and integrated student identities, without which there is no sense, no directivity in life. This means reasserting the relevance of orienting narratives, which today are neglected, displaced by the overemphasis on skills and information.
- Design activities that integrate school culture with everyday culture and balance cognitive with directive higher mental functions, recognizing that both are dimensions of the same historical–cultural trajectory of development.

Redesigning education from a CHAT perspective will not be an easy task, but it can be expected to yield a substantial dividend. We have certainly found this to be true in our own attempts.

Conclusion

The fading of integral and directive productive activities is one of contemporary culture's biggest problems. If inactivity and sedentarism are hard for an adult to withstand, they are even more troubling and debilitating for the developing and learning child. To combat these negative influences, the CHAT perspective offers a cultural constructivism in which cognition is merged with directivity, reason with passion, and in which the mere accumulation of encyclopedic information is replaced by activities in which cultural artifacts are put to purposeful use by human hands. Re-establishing meaningful and productive activity in this way also leads to the re-emergence of engaged involvement.

CHAT conceives of a teacher as one who is capable of achieving this reconciliation: bringing together physical and mental action, affectively as well as intellectually charged, and socially as well as instrumentally mediated An architect of meaning, a poet of science and a scientist of poetry, a teacher of life. Instead of aiming for impersonal, 'teacher-proof' materials, the CHAT perspective emphasizes the leading role of people – educators and students – in education and seeks to arouse their passion for learning, conscience and life.

6

Sociocultural Perspectives on Assessment

Caroline Gipps

This chapter takes a sociocultural perspective on assessment, looking first at the critical role of assessment in a CHAT approach to education, and then at what this implies for assessment practice. I use assessment as a general term: assessment incorporates a wide range of methods for evaluating pupil performance and attainment, including formal testing and examinations, practical and oral assessment, and classroom-based assessment carried out by teachers. I shall use specific terms (e.g. standardized tests, portfolio assessment) where the discussion is about specific forms of assessment.

Two important developments have underpinned recent evolution of the study of assessment. The first is increased understanding of the relationship between assessment and learning; the second is a growing interest in the use of informal assessment in the classroom. Of course these two developments are linked, for we know that constructive (as opposed to competitive) assessment in the classroom can be a valuable impetus for learning. Therefore, much of the practice in assessment addressed here will be classroom-based assessment, rather than external testing.

How we see learning taking place is crucial to how we construe teaching as an activity, but it is also crucial to how we construe assessment. There is a growing realization that assessment is not an isolated activity operating independently of, and therefore without impact on, teaching; rather, teaching, learning and assessment are inextricably interrelated. Just as in CHAT theory the human actor operates in a cultural, social, material and technological setting, which poses problems but also offers tools and resources to create solutions, so assessment operates in a social and cultural setting in which it may be seen either as a 'problem' ('examination as hurdle') or as a way of supporting learning (assessment for learning).

Let me unpack this a little. In the traditional model of teaching and learning, the curriculum is seen as a distinct body of information, specified in detail, that can be transmitted to the learner. Assessment here consists of

An earlier version of some of this material can be found in Gipps (1999).

checking whether the information has been received and absorbed. Standard-ized achievement tests evaluate students' abilities to recall the facts learned and to apply them in a routine manner. Even items which are designed to assess higher-level activities often require no more than the ability to recall the appropriate formula and to make substitutions to get the correct answer. Thus students who, on the basis of this form of assessment, conceive of knowledge as collections of facts, will tend to depend on learning strategies that are aimed at successful memorization (Marton and Saljo, 1984) rather than those required for deep learning.

By contrast, constructivist models see learning as requiring personal knowledge construction and meaning making, and as involving complex and diverse processes; such models therefore require assessment to be diverse, in an attempt to characterize in more depth the structure and quality of students' learning and understanding. While, for example, standardized multiple choice or short-answer type tests are efficient at sampling the acquisition of the specific knowledge presented by teachers or textbooks, more intense, even interactive methods, such as essays, performance assessments and small group tasks and projects, are needed to assess understanding and the processes of learning, as well as to encourage a deeper level of learning.

However, sociocultural approaches to learning have additional implications that are significant for assessment practice. These are addressed in the next section. Put most simply, the requirements are that process should be assessed as well as product, that the conception be dynamic rather than static, and that attention must be paid to the social and cultural context of both learning and assessment.

Assessment in Sociocultural Perspective

There are four key aspects of Vygotsky's ideas that relate to assessment and it is on these that I will focus in this chapter. As will be seen, much of my discussion will resonate with material in other chapters in this volume. First is the critical role of tools in human activity, and the implications of offering assistance and guidance during the course of an assessment. Second is the inseparability of the social, affective and cognitive dimensions of action and interaction and hence the implication that learners should be assessed, not in isolation and in competition, but in groups and social settings. Third is the relationship between expert and 'apprentice' around which individual intel-lectual development hinges, and the implications of this for the assessment relationship. Fourth is the role of assessment in identity formation.

The use of tools and assistance

Vygotsky pointed to the importance of tools and assistance from others in human action and hence also in learning. The use and internalization/appropriation of external supports is a key element in his account of the development of mental functions. However, assessment in the traditional examination and psychometric model denies the pupil the use of external tools and this reduces its usefulness and ecological validity. Following Vygotsky's ideas we should develop assessment which allows the use of auxiliary tools (including adult support) and thus produces best performance rather than typical performance. Such assessment is interactive and is termed *dynamic assessment*. As Lunt (1994) explains:

> Dynamic assessment procedures . . . involve a dynamic interactional exploration of a learner's learning and thinking process and aim to investigate a learner's strategies for learning and ways in which these may be extended or enhanced. Since it offers individuals an opportunity to learn, dynamic assessment has the potential to show important information about individual strategies and processes of learning and, therefore, to offer potentially useful suggestions about teaching. (Ibid., p. 152)

Using interactive assessment that elicits elaborated performance – at the upper rather than the lower threshold – resonates with Vygotsky's Zone of Proximal Development (ZPD) (Vygotsky, 1978). In this process, assessor and student collaborate to produce the 'best performance' of which the student is capable: help given by an adult is the rule, in order to obtain best performance. In standardized tests we withhold help in order to produce typical performance.

Interactive assessment can reduce anxiety in the test situation and this too will encourage best performance (Nuttall, 1987). In this respect, it may be particularly beneficial for children from minority groups, who might be disadvantaged in the standardized situation. The experience of the early National Assessment programme in England showed that interactive, classroom-based standard assessment tasks offered minority-group children a better opportunity to show what they knew, understood and could do than standardized tests, despite the former's heavy reliance on language (Gipps, 1994b).

Assessment in social settings

Some researchers in the CHAT perspective who focus on situated learning in the apprenticeship model suggest that assessment is not necessary, while others suggest that individuals must be assessed as part of a group. For example, Lave and Wenger (1991) argue that, where learning takes place through apprenticeship, testing is not necessary since increasing participation has its own use value; in settings such as school, however, learning becomes commoditized and exchange value, demonstrated through testing, comes to be treated as more important than use value:

> The commoditization of learning engenders a fundamental contradiction between the use and exchange values of the outcome of learning, which manifests itself in conflicts between learning to know and learning to display knowledge for evaluation. Testing in schools and trade schools (unnecessary in situations of apprenticeship learning) is perhaps the most pervasive and salient example of a way of establishing the exchange value of knowledge. Test-taking then becomes a new parasitic practice, the goal of which is to increase the exchange value of learning independently of its use value. (Ibid., p. 112)

For those who look to assessing individuals as part of a group, this can be afforded by assessing students in collaborative group activity where they contribute to a task and help others. 'In such assessment, as in instruction using group approaches, the student can observe how others reason and can receive feedback on his or her own efforts. In this context, not only performance, but also the facility with which a student adapts to help and guidance, can be assessed' (Glaser and Silver, 1994, pp. 412–13). Such socially situated collaborative assessment also has the advantage of encouraging students to develop and question their definitions of competence. Brown and colleagues describe collaborative assessment environments as providing aid in the form of 'standardized hints'; in contrast, in collaborative teaching environments aid is opportunistic (Brown et al., 1992).

Cobb and Bowers (1999), too, talk about assessment within the group (using the term 'evaluation'). Within their cognitive and situated perspective on learning, performance is socially situated. Therefore the teacher should evaluate the group's changing beliefs and reasoning and the individual should be evaluated in relation to the group. The issue for Cobb and Bowers is how one views individuals whose (mathematical) reasoning is less effective than that of others in the group. They describe such students as those who have less sophisticated ways of participating in particular classroom practices. Their point is that, since performance is socially situated, the performance resides not just in the student but in the relationship between the teacher and the individual student. They therefore treat academic success and failure in the classroom as the exclusive property neither of individual students nor of the instruction they receive. Instead they see it as a 'relation' between individual students and the practices that they and the teacher construct. So pupil assessment in their model focuses on the individual as part of the group, and the key issue becomes whether/how one interprets the evidence of performance of individuals.

The assessment relationship

In the school setting, teachers are experts and students are novices or apprentices; the relationship between them is crucial to the learning process and it can be constructed in a number of ways.

In traditional assessment the relationship between teacher and student is a hierarchical one. The teacher sets and defines the task and determines how performance should be evaluated. The student's role is to be the object of this activity and, through the completion of tasks and tests, to be graded. However, there are other ways of seeing this relationship. In forms of assessment such as negotiated assessment and self-assessment, the student has a role in discussing and negotiating the terms and outcomes of the assessment – although, in reality, such practice may be rare. The thesis behind such a non-traditional approach is that students need to become involved in the assessment process so that they are encouraged to monitor and reflect on their own performance in order to become self-monitoring and self-regulating learners. Here the teacher is reducing the hierarchical nature of the relationship between expert and apprentice, by bringing the learner into a more active role in which he or she is afforded more responsibility.

Taylor et al. (1997), discussing the communicative relationships between pupils and teachers, draw on the work of Jürgen Habermas to develop the notion of open discourse. In open discourse, communication is oriented towards understanding and respecting the perspectives of others and this provides another perspective on the assessment relationship. As with an interpretative approach, a key issue is the need to understand the learner's response. In relation to informal assessment, this includes the learner's expectations, assumptions and interpretations of the classroom culture, task demands and criteria for success. According to Taylor et al.:

Open discourse gives rise to opportunities for students to:

1   negotiate with the teacher about the nature of their learning activities;
2   participate in the determination of assessment criteria and undertake self-assessment and peer-assessment;
3   engage in collaborative and open-ended enquiry with fellow students; and
4   participate in reconstructing the social norms of the classroom. (Ibid., p. 295)

Taylor and colleagues do not articulate how such a communicative climate might be set up, but have developed a questionnaire to evaluate the learning environment on five key dimensions, including shared control and student negotiation of both learning and assessment activities (but see Wells, 2000, for some suggestions as to how this can be achieved).

Indeed, from a sociocultural perspective the task is, in a sense, constructed by the student, not the teacher/assessor: the situatedness of the individual determines what sense is made of what the assessor provides (Cooper and Dunne, 1998). Ideally, then, there should be opportunities for tasks and criteria to be discussed, clarified, even negotiated with the pupil, so that assessment becomes a more collaborative enterprise, in which the pupil has some input. Such a situation would allow more opportunities for establishing a teacher–pupil relationship based on power *with* the pupil as opposed to power *over* the pupil (Kreisberg, 1992).

Feedback from the teacher to the student, which is a key link between assessment and learning, can also be analysed in terms of the power relationship between teacher and student. Formative assessment is the process of appraising, judging or evaluating students' work or performance, and using this to shape and improve their competence. This means teachers using their judgements of the students' knowledge or understanding to feed back into the teaching process. Sadler's (1989) detailed discussion of the nature of qualitative assessment gives feedback a crucial role in learning; he identifies the way in which feedback should be used by teachers to unpack the notion of excellence, which is part of their 'guild knowledge', and to share it with their students, so that students are able to acquire understanding of standards for themselves.

Research by Tunstall and Gipps (1996) to describe and classify feedback from teachers to young students as part of informal assessment suggests that such feedback can be categorized as either evaluative or descriptive. Evaluative feedback is judgemental, with implicit or explicit use of norms. Descriptive feedback is task-related, making specific reference to the child's actual achievement or competence. Tunstall and Gipps identified two types of descriptive feedback associated with formative assessment. One of these, 'specifying attainment and specifying improvement', shows a mastery-oriented approach to formative assessment. It involves teachers' acknowledgement of specific attainment, the use of models by teachers for work and behaviour, diagnosis using specific criteria, and correcting or checking procedures. The other, 'constructing achievement and constructing the way forward', involves teachers' use of both sharp and 'fuzzy' criteria, teacher–child joint assessment of work, discussion of the way forward, and the use of strategies for self-regulation of learning.

In the feedback categorized as 'specifying', the teacher retains control and power. She tells the pupil how/whether the work is good and what needs to be done to improve on the task. In 'constructing' the teacher is sharing power and responsibility with the pupil. Teachers using this latter feedback conveyed a sense of work in progress, heightening awareness of what was being undertaken and reflecting on it, thus having the effect of bestowing importance on the work. Teachers' use of this feedback shifted the emphasis more to the child's own role in learning, using approaches which passed control to the child. There was more a feel of teacher as 'facilitator' than 'provider' or 'judge' and more of 'teacher *with* the child' than 'teacher *to* the child'. This type of feedback encouraged children to assess their own work and provided them with strategies that they could adopt to develop their work. Teachers, in this approach, were involving the learner in the process of assessment as well as demonstrating power with, rather than power over them. Such a relationship is not only conducive to learning, but also to the development of strategies for self-assessment and self-monitoring.

However, developing such a relationship is not straightforward. In an analysis of teachers' informal assessment of pupils in Switzerland, Perrenoud (1991) claims that, since many pupils are content to do what is minimally required in order to 'get by', attempts by teachers to engage them more deeply in learning, and in sharing power through self-assessment, will require a shift in the established equilibrium. 'Every teacher who wants to practise formative assessment must reconstruct the teaching contracts so as to counteract the habits acquired by his [*sic*] pupils. Moreover, some of the children and adolescents with whom he is dealing are imprisoned in the identity of a bad pupil and an opponent' (ibid., p. 92). Similarly, in an early profiling portfolio scheme which involved student self-assessment and negotiation of target setting, Broadfoot et al. (1988) found that secondary students viewed self-assessment as difficult, partly because they were not used to it, and partly because the assessment criteria were unclear. Pupils' perceptions of teacher expectations, their views on what was socially acceptable, and their anxiety not to lose face affected their self-evaluation. Furthermore, there were differences in approach to the process of self-assessment and 'negotiation' in relation to gender: boys tended to be more likely to challenge a teacher's assessment and have a keen sense of the audience for the final record, while girls tended to enter into a discussion and to negotiate more fully.

So it appears that, if self-assessment of their work is to be empowering to students, considerable development will be required on the part of teachers as well as in preparation of the students. Teachers will need to take a back seat rather than driving and controlling the process, and not only will they need to make the new ground rules clear to pupils, but also persuade them that their contribution to evaluation is valued.

This kind of analysis can also be applied to questioning, another tool that plays a key role in informal assessment.

The 'opening moves' of teachers and students in the negotiation of classroom contracts will be determined by the epistemological, psychological and pedagogical beliefs of both teachers and students (Black and William, 1998). When a teacher questions a student, the teacher's beliefs will influence both the questions asked and the way that answers are interpreted (Tittle, 1994). In turn, the student's responses to questioning will depend on a host of factors. For example, whether the student believes ability to be incremental or fixed will have a strong influence on how the student sees a question: as an opportunity to learn or as a threat to self-esteem (Dweck, 1986). Even where the student has a 'learning' as opposed to 'performance' orientation, the student's belief about what counts as 'academic work' (Doyle, 1988) will have a profound impact on the 'mindfulness' with which that student responds to questions.

Much teacher questioning is 'closed' and students may develop strategies to discover the answer the teacher wants before actually committing themselves to it (Edwards and Mercer, 1987). In such a climate attempts by the teacher to engage in detailed diagnostic questioning may be misinterpreted (Torrance, 1993). Where the teacher's questioning has always been restricted to 'lower-order skills', students may well see questions about understanding or application as unfair, illegitimate, or even meaningless (Schoenfeld, 1985). As Edwards and Mercer (1987, p. 45) point out, 'Repeated questions imply wrong answers', and the student may change tack in order to give the 'correct' answer and stop the questioning process rather than become engaged in an interactive process with the teacher.

Opening up of questioning by the teacher needs to be seen as a sharing of power and control with the students – and indeed of what counts as acceptable knowledge – but, as with bringing students into self-assessment, it will require careful preparation by the teacher (see Mercer, this volume; Nystrand, 1997).

The role of assessment in identity formation

Because of the public nature of much questioning and feedback in the classroom, and the power dynamic in the teacher – student relationship, assessment plays a key role in identity formation. The language of assessment and evaluation is one of the routes by which the identity of young persons is formed – for school purposes at least. The role of assessment as a social process has to be acknowledged in this sphere: identity is socially bestowed, socially sustained and socially transformed (Berger, 1963). Penuel and Wertsch (1995) argue that

> Identity formation must be viewed as shaped by and shaping forms of action, involving a complex interplay among cultural tools employed in the action, the sociocultural and institutional context of the action, and the purposes embedded in the action. Taking human action as the focus of analysis, we are able to provide a more coherent account of identity, not as a static, inflexible structure of the self, but a dynamic dimension or moment in action . . . identity formation is a moment of rhetorical action, concerned with using language in significant interpersonal contexts to form identities. (Ibid., pp. 84–5)

If identity is conceived as concerned with persuading others and oneself about who one is, and what one is able to do, the judgement of others is crucial. Simultaneously reflecting and observing, the individual evaluates himself 'in the light of what he perceives to be the ways in which others judge him in comparison to themselves and to a typology significant to them' (Erikson, 1968, p. 22). Indeed, following Bernstein's (1982) argument about the pervasiveness of covert, informal assessment, it may be that the teacher's regular classroom-based assessment of the pupil has more impact on identity formation than the results of standardized tests and formal examinations/report cards. Ames's (1992) work, too, shows how the classroom assessment climate can affect students' views of themselves. Classrooms in which assessment focuses on comparison and competition with others can lead to 'negative affect directed toward the self' in children who compare unfavourably. Ames argues that students' perceptions of their ability are particularly sensitive to information based on social comparison. Children's evaluations of their ability and feelings towards themselves are more negative when the classroom climate is focused on winning, out-performing one another, or surpassing some normative stand-ard, than when children focus on trying hard, improving their performance, or just participating.

The teacher must be ever mindful of the impact of the assessment regime and classroom climate on the pupils. Involving the pupils in evaluation of their work through a constructive process of feedback is one way in which teachers can show pupils that they are valued and respected rather than objects of classification and grading.

Implications for Classroom Assessment

I now turn to some of the implications of sociocultural perspectives for assessment practice itself. First, let us look at interactive assessment to produce best performance. An example of an assessment approach that was able to elicit best performance appeared from evaluations of the early English National Assessment programme. In the early stages this national assessment programme required the pupils to be assessed across the full range of the National Curriculum, using external tests and teachers' own assessments. The external tests were originally called Standard Assessment Tasks (SATs); those used in 1991 and 1992 were true performance assessments and involved classroom-based, externally set, but teacher-assessed activities and tasks.

An important point emerged from evaluation studies, at both age 7 and 14 (Gipps, 1994a): the SAT-type activity, with its emphasis on active, multi-mode assessment and detailed interaction between teacher and pupil, appeared to offer a good opportunity for children to demonstrate what they knew and could do. In other words, it elicited best performance. The key aspects of the assessment seemed to be:

- a range of activities, offering a wide opportunity to perform;
- match to classroom practice;
- extended interaction between pupil and teacher to explain the task;
- a normal classroom setting which is therefore not unduly threatening;
- a range of response modes other than written.

It was also noted that these characteristics seemed to be particularly signific-ant in supporting the performance of minority and special needs children.

A second requirement of the sociocultural perspective, namely to assess the processes of learning as well as learning in the social setting, can be met in a number of ways. Portfolios can be used to reflect the processes of learning and their development over time. Portfolios, of course, take many forms: they may contain items selected at intervals by the teacher, or 'best' pieces of work chosen by the pupil; and work in the portfolio may be assessed in a more or less standardized way (Koretz et al., 1993).

To support the sociocultural model of learning, a portfolio would need in some way to reflect or articulate the social setting in which the learning took place. Commentary by the teacher and the pupil could be used to describe this. For example, student and teacher commentaries are part of the final portfolio in the PROPEL project (Wolf et al., 1991). These commentaries are focused on the process of learning, on developing achievement, and they encourage reflection on the part of both pupil and teacher. The process is hard, Wolf (1989) argues, because portfolios 'demand intimate and often frighteningly subjective talk with students' (ibid., p. 37). Pupils may be unwilling to engage in the intellectual process, while the teachers may be unable to give up control of the discussion. But where it works, she argues, it is well worth the effort.

With regard to the assessment relationship, Lampert (1990) describes a project in the teaching of mathematics in which the roles and responsibilities of teachers and students within classroom discourse were altered. Sometimes the teacher consciously held back from commenting on answers given by students, and so the class developed discussion around the problems and tasks, made hypotheses about solutions, and took risks in the way that the mathematical community would. The teacher, standing back, refused to be the intellectual authority in the way that is normally the case in school mathematics. This approach to learning in a classroom community entails a different approach to assessment of pupil attainment. The emphasis was on the analysis of the students' language, their assertions and ability to demonstrate that their strategies were valid. In such a group/community learning situation, assessment may be focused as much on the group as on individuals; for example: 'By the end of the lesson, 14 of the 18 students present in the class had had something mathematically substantial to say about exponents...' (ibid., p. 52).

In any sociocultural framework for assessment it is important to acknowledge the complexity of interactions among students, teachers and assessment. Factors such as student perceptions of how testing impacts on them, student and teacher confidence in the veracity of test results, and the differences in student and teacher perceptions of the goals of assessment all need to be considered. Tittle's (1994) framework is one of the broadest so far articulated in this vein. Tittle proposes evaluation of both student and teacher perspectives using questionnaires to assess student feelings and thought in doing mathematical problems. Teachers review these responses using a think-aloud procedure and this information aids the use of assessment for teaching. The assessment result itself is only one piece of the information which the teacher will draw on in making inferences and deciding next steps; the other pieces of information are the pupil's personal and learning history; the realities and constraints of the class or group setting; and the type of assessment information (whether it is detailed or a single figure, criterion-referenced or a standardized score, etc.). The teacher's interpretation of the test score is dependent upon other knowledge that he or she has, including how the pupil responded to the tasks that made up the assessment.

Tittle's (1989) argument is that we need to extend validity enquiry to include the teacher's and student's perspective in the validation of what test scores mean and whether they are useful to teachers and learners, since we cannot assume that the teacher shares the same frame of reference as the test developer.

Conclusion

Within the framework of CHAT theory, assessment is an interactive, dynamic and collaborative activity. Rather than being external and formal in its implementation, assessment is integral to the teaching process and is embedded in the social and cultural life of the classroom. Such an approach can be seen as constructive and enabling because of its focus on assessing the process of learning, its attempt to elicit elaborated performance, and its emphasis on collaborative activity, whether the collaboration is with the teacher or a group of peers. By contrast, traditional testing is controlling and classifying. Much of the work in this field is still at the level of research, however, and a number of issues remain to be clarified. For example, such an approach to assessment is often time-consuming and demands particular skills of the teacher/assessor. The procedures, being unstandardized, do not meet traditional reliability criteria and this has an impact on the purposes for which the assessment can/should be used. Finally, there are many issues to be resolved around the evaluation of individuals within group performance.

What these developments have made clear, however, is that there is an urgent requirement to rethink some of our society's traditional assumptions about assessment. The new approaches, by offering assistance in the assessment task, allow us to see how the process of learning is developing; enable assessments to be made in the social setting of the group; open up the traditional relationship between teacher and student; attempt to recognize the learner's perspective; and give the student an understanding of the assessment process and evaluation criteria. This overall approach to assessment may be seen by traditionalists as somehow improper, giving the student unfair advantage, and amounting to an abrogation of the teacher's responsibilities. But the role of the teacher is not diminished by opening up discussion of assessment with the student; this is an additional role which the teacher must take on in order to develop the students as self-monitoring learners. That is a major challenge for assessment in the twenty-first century.

7

Teaching, Learning, and Development: A Post-Vygotskian Perspective

Anna Stetsenko and Igor Arievitch

> Learning is not development; however, properly organized learning results in mental development and sets in motion a variety of developmental processes that would be impossible apart from learning. (Vygotsky, 1978, p. 90)

These words by Lev Vygotsky address one of the most fundamental concerns for anyone dealing with children – parents, teachers, developmental psychologists and others. How are teaching, learning and the development of children's minds related? Are these processes independent, or do they influence each other, and if the latter, then in what way and by what means? For example, can qualitatively new levels of intelligence be achieved as a result of learning? The way we answer these questions depends on what we believe about such basic theoretical matters as the very nature of mind and its development. These answers also crucially affect the ways we organize the processes of teaching-and-learning. For example, if we believe that children's minds develop according to 'internally driven' laws, then we will be mostly concerned with detecting these laws so as to tailor teaching processes to students' naturally unfolding capacities. If, on the contrary, we believe that children's minds can be developed through teaching-and-learning, then our primary concern should be to construct those forms of teaching-and-learning that do have a developmental impact on the minds of students.

Of course, learning always results in some change, for example, in increased knowledge or the acquisition of a new skill. However, the Vygotskian position is more radical than this simple statement, differing drastically from traditional views in psychology and education. According to Vygotsky, teaching-and-learning is the very pathway through which human mind develops. The aim of this chapter is to explore this radical position, its complex layers and its practical implications.

The contribution of the authors was equal.

We first take a brief look at how the relationships between teaching, learning and development have been approached in several historically prominent psychological theories. Then we discuss how this issue has been conceptualized in sociocultural theory. After that we focus on how these theoretical formulations were elaborated and empirically tested by one of Vygotsky's followers, Piotr Gal'perin. We argue that, by breaking the vicious circle that prevails in traditional thinking about learning, teaching and development, this approach suggests how to arrange teaching-and-learning processes in such a way that they indeed lead to a profound developmental change in children's minds.

Research on Teaching, Learning and Development: Traditional Gaps and Persisting Controversies

The relationship between teaching, learning and development has an interesting history in psychology, characterized more by a shifting of attention and prioritization between these processes than by a focus on their interrelationships. With some notable exceptions, such as the work of John Dewey, these relationships were largely ignored in psychological theories at the beginning of the last century. The role of learning in development came to the fore with the rise of behaviourism, which attempted to specify the learning mechanisms underpinning changes in behaviour. Behaviourists, however, excluded mental processes from their analyses, and therefore had nothing to say about the development of these processes. Besides, behaviourist theories were grounded in research on animals. Children's learning, particularly at school, was not the direct focus. Although some inferences were drawn from animal studies about the teaching and upbringing of children, this approach could not and did not offer much insight into how teaching-and-learning affects cognitive development.

However, by the mid-1970s, with the waning influence of behaviourism and the rise of the new cognitivist theory, learning itself ceased to attract attention (cf. Stevenson, 1983). Discussion of learning was replaced by an interest in the discovery of deep universal laws of mind that were presumed to be hardly affected by any external influences. Cognitivist theories primarily aimed, and continue to aim, at describing context-independent processes common to all humans, regardless of the culturally specific activities in which people engage. For example, from a cognitivist position, what matters in the analysis of memory is a predetermined and virtually unchangeable storage capacity that is thought to be best revealed through research on the memorization of meaningless information (e.g. strings of letters) outside schooling experiences or any other learning practices.

Nevertheless, the issue of how cognitive developmental change comes about has been central in another landmark theory: Jean Piaget's 'genetic epistemology'. Piaget can be credited with the discovery of many important regularities in how the human mind develops through the individual's active engagement with the world. However, this theory largely attributes children's progress in developing mental capacities, such as conceptual understanding, to their own independent experiences and discoveries. Whether and how cognitive development is affected by what children learn at school has not been examined in the Piagetian framework.

Thus the complex role of teaching-and-learning in mental development has essentially been ignored in most of the prominent approaches in psychology. How specific activities in which learners engage, and the mental tools that they learn to use, affect the development of their minds is a question that has rarely been clearly formulated, let alone satisfactorily resolved. Today, teaching, learning and development continue to be viewed by many as processes that are essentially different from each other or only superficially related. For example, despite growing evidence that intelligence can be learned and taught (see Perkins, 1995), there is practically no debate about the mechanisms that underlie and possibly link all three processes: teaching, learning and cognitive development.

As a result of these gaps, the domains of psychological and educational research have not, in our view, profited from each other as much as they could. On the one hand, discoveries about learning processes contribute only very little to our understanding of how and why children's minds develop. For example, new teaching methods are not regarded in terms of their implications for general theories of development. On the other hand, psychological theories of development do not have a large impact on the practice of teaching and learning (cf. Strauss, 1998). Although some ideas from cognitive psychology have influenced educational practice (e.g. the emphasis on metacognition), too often these ideas have not been supported by explicit strategies for implementing them in school. It is somewhat ironic that arguably the greatest contribution of cognitive psychology to education has been summed up in the following principle: 'Think less about teaching and more about learning' (Romig, 1999). However, we believe that the wall between teaching and learning that cognitivism inadvertently encourages can hardly benefit our understanding of either of these processes.

The reason why researchers concerned with teaching, learning and development are still searching for common ground on which their findings could be integrated, we believe, is that there has been a dearth of conceptual space where the relationship between these processes could be conceived. Indeed, when learning is regarded only as the forming of links between stimuli and responses (as in behaviourism), or when the developing mind is viewed as governed merely by internal regularities (as in cognitivism), or when the impact of teaching on development is ignored (as in most of developmental psychology), there is simply no room for the three processes to be conceptually brought together and examined.

It took a whole new approach to human mind and development – socio-cultural theory – to make the analysis of links between teaching, learning and development both possible and necessary. In fact, conceptualizing this relationship has been a pivotal element in this approach.

A Sociocultural Framework for the Study of Teaching, Learning and Development

Sociocultural theory, largely inspired by the seminal works of Lev Vygotsky, can be characterized by its central claim that children's minds develop as a result of constant interactions with the social world – the world of people who do things with and for each other, who learn from each other and use the experiences of previous generations to successfully meet the present demands of life. These experiences are crystallized in 'cultural tools', and children have to master such tools in order to develop specifically human ways of doing things and thereby become competent members of a human community. These tools can be material objects (e.g. items of kitchenware that crystallize specifically human ways of eating), or patterns of behaviour specifically organized in space and time (for example, children's bedtime rituals). Most often, however, such tools are combinations of elements of different orders, and human language is the multi-level tool *par excellence*, combining culturally evolved arrangements of meanings, sounds, rules of communication, and so forth.

Learning such tools is not something that simply helps the mind to develop. Rather, this kind of learning leads to new, more elaborated forms of mental functioning. For example, when children master such a complex cultural tool as human language, this results not only in their ability to talk but leads to completely new levels of thinking, self-regulation and mentality in general. The learning of language calls into being – and in effect shapes and forms – new facets of the child's mind.

Importantly, cultural tools are not merely static 'things' but embodiments of certain ways of acting in human communities. In other words, they represent the functions and meanings of things as discovered in cultural practices: they are 'objects-that-can-be-used-for-certain-purposes' in human societies. As such, they can be appropriated by a child only through acting upon and with them; that is, only in the course of actively reconstructing their meaning and function. Such reconstruction of cultural tools is initially possible only through interaction with other people who already have the knowledge of a given cultural tool.

This short account illustrates the fact that the sociocultural approach, unlike those we have previously discussed, not only allows for a synthesis of teaching, learning and development; it actively calls for it. Teaching leads development because it allows children to learn to use new cultural tools, and such mastery constitutes the very cornerstone of mental development. Children's development is thus inherently linked to teaching-and-learning. Moreover, the relationship between them is made explicit in this approach: it is conceptualized as a three-fold process in which cultural tools are provided, learned and transformed into the building blocks of the mind, all within the space of active interaction and cooperation in the 'zone of proximal development'.[1]

Gal'perin's Perspective on Teaching, Learning and Development

Because such a central role is accorded in the Vygotskian approach to the role of teaching-and-learning in development, it is no wonder that much of the research conducted in this tradition has focused on exactly this issue. Many innovative ideas with vast theoretical and practical implications for education have issued from this research, and continue to do so (cf. Wells, 1999). However, one of the most radical approaches to teaching, learning and development can be found in works by Piotr Gal'perin, who started his career as Vygotsky's close colleague and went on to establish his own theory of development that continued and in many ways expanded Vygotsky's framework.

At the centre of Gal'perin's theory is the issue of the origins of mind and cognitive change. Extending Vygotsky's ideas about human development, Gal'perin contended that mental processes should be understood as transformed and internalized material actions that involve cultural tools. He postulated three stages in the process by which such transformation occurs, progressing from physical action to audible verbalization and, finally, to 'internal speech' and other mental operations (see Gal'perin, 1989). Such internalized actions become 'the very stuff' of the mind by providing it with structure and content.

For example, according to Gal'perin, voluntary attention is not an inherent mental capacity which focuses a mysterious 'mind's eye' on a desired content but, rather, a transformed, initially material process of monitoring one's own activities. Take the case of a child's ability to pay attention while writing. To be sure, many children come to form this ability without being fully aware of all the stumbling blocks they overcome along the way and all the complexities involved in this process. However, as most teachers and less fortunate parents know, a large number of children experience tremendous difficulties in learning how to be attentive while writing. For this ability to emerge, it is not enough to encourage the child to pay attention, because children might simply not know what it takes 'to pay attention'. Instead, children have to be taught how to monitor their writing activity, namely, how to notice and correct their mistakes. This learning, in the early stages, must involve various material 'supports' such as, for example, pencil marks between syllables.

Later, these material supports can be abandoned and children proceed to perform monitoring in detailed overt speech. In the final stages, the whole monitoring activity can be performed without overt verbalization, that is, 'in mind'.

Importantly, as seen from the example just described, the transformation of material actions into internalized 'mental processes' is a complex process that always involves mastery of cultural tools – in this case, knowledge of how to distinguish syllables. Therefore, exploring the process by which cultural tools are learned by children becomes a pivotal element in studying cognitive development (for details, see Arievitch and Stetsenko, 2000).

Based on these theoretical claims, Gal'perin explored concrete regularities in how actions are transformed from material to mental forms in the course of learning cultural tools. It is in these studies that Gal'perin arrived at what became the cornerstone of his approach: the innovative analysis of instructional practices based on different types of cultural tools, and the spelling out of the developmental potential of different kinds of instruction. Although Gal'perin was primarily interested in the basic regularities of cognitive development, his whole research programme took the form of studying how the teaching and learning of specific cultural tools impacts on children's development.

Traditional instruction and its impact on development

While examining existing instructional practices, Gal'perin came to the conclusion that, in all their great variety, such practices far too often fail to provide children with the cultural tools that are most beneficial for the development of their minds. That is, children are not given tools that enable them to construct their actions in a form that is most conducive to the efficient transformation of these actions into the instruments of mind. Instead, school children are often faced with fragmented, poorly generalized phenomena that are supposed to be learned by simply memorizing them.

Typically, instruction in its traditional form is based on: (a) the teacher's presentation of the task, (b) the explanation of a rule to solve the problem as presented in a particular example, (c) learner's memorization of this rule, and finally (d) practice in solving typical tasks. However, many of the implicit rules and regularities that an expert 'automatically' takes into account may well remain hidden from the learner. Each child has to figure out by herself a substantial body of such rules while trying (often unsuccessfully) to solve a given task.

The basic feature – and main deficiency – of this type of instruction is that it does not encourage children to build the actions in a way that would allow them to meaningfully generalize these actions, and hence to internalize them. Trial-and-error is inevitable in this case, allowing only a slow, gradual selection of the 'correct' form of action necessary to solve the task. As a result, children's actions cannot be efficiently transformed into the tools of their minds.

For example, when learning the grammar of a foreign language, students typically have to memorize by rote dozens of rules. The rules are presented one by one and the explanation of each rule is usually reduced to providing an example. The implicit basic relationship underlying different rules that actually exists in each system of grammar (for example, the relationship between aspects of the word's meaning and the word's structural elements) is not revealed to students. In other words, students are not provided with the tools for a meaningful orientation in the implicit rules that govern each language. As a result, the systems of grammar are perceived by children as a meaningless collection of isolated cases rather than as a coherent system of relationships based on general regularities. If students are to begin to discover these relationships, they can do so only in a lengthy, trial-and-error, intuitive kind of way. It usually takes a lot of painful effort and several years of study to master (or fail to master) a foreign language.

This insufficiency in revealing the set of conditions necessary to solve the task is not a minor detail of the instruction process. In fact, it directly affects the quality of a learner's actions and hence the resulting mental processes. Under these conditions, actions often remain unstable, poorly generalized and dependent on incidental variations in the instructional situation (e.g. the teacher's individual style). This inevitably results in large inter-individual differences in children's performance. In this type of instruction it is practically impossible to establish causal connections between any developmental changes and the instructional milieu. As a consequence, it can appear more plausible to explain development in terms of age-related regularities or inborn inter-individual differences in mental abilities, rather than in terms of the impact of instruction and associated learning on development.

Systemic–theoretical instruction

Having analysed the features of typical traditional instruction, Gal'perin concentrated his efforts on developing an alternative type of instruction that would provide children with more psychologically efficient and developmentally beneficial cultural tools. Based on theoretical assumptions about mental development, Gal'perin defined the main criteria for the selection of such cultural tools. In brief, efficient cultural tools are learning materials (i.e. concepts, theories, ideas) that present in a generalized or schematic form the essential features of a given class of phenomena. Typically, these features pertain to general regularities in how phenomena evolve and relate to each other in human practices. Accordingly, efficient cultural tools are typically found in historically evolved knowledge that captures the lengthy evolution of previous generations' practices in dealing with particular phenomena.

For example, there are many features that describe a circle. Most obviously, a circle is simply a flat round area. In the classical scientific definition, however, a circle is a curved line on which every point is equally distant from one fixed point inside the curve. Yet another definition reflects the procedure by which a circle is produced: a circle is produced by two sticks with one fixed end, or by a pair of compasses. In the latter definition, the initial operation underlying the concept of a circle (and thus its genesis) is revealed, thereby making it clear why all the radii of a circle are and have to be equal – namely, because they are actually generated by the same radius revolving around one fixed point (cf. Davydov, 1988). This latter kind of definition is effective because it describes the circle as a product of a specific operation discovered in socio-cultural practices and thus represents its generic essential feature. Gal'perin suggested that providing learners with cultural tools that reflect generic, essential features of phenomena, greatly enhances learners' cognitive development. A whole new type of instruction based on such cultural tools was developed by Gal'perin and his colleagues.

This instruction, termed systemic–theoretical, arms children with a general method to solve a specific class of phenomena by exposing their relevant essential features; that is, by showing their origins in particular practices. Specifically, this form of analysis includes (a) discriminating between different properties of an object or phenomenon, (b) establishing the basic units to analyse a particular property, and (c) revealing the general rules (common to all objects in the studied area) whereby those units are combined into concrete phenomena. The method makes extensive use of symbolic and graphic models to represent basic relations between different properties of objects.

The principles of systemic–theoretical instruction were implemented by Gal'perin and his colleagues in a number of experimental programmes in a variety of subjects, including science, language and history. Perhaps the most illustrative in terms of its effects on cognitive development is the programme of elementary mathematics for 5–6-year-old children (see Gal'perin and Georgiev, 1960). Within this programme children are taught such fundamental concepts as that of number. Traditional instruction often fails to enable children to form genuine mathematical concepts. For example, numbers are often empirically introduced as single discrete objects (i.e. 'one' stands for 'one pen', 'two' for 'two apples'). Children are taught that 'one' (object) is one, not two or more, and this is something to memorize and follow. The logic and function of the concept of number – that is, how and why numbers have evolved in human practices – are not revealed. As a result, children tend to confuse mathematical numbers with discrete objects.

In contrast, within systemic–theoretical instruction children learn the logic and history of numbers – that is, their origin in specific sociocultural practices. Because all the basic types of numbers emerged as a result of measurement, the idea of measurement is systematically introduced to the children. First, children are shown how important measurement is in various everyday situations, for example, in stores to establish the correct amount of goods. Then they learn to use measurement as an analytical tool with which to derive fundamental concepts in elementary mathematics.

Specifically, children are first taught to choose appropriate measures (e.g. cups for the volume of water, strips of paper for length) in order to compare objects in terms of their particular properties (volume, length). In the process of measurement children learn to use some material tokens (e.g. chips) to record the results of every step of measurement. For example, a child checks how many cups of water fit into a given container and sets aside a chip for each cup. The resulting collection of chips then comes to represent in a very easy-to-grasp manner, quantified in a material form, the volume of water in a given container. This helps children to realize how the properties of objects can be transformed into quantities as a result of measurement. As a next step, children learn how to compare two objects by putting two sets of markers (each recording the result of measuring one object) next to each other, in one-to-one correspondence. For example, the amount of water in one container gets represented by three chips (each representing one cup of water), whereas the amount of water in another container is represented by two chips, with the two sets of chips now being directly and immediately comparable. Thus, concepts such as 'larger', 'smaller', 'equal to', 'larger (smaller) by so much', become operationally clear to children.

It is only after such practical–analytical work that the concept of number is introduced. For example, 'one' is explained as the result of measurement when the measured quantity is represented by one chip (i.e. where one chip stands for one cup of water). Other numbers can then be constructed by children themselves according to the rule 'smaller by 1 or greater by 1'. The material markers are soon replaced by more abstract symbols, thus gradually transforming practical comparisons into mental operations. In sum, the fundamental concept of number is introduced to children not through separate objects but generically; that is, by reconstructing the genuine problem and practice that served as the source from which this concept emerged. The final stages of the programme include similar work aimed at the children gaining mastery of the four arithmetic operations, decimal fractions, and so on.

The general result of the programme is that genuine mathematical concepts are formed in children a whole age-period earlier: in 5- and 6-year-olds rather than in 10–12-year-olds, when it has usually been found to occur. Even more importantly, the children's entire view of material objects changes: they come to understand that things need not be judged by their appearance. In other words, children set themselves free from apparent but often misleading impressions and thus advance from immediate (naive–egocentric) thinking to thinking mediated by the concept of measure. For example, children who were initially identified as non-conservers on Piagetian tasks now display a very different understanding. Children who previously thought that the amount of water poured from a tall container into a shorter one decreased as a result of this operation – irrespective of the container's width – now refuse to give an immediate answer and say instead: 'Let's first measure!' These children then proceed to conclude that the amount of water did not change and thus demonstrate the conservation effect, even though this concept was not directly taught to them.

Another programme illustrating principles of systemic–theoretical instruction aims at teaching foreign languages (Kabanova, 1976). The students in this programme are provided with generalized schemes that help them understand and systematically track down the sources of grammatical forms in the contexts of human activities and practices. For example, the complex rules of how to use German modal verbs, instead of being presented as a collection of unrelated cases that have to be memorized, are explained in a systematic way based on revealing the implicit functions of these verbs. In the process, students learn how verbs function in human language to reflect intricacies both of the reality they describe and the human communication they serve to accomplish. Thus, subtle linguistic differences become apparent to students even if their native language does not have a similar system of verbs. Importantly, students are not just 'trained' in how to apply linguistic rules, but are given cultural tools that enable them to discover implicit linguistic regularities. After these schemes are internalized, students use them as powerful tools of orientation in language phenomena. For example, students are able to transfer the acquired method to other linguistic activities such as creating their own 'languages' according to systematic linguistic rules.

In general, as in the teaching of elementary mathematics, this programme has resulted in a spectacular cognitive–developmental change, in that children advance from a naive–empirical way of thinking (i.e. based on apparent but often misleading features) to one that is theoretical (i.e. based on essential characteristics of phenomena). Importantly, the systemic–theoretical teaching in these and many similar programmes leads to substantial progress not just in children's knowledge but also in their wider cognitive functioning. For example, significant improvements occur in children's abilities to analyse, plan and reflect upon their actions, to set goals and systematically control how they are attained. No less significant is that trial-and-error learning, so typical of traditional instruction, becomes rare, and also that the time it takes children to learn new knowledge or skills significantly decreases. In addition, impressive changes occur in children's learning motivation. That is, in contrast to children in classes with traditional instruction, whose motives for learning often remain pragmatically oriented (e.g. to get a good grade, to do better than others), children in experimental classes gradually develop a genuine learning motivation – a strong and stable interest in the exciting process of discovering the hidden regularities in the world and general ways of solving problems.

Teaching experiments based on Gal'perin's principles were mostly carried out from the 1960s to the 1980s, ranging from programmes on limited topics, such as described above, to long-term programmes both for adults and children. Furthermore, Gal'perin's approach has had a direct impact on large-scale teaching experiments, also initiated in the 1960s, by El'konin and

Davydov and continuing until the present in many different parts of the world (see Davydov, 1988). However, given the fundamental nature of implications from Gal'perin's approach, broader replications and further analyses of its methodology are certainly needed. In addition, this approach could greatly benefit from the incorporation of recent developments in research on socio-interactional contexts of learning, such as situated learning (e.g. see the present volume). We shall conclude this chapter, however, by considering some of the implications of Gal'perin's research in more detail.

Implications for Developmental Psychology and Education

Gal'perin's approach integrates the analysis of teaching, learning and development by capitalizing on an element central to all three of these processes. This element concerns the 'cultural tools' provided by teachers and learned by children, thereby inducing activities that can be transformed into powerful instruments of mind. These new instruments provoke development, in the full sense, as they empower learners to become active explorers and thinkers. Thus, the development of the human mind is seen not as a process separate from teaching and learning, but as part of a system that encompasses all three activities. In this sense, Gal'perin's approach fills the gaps so typical of previous frameworks in both psychology and education. It also allows us to understand what lies behind developmental change and thus adds greater specificity to Vygotsky's insight that development is driven by teaching-and-learning. Ultimately, it is in this sense that Gal'perin's theory is a contribution simultaneously to developmental psychology and to education.

Importantly, in contrast to traditional theories, which often ignore how development is contingent on teaching-and-learning practices and thus confuse developmental outcomes achieved within particular educational systems with universal developmental regularities, Gal'perin's approach draws attention to a self-perpetuating 'vicious circle', namely:

Inadequate theories of development → Poor educational practices → Poor development outcomes → Inadequate theories of development

For example, many traditional theories posit that children lack the ability to reason in a reflective way with abstract categories. Given this view, many educators think that children need to be taught in a fashion that best accommodates this allegedly fixed age-related feature of their minds. Thus, traditional instruction typically includes the requirement to teach young children in a 'piecemeal' fashion whereby they are exposed to small bits of information supported by concrete illustrative examples, with no attempt to reveal the general rules and connections that lie behind these examples. As a result, children indeed do not develop the ability to operate with abstract (i.e.

generalized, systematic) concepts. In contrast, research findings by Gal'perin and his colleagues demonstrate that, when children are taught in a systemic–theoretical fashion, as described above, there are spectacular developmental changes, including progress in abstract reflective thinking. In this sense, then, it is the traditional instructional restrictions thought to be grounded in inherent limitations of children's minds that, in fact, themselves produce these limitations!

Gal'perin's research, we would argue, represents a key development in the educational approach originally envisioned by Vygotsky and currently pursued by many working in the sociocultural tradition. For example, Gal'perin's theory provides essential support for theories striving to dispel the old stereotypes that still underlie many educational practices. Specifically, Gal'perin's work helps to undermine the 'seed metaphor' that describes cognitive development as a process driven by inner regularities that can be only slightly (if at all) altered by learning. His studies show that children have a vast developmental potential that can and should be realized within teaching–learning practices that are based on sociocultural principles of development.

Gal'perin's approach is also consistent with theories that emphasize that children need to acquire not only rules and facts (i.e. declarative knowledge) but also procedures of how and where to apply knowledge (i.e. procedural knowledge) (e.g. Bruer, 1993). Gal'perin specifies ways to enable students to grasp not just the surface of things but the regularities of how various phenomena evolve, develop and systematically relate to one another in contexts of human practices. Understanding these essential features entails understanding how knowledge can be applied in various practical domains. For example, and turning again to the programme in mathematics described above, learning the concept of number as part (and product!) of a broader activity of measuring entails understanding how to use numbers for real-life tasks that necessitate measurement. Thus, it becomes possible to bridge the traditional gap between practical and theoretical knowledge. This is achieved not by simply giving students additional 'practice' in applying initially inert knowledge, but by introducing phenomena, right from the beginning, as essential instruments and products of historically evolved human practices.

Furthermore, Gal'perin's principles are in agreement with theories that emphasize that learning is ultimately embedded in cultural practices and distributed among the participants (e.g. Cobb, 1998; Lave and Wenger, 1991; Rogoff, 1990). However, Gal'perin's theory goes further in that it emphasizes the following. To understand the development of mind one needs not only to observe how children participate in practices and make use of cultural tools, but also to construct instructional procedures that specifically provide students with experiences of tool use, in which the evolving histories and functions of the tools are made explicit. Finally, Gal'perin's approach gives an instructive – albeit a counter-intuitive – answer to what is perhaps the most pressing issue concerning education today: why is school learning so abstract and removed from real life? From Gal'perin's perspective the remedy for the schools' failure to produce useful knowledge and know-how should be sought not by substituting the teaching of 'abstract' knowledge by rich and specific 'hands-on' experience. Instead, the demarcating line should be drawn between inert knowledge, regardless of its level of generality, on the one hand, and knowledge – also of varying degree of generality – as an instrument of meaningful, historically evolved cultural practices, on the other. It is this latter knowledge, unlike inert facts or knowledge gained in a 'hands-on' and vivid, but too often fortuitous and unsystematic experiences, that empowers children with methods for constructing *new* knowledge. Therefore, it is also this kind of knowledge that can be actively used by the learners in virtually unlimited expansive cycles of exploration and discovery (cf. Engeström, 1991). Arguably, there is nothing more practical than such knowledge, especially in the twenty-first century in which increasing value is likely to be put on life-long learning.

Note

1   Although the ZPD is not the focus of this chapter, it should be noted that this concept is inextricably linked to that of the cultural tools (for details, see Stetsenko, 1999).

Part II
Pre-School and School-Age Learning and Development

8

Emerging Learning Narratives: A Perspective from Early Childhood Education

Margaret Carr

In the twenty-first century, we might surmise, the role of being a pupil in early childhood settings and schools will become more complex and less well defined, uncertainty of outcome will increasingly be the norm, and patterns of responsibility for learning will shift towards individual and collaborative forms away from instructions and edicts from above. Nurturing learning dispositions in these three domains will help children to become good life-long learners. This chapter explores the relevance of culture and history to this project, using early childhood activities as examples.

Expectations about participation in educational activities develop during early childhood, and many of these expectations appear to be robust, influencing learning in later years. An influential US longitudinal study of children from early childhood to age 27 speculated on the mechanisms of lasting change as follows:

> The essential process connecting early childhood experience to patterns of improved success in school and the community seemed to be the development of habits, traits, and dispositions that allowed the child to interact positively with other people and with tasks. This process was based neither on permanently improved intellectual performance nor on academic knowledge. (Schweinhart and Weikart, 1993, p. 4)

These findings by Schweinhart and Weikart suggest that although skills and knowledge are necessary outcomes of education, they may not be sufficient. Learners have to be ready and willing as well as able (Claxton, 1990, p. 164) to learn. Schweinhart and Weikart also take the stance that learning is about participation and interaction. In New Zealand the national early childhood curriculum takes a similar stance. It emphasizes the critical role of socially and culturally mediated learning and describes learning as 'responsive and reciprocal relationships with people, places and things' (New Zealand Ministry of Education, 1996, p. 9). A number of writers have highlighted the role

This research was partly supported by funding from the Research Division of the New Zealand Ministry of Education.

of dispositions in defining reciprocal and responsive relationships. Katz (1988) commented that 'dispositions are a very different type of learning from skills and knowledge. They can be thought of as habits of mind, tendencies to re-spond to situations in certain ways'. She cites friendliness, curiosity and being bossy as examples of dispositions. I have described 'learning dispositions' in relational terms and defined them as tendencies that dispose learners to inter-pret, edit and respond to learning opportunities in characteristic ways (Carr, 1999); their importance is highlighted in several chapters in this volume.

This chapter explores three domains of learning disposition: (1) intent and meaning, (2) response to challenge or uncertainty and (3) responsibility. These three dispositional domains all refer to participation and interaction between learners and the educational environment, not to temperament free of environmental context. Researching them requires 'interpretive, contextu-ally rich studies of classrooms' (Walsh, Tobin and Graue, 1993, p. 467). It requires close attention to what Wertsch (1991) has called 'mediated action', a unit of analysis that links the individual to the learning environment in a transactional model of learning.

In this chapter activity is given its common meaning as a curricular event, set up for an educational purpose by the teachers in the early childhood centre, and the discussion is about the child's implicit theory of education in a number of activities. The child's implicit theory of education is characterized here as being to do with what the intent, goal or topic is perceived to be; whether she is ready, willing and able to tackle difficulty and risk error; and whether she is ready, willing and able to take responsibility – i.e. the learning dispositions. I have called this the child's learning narrative (Carr, 2000a; after Bruner, 1990b). I will argue that, in one particular early childhood setting, two activities (screen printing and marble painting) had come to reflect different implicit theories of education or learning narratives and were selected by children who held those narratives. In other words, learning nar-ratives adhered to activities as a result of transactions between learners and teachers and artifacts over time. Mercer (this volume) points out that one of the strengths of a sociocultural approach is that it encourages education to be explained in terms of the interactive process of 'teaching-and-learning', and that Vygotsky had at his disposal the Russian word *obuchenie*, which means both teaching and learning. Interestingly, the curriculum development team that developed New Zealand's socioculturally oriented early childhood cur-riculum (Carr and May, 1994) had at their disposal the Maori word *ako*, which also means both teaching and learning.

Two Activities in an Early Childhood Setting

In order to research the learning dispositions of a group of 4-year-olds in an early childhood programme, I observed children in a New Zealand kindergarten (a half-day sessional programme) for six weeks as they worked on everyday construction and craft activities. The children were free to choose their activities for about two hours each morning while adults were on hand to tutor, provide social support and/or participate in collaborative endeavours. The activities were set out but not directed by the teacher, and the context therefore has some similarities with the Fifth Dimension after-school games programme at UC San Diego (Brown and Cole, this volume) and the spontaneous and student-initiated events in school classrooms described by Wells (this volume). In this case, the research question was whether some activities were rich in opportunities for inducting the children into a technologists' community of practice or social intent, encouraging persistence with tackling uncertainty and challenge, and facilitating the development of joint attention and co-construction.

To answer this question I compared a number of activities, two of which are described here. Near to what might be described as a 'cutting, pasting and painting' working table was the screen-printing table. The screen-printing process included cutting out a template, positioning it over the painting paper under the screen, screening the paint in a smooth and vigorous manner and removing the print. Thirty children participated in episodes of screen printing, thirteen of them participated only once, and six children chose screen printing as a favourite activity (each making five or more prints). On a nearby shelf with the staplers, scissors, adhesive tape, paste and paints there was a rather battered looking shallow cardboard box, with two cups of paint that each contained marbles and a teaspoon. These were the ingredients of the activity called 'marble painting'. The process was as follows: a piece of paper was placed in the cardboard box, a marble was spooned in, and the box was moved about to enable the marble to roll lines of paint onto the paper. The effect was somewhat like a Jackson Pollock painting. Three children chose marble-painting as one of their favourite activities. Altogether there were 58 episodes of screen printing, and 17 episodes of marble painting.

As an Apprenticeship for What? Meaning-Making and Social Intent

The screen-printing activity, which a high proportion of children tried only once, did not emerge as an apprenticeship into screen printing. Rather, the activity was an apprenticeship into 'being a kindergartener' (and, especially, being a morning kindergartener, because this activity had not been available to the younger children who came in the afternoons and then 'graduated' to the morning). Being a kindergartener was to a large extent defined as acquiring the skills needed for the next rung up the educational ladder, school: cutting with scissors along a line, writing your name (29 of the screen-printing episodes were observed to include children writing their names), and following a complex sequence. 'Good cutting' was a necessary part of the process.

If 'being a screen printer' had been the intent, then at least one of two capacities or affordances would have been exploited: (1) duplication of image in which the same image is repeated on either the one picture or as different pictures, and (2) silhouetting, in which a drawing or a found object (a leaf, for instance) becomes its 'shadow' or a shape only. The first capacity was not exploited by any of the children during the observation period. No one screen printed the same image more than once, perhaps because at the beginning of the year it was a popular activity and there was a certain amount of queuing at the screen. Experimenting was difficult when there was a queue, and a queue-generated routine (one person, one image, one picture) was established during the early part of the year.

Even the second capacity (silhouetting) passed many of the screen-printing children by (although a teacher suggested to Emily that as a simpler process she might like to use some leaves for printing – 'You just want to do the printing part?' – Emily did not pursue this plan). For many of the children, a 'good' screen print was an evenly painted template: the children almost always kept the template as well as the print, peeling it off the screen and gluing it to a third sheet of paper, writing their name on that and hanging it up to dry. Three children kept the template and threw away the print (even Danny, who later did become interested in the negative shape left behind, was much more interested in the template on his first two attempts). On six occasions there was no template: often an uncut drawing was screened. Samuel screened an uncut drawing on both occasions that he made a print, and many of the children only made a cursory attempt at cutting around a drawn shape (Bridget, for instance, told Amy that her print was a picture of herself, but the shape that emerged was a rectangle with a 'bite' cut out of one corner). Most children interpreted the instruction to 'cut out a shape' as a request for circles, rectangles or triangles, or miscellaneous and unidentifiable (and not expected to be identified) shapes. Teachers often reminded children that the detail was important because 'that's the shape you're going to see'. However, on only one occasion out of the 58 were the unique affordances of screen printing commented on by adults or children: one morning Danny was screen printing a cut-out animal drawing and told Joan that he was 'going to do the shadow of it'.

Surprisingly, marble painting did have the look of a craft apprenticeship. The marble-painting process was transparent, with children able to take in the process rapidly from beginning to end. Molly commented: 'the ball's making me do that'. Children could observe marble painters carefully, understand what was going on, then carry out the process themselves. In its original form there was not much that could go right or wrong. However, one day the box was lost; Jason decided to make a new box, and then the children chose to make a new box each time they wanted to do a marble painting. This painting-box construction, together with assessments of its efficiency during marble painting, became one of the focus points of the activity, with a clear meaning and considerable challenge.

So screen printing and marble painting had each become characterized by very different intent or meaning. Screen printing reflected a 'kindergartener' intent: a successful screen print signalled membership of the community of practice of kindergarteners who are competent in a number of fragmented skills whose purpose is understood by the teacher but seldom by the kindergartener. (Of course, print-making activities in early childhood are not compelled to take on this intent: in another kindergarten with a different culture and a different history, a few years later, the teachers brought in some enthusiastic print-makers who taught the children new techniques and showed them their work. A group of about eight children developed sequences of elaborate and complex prints that included repeated patterns and designs that drew inspiration from South Pacific art forms, and exploited the qualities of a silhouette.) Marble painting reflected a 'technologist' or craftsperson intent; technologists pose and solve problems that have meaning and purpose for them.

Orientation to Challenge

The second disposition of interest was orientation to challenge. As indicated above, when they participated in screen printing many children didn't try to solve problems or tackle difficulty. Thirty-seven of the 58 screen-print episodes began with roughly or randomly cut shapes or no template at all, and only six children persevered with the process to make five or more prints during the observation period. Thirteen of the thirty children who made a print never returned to this activity. Bridget and Rita screened a face or figure, but Rita's was uncut, and Bridget's was minimally cut. However, although children seldom tackled difficulty or ran the risk of error in the screen-printing part of the process, the earlier step, writing one's name, did run the risk of error, and many children persevered with this in spite of its difficulty.

At first glance marble painting did not seem to provide challenging art or craft opportunities. The process was easy, with only five steps (writing your name on the paper before you paint, putting the paper into the box, putting the marbles and paint in, tipping, removing and hanging up to dry). Even the first step, writing your name, was often omitted because no one – children or adults – appeared particularly to value the ownership of paintings that all looked so very similar. It would appear to be an activity that didn't call for much concentration or effort (Nick: 'Is it easy?' Nell: 'It is easy'), calling into play alternative discourses: discussions about friendship for instance. But 'being a technologist' held its own. The marble-painting box is lost. Field notes record the following episode:

Jason elicits the help of the observer to look for the marble-painting box, which we can't find.

Jason: 'I could just get another box!'

He cuts one wide side and then the end flap off a breakfast-food box. Now he has a tray with one side cut off. He tucks some paper into one end, spoons in the painted marble, and rolls it about. The marble rolls onto the table. To solve the problem he (a) controls the marble by pushing it around with the spoon, instead of tilting the box. Then he (b) tilts the box again, catching the marble with his hand. He explains the problem to the observer: 'It needs one up there' (another side to the tray), and he (c) curls the paper insert up to form a fourth side and a curved edge for the marble to roll up onto and back down.

Jason had changed the rules and rituals for the activity. Other children began to incorporate box-making into marble painting, finding and solving new problems.

Pattern of Responsibility

The third learning disposition was to do with the pattern of responsibility or control. Three patterns featured in these two activities: adult tutorials, adult–child collaboration and peer collaboration.

Adult tutorials

In screen printing, adults were much more closely involved than in marble painting. Of the 589 conversational turns in all the screen-printing episodes for which there was a transcript, 44.6 per cent were adults' turns in comparison with 24.3 per cent of 77 in the marble painting. Adult speech turns were not only more frequent, they were longer in screen printing. Typically, in screen printing, the social interchange was between an adult and one, two or three children, and the format was in the nature of a tutorial. In an adult tutorial style, adults were controlling the direction and the level of persistence by using a high level of control: giving instructions and information (when the purpose of the enterprise is not clear to the child), asking questions, and praising. The following interaction between Alison (a teacher) and Rita provides an example. Alison is in the final stages of teaching Rita to do her first screen print.

> Alison: Go back up to the top and make that paint come down to the bottom (*instruction, purpose not yet clear to child*).
> OK. (*Approval of ongoing work: 'that's right'.*)
> Down again, down again, there you go, you've covered your piece of paper up . . . so we'll put this back, lift this up again (*instruction, purpose not yet clear to child*).
> Lift it up (*instruction, purpose not yet clear to child*).

> That's it. (*Approval of ongoing work: 'that's right'.*)
> Come around here Rita, and we're going to pull the piece of paper down (*instruction, purpose not yet clear to child*).
> Start from the top (*instruction, purpose not yet clear to child*) . . .
> There you go, there's your picture! Alright, look at that. (*Approval and enthusiasm about the product.*)

Rita: Yep.
Alison: Yeah! (*General approval and enthusiasm.*)
Rita: Wait 'til I show Mum it.
Alison: That's a screen print. (*Information, giving the label.*)

Alison's comments alternate instructions with approval, and the instructions have a long-term goal in mind that is, during the process, hidden from Rita. All will be revealed at the end. Other research has documented a distinctive discourse/responsibility tutorial pattern at 'circle time' (Kantor, Elgas and Fernie, 1992; Reich, 1993), where children learn the 'school'-oriented (initiation from the adult, response from the child and evaluation from the adult) tutorial pattern. The adult tutorial follows closely the structure of traditional classroom talk: IRE (teacher Initiation, student Response, followed by teacher Evaluation: Mehan, 1979; Greenleaf and Freedman, 1993; Pontecorvo and Sterponi, this volume). Wells (1993) provides a useful discussion of this structure, incorporating discourse analysis and arguing for a distinction between 'low-level' evaluation and 'high-level' evaluation or follow-up. In the above example, the student usually responded with an action, not a comment or answer, and the teacher followed that action with low-level evaluation, praise ('OK', 'That's it' and 'alright, look at that'), and then a new instruction.

Adult–child collaboration

A second responsibility pattern, adult–child collaboration, where both adults and children contribute to a common enterprise, occurred occasionally in both activities. The following is an example during the marble-painting activity:

Alison (*teacher*):   See all the lines, the patterns that the marble's making? (*Comment on detail of ongoing or final work, indicating interest.*)
Molly: You can um get the ball going that way and then put it in there.
Alison: Yeah (*agreement*). It's like lots of roads, isn't it? (*Comment on detail of ongoing or final work, in this case providing an analogy and indicating interest.*)
Molly: Um they fell down there but Myra couldn't find the lellow (*yellow*) one.
Alison: Marble? (*Seeking clarification of child's comment.*)
Molly: Yes.
Alison: Did it pop out did it? (*Seeking clarification.*) Let's see if we can see if it's rolled under the furniture (*offering and giving help*).
Molly: But I didn't see it when it was.
Alison: Look there it is (*offering and giving help*).

The teacher alternated between expressing interest in the specifics of the enterprise ('It's like lots of roads, isn't it?'), clarification of the children's meaning, and new follow-up suggestions ('Let's see if we can'). Molly contributed a commentary about the process and an explanation of difficulty (the yellow marble is lost). It was a collaborative process.

Peer collaboration

New (1994) has reported from the collaborative sociocultural environment of early childhood programmes in Reggio Emilia in northern Italy that children will often provide technical assistance to peers and even add to each other's constructions and drawings. And Rogoff (1998) has outlined the value for learning of collaborative activity among peers. Examples of peer collaboration, with one child suggesting a new idea or direction to another, were rare in screen printing; they were more likely in marble painting. Four (out of 58) screen-printing episodes but six (out of 17) marble-painting episodes included peers giving each other technical assistance. The following provides an example that occurred when Nell taught Jinny to construct a box and Jinny taught Nick to make a marble painting. The apprentice (Nick) asked about the process and then took on some of the responsibility, spooning marbles in for Jinny. In the following transcript, explanations of process and/or possible difficulty from one child to another and questions (mostly from Nick) seeking explanation or a request for participation are common.

The scenario: Jinny has come over to the construction table where Nell is marble painting in a box she has constructed, and Jason is nearby, making a kite. She tells Nell that she wants to do a marble painting.

Nell: I (*you?*) can't do one yet, Jinny, 'cos you've got to make a box (*explanation*). You've got to get some of these scissors (*instruction*). Go and get a box (*instruction*). As big as this prob'ly or like that (*instruction*). And then you can cut it (*instruction*).

Jason: (Looks up from his kite making) Ah, only off the tops, not these. (*He points to the sides of Nell's box, pinpointing difficulty*.)

Nell: No, not the sides (*pinpointing difficulty*). (*Jinny goes off to find a box, and then returns to cut one 'top' side off. Nick arrives*.)

Nick: Where did you get that box from?

Nell: I don't know. On the shelf (*explaining process*). (*Nick watches Nell marble painting*.)

Nick: Is there two balls in there?

Nell: Yep.

Nick: What are those, do those, balls do that?

Nell: Marbles. (*Nell is giving Nick the correct word*.)

Nick: painting? (*Same time*) (*Jinny has completed her cutting, pushes a piece of paper into the base of the shallow box she has made, adds marbles from the yellow and blue paint containers, and rolls them about*.)

Nell: Yeah. They make it (*sound of marbles rolling about*).
Jinny: green in there (*explanation of process*). . . .
Nell: (*To Jinny*) And put some of that colour into the green. (*instruction*).
            (*Sound of marbles rolling about.*)
Nick: Is it easy?
Nell: It is easy.
Nick: (*To Jinny*) Can I've a turn now? . . .
Nick: Do I put a bit of this in? (*Nick adds paint to Jinny's painting; she tilts the box.*)
Nick: Shall I put the ball in? . . . (*He spoons another marble in, and she tilts the box.*)
Nick: Shall I put a bit more paint in? . . . (*Jinny removes her painting and puts a fresh piece of paper in for Nick. He adds marbles and paint and tilts the box, increasingly vigorously so that the marble is thrown into the air. Alison, a teacher, arrives.*)
Alison: (*Sound of marble dropping*) Ooh that went high.
Nick: Well. It landed in the box (*explanation of process*).
Alison: Uh huh.

Nell took the lead, giving Jinny an explanation about why she could not do a marble painting straight away (she has to make a box), and then gave her four instructions. Jason warned of possible difficulty, a warning confirmed by Nell. Nick then shared the responsibility by asking a number of questions about the process, asked if he could have a turn, then did some of the work for Jinny (checking with her that this was acceptable). The field notes record that 'Nick now does one, absorbed by it. He asks Alison (the teacher) to look at it, and they talk about the tracks the balls have made, where they have turned a corner.'

In screen printing the responsibility, constrained by the technology and generally interpreted as being about being a kindergartener, belonged with the adults. Unlike a marble painting, the product was named, valued and personal. Adult comments were coded for 'level of power' at four levels (Wood and Wood, 1983; Carr, 2000b). The proportion of adult utterances at the highest high level of power was 22.8 per cent for screen printing and 8.5 per cent in marble painting. Evaluative comments (judgements, queries about purpose, praise and focused evaluative comments) were divided into those comments that referred to the task at hand ('stapling would have been better than sellotape because . . .') and personal praise or comments that referred to the judgement of another person ('good girl'; 'your Mum will be pleased with you'). Of all the adult evaluative comments in screen printing, 33.2 per cent were of the latter category: personal or general praise, or comments that called on an another person's judgement. Studies cited in Heyman and Dweck's (1998) study of children's thinking about traits, and in Black and William's (1998) review of assessment and classroom learning, suggest that praise and evaluation feedback that focuses on traits of the child such as being good or being clever afford 'performance goals' in which children strive to display their goodness or their ability, and avoid difficult tasks in case they make an error and are perceived to be unable. Only 0.8 per cent of the adult evaluative comments in marble painting were in this category.

In summary, then, screen printing was characterized by tutorials in which adults were in control and assessments were both external and general or person-oriented. Marble painting was characterized by peer collaboration, assessment by adults that referred to the task, and self-evaluation of success by the children, often assisted by their peers.

Learning Niches: Issues of Continuity and Transfer

This research indicated that a number of different learning narratives were being established in one area of this kindergarten. Screen printing was an activity characterized by kindergartener (being a good student) goals, little technological challenge, and adult tutorials. Marble painting was an activity characterized by technological intent, finding difficulty, and collaboration. Which of these, if any, might children take on to school? Edwards and Mercer (1987, p. 10) had commented that

> structures which typified the talk in secondary classrooms . . . can be seen emerg-
> ing in the talk of infant classrooms, with the implication that children are very
> quickly socialized into fairly rigid pupil roles which they act out for the rest of
> their school careers.

To say that children 'are socialized' into pupil roles underestimates the complexity of the transactions between adult and child, child and child, and child and activity. In this study, children were also socializing the activities, fitting them to the dispositions that they have brought to the centre and forming them into what we might call 'learning niches' (Scarr and McCartney, 1983; Gauvain, 1995). A Swedish longitudinal study (Broberg et al., 1997, p. 67) suggested that children's later development (closer to age 8) is driven by the 'child's ability to choose her or his own environment'. This study confirms Smiley and Dweck's (1994) suggestion that the process begins early. One possible answer to the question about which learning narratives children will take to school is that learners have already established privileged dispositional patterns of learning at home, have selected and edited experiences in the early child-hood centre in order to confirm them, and will carry these patterns with them to school. I searched for the children's apparent learning niches – favourite dispositions across a number of construction activities (with occasional reference to the children's participation in nearby block and dramatic play). Two processes appeared to be at work: niche-forming or niche-choosing, and resistance.

Niche-forming and niche-choosing

Lisa was a major player in screen printing. In screen printing and other activities her privileged learning narrative appeared to be a 'good kinder-gartener'; she kept close to adults for reassurance and approval. Nell and Jason were major players in marble painting and in other art and craft activities (but not in screen printing). Jason typified the marble painting dispositional milieu in 15 episodes observed (he left to go on to school during the observations): he often tutored or provided help for others and he enjoyed finding and solving difficulties. Nell featured in 34 episodes, favoured collaborative enterprises and discussions, but almost always avoided technical difficulty. Once, however, during marble painting, she asked Jason how to make a box and admitted that she did not know how to do it. Jason had taken the lead to 'socialize' this activity towards 'learning' and self-evaluating in many ways, and Nell appeared to be experimenting with a new disposition towards technical difficulty and risk of error – this was the first time that she had been heard to say that she did not know how to do something.

Resistance

Linda and Danny both persevered with screen printing and could be described as finally resisting the 'good student' intention as they began to practise being apprentice screen printers. This took some time for Linda: in most episodes (she appeared in 35) Linda was typically concerned with 'being good' and liked to be told what to do, but towards the end of the observations, when adults were busy elsewhere, she completed a detailed template for a screen print and made the print without seeking permission or approval. There were five episodes where Danny made screen prints. He began by keeping the painted template and throwing away the print, but by the fourth and fifth episodes he was beginning to exploit the silhouetting affordance of this medium. Perhaps because of an interest in drawing, he had become interested in learning to be a screen printer.

If children bring dispositions from home and establish comfortable niches for them in the early childhood setting, then it is possible that they may also take them from early childhood to school. We need more research on this. Some research suggests that the social intent or goal orientation (the first domain of disposition considered here) in each place may be central. For example, Beach (1995; cited in Cobb and Bowers, 1999), researching transfer of learning between work and school, found that the goal structures in different places were important. Beach's research focused on the adult education of shopkeepers. Those students in the adult education class who continued to identify themselves as shopkeepers in a new setting (the adult education class) transferred arithmetical competencies from one setting to another; but students who defined themselves as students in one place but as shopkeepers in another did not. The social intent or goals (learning arithmetic as an end in itself versus generating profit as a shopkeeper) in the different places were different and the competencies remained goal-specific.

For the 4-year-olds in transition to school, if school activities appear to be similar to most of the screen-printing episodes, characterized by a 'being a (good) student' agenda, equivalent to being a (good) kindergartener, where the children were following instructions and individually completing a mysterious task because the teacher encouraged and praised this, then the patterns of responsibility and response to difficulty characteristic of screen printing might be carried over into the school setting. If school activities appear to be about 'being a technologist', equivalent to the goal in marble painting where the children were inventing and solving problems, engaging in and self-evaluating meaningful tasks, often with the assistance of others, then peer collaboration and tackling difficulty with enthusiasm might be learning narratives for school as well as for some activities in the early childhood setting.

Implications for Education

To return to the question that I raised earlier in the chapter: were some activities (by their physical and technological nature) rich in opportunities for inducting the children into a technologists' community of practice or social intent, encouraging persistence with tackling uncertainty and challenge, and facilitating the development of joint attention and co-construction? The answer was yes and no. The mediation of physical materials and tools was influential, but it was not enough to determine a community of learners. The materials and tools variously afforded (Gibson, 1979) technological endeavours, persistence and collaboration. However, the children viewed the range of activities through their own dispositional lenses. They interpreted, selected and edited the curriculum on offer, and responded to the interpretations, selections and editings of others. Langer (1989, 1997) provides some beautiful examples of the affordance of artifacts being 'mindfully' opened up by pedagogical practice that alters rigid or closed dispositional mindsets. The research on 4-year-olds provided examples of this too (Jason transformed the marble-painting activity through his enthusiasm for tackling difficulties), and of mindsets 'mindlessly' closing down activities and pedagogical practice (the notion that completing a screen print signified being nearly at school).

In early childhood programmes children are being introduced to literacy, numeracy, music, art, technology, dance and drama, and other ways of doing things or representing experience. Writing about middle-class children learning literacy at home, Gee says:

> [The parent is introducing] the child into a characteristic (socially and culturally specific) *way of doing things*, into a particular *form of life*, in this case, how

people 'like us' approach books (talk about, read, value, use, and integrate them with other activities). (Gee, 1992, p. 124; emphasis in the original)

At the same time as they are being introduced to ways of doing things, children are co-constructing (with adults, peers and tools) ways of learning things, in this case how people 'like us' (in this case study nearly-5-year-olds, girls, boys, kindergarteners, print makers, marble painters) approach learning. This chapter has painted a complex picture of learning in an early childhood setting. The perceived goal orientation of an activity, or the community of practice that culture and history have attached to the activity, appears to be a central determinant of two other dispositions: perseverance and responsibility for learning. Children in early childhood settings are often presented with a rich array of activities and diverse dispositional milieux. In a 'free play' environment many 3- and 4-year-olds will select only the familiar. A critical approach to curriculum, however, will dispose both adults and children to be reflective about their disposition to choose particular goals, and will encourage new definitions of old and familiar goals or communities: kindergarteners-preparing-for-school, for example, might include peer collaboration; or being a 'good' student might include risking being wrong. And where the goals or ways of being in early childhood settings and school classrooms orient learners to persevere with difficulty and uncertainty, and collaborate with others in joint enterprises, these may form lifelong positive learning dispositions.

9

Semiotic Mediation and Mental Development in Pluralistic Societies: Some Implications for Tomorrow's Schooling

Ruqaiya Hasan

What gives Vygotsky's theoretical approach to mental development its enormous reach is the concept of semiotic mediation, which establishes connections across some of the most important areas of human social existence and foregrounds the fundamental relationship between mental functions and linguistic discourse within social/cultural activity. However, in thus attaching greater importance to language than to other modalities of meaning, Vygotsky invites us to ask what it is that language enables us to do which other semiotic modalities do not – or at least not to the same extent, or with the same facility. Similarly, his identification of social/cultural activity as the essential site for the operation of semiotic mediation opens up interesting questions, such as the relation between cultural activities and language, and whether different kinds of activities encourage different forms of semiotic mediation. Since contemporary societies are pluralistic, with multiple groupings whose boundaries are drawn by reference to interest, race, gender, occupation and socio-economic status, it is important to ask whether cultural activities and their linguistic performance differ across these social groups, and if so, whether this influences children's development, and particularly their readiness to engage with formal education. It is the aim of this chapter to explore these questions and, by revealing some important implications of accepting semiotic mediation as the essential means of making human minds, to suggest avenues for conceptualizing better programmes for truly egalitarian education.

Semiotic Mediation: One Process, Two Manifestations

I shall use the term 'semiotic mediation' throughout this chapter as a short form for *semiotic mediation by means of the modality of language*. In assigning this crucial place to language in the processes of semiotic mediation, I do not wish to prejudge the role of other semiotic modalities in the formation of higher mental functions, but simply to respect Vygotsky's own usage. Using the term in this sense, I take it as axiomatic that semiotic mediation is a constant feature of human social life.

In the writings of Vygotsky and his colleagues, as well as in current discussions and applications, it has been customary to invoke the agency of semiotic mediation with specific reference to concept formation and/or some form of problem solving, typically in officially recognized educational sites. But to emphasize its function only in such contexts is to encourage the questionable view that semiotic mediation is restricted to cultural activities which call for explicit, deliberate teaching of specific concepts, knowledge structures and the like. This underestimates the full power of the concept, however, since semiotic mediation occurs wherever discourse occurs, and discourse is ubiquitous in the living of social life. Properly understood, then, the most important role of (linguistic) semiotic mediation is to enable the speaking subjects to internalize the world they experience in the living of their lives.

Seen from this perspective, the most basic and foundational achievement – but certainly not the only achievement – of semiotic mediation is the inculcation of mental dispositions, that is to say, tendencies to respond to situations in certain ways and beliefs about what things are worth doing in one's community, and how they are to be done (see Carr, and also Claxton, this volume). However, these mental dispositions – the readiness with which learners engage in the appropriation of some concepts rather than others, as well as the mode of negotiation they habitually bring to the learning situation – are just as relevant in the context of educational learning, for they will constitute the foundation for what Vygotsky (1987) called 'scientific concepts' and for specialized knowledge structures of many kinds.

Nevertheless, as I will argue, there are good reasons for attending to the differences between these two modes of the operation of semiotic mediation, which I will refer to as *invisible* and *visible* mediation, respectively. As the label suggests, visible mediation is deliberate and relatively more clearly focused on some specific concept or problem: interactants can actually 'see' what they are doing. Typically, at least one of the interactants is aware that she or he is teaching or explaining something specific to someone; further, an essential requirement for success is the learner's voluntary attention and active participation. This is in contrast to invisible mediation, where interactants are aware of neither the teaching nor the learning of any concept in particular, much less of any specific goal to be achieved – or, at least, the goal uppermost in the mind is not directly relevant to what language is mediating, as in the following example:

Extract 1
Mother: Put it up on the stove and leave it there.
Karen: Why?
Mother: 'cause.

Karen: That's where it goes?
Mother: Yeah

Here the interactants do not 'see' what is being mediated; what they 'see' is some process of everyday living in which discourse is of no independent significance.

Together, these forms of semiotic mediation serve important purposes in the creation of culture, and in giving social subjects a lived sense of belonging to the culture in which they are located – which latter is, of course, a condition for the maintenance of culture. However, from the point of view of individual development, invisible mediation is primary, both in terms of time and in terms of its pervasiveness, for it begins in very early infancy and occurs across a large number of cultural activities. However, since the habits of mind thus created are crucial to an individual's ways of engaging in visible semiotic mediation, it is reasonable to suggest that visible mediation is not entirely independent of invisible mediation.

To support these claims, I will discuss examples of discourse as it operates in the context of a variety of cultural activities. These examples are taken from a corpus of naturally occurring dialogues between mothers and their young children, which formed the database for a sociolinguistic research project I conducted to examine 'The Role of Everyday Talk between Mothers and Children in Establishing Ways of Learning' (see Hasan, 1989; Hasan and Cloran, 1990).

Semiotic Mediation and Cultural Activities

The two modes of semiotic mediation identified above – visible and invisible – are typically associated with distinct contexts of cultural activities, which vary along several dimensions. Due to lack of space, however, I will consider only two. The first is the dimension that I have referred to as the *sphere of activity* (Hasan, 1999). Cultural activities range from everyday ones to those that are highly specialized. Everyday activities extend over a whole cultural community and are so basic and ubiquitous that we may think of them as universal. Examples include preparing and eating food, minding children, cleaning, washing and shopping and, equally importantly, taking steps to indicate membership of one's local 'village' (Lemke, this volume) – though of course the details of how these things are done vary to different degrees across cultures and subcultures. What is common, however, is the fact that everywhere the conducting of these activities becomes highly routinized, scarcely requiring concentrated attention.

By contrast, specialized activities do not extend over the whole community. One manifestation of the division of labour in society is precisely that certain activities are typically performed by certain social groups and not by others. Activities of the professional type such as lecturing, welding and banking are clear examples. And although in some cases – especially where the activity is physical, for example welding – the various actions in its perform-ance can become routinized, specialized activities typically require reflection on how they are to be performed and, in all cases, the actants are aware of the endpoint of the game they are engaged in.

Cutting across this dimension is the dimension of the *form of action*. Here two major forms are acting by doing and acting by saying. There are times when the interactants' action is entirely material (i.e. carried out physically, such as when mowing the lawn), and others when it is entirely verbal, carried out purely linguistically (such as when talking on the phone, conducting a seminar, participating in a talk-back radio programme, etc.). But very often both material and verbal actions co-occur. This co-occurrence can be of different kinds, of which two are particularly relevant to the present discus-sion since they have different significance from the point of view of cultural activity: one is where language is used in aid of performing the material activity, and the other is where verbal and material action run side by side without either being relevant to the other. In the first case a single cultural activity is at stake, while in the second, strictly speaking, two activities are being performed in parallel, one material, the other verbal.

It is important to recognize that in real life – as opposed to academic analysis – there is no clearly demarcated division between one activity and the next: distinct activities weave in and out of one another and sometimes there may be no indication of a shift except in the language used. Consider the following example, taken from an interaction between mother and Helen (3 years 11 months) as they wash and dry up dishes:

Extract 2

1	*Mother*:	No, I'll wash 'em up darling, you can dry some little ones and put them [? here] for me, wait till I get a clean towel out . . . there you go . . .
2	*Helen*:	Thank you
3	*Mother*:	I'll put the little ones up here that you can dry up, OK?
4	*Helen*:	The dish . . . the dish first . . .
5	*Mother*:	(*Coughs*) Pardon me . . . hurry up because I've got a big dinner to get tonight.
6	*Helen*:	What kind of dinner?
7	*Mother*:	we'll have a roast leg of ham.
8	*Helen*:	Goody!
9	*Mother*:	And roast veggies.
10	*Helen*:	Goody!
11	*Mother*:	I might ring up daddy and ask him to bring some peas home [?]
12	*Helen*:	Goody!
13	*Mother*:	He'd like a nice feed of peas.
14	*Helen*:	[?]
15	*Mother*:	I think you children can make some fruit salad, how about that?
16	*Helen*:	Yeah, goody! I'll make it for you.

In turns 1–4 of this extract verbal action is assisting in the conduct of the ongoing material activity of washing up: this is the *ancillary* use of language, and at this point only one activity is being performed. However, at turn 5 a shift (Hasan, 2000) occurs as the new topic of dinner is broached, and the remaining turns constitute a discussion of that evening's dinner. So at this point, side by side with the ongoing material activity of washing up, we have the verbal activity of discussion running in parallel. This latter activity is not ancillary but *constitutive* of discussion.

In the above extract the discussion in 6–16 moves around in the general domain of food, but it is not necessary for the two parallel activities to share the same domain. This can be seen in the following example where, with her mother's guidance, Helen was washing a saucepan lid which apparently needed a good deal of scrubbing:

Extract 3
1 *Helen*:   You have to do it hard, don't you?
2 *Mother*:   Mm, you do, don't you, yes . . .
3 *Helen*:   Doesn't matter for you and me to do these.
4 *Mother*:   No.
5 *Helen*:   Because we can do it the right way, God teaches us.
6 *Mother*:   No, God doesn't teach you things like that, it's mummy's job to teach you things like that.

The mother's comment in the last turn – 'It's mummy's job to teach you things like that' – is very far removed from the business of washing up. As an adult well versed in the ways of her culture, she is telling her daughter explicitly about an expectation attached to being a mother. Casual conversation abounds in such explicit aphorisms, which nevertheless hardly reach the point of conscious, deliberate reflection. However, over time, the continuing occurrence of talk of this kind constructs a design for ways of being, doing and saying that are viewed as legitimate within the speakers' community. In this sense, such talk is a site for one kind of invisible semiotic mediation. What it mediates is elements of mental maps for living in the culture of one's immediate community.

Such explicit teaching, referred to by Bernstein (1990, 1996) as *local pedagogy*, occurs often, especially in the discourse of adults and children.[1] However, more relevant to the production of children's mental habits are forms of interaction where *no* cultural rules are being explicitly enunciated. This does not mean that culture is irrelevant to these encounters; it is simply that it goes underground: sayings which pertain to everyday activities and seem to be 'of no great importance' depend largely on taken-for-granted 'truths' whose validity is treated as self-evident. It is this experience of the *facticity* (Berger and Luckman, 1971) of the world that underlies the everyday discourse in which young children ordinarily and continually participate, which in its turn produces an understanding of what their social universe is like, and of what ways of being, doing, saying and even thinking are favoured by those in their immediate social group. The appropriation of a certain set of mental habits is not so much the result of explicit injunctions, therefore; rather, it is nourished by sayings which scarcely seem to say anything significant, for example sayings of the kind presented in extract 1.

Everyday activities are the most hospitable environment for such sayings because, in the nature of things, everyday activities neither require nor allow the opportunity for deliberation, much less for argumentation. Their near automatization – their unquestioned, almost unquestionable rationality for social subjects already initiated in the culture – leads to an absence of reflection, to the certainty that what one is saying and/or doing is the most rational, the most normal thing to say and do. Mental dispositions come about in the primary experience of internalizing the implications of such meanings unselfconsciously worded by speakers in precisely such environments.

In the next section I exemplify the sorts of things that mothers say to their children while engaged in everyday material activities; at the same time I introduce an important distinction between two types of questions.

Two Styles of Questioning: Prefaced and Assumptive

Consider, for example, a mother asking her child 'Did you know that they are going to leave?' There is nothing extraordinary about such a question: people ask such questions all the time. But consider what it is that the mother has actually done. She hasn't asked to be informed of some state of affairs that is unfolding in the world, nor whether or not something is the case. Her concern is to find out the mental state of her child – what the child knows. I have referred to such questions as *prefaced questions* (Hasan, 1989). The asking of such a question implies, among other things, that knowledge about the child's mental state is not available to the mother unless the child explicitly tells her. To many of us, this is a self-evident fact; we believe it is entirely natural for us not to know other people's mental states unless they choose to inform us. However, below, I will discuss examples (see extracts 5.1 and 5.2) which suggest that this belief is far from universal.

For the moment, let me pursue the chain of implications that seems to follow from a prefaced question. If you believe that another's mental state is unknowable without the use of language, this in turn implies that language would be treated as the essential bridge spanning two individual minds. That being the case, one would expect such speakers to habitually use language so as to make the meaning of their messages as precise as possible. In most languages the way to do this is to qualify the state of affairs, specifying its manner, location, time, etc. Further, because language is seen as an important means of getting to know the other, it follows that others' questions must be attended to, comments and assertions must be heeded, and answers should be provided that address the query point.

In the analysis of some 2,000 maternal questions and their answers, we found that the mothers who habitually asked prefaced questions were also the ones who asked highly qualified questions, and provided highly developed answers. Consider the following example (paired asterisks following a question indicate that no time was allowed for a response; paired asterisks on adjacent turns indicate turn overlap):

Extract 4
 1 *Mother*: Did you know that they are going to leave?
 2 *Kristy*: No.
 3 *Mother*: They've been building a house.
 4 *Kristy*: Mm.
 5 *Mother*: Oh, they haven't been building it, somebody else has been build-
              ing it for them, and it's nearly finished, and they're going to move
              to their house in May.
 6 *Kristy*: Why in May?
 7 *Mother*: They're going to wait until the end of the school term.
 8 *Kristy*: Mm.
 9 *Mother*: Because Cathy goes to school now, and then she will change to
              her new school after **the holidays.
10 *Kristy*: **Mm.
11 *Mother*: If they'd moved earlier she'd only go to the new school for a
              week or two, and then they'd have holidays, you see, it would
              mess it up a bit for her.

Note how the mother is careful to clarify the sense of her claim that 'they've been building a house', something that at 3-and-a-half years of age Kristy might well have misinterpreted. Note also how, in response to Kristy's 'why?', she meticulously lays out the reasoning behind her friends' decision to move to their new house in May, not earlier.

The mothers who ask prefaced and qualified questions rarely ignore the questions asked by their children, and overwhelmingly offer relevant and developed answers rather than minimal ones. There is significant statistical proof from my research as well as that of Williams (1995) that the massive experience of engaging in discourse of this kind produces in the children a particular kind of orientation to meanings, a tendency to respond to questions and to information in ways that are qualitatively different from those of children whose mental habits and experience of everyday discourse is differ- ent. To appreciate how different the experience of discourse is for this other group of children consider the following:

Extract 5.1
1 *Karen*:   How did you get that?** You didn't get out of [?]
2 *Mother*: I walked over and got it, didn't you see me?

    3 *Karen*:   Nup.
    4 *Mother*:   you must be blind.

Extract 5.2
    1 *Mother*:   D'you love daddy? . . . D'you love daddy?
    2 *Julian*:   Mm. (*Affirmative*)
    3 *Mother*:   D'you love Rosemary?[2]
    4 *Julian*:   No.
    5 *Mother*:   Why don't you love Rosemary?
    6 *Julian*:   (*Laughs*)
    7 *Mother*:   Why don't you love Rosemary?
    8 *Julian*:   (*Continues to laugh*)
    9 *Mother*:   You're a rat-bag. (*Realizes that Julian was teasing*)
   10 *Julian*:   I do.
   11 *Mother*:   [?]
   12 *Julian*:   Who else do you want me to love?

In these extracts the mother asks what I have called an *assumptive question*. Such questions are realized grammatically by a negative interrogative. I call these questions 'assumptive' (Hasan, 1989) because the person asking appears to have already made an assumption about what the correct answer should be. In extract 5.1 the mother's expectation is that the answer to 'Didn't you see me?' should be 'Yes I did', otherwise 'You must be blind', and we know that Karen is not blind. Here the mother assumes that, had Karen been behaving according to normal expectations, she would have seen her mother go out to get the object. In extract 5.2 the mother's question 'Why don't you love Rosemary?' assumes that, as a normal brother, Julian ought to love Rosemary. It does not seem far-fetched to suggest that mothers asking such questions assume they know what their child's mental state is. Julian understands this – as is clear from turn 12, which we may paraphrase as: 'It is clear to me by your ways of questioning that you think I should love Rosemary; this implies that you also have views on who else I should love; so who are those people that in your opinion I should love?'

It is perhaps obvious that assumptive questions are the converse of prefaced ones. If a mother habitually asks assumptive questions, she implies that she knows her child's mental state – what her child knows, feels or senses. In an important sense the child's answer is irrelevant; the mother already knows without explicitly being told. This in turn implies that language has a less critical status in the creation of intersubjective relations between them. Interestingly, mothers who very frequently ask assumptive questions are also relatively less concerned about attending to their children's questions; they also put less effort into making their own questions precise or their answers developed. In fact, minimal and what one might think of as inadequate answers are quite likely, as already exemplified in extract 1. What I am suggesting, then, is that sayings as trite as the exchange 'why' and ''cause' (extract 1) are not without importance in the formation of mental attitudes. It is a common-place that questions are a way of finding out, but perhaps some children's experience might discourage the formation of this attitude to questions.

Lest it seem that too much is being claimed on the basis of these few examples, it needs to be emphasized that the extracts cited above are representative of a much larger corpus of children's talk, observed in three settings: (1) talk with their mothers in the same everyday environments, (2) their negotiations with familiar neighbourhood peers during spontaneous play, and (3) their discourse in the classroom during the first few weeks after entry into the school at around the age of 5. Furthermore, the main thrust of my finding has also been validated by the results of colleagues (Cloran, 1994, 1999; Williams, 1995, 1999). In addition, the semantic features I have picked out above form parts of larger clusters, whose pattern of occurrence tends to differentiate significantly the speech of the two groups of mothers.

There is thus consistent and strong evidence that, at this early stage of 3-and-a-half to 4 years, the children belonging to these two groups have had a massive experience of specific ways of saying and meaning that, orienting them to certain ways of being, doing and saying as legitimate and reasonable in their communities, has established different ways of learning, different ways of solving problems, different forms of mental disposition. True, the patterns of language I have singled out are very ordinary, but this, in a way, vindicates the claim that the production of mental disposition is brought about by the invisible semiotic mediation of unselfconscious discourse embedded in everyday cultural activities. Such discourse *is* ordinary and that is why it is so effective. Furthermore, as this process begins in early infancy, the invisible mediation which occurs in the course of everyday activities attains a primary status in the life of the individual. It becomes in effect the ruler of attention and interest, of motivation and relevance. Thus, the child's ways of participating in the negotiation and appropriation of technical concepts or specific knowledge structures, etc., is coloured initially – though not necessarily finally – by the experience of this primary mediation.

Before leaving this section, it remains to point out one very important feature of this mode of semiotic mediation which is instrumental in producing primary mental disposition. The everyday cultural activities in which it is embedded are overwhelmingly culture-maintaining, since their efficient performance depends on routinization, which means a suspension of reflection. This encourages the tendency towards preserving existing templates. Thus the two groups of mothers each semiotically mediates precisely the ways of being, doing and saying that come naturally to them, that are their ways of coping with everyday reality. Through this mediation the mother's culture becomes the growing child's map of reality, thus ensuring its own continuance. And it is this history of semiotic engagement that children bring to their encounters with the discourse of the school.

Semiotic Mediation, Higher Mental Functions and Specialized Cultural Activities

One way in which the cycle of cultural reproduction just described can be given a different shape is through the working of 'visible' semiotic mediation. This is, in fact, one of the major functions of schools and universities. For reasons of space, however, I shall focus here only on visible semiotic mediation at home.

Consider the following extract, which is taken from a very lengthy discussion between Kristy and her mother. The origins of this dialogue go back to an earlier scene where Kristy was having a meal. At that earlier point, a moth had just died a soggy death by flying low over a steaming cup. Kristy was distressed by this death.

Extract 6

1	*Kristy:*	Why did he die there?** Why did he die there?** He wouldn't have wanted to die, do you know that?
2	*Mother:*	That's right, most things don't want to die.
3	*Kristy:*	Mm, a dog will get killed by something that wanted to eat a doggie.
4	*Mother:*	Yeah, sometimes people want to die, or animals want to die if they are very sick and it's hurting them.
5	*Kristy:*	Mm.
6	*Mother:*	But yeah, usually animals and people don't want to die, so –
7	*Kristy:*	Mm.
8	*Mother:*	Everyone has to die sometime, and sometimes people or animals have accidents.
9	*Kristy:*	Mm.
10	*Mother:*	Or sometimes other things eat them, so other moths get eaten by birds.
11	*Kristy:*	Why do they?
12	*Mother:*	well, birds need to eat **and –
13	*Kristy:*	**Yeah and –
14	*Mother:*	Mm?
15	*Kristy:*	they [? should've] eat bigger things um mice.
16	*Mother:*	You think birds should eat mice?
17	*Kristy:*	Yeah.
18	*Mother:*	well, you got upset the other day about the eagle at the museum eating the rabbit didn't you?
19	*Kristy:*	Mm.
20	*Mother:*	see, there's not much difference is there?

At this point there is a digression to a different topic, but a minute or so later Kristy returns to the matter that is obviously of concern to her.

35	*Kristy*:	Why did the eagle eat the rabbit?
36	*Mother*:	Because rabbits are the sort of animals that eagles eat, different animals eat different food, they eat food that lives where they can catch it and food that's the right size for them to catch.
37	*Kristy*:	Mm.
38	*Mother*:	An eagle couldn't eat a cow because a cow would be too big, but eagles can eat rabbits, they're a nice size for eagles, they give them plenty to eat, and they're small enough for eagles to catch, but most animals eat other animals, even you eat chickens and every time you eat a chicken a little chicken has to die.

There is much more of this discussion, but we can stop at this stage of what is surely a model lesson on the grim rudiments of natural selection. I would like to use this extract to draw attention to some important points. First, compare this with extract 3. In both cases the discussion runs parallel to some other everyday material activity, and it goes without saying that the verbal action is constitutive. There are, however, some major differences between them. In extract 3 the move into the constitutive is evanescent, hardly receiving conscious attention, whereas in 6 the constitutive activity of discussion is much more developed. Had the mother been asked what she was doing, very likely she would have said that she was explaining to Kristy why every living thing has to die some time, and how in order for one thing to live another thing might have to die. In 3 the aphoristic comment is no more than the beginning of a specialized activity – explaining about maternal obligations – whereas in 6 the activity of explanation is full-fledged. This latter is a case of local pedagogy too, but unlike 3 it displays a more deliberate and sustained effort at 'getting some point across' and at the same time it makes contact with a fragment of educational knowledge. In short, in 6, running parallel to an everyday cultural activity, we have an instance of a specialized one. This local pedagogic activity is not exactly like a lesson in a classroom, but it is as close to that activity as you can get at home, especially where one participant is relatively immature. This is thus a classic example of visible semiotic mediation, which occurs by means of discourse embedded in specialized cultural activities calling for sustained attention by participants.

As pointed out earlier, specialized cultural activities – unlike everyday ones – do not extend over the whole cultural community. There is an interesting paradox here: everyday activities are near universal, though the way they are carried out varies across different communities. By contrast, specialized cultural activities are restricted in their distribution within a culture: not everyone engages in them; however, wherever a category of such activity is found, the form of its manifestation is near universal. Specialized activities depend fundamentally upon verbal action although, very often, they enlist other semiotic modalities in their performance. For example, figures, images, charts, scale models, logical and mathematical symbols, ritual representations of superhuman forces, etc., are instances of non-verbal semiotic modalities pressed into service as abstract tools for the semiotic mediation of 'uncommonsense' concepts and knowledge structures.

For most of us today, by far the most common specialized activities are those first experienced regularly in schooling. At least in so-called advanced societies the school has for decades been the major official site for the production and distribution of such knowledge. But it is really at home that the ontogenesis of what Claxton (this volume) calls *epistemic mentality* takes its first halting steps. Mercer (this volume) presents an example of such an interactive episode, and my data, too, provide rich support for making this claim. However, with my colleagues, Cloran (1994, 1999) and Williams (1995, 1999), I find that the occurrence of such interactive episodes is selective: it is not children, as a general category, but *some* children belonging to a particular group, who typically experience discourse of this kind – as a comparison of extracts 6 and 7 will confirm.

Extract 6 is representative of how discourse between mothers and children moves in one social group. Time and time again in my data, the discourse of *quasi*-specialized knowledge occurs in the 'middle of' daily activities, and by necessity it calls for a readiness on the mother's part to entertain contextual shifts, to be willing to reclassify the context of the ongoing discourse (Cloran, 1999; Hasan, 1999, 2000). The tendency to move with the child's moving discourse, the readiness to reclassify context, is a discourse characteristic of the same group of mothers who frequently ask prefaced questions made precise by qualification, and who attend to their children's questions, and provide them with well developed answers. By contrast, the second group of mothers is significantly less willing to entertain contextual shift, as is seen in extracts 7.1 and 7.2.

Extract 7.1

1	*Mother*:	Come on, eat your tea please . . .
2	*Karen*:	Could you put some more[3] in there? . . .
3	*Mother*:	(*Warningly*) Karen! . . . give me it, eat your tea.
4	*Karen*:	[?]
5	*Mother*:	Mm?
6	*Karen*:	[? put] lemon in it.
7	*Mother*:	Well, eat some tea, or you don't get nothing.
8	*Karen*:	I see how many [?] there are. (*Talks to herself as mother pours drink*)
9	*Mother*:	Quick . . . want the lid on it?
10	*Karen*:	No.
11	*Mother*:	Come on, eat your tea, less drink and more eat . . . did you hear what I said Karen?
12	*Karen*:	Mm.
13	*Mother*:	Well, do it.

Extract 7.1 is fairly typical of this group of mothers, who appear to have a well defined idea of the boundaries between contexts and are normally reluctant

to permit the interpenetration of one context by another. If I understand Claxton (this volume) right, it would seem that the two groups of mothers belong to the two distinct cultures described by Edward Hall (1959) as *monochronic* and *polychronic*. Karen's mother belongs to the group that, at least in this respect, may be said to have a monochronic culture. In this 20-minute recording of the mealtime discourse, the mother produces 20 injunctions to the daughter to 'eat her tea'; she studiously ignores any opening of the discourse in directions other than those specifically pertaining to the mealtime activity. In characteristic fashion, questions are disposed of with an alacrity that misses their real query point.

But does this mean that in such cases there is no contextual shift, no reclassification of context at all? As Bernstein (1990) perceptively remarked, the maintenance of the boundary between categories requires the exertion of power and control. Our example here is no exception. Elsewhere (Hasan, 2000), I have claimed that the context does shift, but the direction of its shift is quite predictable: in order to preserve what she considers to be the boundaries of this activity, Karen's mother's discourse moves resolutely into the regulative mode, as shown by extract 7.2, which occurs only a few seconds after extract 7.1.

Extract 7.2

1 *Mother*: Give me your spoon, and I'll feed you, like a big baby, come on, baby! Give me your spoon.
2 *Karen*: (*Scandalized tone*) No.
3 *Mother*: Well sit up properly, and eat your tea . . . Karen! (*Warning tone*)
4 *Karen*: I'm falling down (*i.e. off the chair*).
5 *Mother*: You're not falling down.
6 *Karen*: Yes I am, I always fall down . . . **I am falling down.
7 *Mother*: **Eat your tea.
8 *Karen*: I am falling down.
9 *Mother*: Sit up, before I get a stick and smack you.

If contextual shift is an invariable condition for moving from the quotidian to the specialized discourse at this early stage in the child's life, clearly the reluctance to allow such shifts is likely to have significant consequences for the ontogenesis of specialized discourse. The final section consists of a brief word on the implications of this situation and offers a suggestion for an approach to schooling that might go some way towards the ideal of equal opportunity.

Schooling for Tomorrow: Concluding Remarks

In the preceding sections I have attempted to show that 'any learning a child encounters in school has a previous history'. It seems to me beyond doubt that this history favours children differentially in today's industrialized, pluralistic societies. The pre-school learning history of the first group of children favours an easier engagement with the specialized discourses of the school; by contrast, that of the second group favours easier adjustment to the regulatory aspect of the pedagogic discourse. To the extent that the real aim of education is to enable pupils not to reproduce knowledge but to produce it, not simply to replicate but to create, this appears to place the first group in an advantageous position. Thus, although educational systems claim to provide equal opportunity for all to acquire the competence for engaging in specialized activities, this remains an ideal goal, as yet never achieved in reality, anywhere.

It would be a simplification of the complexities of the educational system to claim that the only reason it fails to achieve its ideal goal is the differential learning history of the pupils; but that this is one major reason for the schools' failure cannot be denied. Nevertheless, to accept this is not to imply that the learning the child brings to the classroom is final, that the forms of consciousness – the mental dispositions – are graven images which are no longer susceptible to the very instrument of semiotic mediation which has produced them in the first place. As complex self-organizing systems, human brains learn by learning; there is, as Wells (this volume) points out, a spiral of learning. But an initial effort is required to create a situation in the classroom which recognizes the nature of the challenge to draw all children into the activity of learning. The challenge is that those for whom the educational system is ostensibly designed bring many voices into the classroom; however, even a cursory look at classroom practices reveals that it privileges one single voice. This happens to be the voice of the more powerful segment of society. Those who do not recognize this voice cannot truly participate in the specialized discourse of knowledge production and must strive to master this other epistemic dialect on their own.

In the continuation of my research, in which these children were followed into the first year of schooling, we found that across the spectrum of schools the teachers showed no significant variation in their ways of saying: the variation in the data was totally accounted for by the difference in how the children talked during lesson time. The challenge for tomorrow's education is to correct this situation. And one way of achieving this is to encourage pupils to question the taken-for-granted realities. By this I mean both the reality cherished by the mothers of the first group as well as that cherished by the second group. It is often pointed out that in the classroom it is the teacher who asks questions. I have no objection to this so long as the teacher knows how to respect the answers – to respect them to the extent of actually involving pupils in reflecting on the assumptions that underlie their answers, and involving them in articulating those assumptions, thus making them available for conscious reflection and questioning. This reflective mode has the potential of questioning all voices, listening to all voices and probing into all assumptions.

A programme of this kind is what I described some time ago under the label of reflection literacy (Hasan, 1996). But to be able to encourage reflection literacy, those who educate teachers need to rethink the interconnections between the semiotic, the social and the cognitive.

Notes

My thanks are due to Gordon Wells for this condensed version of the chapter based on an earlier draft.

1   A good example of such pedagogy will be found in the conversational sequences in Mercer (this volume).
2   Rosemary is Julian's sister.
3   On the basis of the preceding dialogue, it would appear that Karen is referring to some sauce.

10

Learning to Argue and Reason Through Discourse in Educational Settings

Clotilde Pontecorvo and Laura Sterponi

The exploration of cognitive processes as they occur in natural contexts constitutes an intriguing enterprise for researchers who embrace a sociocultural perspective (Lave, 1988). Within this framework cognitive development is conceived, not as taking place within individuals' minds, but rather through the processes involved in contributing more effectively to jointly undertaken activities (Resnick, Levine and Teasley, 1991). Cognitive development is seen, therefore, as an inherently cultural and historical phenomenon. Thus, learning is viewed not merely as the acquisition of higher mental skills as a result of maturation; rather, it is understood in terms of a wider process of socialization through which children become members of communities of practice (Lave and Wenger, 1991) and take up increasingly more active and central roles in the sociocultural activities of their communities.

This view entails a revolutionary conception of what is involved in education and it has significant implications for the conduct of the activity of learning-and-teaching. Since higher cognitive capacities are inherently cultural and historical in origin, they do not arise naturally within every individual. Human beings are *educated* to think and reason, and specifically to think and reason in ways that may differ across cultures and epochs. Given that there is not one universal way of thinking and reasoning, teachers, curriculum workers and educators need to rethink what and how teaching is usually carried out in different contexts, and what are the criteria for promoting and nurturing certain reasoning practices and for marginalizing or even censoring others.

In line with this critical perspective the study to be reported here explores how young Italian children (between 4 and 5 years of age) are socialized to argumentative discourse. This approach differs from the traditional cognitive approach in which argumentative reasoning is conceived as an abstract logical skill and examined in decontextualized settings. In contrast, we approach argumentative discourse as a *language-game* (Wittgenstein, 1958), namely a procedure of reasoning which is used in various speech activities across a variety of contexts. It is in these contexts that children enter into contact with the discursive/cognitive operations of argumentation used in their culture and, through participation in these activities, progressively acquire them.

This study focuses on two prominent loci of linguistic and cognitive socialization, namely pre-school and family settings. Within these contexts we will examine collective narrative activity and the ways in which it can serve to develop arguing and reasoning abilities, which children can apply in their future school and life experiences. We will start with an analysis of a pre-school speech event (Hymes, 1972), describing its main features in terms of the structural organization of the activity, the modalities of participation and the discursive devices/procedures of reasoning. We will then turn our attention to the context of family dinner conversation. Adopting a comparative stance, we will try to single out similarities and differences between the two speech events. In general, through this study we aim to show the inherently discursive and cultural nature of cognitive activities, and particularly that of argumentation. In addition, we aim to throw light on how cognitive development unfolds within everyday human activities.

Methodologically, our study relies upon the methods of conversational analysis (Atkinson and Heritage, 1984; Sacks, Schegloff and Jefferson, 1974). They constitute powerful tools for a truly sociocultural and ecological psychology, since the use of conversation analysis does not dismiss our psychological interest in understanding cognitive development and mental operations, but rather explores these topics as they naturally occur in social activities.

General Features of the Pre-school and Family Contexts

Family and school are surely the two most prominent loci of children's socialization. However, there are several differences between the two settings. We start, therefore, by focusing attention on some general structural and discursive characteristics that are relevant for our study.

In each setting the children observed were between 3 and 5 years of age. The families observed in the home setting consisted of two parents and at least two children (one of them between 3 and 5 years of age). In the pre-school setting we observed a group of 12 children of the same age with one teacher.

It is well known that school, and kindergarten as well, is characterized by the frequent use of a typical type of *speech exchange system* (Sacks, Schegloff and Jefferson, 1974; Wells, 1993). Sinclair and Coulthard (1975) described it as the IRF triplet: teacher question, child answer and teacher follow-up. However, within the pre-school speech event we examine, the teacher does not enact such a traditional pattern of teaching. In contrast, she has been trained to employ a different interaction pattern and, instead of evaluating the children's contributions, she often repeats, recycles or rephrases them in order to have children continue the discussion among themselves (see Nassaji and Wells, 2000).

Although both parents and teachers share the common aim of educating children, they differ in their priorities and in the strategies they use. A significant difference results from the fact that children's accountability – that is the need to give account – is in the family linked to 'doing' and to the possible negative consequences of their actions, while in school it is more linked to 'knowing', that is to say to a sphere which can be set up as a virtual space, independent of action and its consequences.

Exploring the Pre-school Speech Event

In the pre-school setting we focused our attention on a narrative activity that children are recurrently engaged in. It consists of two different phases: in the first phase, small groups of children were read a fairy tale (the story of 'Mascia and the bear'). The reading was interrupted at crucial points (see below) and the children were asked to predict how the story would continue. Immediately after the listening–predicting phase, there followed a discussion. In this second phase, the teacher asked children (a) to explain the intentions and the motives behind the actions of the characters in the story; (b) to evaluate what other actions might be plausible given those motives; (c) to evaluate the cleverness of the central character and her adversary.

Contrasting hypotheses and co-constructing reasoning

From its start the narrative activity has a strong hypothetical flavour. Children enthusiastically suggest various alternative ways in which the story might develop. Different narrative versions emerge and a lively discussion ensues. Other children's hypotheses are criticized and new versions are counterposed. Faced with the need to defend their positions and to undermine those of others, the participants have the opportunity to exercise their argumentative skills and to improve their capacity to handle narrative materials. The following excerpt vividly illustrates how the participants co-construct a plausible (to them) continuation of the story.

Excerpt 1

Teacher: Come ha fatto a scappare da dentro – dalla casetta dell'orso?
(How could she flee from within – from the bear's little house?)

Fabiola: Stava a vedere se pioveva, allora lui, il cestino era aperto, allora lei, zacchete! se ficca dentro, però così – e in testa ce mette le frittelle. ma se è grande (*Mascia*) se rompe el cestino però!
(He was looking to see whether it was raining, then he – the basket was open then she zacchete! (*Italian onomatopoeia*) she slips in, but so – and she puts the fritters on her head but if she is big the basket will break!)
[. . .]

Walter: Perché se Mascia era come noi o come te poteva rompe' il cestino uguale perché il cestino sarà così o così.
(Because if Mascia was like us or like you she could have broken the basket anyway because the basket was like this (*shaping with his hands the form of a little basket*)).

Sabrina: Il cestino era grande, se no non ce metteva neanche le frittelle. Ce n'ha messo tre o quattro o cinque o sei!
(The basket was big, otherwise she could not even put the fritters in it. She has put three or four or five or six in it!)

Fabiola: O sei! Almeno dopo il cestino: ciacchete!
(Or six! So that after the basket: ciacchete! (*Italian onomatopoeia indexing crashing down*)).

Walter: See, così il sei è più grande, sei chili pesa, no? co' le frittelle, così ce se mette Mascia che pesa almeno sette chili e quello se sfascia tutto. sette chili, quaranta chili!
(What? So 6 is bigger, it weighs 6 kilos, doesn't it? with the fritters, so Mascia who weighs at least 7 kilos puts herself in and that (*the basket*) will all crash down, 7 kilos, 40 kilos!)

These few turns show the complexity of narrative activity and how it is jointly accomplished. Fabiola, who is the first to answer the teacher's question, provides her narrative version by constructing what Bruner (1986) has called a *dual landscape* and by switching back and forth between the *landscape of action* and the *landscape of consciousness*. Her narrative is rather complex, as it considers both the protagonists' actions and their thoughts and feelings. Furthermore, at the end of her contribution she adds her own perspective as narrator. As Bruner has pointed out, the landscape of consciousness illuminates protagonists' doings and offers to the audience the narrator's understanding and interpretation of events.

The other children's subsequent contributions also wander through the dual landscape, thereby deploying and enriching their collective reasoning. Different plots are projected and then discussed. In so far as they respect the criterion of internal consistency, these imaginary narrative paths can all be considered equally possible and acceptable.

This is a crucial educative value that narrative activity frequently entails. It organizes experience, imbues it with meaning, and it also reveals that a multiplicity of interpretative frames are possible (Ochs, 1997; Ochs and Capps, 1996). Therefore, narrative activity can be a powerful educational tool for promoting plurality of perspective and cultivating critical thinking. It also encourages comparisons among the different viewpoints and understandings; it may also bring different voices into dialogue without the aim of making them into a unison chorus.

Hypothetical and counter-factual reasoning

In practice, children's collaborative reasoning, rather than emerging from mutual agreement, is realized through oppositions and explanations of a counter-factual nature. Going back again to Fabiola's first turn in excerpt 1, it can be seen that, after having put forward her hypothesis, she formulates a possible objection to her proposal: it wouldn't work if Mascia was too big. In the discussion of 'grande' (= big/grown-up) that follows, the two notions of size and age are collapsed and the children consider both aspects together (see excerpt 2). In this brief sequence it is possible to observe the typical use of conditional forms from which negative effects can be derived. Fabiola and, later, other children choose them as the more compelling forms when they want to deny an alternative hypothesis produced by another participant.

Challenges, oppositions and counter-proposals, however, do not prevent reasoning from unfolding. Rather, it is evident that this very opposition of hypotheses, the accounting activity it triggers, and the seeking for consensus, allow the children to reach collectively an articulation of reasoning far more complex than any one of them would have achieved alone. In sum, through the contrasting of perspectives they succeed in co-constructing reasoning. After some insistence on the point of the combined weight of Mascia and of the fritters, the children shift their collective attention to the question of age, which becomes the object of another piece of articulated dispute.

Excerpt 2
Fabiola: Ma Mascia è piccola!
              (But Mascia is [a] little [child]!)
Sabrina: C'ha tre anni! Forse.
              (She's 3 . . . maybe.)
              [. . .]
Walter: Se c'aveva cinque anni vol dì' che era poco intelligente. Invece c'ha
              tre anni è tanto intelligente. però se c'aveva,
              (If she was 5 years old it means that she was not clever enough.
              Instead if she is 3 years old she is very clever. But if she was,)
Teacher: Perché se c'aveva tre anni era tanto intelligente, se c'aveva cinque
              anni era poco intelligente? Invece se c'ha d –
              (why if she was 3 she was very clever, if she was 5 she was not clever
              enough? Instead if she was t –)
Walter: No, me so' sbajato. Se Mascia aveva tre anni come fa a esse intelligente
              se è piccola. Ancora non sa le idee, je le deve dì' la nonna.
              (was wrong. If Mascia was 3 how can she be clever if she is little
              (young). She doesn't have ideas yet, the grandmother has to tell her
              them.)
              [. . .]
Teacher: Se, se?
              (If, if?)
Sabrina: Te che ne sai quanti ce n'ha de anni mica c'è scritto?
              (How do you know how old she is? It's not written down.)
Walter: E che te ce l'hai? che te lo sai quanti ce n'ha? Dai dimmelo quanti ce
              n'ha, dimmelo!
              (And what do you know about it? How do you know how old she
              is? Come on, tell me how old she is, tell me!)

Fabiola: C'ha cinque!
             (She's 5!)
Walter: Beh, dimmelo quanti c'ha!?
             (Well tell me how old she is.)
Sabrina: Se se c'era scritto ce lo leggeva la maestra.
             (If it was written down, the teacher would have read it to us.)

This excerpt shows that children's reasoning can be deployed through pointing out possible negative consequences of different hypothetical conditions (e.g. Walter's turn: if Mascia is too young, she cannot be clever enough to flee away) and through using counter-factual forms (e.g. Sabrina's turn: you cannot say how old she is because it was not written, given that if it was written down the teacher would have read it to us). Hypothetical and counter-factual constructions are rather complex patterns of reasoning that are found not only in narrative activity across contexts but in scientific practices as well. Scientific knowledge thrives on challenging matters of fact, on refuting certain theoretical assumptions and on replacing them with new ones considered more accurate and adequate. Moreover, sociologists of science (Gilbert and Mulkay, 1982; Latour and Woolgar, 1979) have revealed that scientific theories are themselves constructed according to a particular narrative genre. Drawing on these remarks, we would emphasize the fact that narrative activity may not only socialize children into prototypical narrative thinking – with its meaning-making force – but may also provide the rudiments of scientific reasoning and practice (Ochs and Taylor, 1995; Ochs et al., 1992).

Last but not least, it can be observed that narrative activity, in so far as it encompasses the challenging, defending and redrafting of alternative narrative versions, promotes metacognitive thinking and cultivates metalinguistic ability.

Categorization as a situated rhetorical activity

Excerpt 2 reveals another crucial aspect of reasoning and arguing: the process of categorization. The children discuss the meaning of the categories *piccolo* and *grande*. Not only are the temporal and spatial dimensions concurrently evoked and contrasted; within each dimension the categories' boundaries are questioned and negotiated.

These aspects show that categorization, rather than being an abstract cognitive process, is a situated interactional activity (Goodwin, 1994). Categorization is something we *do* in social context in order to pursue social goals (e.g. persuading, accusing) (Edwards, 1991). Therefore, categories are flexible and do not have fixed and unequivocal membership demarcations; they are rhetorically handled and their meaning is contextually contingent.

In excerpt 2 it is possible to appreciate how even young children are able to strategically deploy category systems: they use the fact that the categories *piccolo* and *grande* do not have unique semantic content nor imply well-defined sets of features as a resource for justifying and sustaining their clashing positions about the bear's intelligence and, ultimately, to achieve agreement and consensus.

Preliminary Conclusions

From our analysis of pre-school activity three fundamental aspects of children's reasoning emerge:

1   It is highly co-constructed: children's narrative activity is co-authored and multi-voiced. Children's clashing positions are never simply juxtaposed but are negotiated, transformed and often blended in new reasoning paths.
2   It unfolds through complex argumentative patterns; overwhelmingly, hypothetical format and counter-factual structure are used.
3   It is rhetorically shaped: participants make use of refined discursive strategies and rhetorical moves for achieving agreement and consensus.

These three features of children's reasoning are surely closely linked with the particular narrative activity the children are engaged in, i.e. the construction and reconstruction of the story of Mascia and the bear. Indeed, several studies have already shown that narrative activity in a wide range of human contexts is highly co-constructed (Goodwin, 1984; Ochs, 1997; Ochs and Taylor, 1992; Pontecorvo, Amendola and Fasulo, 1994; Sacks, 1992). Moreover, it often stimulates hypothetical thinking (Ochs, et al., 1992) and promotes plurality and critical interpretation, thereby constituting a privileged tool for cognitive and linguistic socialization (Lucariello and Nelson, 1987; Orsolini and Pontecorvo, 1992; Pontecorvo and Fasulo, 1997).

Furthermore, we would argue that these important elements of children's reasoning are also prompted and subsequently reinforced by the teacher's mediation: through reformulations and repetitions of children's contributions, the teacher plays the role of catalyst of the unfolding discussion, so that children's voices are not simply juxtaposed but are brought into a dialectical confrontation. This mediational role requires the teacher both to be very responsive to the children's utterances – e.g. by using mirroring (Rogers, 1951), and only semantically contingent queries (Orsolini and Pontecorvo, 1992) – and to withdraw her intervention when the children are developing a collective path of arguing and reasoning. From an educational perspective, in sum, we would suggest that narrative activity and peer-group discussions are activities to be promoted and cultivated in the pre-school setting and, indeed, in later years as well.

Next, we turn our attention to the family setting to see whether, to what extent and where the features of children's reasoning in the pre-school setting are also present in dinner conversations.

Exploring Family Dinner Talk

Do children learn to argue before they go to school, and when can we say that they are learning? How are they socialized to the discursive tools and the rhetorical devices of reasoning?

In trying to answer these questions we have analysed Italian family dinner conversations. In particular, in the present study we have focused our attention on the narrative and the argumentative sequences in which children are engaged as ratified participants (regardless of whether they are talking or just listening).

Joint narrating

Remarkable studies of the activity of storytelling (Goodwin, 1984; Jefferson, 1978; Sacks, 1992) have shown that narratives are interactional accomplishments: the launching of a narrative, its actual unfolding and its closings alike require the contribution of all the participants, i.e. the recipients, the audience, as well as the storytellers. Even when speakers do not share the same view of the reported events the narrative is most of the time co-constructed through the quick exchange of turns, opposing of descriptions, and negotiation of memories. Indeed, also in family dinner conversations there is a remarkable amount of narratives (Lucariello and Nelson, 1987; Pontecorvo, Amendola and Fasulo, 1994; Ochs and Taylor, 1992). As well as in the pre-school context, narrative activity in the family setting is highly co-constructed. Therefore, by participating in family narratives, children acquire the conventions of storytelling and the discursive devices for narratively constructing reality (Bruner, 1991); last but not least, they practise different forms of participation in collective activities (Lave and Wenger, 1991).

In comparison with the pre-school context we have observed that, in Italian family narratives, participation roles are more flexible and often exchanged: within the same storytelling, not only is the role of narrator shared and passed among participants, children included, but challenging moves, such as problematizations and critiques, are also performed by all the members of the family. This observation resonates with Ochs and Taylor's (1995) suggestion that *social familiarity* encourages complex reasoning. The two authors have analysed American dinner conversations, revealing that, during such 'hectic, seemingly chaotic' speech events, complex cognitive processes are accomplished (ibid., p. 44):

> Where participants know one another well, they may be less hesitant to express uncertainty or perplexity over the problematic affairs in the narration and more open to invite the help of others in explaining the narrated events. Where participants know one another well they are able within limits to enter into the other's telling of events and reconfigure the other's version without dissolving the relationship. (Ibid., p. 43)

This aspect has a significant educative implication: familiarity among children and between teachers and children is not only to be pursued because it offers to all the participants a positive emotive environment for their everyday experience, but also because it encourages complex cognitive processes. Thus, social familiarity should be one of the primary aims of educators. Familiarity grows through practices of social interaction and dialogue, namely through group activities of different kinds, such as the one we examined in previous sections of this chapter.

Violation of rules and negative consequences

Family narrative and pre-school storytelling are both collaborative accomplishments, but they present relevant distinctive features. In fact, we did not find in family narratives the kind of articulated hypothetical and counter-factual procedures we found in the pre-school narrative activity.

This might lead to the conclusion that hypothetical and counter-factual reasoning is peculiar to the school setting. However, if we do not limit our analysis to narrative sequences, but also turn our attention to argumentative sequences, which also frequently occur in family dinner conversation, this conclusion is immediately contradicted.

We have noticed that in some kinds of argumentative sequences – in general, when an account of a violation of the normal is either requested or provided – a similar procedure of reasoning/discursive device to the one we have documented in children's pre-school narrative activity frequently occurs:

If you do not do X the negative event Y will occur.
If you do non-X the negative event Z will occur.

In what follows we present vivid examples of such a procedure. In excerpt 3 the participants are the Nacchi family: dad, mum, daughters (Ludovica, 14; Irma, 10; Antonia, 3 years 6 months). Antonia looks tired and is not eating.

Excerpt 3

Mum: Senti. Ma hai ancora tanto sonno? Poi ti faccio dormire in braccio a me. Va bene?
(Listen, are you still very sleepy? Later I'll let you sleep in my arms. All right?)

Antonia: No: [dormo nel letto].
(No: [I'm going to bed]).

Mum: [Eh si amore] eh si però devi dormire presto. Non facciamo come l'altra volta che ti sei addormentata a mezzanotte e poi ti senti male d'accordo?
([Eh yes my love] eh yes but you must sleep soon. Let's not do what we did last time when you fell asleep at midnight and then you feel sick all right.)

In this excerpt the 3-and-a-half year old girl disdains her mother's offer to let her go to sleep in her arms. Antonia's refusal is initially accepted and counter-argued by the mother, who then also articulates a warning: Antonia has to sleep soon without waiting until late as she did another time, which resulted in her feeling sick. The warning has the typical form of showing the negative consequences of a possible misbehaviour.

The informative relevance of negative assertions brings us directly to the core of narrative activity. Indeed, negative episodes have a crucial role in narrative, as they very often have the function of initiating events from which the main plot of the narrative develops (Bruner, 1991; Labov, 1972; Ochs, 1997; Stein and Glenn, 1979). Without a negative or problematic event we would hardly have any type of narrative.

We would like to suggest here that the conditional structure and negative format we found in family discourse resembles the hypothetical and counter-factual pattern we found in children's pre-school discourse. Thus, when children enter pre-school they have already been exposed to complex patterns of reasoning. Within a domain of practical reasoning they experience the discursive devices that will recur within other speech activities in other contexts (e.g. the classroom).

However, there is more to say: in family conversation, children not only listen and assimilate certain patterns of reasoning and discursive devices; they also have the chance actively to perform and practise these very same devices. In the following excerpt, the complex strategy of uttering the negative consequences of something that the other has done is performed rather astonishingly by the not-yet 4-year-old girl, Luisa.

Excerpt 4
Minelli family: Dad, mum, son Luca, 10 years 9 months, daughter Luisa, 3 years 10 months. Luca has just tried to serve himself the water from the bottle by handling it with just one finger. The bottle is likely to fall on the table. Both parents scold Luca severely.

Mum: Va bene la prossima volta te lo facciamo capire meglio con uno schiaffone.
(OK, the next time we'll make you understand it better with a big slap.)

Dad: Visto che continui a fare lo stupido.
(As you continue to act stupidly.)

Luisa: Guarda non si fa non si ri non si dice così al fratellino. Me lo ha spiegato la nonna.
(Look you don't do, you don't re-you it don't say so to the nice little brother. Grandma explained it to me (*sighing excitedly*)).

Mum: Fratellino perché ci fa disperare. Versa l'acqua con un dito.
(Nice little brother because he drives us to despair. He pours out the water with one finger.)

Luisa: Non è vero. Adesso glielo spiego io.
       (It's not true now let me explain it to him.)
Mum: Eh spiegaglielo.
       (Eh, explain to him.)
Luisa: Luca così non si fa perché la bottiglia se la versi con un dito non si fa
       perché si può cadere il bicchiere con tutta la bottiglia. Capito?
       (Luca you don't do it so because if you pour it out the bottle with one
       finger you can't do it because the glass with all the bottle can fall
       down. Did you get it?)
Luca: (*Vertical headshakes*)

In this excerpt young Luisa performs effectively the language-game of education: she (1) uses a conditional form, (2) displays possible negative consequences, (3) ends with a tag question. Her intervention is surely courageous: she reproaches her parents for the rough expressions they used in scolding her brother. However, her explanatory and rhetorical abilities are so sharp that her parents are wordless and Luca has to give his consent!

Categorization and Other Rhetorical Devices

Within the discursive context of rule violation and the statement of rules, children are often requested to account for their acts (Pontecorvo, Fasulo and Sterponi, in press). In accounts, rules are negotiated and differently interpreted, exceptions are invoked and denied (Garfinkel, 1967). In order to perform this activity effectively, rhetorical skill and persuasive ability are necessary. Therefore, in family dinner conversation children can learn and practise the rhetorical devices and the patterns of reasoning that they will be using in other social contexts (e.g. in the classroom).

As an example we present here a brief excerpt of family conversation in which the same categories of *piccolo* and *grande* that we commented on before (see excerpt 2) are differently deployed by participants

Excerpt 5
Traverso family: dad, mum, daughters Carla, 7 years, Federica, 4 years.

Carla: Dovremmo eliminare tutti i pupazzi. Darli ai poveri. Regalarli.
         Pupazzi che sono in buona salute li regaliamo.
         (We should eliminate all the puppets. Give them to the poor people.
         Give them away. Puppets that are in good health give them away).
         [. . .]
Federica: Ma io ci voglio giocare.
         (But I want to play with them (*whining*)).
Carla: Eh Federì ma tu sei grande. Hai cinque anni mo.
         (Eh Federi but you're grown-up. You're 5 years old now).

Federica: Ma io ci gioco lo stesso. Vero mamma?
              (But I play with them all the same. Isn't it true mum?)

In this excerpt the older daughter, Carla, in order to get her sister's agreement to giving away all the puppets, cunningly tells her that she is grown-up.
Carla knows that Federica wants to be considered *grande* and she attempts
to take advantage from the implication of this attribution (i.e. when one is
grown-up one doesn't play with puppets). As a matter of fact, Federica does
not want to give the puppets away, but she does not refuse her sister's attribution: even though she is grown-up now she nevertheless continues to play
with puppets! In sum, in this excerpt the two daughters, in order to achieve
their opposite goals, give different meanings and underline distinct implications linked with the same category of *grande*.

The description of events is another profoundly rhetorical speech activity.
In everyday conversation the way events are reported does not depend only
on one's own knowledge and experience but also on other elements, such as
the reasons why the episode is recounted, the recipients of the storytelling,
etc. In the following excerpt four different versions of an event are provided
by different members of the family!

Excerpt 6
Bianucci family: dad, mum, daughters Silvia, 4 years old, Fabiana, 9 years old.

Mum: Silvia (.) Raccontaci bene quello che stavifacendo con Clara in stanza
             prima che venisse su Fabiana.
             (Silvia, tell us precisely what you were doing with Clara in your
             room before Fabiana came up.)
Dad: (   )
Silvia: Stavamo giocando a polizia. E poi uno c'ha disturbato. Ch'eri tu.
             (We were playing police then someone came to disturb us who was
             you (*to Fabiana*)).
Fabiana: Ti stavi per rompere la testa. Ho disturbato.
             (You were just breaking your head. I disturbed you).
Dad: Ma io l'ho lasciate che volevano farsi un riposino.
             (But when I left them they wanted to take a nap).
Fabiana: No.
Mum: A disfare i letti.
             (To undo the beds).

The mother solicits Silvia's telling of what happened in the afternoon.
Mother's request for a precise report reveals the inquiring character of her
invitation. Though indirectly, the mother is asking for an account. As a matter
of fact, Silvia's reply is both a report of what she did and a justification for it.
Categorizing what she was doing in the afternoon as playing police, Silvia is
claiming the permissibility of her presumably animated behaviour (it is not

possible to play police quietly). However, Fabiana immediately supplies a contrasting version of what was going on between Silvia and Clara in the afternoon. Like Silvia's version, Fabiana's report provides a justification of her behaviour (she presumably intervened to interrupt the game). A similar interpretation can be given to the father's report to the mother, in which he denies responsibility for what happened in the afternoon.

Conclusions: Educational Implications

Starting from a perspective that considers cognitive development as part of a complex process of socialization, this study has shown that pre-school narrative activity socializes children into complex patterns of reasoning. It emerged that, in collectively dealing with the construction and reconstruction of narrative, children frequently use hypothetical and counter-factual devices. Furthermore, conflicting perspectives are opposed and children are called to account for their positions. The clashing of viewpoints and their subsequent negotiation facilitate metacognitive awareness and trigger the achievement of complex modalities of reasoning. Thinking is carried out collectively, thereby achieving more complex levels of reasoning. Moreover, subtle rhetorical devices are used for gaining agreement and consensus.

These findings invite teachers and curricula workers to grant narrative activity a central role in everyday classroom practices. However, narrative activity does not always, or automatically, bring about, for apprentices, the rich potentialities we have just summarized above. The way the teacher organizes and manages the narrative activity is critical in making it meaningful. It is important that the teacher promotes co-narration and multi-voicedness, orchestrates the participants' contributions and scaffolds the co-constructing of meanings. In other words, it is necessary to develop teachers' awareness and mastery of the discursive resources which facilitate pupils' participation in collective reasoning. Mirroring interventions, reformulations and semantically contingent queries have been identified and proved to function as powerful tools for sustaining and enhancing children's cognitive development.

Our analysis of Italian family dinner conversations has revealed that complex argumentative and rhetorical devices are also present in everyday family discourse. Indeed, at dinner table young children are exposed to, and can acquire, crucial rhetorical and reasoning skills, given that parents prefer to regulate children's behaviour through the use of counter-factual statements to discourage rule violations. Furthermore, in contributing to family narratives, children learn and practise different forms of participation in social activities, thereby improving their argumentative and cognitive ability.

Teachers should be aware of the patterns of reasoning and the rhetorical devices children acquire in the family context so that schools may become places in which children will find large possibilities to practise, enrich and refine the argumentative resources they have already acquired at home, in their everyday life. If it is agreed upon that all students, by the end of the compulsory curriculum, have to master a range of skills that enable them to be active participants in the public life of their community and masters of their own and of others' rights of citizenship, the awareness and understanding of the multiplicity of viewpoints become a central educative aim. In such a perspective, the statement of a 4-year-old child some years ago in a Reggio Emilia nursery school, who said that 'words are good for disputing without beating each other up', is still of the utmost importance!

11
Developing Dialogues

Neil Mercer

This chapter is about how children learn to use language as a tool for thinking, collectively and alone, and how other people use language to help them do so. I want to argue two main points: first, that the prime aim of education ought to be to help children learn how to use language effectively as a tool for thinking collectively; and second, that classroom-based involvement in culturally based ways of thinking collectively can make a significant contribution to the development of individual children's intellectual ability. Drawing mainly on classroom-based research, I describe classroom-based education as a dialogic process, in which both talk between teachers and learners and talk among learners have important roles to play. In these ways I intend to illustrate the practical educational value of research based on a sociocultural or CHAT perspective. But as well as serving some useful practical ends, I also hope to show how this kind of research can provide answers to some intriguing theoretical questions about the relationship between thought, language and social activity.

The founding father of sociocultural research, Lev Vygotsky (1978), proposed that there is a close relationship between the use of language as a cultural tool (in social interaction) and the use of language as a psychological tool (for organizing our own, individual thinking). He also suggested that our involvement in joint activities can generate new understandings which we then 'internalize' as individual knowledge and capabilities. Although developmental psychologists have treated his claims about the connections between 'intermental' and 'intramental' activity with great interest, surprisingly little evidence has been offered to support or refute them. Towards the end of this chapter I will describe some classroom-based research which has provided such evidence.

Development from a Sociocultural Perspective

The central idea underpinning the sociocultural perspective on human intellectual development is that individual development is integrated with the longer-term historical development of our species and that language plays a vital role in achieving this integration. Psychological and anthropological studies of adult–child relations, observed in many cultures, support the view that growing up is an 'apprenticeship in thinking', an induction into ways with words and ways of thinking which is achieved through dialogue (for example, Heath, 1983; Rogoff, 1990, 1995; Wells, 1986). This research has highlighted the importance of the role that parents and other people play in helping children learn, in the course of everyday joint activity. However, little of that research has been concerned with the activity of adults as self-conscious teachers or instructors, or with the ways children seek guidance or information to improve their understanding. Adults do not only allow children to participate in family activities, they also deliberately provide them with information and explanations and instruct them in ways to behave. And children, for their part, may take active roles in soliciting help or obtaining information and transforming what they are given into their own new understanding. Of course, the extent to which they are able and willing to be active participants in teaching-and-learning dialogues will depend on the social circumstances of particular interactions and the interpersonal relations which exist within them.

How Teachers Use Language

Research in schools has revealed that teachers depend on the use of particular linguistic strategies for guiding, monitoring and assessing the activities they organize for their pupils (in ways described in Edwards and Mercer, 1987; Mercer, 1995). All teachers ask their pupils a lot of questions. Most teachers also regularly offer their classes recaps – summaries of what they consider to be the salient features of a past event – which can help students to relate current activity to past experience. Teachers also often elaborate and reformulate the contributions made to classroom dialogue by pupils (for example in response to a teacher's questions) as a way of clarifying what has been said for the benefit of others, and also of making connections between the content of children's utterances and the technical terminology of the curriculum (Lemke, 1990; Wells, 1999). These strategies seem to be in common use throughout the world, even though teaching styles and ways of organizing classrooms vary within and across cultures (see Edwards and Westgate, 1994, and Mercer, 1995, for a review of relevant research).

Of course, as with the tools of any trade, teachers can use these common discursive strategies relatively well or badly. To make such an evaluation we need to consider what their intended educational purpose might be. For a teacher to teach and a learner to learn, both partners need to use talk and joint activity to create a shared framework of understanding from the resources of their common knowledge and common interests or goals. Talk is the principal tool for creating this framework, and by questioning, recapping, reformulating, elaborating and so on, teachers are usually seeking to draw pupils into a shared understanding of the activities in which they are engaged. I find it useful to think of this shared understanding as an Intermental Development Zone (IDZ) in which educational activity takes place. The IDZ is a dynamic frame of reference which is reconstituted constantly as the dialogue continues, so enabling the teacher and learner to think together through the activity in which they are involved. If the quality of the IDZ is successfully maintained, misunderstandings will be minimized and motivations will be maximized. If this is successful, the teacher will be able to help the learner transcend their established capabilities and to consolidate their experience in the zone as improved capability and understanding. If the dialogue fails to keep minds mutually attuned, however, the IDZ collapses and the scaffolded learning grinds to a halt.

The IDZ is a mutual achievement, dependent on the interactive participation and commitment of both teacher and learner; but a teacher must take special responsibility for its creation and maintenance. It is a continuing, contextualizing framework for joint activity, whose effectiveness is likely to depend on how well a teacher can create and maintain connections between the curriculum-based goals of activity and a learner's existing knowledge, capabilities and motivations (Mercer, 2000, ch. 6.) In the next section I will describe some ways in which teachers can most successfully develop an IDZ with their pupils and help them make the most of their educational experience.

Some Characteristics of Effective Teaching

For several years now, I have been involved in research on how teachers use language as the principal tool of their trade. Based in primary schools in England and in Mexico, one of the aims of this research has been to improve the quality of classroom education. The Mexican strand of this research, led by Sylvia Rojas-Drummond at the Autonomous University of Mexico (UNAM), has compared teachers in state schools whose pupils had been found to develop particularly well in reading comprehension and mathematical problem-solving, with teachers in similar schools whose pupils have not made such significant achievements. Using video recordings of classroom interactions, the Mexican researchers and I tried to discover if the better teachers differed from those who were less successful in the ways they interacted with their pupils. Essentially, we were trying to see if the better teachers were providing a more effective 'scaffolding' for their pupils' learning. We were also interested in what kinds of learning teachers appeared to be encouraging.

Our analysis covered several features of classroom interaction, including teachers' uses of questions. We looked at the content of tasks, activities and discussions, at the extent to which teachers encouraged pupils to talk together, and the kinds of explanations and instructions teachers provided to pupils for the tasks they set them. The results of this time-consuming and complex analysis (described in more detail in Rojas-Drummond, Mercer and Dabrowski, 2001) can be summarized as follows. We found that the more effective teachers could be distinguished by the following characteristics:

1   They used question-and-answer sequences not just to test knowledge, but also to guide the development of understanding. These teachers often used questions to discover the initial levels of pupils' understanding and adjust their teaching accordingly, and used 'why' questions to get pupils to reason and reflect about what they were doing.

2   They taught not just 'subject content', but also procedures for solving problems and making sense of experience. This included teachers demonstrating the use of problem-solving strategies for children, explaining to children the meaning and purpose of classroom activities, and using their interactions with children as opportunities for encouraging children to make explicit their own thought processes.

3   They treated learning as a social, communicative process. As I mentioned, earlier research has shown that most teachers make regular use of a set of conventional dialogic techniques – question-and-answer sessions, recaps, reformulations and so on. The more effective teachers used these effectively to do such things as encouraging pupils to give reasons for their views, organizing interchanges of ideas and mutual support among pupils, and generally encouraging pupils to take a more active, vocal role in classroom events.

The findings of our research are in accord with those of other researchers (see, for example, Brown and Palinscar, 1989). This has encouraged my colleagues and I – and the teachers with whom we have been working closely in both the UK and Mexico – to believe that it is useful for teachers to become aware of the techniques they use in dialogue and what they are trying to achieve through using them. Teachers have found this approach useful for examining their own practice. Even very good teachers, who probably do these things without being aware that they do so, seem nevertheless to appreciate gaining this meta-awareness.

As I suggested earlier, effective teaching does not simply depend on the use of particular language techniques – it depends on how they are used to create and maintain IDZs. The better Mexican teachers and those who were less effective were all using elicitations, recaps, reformulations and other conventional features of the everyday language of classroom life. The crucial difference between the two sets of teachers was how and when they used them, and what they used them to teach. They differed significantly in the extent they used dialogue to help children see the relevance of past experience and common knowledge, and in the opportunities they provided for children to explain their own understanding or misunderstanding. When setting up activities or reviewing them with children, the most effective teachers used language to support and guide the children's activity. They also encouraged more active and extended participation in dialogue on the part of the children.

The extent to which the children themselves contribute to the establishment and maintenance of an IDZ is of course crucial. That is, the 'ground rules' of classroom interaction must offer them legitimate opportunities to express their uncertainties and reveal their confusions, and to request information and explanations from others who are more knowledgeable. We concluded that the quality of children's educational experience is significantly affected by the extent to which their dialogue with the teacher gives what they are doing in class a continuity of meaning (so that activity is contextualized by the history of past experience) and a comprehensible and worthwhile purpose.

These findings encouraged us to conclude that a good primary school teacher is not simply the instructor or facilitator of the learning of a large and disparate set of individuals, but rather the creator of a particular quality of intermental environment – a 'community of enquiry' (Lipman, 1970; Wells, 1999; this volume) in which students can take active and reflective roles in the development of their own understanding. In such classrooms the students are apprentices in collective thinking under the expert guidance of their teacher. I will return to these matters shortly, after some consideration of talk among children when a teacher or other 'expert' adult is not involved.

Talk Among Learners

A sociocultural perspective helps us appreciate the reciprocal relationship between individual thinking and the collective intellectual activities of groups. We use language to transform individual thought into collective thought and action, and also to make personal interpretations of shared experience. Not only the intellectual development of early childhood but the whole of human life depends on the maintenance of a dynamic relationship between the 'intramental' and the 'intermental'. So far, I have focused on how the pursuit of intermentality figures in the relationships between adults as 'experts' and children as 'novices'. But as well as learning from the guidance and example of adults, children (and novices of all ages) also learn the skills of thinking collectively by acting and talking with each other. Any account of intellectual development which was based only on the study of dialogues between older and younger generations of a community would therefore be inadequate. Members of a younger generation use language among themselves to generate their own, shared understandings and to pursue their own interests. Each generation is active in creating the new knowledge they want and, in doing so, the communal resources of the language toolkit may be transformed. Yet even the rebellious creativity of a new generation is, in part, the product of a dialogue between generations.

Language offers children a means for simulating events together in play, in ways which may enable the participants to make better sense of the actual experiences on which the play is based. Elbers (1994) provides some excellent examples of children engaged in this kind of play activity. Like many children, when they were aged 6 and 7, his two daughters enjoyed setting up play 'schools' together with toy animals. They would act out scenarios in which, with one of them as the teacher, the assembled creatures would act out the routines of a school day. But Elbers noticed that one typical feature of their play school was that incidents that disrupted classroom life took place with surprising frequency. Here is one such example (translated by Elbers from the Dutch). Margareet is the elder girl, being nearly 8 years old, and here takes the role of the teacher. Elisabeth, her younger (6-year-old) sister, acts out the role of a rather naughty pupil.

Sequence 1: Play school

Margareet:	Children, sit down.
Elisabeth:	I have to go to the toilet, Miss.
Margareet:	Now, children, be quiet.
Elisabeth:	I have to go to the toilet.
Margareet:	I want to tell you something.
Elisabeth:	(*Loud*) I have to go to the toilet!
Margareet:	(*Chuckles*) Wait a second.
Elisabeth:	(*With emphasis*) Miss, I have to go to the toilet!!
Margareet:	OK, you can go.
Elisabeth:	(*Cheekily*) Where is it? (*Laughs*)
Margareet:	Over there, under that box, the one with the animals on, where the dangerous animals . . . (*Chuckles*) under there.
Elisabeth:	Really?
Margareet:	Yes.
	(Ibid., p. 230)

In this sequence we can see a child appropriating an adult's way with words. 'Now, children, be quiet' is exactly the kind of teacher-talk that Margareet will have heard every day in 'real' school. But Elbers suggests we can also interpret this sequence as an example of children reflecting together on the rules which govern their behaviour in school, and how the robustness of these rules can be tested. They can play with ideas of power and control without risking the community sanctions which such behaviour would incur in 'real life'. Teachers normally have to be obeyed, and children are not meant to leave the class during lessons – but given the legitimate excuse of having to go to the toilet, how can a child not get her way? Sometimes, in setting up this kind of activity, the girls (out of role) would discuss how best to ensure that such disruptive incidents occurred. For example:

> *Sequence 2: Setting up the play school*
> *Margareet*:   You should choose four children who always talk the most; those children must sit at the front near the teacher. It'll be fun if they talk.
> *Elisabeth*:   (*To one of the toy pupils*) You, you sit here and talk, right?
> *Margareet*:   The desks are behind each other, then they can only . . . then I have to turn round all the time, if the children talk.
> (Ibid., p. 231)

These kinds of examples illustrate something important about how language use in play activities may contribute to children's development. Language can be used by them to simulate social life, to create virtual contexts in which they can practise using the genres of their culture to think together about their shared experience in the communities in which they are cultural apprentices. That is, language enables children to think together about social experience; and social experience enables them to acquire and practise ways of using language to think collectively. For children, playing with discourses is an important way of assimilating the language resources of the community in which they are growing up. This kind of 'adult' talk is particularly common in the classroom 'home' corner in the early years of school.

Learning to Engage in Collective Reasoning

Outside school, the 'ground rules' of everyday communication are usually taken for granted, and there is little meta-discussion or joint reflection on how things are normally done. This indicates a clear and useful role for schools, which are special institutional settings created for guiding intellectual development and understanding. Education should help children gain a greater awareness and appreciation of the discourse repertoire of wider society and how it is used to create knowledge and to get things done. Some valuable, practical ways of using language may not be used much in the informal activities of everyday childhood life, and so children can hardly be expected to learn them there. School life should give them access to ways of using language which their out-of-school experience may not have revealed. It should help them extend their repertoire of language genres and so enable them to use language more effectively as a means for learning, pursuing interests, developing shared understanding and – crucially – reasoning and solving problems together. There is little evidence, however, that this role is recognized within most education systems, or carried out by most teachers. The use of language as a toolkit for collective reasoning is not a common topic in classroom talk, nor does it figure explicitly in any school curriculum I have seen (but see Pontecorvo and Sterponi, this volume). In all levels of education, from primary school to university, students usually seem to be expected to work out the 'ground rules' of effective discussion for themselves.

Classroom research has also shown very clearly that in most of the dialogue between teachers and pupils it is rare for pupils to ask the teacher questions, and even less common for pupils to challenge explanations or interpretations of events that are offered by teachers. Reasons for this, in terms of power relations and conventional norms of social behaviour, are not hard to find, but the fact is that teacher–pupil dialogues do not offer much opportunity for pupils to practise their use of language as a tool for reasoning more generally. A more suitable setting for productive argumentative dialogue, one might expect, would be collaborative activity among pupils without a teacher present. However, observational research in classrooms suggests that when pupils are allowed to work together in groups most of their talk is either disputational or blandly and unreflectively cooperative, only involving some of the children and providing no more than a brief and superficial consideration of the relevant topics (Barnes and Todd, 1995; Bennett and Cass, 1989; Wegerif and Scrimshaw, 1997).

Over the last ten or so years, Lyn Dawes, Rupert Wegerif, Karen Littleton and I have been working closely with primary teachers in the UK to develop a practical programme of 'Talk Lessons' for children aged 8–11. The Talk Lessons are designed with a careful balance of teacher-led and group-based activities. Drawing from the research on teacher–pupil communication which I described earlier, we have designed teacher-led whole-class activities to raise children's awareness of how they talk together and how language can be used in joint activity for reasoning and problem-solving. These teacher-led activities are coupled with group-based tasks, in which children have the opportunity to practise ways of talking and collaborating, and these in turn feed into other whole-class sessions, in which teachers and children reflect together on what has been learned. The group tasks include topics directly relevant to the National Curriculum for English, science and citizenship (cf. Dawes, 1997, 1998, for a teacher's account of these lessons and activities in a curriculum context). We have also created computer-based activities using specially designed software (as described in Wegerif, Mercer and Dawes, 1998; the Talk Lessons and associated software are available as Dawes, Mercer and Wegerif, 2000).

In order to evaluate the Talk Lessons programme, we made comparisons between children in 'target' classes (those using the Talk Lessons) with 'control' classes (of similar children in schools not involved in the programme). One specific kind of comparison we made was to video-record groups of both target and control children doing the same computer-based activities. This comparison reveals striking differences between the two sets of children. Children who took part in the programme are seen to discuss issues in more depth and for longer, participate more equally and fully, and provide more reasons to support their views. (The findings of this research are reported in detail in Mercer, Wegerif and Dawes, 1999; our methods of analysis are described in Wegerif and Mercer, 1997.) Our analysis of recordings of the group activities shows that the improved ability of the target children to think together critically and constructively can be related directly to the structure and content of their talk.

Our target and control classes were also both given a psychological test, the Raven's Progressive Matrices, which has been commonly used as a general measure of non-verbal reasoning (Raven, Court and Raven, 1995). As an additional way of assessing any effects of the Talk Lessons on children's problem-solving skills, we gave both sets of children this test before the target children did the Talk Lessons, and then again after the series of lessons had been completed. A group of children in each target class was also video-recorded, before and after the programme, as they tackled the test. In this way we were able to observe, analyse and assess these children's joint problem-solving activity. When we compared groups in target classes who had failed on specific problems in the pre-lessons test with their successes in the post-lessons test, we could see from the transcripts of their discussions how the quality of their collective reasoning had enabled them to do so. Here, for illustration, are two sequences from the talk of children in the same group. They are doing one of the Raven's puzzles (D9). Sequence 3 was recorded before they did the series of Talk Lessons, while sequence 4 was recorded after they had done so.

Sequence 3: Graham, Suzie and Tess doing Raven's test item D9 (before the Talk Lessons)

Tess:	It's that.
Graham:	It's that, 2.
Tess:	2 is there.
Graham:	It's 2.
Tess:	2 is there Graham.
Graham:	It's 2.
Tess:	2 is there.
Graham:	What number do you want then?
Tess:	It's that because there ain't two of them.
Graham:	It's number 2, look one, two.
Tess:	I can count, are we all in agree on it? (*Suzie rings number 2 – an incorrect choice – on the answer sheet.*)
Suzie:	No.
Graham:	Oh, after she's circled it!

Sequence 4: Graham, Suzie and Tess doing Raven's test item D9 (after the Talk Lessons)

Suzie:	D9 now, that's a bit complicated it's got to be.
Graham:	A line like that, a line like that and it ain't got a line with that.

Tess:	It's got to be that one.
Graham:	It's going to be that don't you think? Because look all the rest have got a line like that and like that, I think it's going to be that because . . .
Tess:	I think it's number 6.
Suzie:	No I think it's number 1.
Graham:	Wait no, we've got number 6, wait stop, do you agree that it's number 1? Because look that one there is blank, that one there has got them, that one there has to be number 1, because that is the one like that. Yes. Do you agree? [Tess nods in agreement]
Suzie:	D9 number 1. (*She writes '1', which is the correct answer.*)

In sequence 3 we can see that Tess does offer a reason – a good reason – for her view, but Graham ignores it and she seems to give up in the face of his stubbornness. Suzie has taken the role of writer and she says little. At the end, having ringed the answer Graham wanted, she disagrees with it. It is not the right answer; but they all move on to the next problem anyway. Sequence 4 illustrates some ways that the talk of the same children changed after the programme of Talk Lessons and how this helped them to solve the problem. Graham responds to opposition from Tess by giving an elaborated explanation of why he thinks 'number 1' is the correct choice. This clear articulation of reasons leads the group to agree on the right answer. Such explanations involve a series of linked clauses and so lead to longer utterances. All three children are now more equally involved in the discussion. They make more effective rhetorical use of language for expressing their opinions and persuading others of their value. Compared with their earlier attempt, language is being used more effectively by the group as a tool for thinking together about the task they are engaged in.

The quality of the discussion of the children who were most successful in solving the Raven's problems can be related to the concept of 'exploratory talk', a way of using language for reasoning which was first identified by the pioneering British educational researcher Douglas Barnes (e.g. Barnes and Todd, 1995). My own conception of this way of communicating is as follows:

> Exploratory talk is that in which partners engage critically but constructively with each other's ideas. Relevant information is offered for joint consideration. Proposals may be challenged and counter-challenged but, if so, reasons are given and alternatives are offered. Agreement is sought as a basis for joint progress. Knowledge is made publicly accountable and reasoning is visible in the talk.

There are good reasons for wanting children to use this kind of talk in group activities because it is a very functional kind of language genre, with speakers following ground rules which help them share knowledge, evaluate evidence and consider options in a reasonable and equitable way. That is, exploratory talk represents a way in which partners involved in problem-solving activity can use language to think collectively – to 'interthink' effectively, with their activity encapsulated in an intermental zone of their own construction. Other experimental and observational studies have demonstrated the value of talk of this kind in problem solving (Teasley, 1997; Lyle, 1993; see also Littleton and Light, 1999). As a result of some recent convergence between sociocultural research and systemic functional linguistics, the relationship between the language genres of a community, the organization of social activity and the pursuit of education has become clear (Gibbons, in press; Russell, 1997; Wells, 1999). Exploratory talk is embodied in some important social practices, such as those used in science, law and business, and it is reasonable to expect that education should help every child to become aware of its value and become able to use it effectively.

From the Intermental to the Intramental

The comparisons between the talk of the children in target and control classes, and between the 'before' and 'after' talk of children in the target classes, confirmed that the Talk Lessons were changing the ways language was used as a tool for collective reasoning. In a nutshell, the lessons led to the children using more 'exploratory talk', and the increased use of this kind of talk was associated with improved joint problem solving. But, as I mentioned at the very beginning of this chapter, the results of this research also provide some evidence about Vygotsky's hypothesis about the link between social activity (the 'intermental') and individual development (the 'intramental'). This aspect of the research depended again on the use of the Raven's test. Two versions of this test are available and so, as well as giving one version of the test to groups of children in both target and control classes before and after the Talk Lessons programme had been implemented (with the target classes), we also set each child in the target and control classes the other version of the test as an individual problem-solving activity. We found that target children became significantly better at doing the problems individually, when compared with the control children. That is, the children who had experienced the Talk Lessons appeared to have improved their reasoning capabilities by taking part in the group experience of explicit, rational, collaborative problem solving. This is despite the fact that these children had no more experience or training in doing the Raven's puzzles, together or alone, than the children in the control classes.

Of course, we cannot be sure exactly what the target children learned from their experience that made the difference. It may be that some gained from having new, successful problem-solving strategies explained to them by their partners, while others may have benefited from having to justify and make explicit their own reasons. But a more radical and intriguing possibility is that children may have improved their reasoning skills by 'internalizing' the ground rules of exploratory talk, so that they become able to carry on a kind of silent rational dialogue with themselves. That is, the Talk Lessons may have helped them become more able to generate the kind of rational thinking which depends on the explicit, dispassionate consideration of evidence and competing options. That interpretation is consistent with Vygotsky's claims about the link between the social and the individual; collective thinking has a shaping influence on individual cognition.

Conclusions

One of the strengths of bringing a sociocultural perspective to bear on education, I believe, is that it encourages us to recognize that the quality of education cannot be explained in terms of 'learning' or 'teaching' as separate processes, but rather in terms of the interactive process of 'teaching-and-learning'. (The English language offers no elegant way of referring to this process. Interestingly, Vygotsky had at his disposal the Russian word *obuchenie*, which means both teaching and learning.) While the focus of attention of educational research may at any particular time be on the teacher or on the learner, we need to consider the active contributions of both these partners to *obuchenie* in any account of events and their outcomes. I have introduced the notion of an 'intermental development zone' to highlight the way that the success of education can be very dependent on partners creating and maintaining shared knowledge resources and a common frame of reference for their joint activity. For an applied researcher or teacher who is concerned with assessing and improving the quality of education, a sociocultural perspective helps avoid any tendency to attribute problems or solutions to the separate actions of teachers or learners, or to account for events without reference to the historical, cultural and institutional frameworks in which they take place.

In relation to classroom education, a sociocultural perspective may also help us transcend the persistent, unfortunate and unhelpful debate about the relative benefits of teacher-led, whole-class sessions and activities where learners work together without the teacher in small groups. Group activities offer learners good opportunities to practise and evaluate ways of using language to think collectively, away from the teacher's authoritative presence. But they need first to be guided in how to talk and work together if these activities are to be of most benefit for their learning; and they may later need the intellectual leadership of a teacher to help them consolidate what they have learned from their joint efforts and relate it to the curriculum and other cultural reference frames. Thus in the Talk Lessons programme, teachers organize and lead activities, provide children with information and guidance and help them recognize and reflect on what they have learned. They talk explicitly with children about the goals of classroom activities. Each teacher models 'exploratory' ways of talking for the children in whole-class sessions – for example, asking 'Why?' at appropriate times, giving examples of reasons for opinions, and checking that a range of views is heard. The success of the Talk Lessons programme depends very much, I believe, on its careful balance between teacher-led, whole-class sessions and 'talk groups' in which children work and talk together, without constant teacher supervision, on problem-solving activities. The organized continuity of this experience helps children to consolidate learning, gain educational benefit from their experience and hopefully helps them understand better how language can be used, in many kinds of social situation, for thinking together and getting things done.

The sociocultural or CHAT perspective on intellectual development asserts that we are essentially social, communicative creatures who gain much of what we know from others and whose thoughts and actions are shaped by our interactions. It also highlights the ways that, through involvement in the taken-for-granted normality of social life, each new generation is influenced by the habits of its predecessors. The role of language as a cultural toolkit for joint intellectual activity is emphasized by this perspective – and so is the relationship between the social and psychological uses of language. All these ideas can be traced back to the original work of Vygotsky. But we need now to go further, following Vygotsky's pioneering example by developing a more radical conception of the relationship between language and thinking. My own suggestion is that we focus our attention directly upon language as a means for thinking collectively – a process which we might, by analogy with 'interaction', call 'interthinking' (Mercer, 2000). This would involve the study of many other kinds of social interaction, not only those which are in any obvious sense 'educational'. Such studies could help us bring the intellectual, developmental, pragmatic, social and cultural functions of language within one theoretical framework. We could then, with increasing confidence, apply this framework in educational and other applied fields of research.

12

Supporting Students' Learning of Significant Mathematical Ideas

Paul Cobb and Kay McClain

Our purpose in this chapter is to illustrate the relevance of Cultural Historical Activity Theory (CHAT) to our work as mathematics educators and instructional designers. The type of research that we conduct involves classroom teaching or design experiments of up to a year in duration. In these experiments, the teacher is a full member of the research team that collectively assumes responsibility for supporting the students' mathematical learning. One of our primary motivations when conducting a design experiment is to explore the prospects for reform at the classroom level by investigating what might be possible for students' learning in a particular mathematical domain. To this end, we develop, test and revise sequences of instructional activities and associated resources, such as computer-based tools, while the experiment is in progress. These ongoing modifications and adjustments are informed by the analyses of classroom events that we discuss in debriefing meetings held after every classroom session. As it transpires, this daily cycle of planning, instruction and analysis is highly consistent with the practices of skilled teachers whose overriding goal is to nurture their students' development of relatively deep mathematical understandings (cf. Ball, 1993; Franke et al., 1998; Lampert, 1990; Simon, 1995; Stigler and Hiebert, 1999). As a consequence, the implications of this type of research are usually relatively immediate because the findings are grounded in the reality of learning and teaching in school classrooms.

When we began conducting design experiments thirteen years ago we did not consciously decide to try to apply CHAT to the problems of mathematics learning and teaching in what might be termed a top-down manner. Our increasing appreciation of the potential relevance of CHAT has been highly pragmatic. We take a similarly pragmatic approach in this chapter by framing a recent seventh-grade design experiment that focused on statistical data analysis as a paradigm case in which to illustrate the compatibility of our approach to instructional design with the basic tenets of CHAT. In doing so, we will discuss four aspects of the classroom learning environment that proved critical in supporting the students' mathematical development: the instructional tasks, the general classroom activity structure, the computer-based tools the students used, and the classroom discourse.

We first provide an overview of the experiment and then focus on each of these means of support in turn. In the final part of the chapter, we step back to consider issues of equity by placing the design experiment in broader context.

Background to the Design Experiment

In preparing for the design experiment, we conducted interviews and whole-class performance assessments with a group of seventh graders from the school in which we planned to work. These assessments indicated that data analysis for most of these students involved 'doing something with the numbers' (McGatha, Cobb and McClain, 1999). In other words, they did not view data as measures generated in order to understand a phenomenon or make a judgement (e.g. the points that a player scores in a series of basketball games as a measure of his skill at the game). The students were manipulating numbers that were divorced from the situation in which they had meaning. Further, when the students compared two data sets (e.g. the points scored by two basketball players in a series of games), they typically calculated the means irrespective of whether this would enable them to address the question or issue at hand.

We should stress that in interpreting these findings, we did not view ourselves as documenting a psychological stage in seventh graders' reasoning about data. Instead, we were documenting the consequences of the students' prior instruction in statistics. They had, for example, previously studied measures of centre (i.e. mean, mode and median) as well as several types of statistical graphs (e.g. bar graphs, histograms and pie charts). Our assessments tell us something about not just the content but the quality of that prior instruction. They indicate, for example, that classroom activities had emphasized calculational procedures and conventions for drawing graphs. This view of the students' reasoning as situated with respect to prior instruction was useful in that it enabled us to clarify the starting points for the design experiment. For example, we concluded from the assessments that our immediate goal was not one of merely remediating certain competencies and skills. Instead, the challenge was to influence the students' beliefs about what it means to do statistics in school. In doing so, it would be essential that they actually begin to analyse data in order to address a significant question rather than simply manipulate numbers that have little significance.

The students' reasoning in these initial assessments contrasts sharply with the ways in which they analysed data at the end of the ten-week experiment. As an illustration, in one instructional activity the students compared two treatment protocols for AIDS patients by analysing the T-cell counts of people who had enrolled in one of the two protocols. Their task was to assess

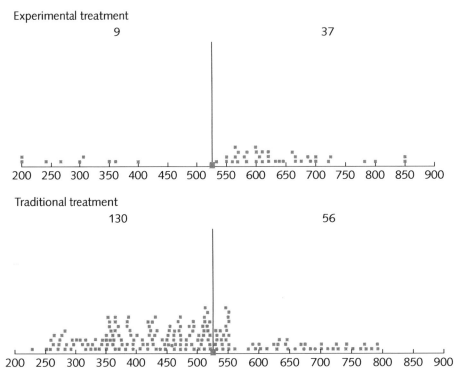

Figure 12.1   The AIDS protocol data partitioned at T-cell counts of 525.

whether a new experimental protocol in which 46 people had enrolled was more successful in raising T-cell counts than a standard protocol in which 186 people had enrolled. The data the students analysed are shown in figure 12.1 as they were displayed in the second of two computer-based minitools that they used.

All 29 students in the class concluded from their analyses that the experimental treatment protocol was more effective. Nonetheless, the subsequent whole-class discussion lasted for over an hour, during which the focus was on both the adequacy of the reports the students had written for a chief medical officer and the soundness of their arguments. For example, one group of students had partitioned the two data sets at T-cell counts of 525 by using one of the options on the minitool, as shown in figure 12.1. In the course of the discussion it became clear that their choice of 525 was not arbitrary. Instead, they had observed that what they referred to as the 'hill' in the experimental treatment data was above 525, whereas the 'hill' in the standard treatment data was below 525. In other words, they had partitioned the data in this way in order to quantify a pattern in the data.

This analysis was one of the most elementary that the students produced. Another group had used a second option on the computer minitool to partition the two data sets into four groups of equal size, as shown in figure 12.2.

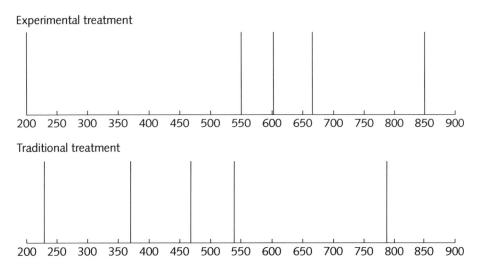

Figure 12.2 The AIDS protocol data organized into four equal groups with the individual data points hidden.

In this option, 25 per cent of the data in each data set are located in each of the four intervals bounded by the vertical bars. As one student explained, these graphs show that the experimental treatment is more effective because the T-cell counts of 75 per cent of the patients in this treatment were in approximately the same interval as the T-cell counts of only 25 per cent of the patients who had enrolled in the standard treatment. This student, like many who contributed to the discussion, was clearly reasoning about the data rather than attempting to recall procedures for manipulating numerical values.

As we have reported elsewhere, we also conducted individual interviews with the students at the end of the experiment (Cobb, 1999; McClain, Cobb and Gravemeijer, in press). The analysis of these interviews corroborates our classroom observations and indicates that a significant majority of the students came to reason about data in relatively sophisticated ways. It is also worth noting that the next school year, when we conducted a follow-up design experiment focusing on statistical covariation with some of the same students, there had been no regression in the students' reasoning about data during the nine-month gap between the two experiments (Cobb, McClain and Gravemeijer, 2000).

This overview gives some indication of how the students' reasoning about data changed during the ten-week experiment. We now turn our attention to the process of that change and the means by which it was supported and organized.

Instructional Tasks

In preparing for the design experiment we took account of the recent profound changes in the discipline of statistics. Statisticians now use computer-based analysis tools to search for trends and patterns in data in a post hoc manner that had previously been considered illegitimate (Cobb, G., 1997). This process of 'data snooping' or 'exploratory data analysis' (EDA) complements traditional computational methods with new techniques that involve creating and manipulating graphical representations of data (Moore, 1996). Biehler and Steinbring (1991) use the metaphor of detective work to characterize EDA in that the purpose is to search for evidence, whereas traditional methods of statistical inference play the role of the jury that decides on the basis of evidence. As they make clear, this exploratory orientation is central to data analysis and constitutes an important instructional goal in its own right. From this, we concluded that it would be essential for students' activity in the design experiment classroom to be imbued with the spirit of genuine data analysis from the outset. This in turn implied that the instructional tasks should all involve analysing realistic data sets for a purpose that the students deemed reasonable. As a consequence, the tasks we developed involved analysing either (1) a single data set in order to understand a phenomenon, or (2) comparing two data sets in order to make a decision or judgement. The example of the two AIDS treatment protocols illustrates the second of the two types of instructional tasks.

Our concern that the students' activity should involve a genuine spirit of data analysis highlights the importance that CHAT gives to the overall goal or motive of an activity (cf. Leont'ev, 1978). Our motive for searching for trends and patterns in data had concrete implications for our instructional design. It is also worth noting that the changes we discussed in statistics as a discipline illustrate a second basic tenet of CHAT, namely that the use of new tools does not merely amplify an activity by making it more efficient but can change the very nature of the activity. It was only as desktop computers became commonplace that the general approach of EDA originally proposed by Tukey (1977) became feasible and in turn led to the further development of data analysis methods. In this case, the changes were in the activities of an entire disciplinary community. As we will see, this tenet of CHAT also has implications for instructional design in which the goal is to support and organize changes in the activities of classroom communities.

The Classroom Activity Structure

Our concern that students should be involved in analysing data rather than merely manipulating numbers led to the development of an approach in which the teacher talked through the data generation process with the students. These conversations often involved protracted discussions during which the teacher and students together framed the particular phenomenon under investigation (e.g. AIDS), clarified its significance (e.g. the importance of developing more effective treatments), delineated relevant aspects of the situation that should be measured (e.g. T-cell counts) and considered how they might be measured (e.g. taking blood samples). The teacher then introduced the data the students were to analyse as being produced by this process. The resulting structure of classroom activities, which often spanned two or more class sessions, was therefore (1) a whole-class discussion of the data creation process, (2) individual or small-group activity in which the students worked at computers to analyse data, and (3) a whole-class discussion of the students' analyses.

We conjectured that, as a consequence of participating in discussions of the data creation process, the data would come to have greater meaning for the students in terms of the interests and purposes for which it was generated (cf. Latour, 1987; Lehrer and Romberg, 1996; Roth, 1997). This conjecture proved to be well founded. For example, we have clear indications that, within a week of the beginning of the design experiment, doing statistics in the project classroom actually involved analysing data (Cobb, 1999; McClain, Cobb and Gravemeijer, in press). In addition, as the experiment progressed, there was a progressive handover of responsibility from the teacher to the students (Tzou, 2000). Initially, the teacher had to take an extremely proactive role in the discussions. However, later in the experiment the students increasingly raised their own concerns about, for example, the need to control extraneous variables and about sampling methods. These contributions suggest that most if not all the students had developed some awareness that the legitimacy of the conclusions drawn from data depends crucially on the data generation process (cf. G. Cobb and Moore, 1997).

We should stress that the teacher did not attempt to teach the students how to generate sound data directly. Instead, she subtly guided the emergence of a classroom culture in which a premium was placed on the development of data-based arguments. It was against this background that the students gradually became able to anticipate the implications of the data generation process for the conclusions that they would be able to draw from data. Thus, in line with the basic tenets of CHAT, the teacher's orchestration of conversations about the data generation process was the primary means by which she supported this learning.

Tool Use

As we have noted, the use of computer-based tools to create and manipulate graphical representations of data is central to EDA. In the teaching experiment the students used two computer minitools that were explicitly designed as means of supporting the development of their reasoning. We conjectured that, as the students used these minitools, they would come to reason about data in increasingly sophisticated ways. We described the second of these tools when we discussed students' analyses of the AIDS treatment data. The interface for the first minitool is shown in figure 12.3.

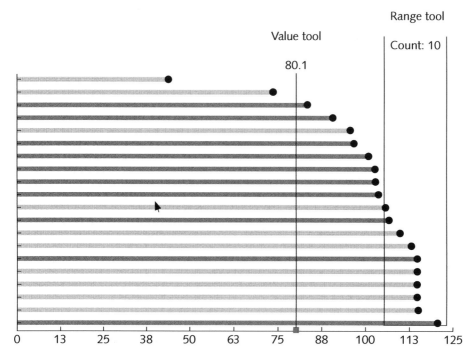

Figure 12.3 The first computer minitool.

This minitool enabled the students to order, partition and otherwise organize sets of up to 40 data points in a relatively immediate way. When data are entered each individual data point is inscribed as a horizontal bar. The students could select the colour of each bar to be either pink or green, thus enabling them to enter and compare two data sets. In addition, they could sort the data both by size and colour. Our choice of this relatively elementary way of inscribing individual data values reflected our goal of ensuring the students were actually analysing data. To this end, the initial data sets the students analysed were also selected so that the measurements made when generating the data had a sense of linearity and thus lent themselves to being inscribed as horizontal bars. For example, figure 12.3 shows data that were generated to compare how long two different brands of batteries last. Each bar shows a single case. In this instance, the case is the life span of one of the ten batteries of each brand that was tested. The students' task was to assess the relative merits of the two brands. As we have indicated, the choice of this inscription together with the approach of talking through the data creation process proved to be effective in that the students began to actually reason about data shortly after this minitool was introduced.

In addition to the options we have described thus far, the students used what they called the value tool to find the value of any data point by dragging a vertical red bar along the horizontal axis as shown in figure 12.3.

Further, they could find the number of data points in any horizontal interval by using what they called the range tool. Our intent in developing the value tool was to provide the students with a way of 'eyeballing' the centre or balance point of a set of data points. However, the students used it to partition data sets and to find the value of specific data points. In the case of the range tool our intent was to provide the students with a means of investigating the 'spreadoutness' of data sets. Although the students used the range tool in this way to some extent, they also used it to isolate the data points within a particular interval. As the students used these two options, they began to reason about (1) the range, and maximum and minimum values of data sets, (2) the number of data points above or below a particular value or within a specified interval, and (3) the median and its relation to the mean. Against this background, the teacher introduced the second minitool in which data points were inscribed as dots in an axis plot (see figure 12.1).

Our intention in designing the second minitool was to build on the ways of reasoning about data that the students had developed as they used the first minitool. For example, the dots at the end of the bars in the first minitool have, in effect, been collapsed down onto the axis in the second minitool. In fact, the teacher introduced this new way of inscribing data by first showing a data set inscribed as horizontal bars, then removing the bars to leave only the dots, and finally transposing the dots onto the horizontal axis. As we had hoped, the students were able to use the second minitool to analyse data almost immediately, and it was apparent that the axis plot inscription signi-fied a set of data values rather than merely a collection of numbers marked on a line. In our view, this development cannot be explained solely in terms of the teacher's careful introduction of the new minitool. Instead, we have to consider what the students learned as they used the first minitool.

We can tease out this learning by focusing on the students' reasoning as they compared data sets in terms of the number of data points either within a particular interval or above or below a particular value. In the case of the battery data, for example, the first student who explained her reasoning said that she had focused on the ten highest data values (i.e. those bounded by the range tool in figure 12.3). She went on to note that seven of the ten longest-lasting batteries were of one brand and concluded that this brand was better. Assisted by the teacher, another student challenged her argument by observ-ing that the next four longest-lasting batteries were of the other brand and that if they were included, there would be seven batteries of each brand. The next student to explain his analysis said that he had partitioned the data at 80 hours as shown by the value tool in figure 12.3. He then argued that some of the batteries of one brand were below 80 hours, whereas all those of the other brand lasted more than 80 hours. He judged this latter brand to be superior because, as he put it, he wanted a consistent battery.

The crucial point to note is that, in making these arguments, the students were focusing on the location of the dots at the end of the bars with respect to the axis. In other words, a subtle but important shift occurred as the students used the first minitool. Originally, the individual data values were represented by the lengths of the bars. However, in the very process of using the minitool, these values came to be signified by the endpoints of the bars. As a consequence, the students could readily understand the teacher's explanation when she introduced the second minitool by collapsing dots down onto the axis. Further, as the options in this new minitool involved partitioning data sets in various ways, students could use it immediately because they had routinely partitioned data sets when they used range and value options on the first minitool.

It is almost impossible to deduce this significant step in the students' learning by inspecting the physical characteristics of the first minitool. As a basic design principle, we do not in fact attempt to build the mathematics we want students to learn into tools and then hope that they might somehow come to see it in some mysterious and unexplained way. Instead, when designing tools, we focus squarely on how students might actually use the tools and what they might learn as they do so. This emphasis on the nature of students' activity with tools rather than on the tools in and of themselves is entirely consistent with CHAT. The contention that the tools students use profoundly influence not only the process of their learning but also its product and the types of reasoning that they develop is not merely a theoretical commitment for us. Instead, it is a basic feature of the world in which we work as we attempt to support students' mathematical learning in classrooms. As we have illustrated, students' use of the tools we develop is a primary means of supporting their development along learning trajectories that aim at significant mathematical ideas. In the case of the statistics design experiment, the significant idea that emerged as the students used the second minitool was that of data sets as distributions (Cobb, 1999; McClain, Cobb and Gravemeijer, in press). Had the design of the two minitools been substantially different, it is doubtful that this idea would have become routine in the project classroom.

Classroom Discourse

The most important feature of the classroom environment, which we have overlooked to this point, concerns the classroom discourse – the ways in which the teacher and students talked about data. As several chapters in this volume focus on aspects of classroom discourse that span a range of content areas, we will restrict our focus to two characteristics that relate specifically to mathematical learning. The first of these concerns the norms or standards for what counts as an acceptable mathematical explanation, while the second deals more directly with what might be termed the content of whole-class discussions.

Earlier, we noted that the overall motive for doing statistics in the project classroom was to identify trends and patterns in data. However, explanations in which students indicated such a pattern were not necessarily treated as legitimate. We can illustrate this point by returning to the students' analyses of the battery data. Recall that the first student who explained her reasoning argued that one of the brands was better because seven of the ten longest-lasting batteries were of that brand. During the ensuing discussion, it became apparent that her decision to focus on the ten rather than, say, the twelve longest-lasting batteries was relatively arbitrary. In contrast, the next student who presented an analysis explained that he had partitioned the data at 80 hours because he wanted a consistent battery that lasted at least 80 hours. In doing so, he clarified why the way in which he had organized the data was relevant with respect to the question at hand – that of deciding which of the two brands was superior.

As the classroom discussion continued, the obligation to give a justification of this type became increasingly explicit. For example, a third student compared the two analyses by commenting that, although seven of the ten longest-lasting batteries were of one brand, the two lowest batteries were also of that brand and 'if you were using the batteries for something important, you could end up with one of those bad batteries'. As a consequence of exchanges such as this, the teacher and students established relatively early in the design experiment that to be acceptable, an argument had to justify why the way in which the data had been structured was relevant to the question under investigation. In the process, the students were inducted into an important disciplinary norm, namely that the appropriateness of the statistics used when conducting an analysis has to be justified with respect to the question at hand.

In switching our focus now from the general characteristics of mathematical explanations to the specific content of what the teacher and students talked about, it is helpful if we outline the approach we took when planning for the whole-class discussions. Typically, while the students were analysing data at the computers, the teacher and a second member of the research team circulated around the classroom to gain a sense of the various ways in which the students were organizing and reasoning about the data. Towards the end of the small-group work, they then conferred briefly to develop conjectures about mathematically significant issues that might emerge as topics of conversation in the subsequent whole-class discussion. Their intent was to capitalize on the students' reasoning by identifying data analyses that, when compared and contrasted, might give rise to substantive mathematical conversations. In the discussion of the battery data, for example, the issue of justifying the way in which the data had been structured emerged from the contrast between the two analyses. In the case of the AIDS data, a sequence of four analyses was selected so that the issue of reasoning about data multiplicatively rather than additively came to the fore.

This opportunistic approach to instructional planning clearly takes account of the diversity in students' reasoning. However, it should also be apparent that our intent in including whole-class discussions in the classroom activity structure was not simply to provide the students with an occasion to share their reasoning. Instead, our overriding concern was with the quality of discussions as social events in which the students participated. In our view, the value of such discussion is open to question unless mathematically significant issues that advance the instructional agenda become explicit topics of conversation. Conversely, students' participation in substantive discussions can serve as primary means of supporting their induction into the values, beliefs and ways of knowing of the discipline. In this regard, we find ourselves in full agreement with CHAT's emphasis on the nature of the cultures in which learning takes place. In our work as instructional designers our immediate focus is on the culture of the classroom, which encompasses general norms of participation, such as those for argumentation, as well as the specific mathematical issues that are judged to be worthy of serious discussion.

Democratic Participation and Equity

The primary function of formal schooling is (or should be) to prepare students for participation not just in classroom activities, but in out-of-school activities that are valued within our society. So we had to ask ourselves what was the real-world value of learning statistics. Mathematics educators typically give two general types of justification. The first appeals to the idea of students as apprentice research statisticians. A second type of justification refers to the increasingly prominent role of statistical reasoning in both work-related activities and informed citizenship, and sees students more as consumers of analysis techniques and arguments developed by others.

In contrast to these two common rationales, we find a third justification to be far more compelling. Briefly, the increasing use of computers, not just within the discipline but in society more broadly, has placed a higher premium on quantitative reasoning in general and on statistical reasoning in particular. There is, for example, much talk of preparing students for the 'information age', but without fully appreciating that the information in this new era is largely quantitative in nature. It is already apparent that many debates about public policy issues tend to involve reasoning with statistical data and that this discourse is increasingly becoming the language of power. Inability to participate in this discourse thus results in de facto disenfranchisement that can lead to alienation from, and cynicism about, the political process. Cast in these terms, statistical literacy that involves reasoning with data in relatively sophisticated ways bears directly on both equity and participatory democracy. On this view, the image that emerges is of students as potential participants in the discourse of public policy. The important competencies for this participation are those of developing and critiquing data-based arguments.

This image led us to make several significant design decisions. For example, we decided against an open-ended project approach in which students would investigate issues of personal interest by generating data themselves, and instead developed instructional activities in which the students analysed data sets created by others. Further, we developed a number of instructional activities in which the students were asked to write reports that had social policy implications (e.g. the analysis of the AIDS data). In addition to ensuring that the students were actually analysing data, the often lengthy discussions of the data generation process in fact served to cultivate the students' interest in issues of this type. Finally, the students engaged in the activities that we judged important, those of developing and critiquing data-based arguments, as they participated in the whole-class discussions.

In terms of the broader literature on equity, the approach we took to statistics instruction is compatible with Delpit's (1988) admonition that students should be systematically inducted into what she calls the culture of power. It also makes contact with Banks's (1995) equity pedagogy which aims to help students from diverse cultural backgrounds develop the ways of knowing needed to participate effectively within and maintain a just, demo-cratic society. We would therefore argue that instructional designs of the type that we have illustrated have the potential to contribute to the reconstruction of schools as institutions that redress rather than regenerate inequities.

Clearly, we have been concerned with what is traditionally termed the transfer of school learning to out-of-school settings. However, we did not frame the design challenge as that of ensuring that students first acquire relatively abstract knowledge and skills in school and then apply them in out-of-school situations. Instead, we focused on an out-of-school activity that we consider important, public policy discourse, and considered what might be involved in participating in it in a relatively substantial way. Rather than attempting to teach the students relatively decontextualized knowledge and skills, our primary concern was therefore to ensure that classroom learning situations were relatively congruent with important out-of-school experiences. We contend that such an approach is far more tenable than one that emphas-izes the transportation of abstract knowledge and skills to highly incongruent out-of-school situations.

Conclusion

In this chapter, having shown that our students' learning during the design experiment was reasonably impressive, we have teased out the various means by which that learning was supported and organized. Though we have dealt with these factors separately, they are in fact highly interrelated. For example, the instructional tasks – as they were actually realized in the class-room – depended on the overall motive for doing statistics (i.e. to identify patterns in data that are relevant to the question or issue at hand), the struc-ture of classroom activities (e.g. talking through the data creation process), the computer minitools that the students used to conduct their analyses, and the nature of the classroom discourse (e.g. engaging in discussion in which mathematically significant issues emerged as topics of conversation). Given these interdependencies, it is reasonable to view the various means of support we have discussed as constituting a single classroom activity system. The comprehensive nature of this system indicates that an approach to instructional design compatible with CHAT extends far beyond the traditional focus on curricular materials. It is designed to produce both the learning of significant ideas and the cultivation of the relevant dispositions.

As a final observation, we should clarify that, in addition to providing an orientation to instructional design, CHAT offers a perspective on classroom events that can inform the ongoing improvement of designs and, thus, teaching. We noted when giving an initial overview of the statistics design experiment that, in line with CHAT, we view students' reasoning as situated with respect to instruction. In taking this perspective, we see students' learning as intimately related to the means by which that learning was supported (i.e. the classroom activity system in which they participated). For our purposes as designers, this situated view is a strength rather than a weakness, in that it enables us to tease out aspects of the actual classroom environment that served to support and organize the students' learning. This in turn makes it possible for us to develop conjectures about how we might be able to improve those means of support and thus students' learning of significant ideas. We therefore contend that CHAT has much to offer if we want to move beyond the pendulum swings that have characterized educational reform throughout the twentieth century. The fundamental problem in our view is not so much with the current level of student achievement and the quality of teaching as it is that we do not have a systematic way of bringing about improvement (Stigler and Hiebert, 1999). CHAT makes it possible for reform to become an ongoing, iterative process of continual improvement. This, for us, is the most compelling reason why educators might want to explore the potential relevance of CHAT.

13

A Developmental Teaching Approach to Schooling

Seth Chaiklin

The institution of schooling, as currently practised in virtually all modern societies, aims ideologically to prepare children and young persons to better participate in and further develop the societal practices they will subsequently encounter. In this respect, the practice of education as a whole – at least for primary and secondary levels – is concerned with the development of the whole person, or what in this chapter will be called 'personality development'. However, the main substance of children's daily life in school is (and should be) work with subject-matter content. Classroom practices are organized largely to create conditions that enable children to work with subject-matter content. Therefore, to realize more general ends, like personality development, instructional practice must be based primarily on working with subject-matter content. This seemingly simple practical demand raises a serious problem for most existing theoretical approaches in psychology and education. It is rare to find a theory of subject-matter teaching and learning that also provides a conceptual analysis for how to organize specific instructional activities for supporting personality development.

Developmental teaching, with its cultural–historical focus on human development through participation in societal practices, provides a way to link more general societal goals with a concrete subject-matter instructional practice. This chapter aims to illustrate this idea by first sketching a cultural–historical approach toward analysing schooling, personality development and teaching/learning, and then presenting a detailed example of the essential role of subject-matter analysis in developing teaching interventions that contribute to personality development.

Thanks to Joachim Lompscher for many critical comments along the way.

Ideals of Schooling

Because the practice of schooling embodies a historically accumulated complex of cultural values and norms, we must look at the historical development of the institution of schooling as obligatory for all children as part of under-standing the relation of schooling to personality development.

Obligatory schooling was first created and maintained by European states in order to develop the personalities of children in relation to the state (e.g. Boli and Ramirez, 1992). That original nationalist interest is still evident in contemporary school systems. Other ideological demands can also influence schooling practices. The utilitarian, moral and liberal ideologies serve to focus thinking in certain directions, creating a climate in which teaching is conducted. Ideological interests – manifested in material demands such as desired levels of standardized test performance, literacy levels, technical competencies – often serve as powerful constraints on the range of permitted or imagined practices within governmentally supported (or regulated) schools.

Let us therefore take an imaginary step away from the historically estab-lished ideological values and consider a school whose primary motive is to help pupils realize their vocation as a person (i.e. humanization). This motive is not especially novel, nor unique to the cultural–historical approach. Many have expressed similar ideas, and in some cases have created educational practices that try to realize this ideal (e.g. Freinet, 1969; Freire, 1970). I suspect many school professionals would express a similar ideal as a personal value. And sometimes it can be found as an explicit part of official national policy (which is not always identical with a well-embedded societal practice). For example, the purpose of the comprehensive school (*folkeskolen*) according to current Danish law includes developing 'democratic, critical, independent-thinking citizens'. But how are these intentions to be made concrete through subject-matter teaching?

Personality Development and Schooling

The idea of personality development as found in the cultural–historical tradi-tion focuses on the development of motives in relation to societal practices (Leontiev, 1978; Chaiklin, 2001). Because motives are acquired through par-ticipation in societal practices, it is easy to see how and why formal schooling can be important for the development of motives, and hence of personality. The process of personality development gives a concrete psychological analysis for this humanization process. Personality is developed through the acquisition of psychological capabilities in relation to societally meaningful practices. These psychological functions are not developed in a general or abstract way, but only through working with specific substantive content – subject-matter content in the case of schooling. Therefore, subject-matter teaching that develops learning activity for specific contents is fundamental for the development of personality.

Of course it is also quite easy to work with subject-matter teaching in a way that does not develop psychological capabilities. For example, if children's requests for the reasons for learning a particular topic are met with a bland, half-hearted assertion of its future value, then no connection is made with their current interests and motivation. In such a situation, they may conclude that learning without personal purposes is acceptable, maybe even desirable. Learning that takes place under these conditions may result in the accumulation of knowledge, but it is unlikely to contribute to humanization.

Developmental Teaching

The term 'developmental teaching' reflects the essential theoretical proposition, formulated by Vygotsky (1987, pp. 210–11), that teaching should take a leading role in relation to mental development. The practice of developmental teaching is organized around the idea of theoretical thinking. To think theoretically is to understand the general relations manifest in the surface appearance of a phenomenon. Modelling is used as a way to think theoretically. The initial, primary relations in a model are used to organize investigations of the development and transformation of these abstract relations in concrete forms (Davydov, 1990, ch. 7; Stetsenko and Arievitch, this volume). For example, in analysing sociological conditions of community development, some primary relations are family structure, means of production and local living conditions. With these general relations one can then start to model concrete surface appearances, such as life in Puerto Rico and New York City at the beginning and the end of the twentieth century. Such relations were used as the basis for a teaching experiment in an after-school programme in East Harlem, New York (Hedegaard, Chaiklin and Pedraza, in press).

The knowing process involves formulating, investigating and reflecting about models. Teaching involves creating opportunities for pupils to investigate problems that enable them to develop a theoretical relation to specific subject matter. In this respect, developmental teaching is like other problem-based approaches to instruction, and its classroom activities are likely therefore to have similar appearances to such approaches. However, unlike most problem-based approaches, the developmental teaching approach selects problems for investigation based on its subject-matter analysis, and the specific teaching interactions are motivated by a focus on personality development (Davydov, 1988, pp. 17–19). Therefore, the ways in which classroom interactions are organised are likely to be different in ways that are not readily visible at a quick glance, but appear over a longer period.

In constructing concrete developmental teaching programmes many aspects are involved (beyond those that will be discussed here), including principles for organising classroom interactions that support intellectual development. For more extensive examples, see Aidarova (1982), Hedegaard (1988, 1990), Lompscher (1999) and Markova (1979).

Subject-Matter Analysis

The development of personality through schooling should be approached primarily through the organization and response to pupils' actions during subject-matter teaching. To elaborate this idea more concretely, I will first outline the general idea of subject-matter analysis and its relation to curriculum development, and then discuss an example of how subject-matter analysis was used in planning a unit of upper-secondary school physics teaching.

Subject-matter analysis is a general term that covers several different, but interrelated, rational analyses that teachers and/or curriculum designers should make in conceptualizing and implementing the subject matter, or 'content', of teaching. The main task and focus of subject-matter analysis is to identify the fundamental ideas that organize a subject-matter area, and the conceptual relationships between these ideas. The analyses can range from global principles – such as the role of communication in language or the importance of organism–environment relations in biology – to detailed analyses of specific necessary or essential relations, such as how verb tenses are used to communicate concisely about the temporal (and sometimes spatial) occurrence of events, or processes by which organisms develop protective colouration. What is more difficult to explain briefly is that the analyses should try to show the relations between the general and the specific – such as shown in the two previous examples. The ideal is to develop a 'kernel' model that integrates the various conceptual relations in a problem field. Such models must be worked out according to the current state of knowledge and conceptual logic found in a particular discipline. In other words, there are no predefined templates. However, in the developmental teaching tradition, one tries to draw upon the conceptual resources found in dialectical logic when constructing these analyses (e.g. Ilyenkov, 1977).

Curriculum development – the systematic description of the topical knowledge and skills to be acquired from teaching – should be carried out in coordination with subject-matter analysis. In principle, many of the tasks of curriculum development – such as considerations of what disciplines should be included in a school programme and what topics should be taught for the selected disciplines – cannot be done without at least an informal or superficial subject-matter analysis. Therefore, it is not surprising if some overlap appears between curriculum development and subject-matter analysis. Ideally, one would want curricular decisions to be based on a more systematic consideration of subject-matter knowledge and its relations to societal practices. These considerations are instances of subject-matter analysis.

In practice, most global curricular questions are already decided and institutionalized in various ways through such instruments as national curriculum plans, examination demands, and textbooks – seemingly beyond the grasp of classroom teachers. From that perspective, it would seem that subject-matter analysis is merely another tool for realizing predefined institutional goals, which in practice are often skewed toward specific kinds of reproductive and problem-solving performance. However, let us retain a focus on the idea that subject-matter instruction should contribute to humanization, through personality development, and consider how it could be used to work toward those ends.

Teaching should aim to develop understanding of the central topics in a problem area. This is one aspect of giving pupils tools needed to participate in societal practices. Other important and integral aspects are to develop an interest among pupils for wanting to acquire this knowledge, and an interest to use this knowledge actively while participating in those practices. Subject-matter analysis is important for achieving these goals. By using subject-matter analysis, teachers and/or instructional designers can organize teaching activities in the classroom to create conditions for pupils to embody the conceptual relations identified in the subject-matter analysis, and to appreciate the conceptual problems of the discipline. In developmental teaching such analyses are used during the planning process, both prior to the school year when teachers are selecting and structuring topics, and during the actual teaching when they need to prepare the next day's classroom activity in response to an unexpected question or problem that the pupils have brought forward.

An Example of Subject-Matter Analysis

I will describe a 45-minute classroom session from a six-week developmental teaching experiment that I conducted with Niels-Henrik Würtz in his physics class in a Danish upper-secondary school (gymnasium). By choosing to describe a single classroom session I have tried to give some feeling for the general organization of subject-matter teaching in the developmental teaching tradition. In the present case I will try to show how a focus on subject-matter analysis can help to organize instructional activities that support personality development through subject-matter learning. Although the principles that organize the teaching may be different, the observable classroom practices may often appear, on the surface, to be familiar or unexceptional. Thus, in evaluating this teaching approach, one cannot only consider the overt organization of classroom activities, but must also consider the instructional goals and how the teaching activities are organized to realize these goals.

In this example, the class was learning Newtonian mechanics, as specified in the national curriculum outline. Some of the more general goals of this curriculum include achieving insight into (a) physics as a means to understanding the world around one, (b) a natural scientific way of thinking, and (c) the world image of physics. From this perspective, the way in which one develops knowledge about Newtonian mechanics may be more important than the problem-solving ability itself. However, pupils can only appreciate the methods by which these ideas are developed by entering into and reflecting upon an investigation of the concrete problems that Newtonian mechanics are designed to handle.

Subject-matter analysis, in which one identifies the essential conceptual relationships in the subject matter, is a necessary part of realizing these goals. Without such an analysis the teacher is left having to assert conceptual relationships to pupils without being able to justify them in action. With such an analysis one can plan a structure of teaching activities that can in fact embody general goals for physics instruction, because the focus shifts from the teacher transmitting the results of scientific thought to having the pupils encounter the kinds of problems that gave rise to this thought. With assistance from the teacher, pupils can then work to build up their understanding of the conceptual system used to handle such problems, which in turn contributes to developing new motives in relation to physics in particular and knowledge in general. These are aspects of personality development.

To appreciate the example presented here, it is necessary to explicate some details of the subject-matter analysis. The general problem in Newtonian mechanics is to describe and explain motion. More precisely, the main interest is not in motion in general, but in 'displacement' (i.e. the translation from one spatial position to another). Newton's analysis assumes that displacing bodies are homogeneous. The homogeneity assumption is useful because we can ignore the physical shape of an object, and treat it as though its mass was concentrated in a single point. (Violations of this assumption, e.g. a can of vegetable soup rolling down a slope, require additional conceptual analyses in physics and additional subject-matter analysis for planning instructional activities.)

The traditional way to describe displacement of a single point is with a graph. Graphical representations of displacement have the important property that they describe the exact position of an object at any moment of time. This is impossible to do with verbal descriptions, because we cannot describe the infinite number of positions that an object occupies while it displaces. If an object displaces the same distance for the same unit of time, without changing direction, then we say that the object has 'constant velocity'. Figure 13.1 shows a graph of two different constant velocities for one-dimensional motion. The straight line reflects the fact that the same distance is traversed for each unit of time. The steeper line indicates that more distance (25 m) is traversed in the same unit (5 sec) of time compared to the less steep line (10 m in 5 sec).

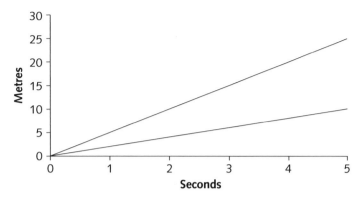

Figure 13.1   Two graphs of position × time, each with constant velocity, but with different speed.

Given that the lines in the graph represent constant velocities, we can now ask what has to happen physically so that the steepness of a given line changes? To explain changes in steepness a concept of force is needed. That is, the concept of force in Newton's analysis is used to explain *changes* in the distance that an object displaces for a given time unit (as opposed to explaining the motion itself). (Force is also used to explain changes of direction, but this aspect is not involved in the example presented here.) Most pupils come to introductory physics instruction with an idea that force must be the cause of motion. It is therefore difficult for them to acquire the Newtonian conception of force as a cause of changes in an object's rate of displacement.

This (partial) analysis of the subject matter enables us to see that as part of the psychological process of understanding the necessity of Newton's concept of force, pupils must understand why graphs are needed to describe motion, and have a concrete understanding of the relation between the physical phenomenon and the position–time graph used to describe it.

In planning the teaching, one must also consider the pupils' background knowledge and capabilities. The subject-matter analysis only identifies the conceptual relations, not the pupils' relations to this content. If the teaching is going to be developmental, then it has to be related to their current capabilities. In the example, the pupils are 17–18 years old and in their second year of the mathematics line in the gymnasium. They already know procedures for producing and interpreting graphs with two continuous variables. Presumably, if requested, they could produce graphs to describe displacement. Therefore, the pedagogical interests are to develop the pupils' awareness of why it is necessary to use a graph, to reflect about the advantages and disadvantages, and to clarify the relationship between the graph and the physical phenomena (remember the homogeneity assumption). These developments will require that the pupils encounter and investigate a genuine problem whose solution provides an opportunity to develop their understanding. These specifications motivate the instructional planner to search for a problem that can only (or best) be solved by creating a graphical description of motion because such a problem helps to motivate the necessity and significance of the graph.

The teaching experiment started with the teacher giving the following problem to the pupils: can you describe a movement so that others can reproduce the same movement exactly without having seen the original movement? This simple (and intentionally vague) problem does not specify what kind of movement. More importantly, regardless of how the pupils interpret the problem, it cannot be solved without using a graph to describe position and time. As a simple illustration, move your finger from left to right. Can you describe, verbally, how fast your finger moved?

The class had been working for two weeks with this problem prior to the classroom session to be described here. The pupils had come up with the idea that studying a motion in one dimension might solve the problem. Unlike typical teaching approaches – where pupils object to the seeming artificiality and irrelevance of one-dimensional motion – this class was actually grateful and excited about the idea of working with one-dimensional motion, because they saw the possibility of being able to solve the original problem.

A classroom session

At the beginning of the session three pupils are standing in front of the class, giving a detailed summary of what the class had been working on in the previous class session. They explain that the class had been looking for what they had designated a 'simple movement' – as simple as possible – and that they had decided that it must be one-dimensional motion. They had also discussed relations between speed and motion, and decided that motion (i.e. the path that is followed) was the same regardless of speed. Finally, the class had decided that they wanted to do an experiment in which they would drop a weight attached to a strip of paper which could be marked with a spark timer (thereby registering position over time). This would be a way to describe a simple movement.

The teacher asks the class what requirement they should have for the description they will make (from the results of their experiment). One boy says 'describe the movement from the first point'. Another says 'describe movement'. The teacher reiterates the question that there should be a requirement. No one volunteers an idea. The teacher writes on the blackboard: 'the point's movement', and then underneath 'position and time'. At this moment, a pupil raises his hand. The teacher asks if he has something to add. The pupil says that his idea was the same as the teacher had written on the blackboard. The teacher asks the pupils what they should concentrate on (when they conduct the experiment). One pupil says 'simple movement'. Another says 'something with speed'. A third says 'position and time'. The teacher then asks what position and time mean in practice, and the third pupil says 'the same as average speed'. The teacher does not challenge this incorrect answer, but suggests that this is what should be investigated.

Within eight minutes after the start of the class the pupils have started to work on the experiment. The teacher provides all the equipment, but gives no instructions about how to use it or what to use it for. The pupils start working without any further discussion in the class, and organize themselves into work groups (one group of four, one group of five and one group of six, which was actually two groups working together to collect data) without any intervention from the teacher. All the pupils participate in conducting the experiments, or observe attentively. When technical problems arise in using the equipment, all the pupils in the work group seem to be involved in discussing and resolving the problems. Once the pupils had collected their data (i.e. the long strips of paper with marks on them), they start to measure between the marks, again without any class discussion or instructions from the teacher. Some groups measure the distance between every point, other groups measured distances between every five or ten points.

With three minutes left in the class period, the teacher interrupts and asks one of the groups to make a summary of what the class had done today. The girl who summarizes starts by referring to the summary given at the beginning of the class session, noting that the idea was to do this exercise as discussed in the previous class session. She then attempts to explain what they were trying to find out, saying: 'It comes from the movement position, from where it starts. I can't remember what we should do.' The teacher asks her and the class, 'What should we say?' One boy says 'position and time' and the summarizer says 'Oh, we should find speed from position and time'. 'Others?' the teacher asks. Another girl says, 'It was not speed, we should find out if speed has something to do with movement'. 'What are we trying to produce here?' the teacher asks. At first, no one from the class can answer the question, but then one person says that they should describe movement in relation to position. The teacher says 'Next time we should see if we have all made the same description. It should be interesting because we have all looked at the same movement.'

Interpretation of the example

In the example presented here the class, not the teacher, had proposed the experiment of measuring the movement of a falling object. Apparently some of the pupils had done this experiment three or four years ago in comprehensive school. They proposed this idea as a way to realize their idea of describing motion in one dimension, and thereby solve the original problem that had initiated the investigation. The pupils were interested and engaged in the work they were doing. This could be seen from the fact that they were able to organize work groups, conduct the experiment and analyse the results without intervention from the teacher, and all were engaged in the process, even if only one or two could physically manipulate the equipment or make the measurements. These characteristics of the pupils' work in this specific case cannot be explained as reflecting some general capabilities or orientation of Danish upper-secondary pupils in general, or of these pupils in particular. Rather, these characteristics indicate that the pupils understand what they are trying to find out and that they are motivated to do it.

But what was so special about the subject-matter content in this example? It appears as though the pupils are doing a traditional experiment, and the class organization seems to reflect well-known 'learning by discovery' traditions. However, the familiar surface appearance of the example becomes much more complicated once we examine the underlying subject-matter relations that organized the tasks and questions that brought the class investigation to this point. With an understanding of the necessary relationships in the subject matter, it is easier for teachers (or instructional designers) to create problems and situations that require pupils to confront the essential relationships that organize a subject matter, which in turn can be used to create a dynamic in the class that serves to develop certain intellectual characteristics and thereby contribute to personality development.

The learning and teaching situation described here was organized by a genuine problem, which after two weeks had still not been solved. This difficulty was motivating for the pupils, perhaps because it was so difficult to solve what appeared initially to be a trivial problem. The pupils are interested in solving the problem as indicated by the fact that they formulated and conducted the experiment described here without any suggestion or advice from the teacher. In terms of personality development, the pupils are learning that (a) their school knowledge can be used to investigate meaningful problems, and (b) they can formulate applications themselves. Of course, this is not learned from this single experience, but if disciplinary work in school is consistently directed to the investigation of meaningful problems, and pupils have the possibility to develop an understanding of the problem as meaningful (i.e. not simply invented and imposed arbitrarily by the teacher), then it is possible for them to develop these motives. In turn, if pupils start to recognize that they can use their knowledge to solve genuine problems, it is more likely that they will be interested to further develop their knowledge and ability to control their actions in the problem field. The development of this interest is one of the main general goals of schooling, as discussed previously.

By the time the pupils are finished with this problem, they have a theoretically concrete understanding of the relationship between a graph of displacement and the physical phenomenon it describes. Or at least they think they do. The teacher now asks them where the observer is in relation to the graph. This creates real panic in the class. They had struggled for three weeks to solve the original problem, and it looks as though their hard-won solution is in danger. The question – which was motivated by another part of the subject-matter analysis – was not designed, however, to create panic, but rather to introduce the idea of 'frame of reference'. (Curiously, frame of reference is not usually discussed in introductory textbooks in connection with force, although it is necessary in order to understand the necessity of the concept.) The teacher's question does not need to be explained. The pupils can see their solution has not considered this aspect, and they are motivated to find a solution.

The teacher's question has created a zone of proximal development for the class by pinpointing a problem that is slightly beyond what they currently understand, yet that can be handled by building on their existing knowledge. This serves to initiate a new round of investigations that will elaborate the class's understanding of the description of motion in a way needed for understanding the necessity of the concept of force. The formulation of this question was possible because the subject-matter analysis gave the teacher (or planner) insight into the next conceptual step in the subject matter, which was used to generate a task that maintained a dynamic tension between the pupils' capabilities and the demands in the subject matter. In practice, this tension often serves to make the pupils motivated and interested in the work.

Questions and Implications Arising from the Example

Perhaps it seems that this teaching approach takes a long time. After all, it took three weeks just to get to the idea of a graph in one dimension. At that rate, it would seem difficult to teach much subject-matter content. In practice, at the beginning of a teaching unit, a developmental teaching approach often moves more slowly than do traditional teaching methods, in terms of the amount of subject-matter content investigated. What cannot be readily seen is that this phase is used for helping the pupils form an understanding of the problem field. In our experience, the amount of material handled increases as the pupils get further into the investigation of a problem. In this particular case, after the pupils started to control description of motion in one dimension, they asked how to handle two- and three-dimensional movement (normally never addressed in introductory physics teaching). It took about 30 minutes in a class discussion for the pupils, with a little support from the teacher, to formulate the technique for describing this motion, which they subsequently used in their further investigations of movement. This increased learning rate comes about because (a) the teaching problems and approach enable the pupils to keep their focus on the central themes identified in the subject-matter analysis, and (b) the pupils are acquiring conceptual tools that are relevant for describing and analysing problems in the subject-matter area. More importantly, by responding to their request, the teacher supports the pupils in learning to trust and use their conceptual knowledge to investigate genuine problems.

If pupils are allowed to freely investigate a problem, then how can the teacher control what they will discover, or whether they will cover the 'right' topics? There are two answers to this question. First, if teachers have a good subject-matter analysis, and have formulated a problem for investigation that grows out of this analysis, then they can be reasonably certain that the class will unavoidably meet many of the topics that might be on an 'official' curriculum list. From this point of view, there is not a 'fixed' amount of material to be covered, but an interest in building up a working understanding of the conceptual relations that organize a subject-matter field. Second, in a cultural–historical perspective, one is interested in evaluating not only what pupils can produce or perform, but also the pupils' self-evaluation of the products of their work, and their self-critique of what needs to be further investigated or developed. These capabilities are developed in the investigations and not from the content alone.

The ability to make good self-evaluations is an example of learning to control one's actions, and awareness of this capability contributes to developing a positive personal sense for working with the subject matter. Both these qualities are aspects of personality development. To encourage this kind of reflective understanding, a simple technique is often used in which each class session starts and finishes with a brief reflection by one or more of the pupils about what the class is trying to accomplish or has accomplished. These short reflections, which may appear to be insignificant and unnecessary, are an important part of the process of helping the pupils become conscious of the knowledge they are acquiring and what it can be used for. The non-triviality of reflection can be seen in the classroom session described above, where the pupils had trouble formulating why they were doing the experiment and what they were trying to find out – even though they were the ones who initiated the idea! When pupils are given the opportunity to engage in these reflections, they often become much more deeply engaged in the material, focusing on its underlying significance and meaning (Chaiklin, 1999). If pupils can identify the strengths and weaknesses in their work, then they are in a better position to identify the knowledge they really need, and to be motivated to acquire what is necessary.

More General Questions and Comments about Subject-Matter Analysis

The example of subject-matter analysis presented here comes from natural-science teaching. However, it is possible to make subject-matter analyses for all subject-matter areas and at all levels of instruction, because it is always possible to take a theoretical approach to a content domain. One of the editors of this volume challenged me to give an example from a different subject domain, such as teaching Shakespeare's *Hamlet*. First, one would have to consider that *Hamlet* is only a surface appearance, a concrete instance of many different universal (or general) relations. Thus subject-matter analysis would have to begin by asking: are we studying *Hamlet* to better understand the historical period during which it was produced? Or for the dramatic techniques being used? Or for relations between fathers and sons? Or for the poetic structure of its language? The specific focus in instruction depends on what conceptual relationships one is forming and investigating, where, in each case, one is seeking to understand the general relationships in the problem field being studied. The particular object *Hamlet* would be a concrete example of those relations.

This preliminary analysis of *Hamlet* helps to see that subject-matter analysis is a difficult, time-consuming process because it requires that one must work through the surface forms. Subject-matter experts are not used to thinking didactically about their subject matter in this relational way. This was illustrated before in the case of 'frame of reference'. Within the developmental teaching tradition, several analyses are available. Davydov (1975) produced one for early arithmetic (presumably inspired by the analysis used by his teacher Gal'perin in laboratory experiments with Georgiev: see Stetsenko and Arievitch, this volume). Markova (1979) and Aidarova (1982) have analysed mother-tongue language learning (also see Stetsenko and Arievitch's description of Kabanova's work). Hedegaard (1996) made one for evolution, and another for describing the historical development of human societies (1988). Van Aalsvoort (2000), working in the cultural–historical tradition, has made an interesting analysis of the relation between chemistry and societal practices.

However, for the most part, these analyses have not been made before. It often means that one must reconstruct the conceptual relations of the subject matter for oneself; it is not simply a matter of looking up what topics are offered in a textbook. Even where subject-matter analyses do exist, it is still important for teachers to have actively constructed (or reconstructed) the analysis for themselves.

This chapter has introduced the idea of developmental teaching as an approach to subject-matter teaching, where subject-matter learning should be understood as part of a process of humanization. In developmental teaching situations, teachers need to be actively participating with pupils in investigating problems. In genuine investigations one cannot usually anticipate all the questions and problems that will arise, even if one has previously taught the same subject matter. In principle, if essential relations have been truly identified in a subject-matter analysis, then a teacher (or planner) should be able to accommodate the unanticipated problems that arise from investigating problems motivated by that analysis (which sometimes may involve the extension or elaboration of the model). If the teacher does not have a working understanding of the subject matter, and of the pedagogical goals to be realized through working with this subject-matter, then it is difficult to handle the modifications and improvisations that necessarily appear in genuine investigations, and still maintain a focus that contributes to pedagogical goals, such as personality development.

14

Standards for Pedagogy: Research, Theory and Practice

Stephanie Stoll Dalton and Roland G. Tharp

The dominant form of pedagogy in the classrooms of America, Japan and other industrialized countries continues to be whole-class instruction. The pervasive assumption is that knowledge is transmitted to students through direct instruction with occasional individual assistance. Students are seen as individuals, and the success or otherwise of learning as predominantly reflecting their individual attributes and talents. In contrast, the Cultural Historical Activity Theory (CHAT) of learning and development takes the view that knowledge emerges through social and cultural activity during community participation. To the focus on individual attributes this perspective adds an emphasis on the ways students' attributes play out in interaction and activity with others (Boaler, 1999; Tharp and Gallimore, 1988; Wells, 2000). This view of knowledge development demands a different pattern of classroom activity settings, a different vision.

The CHAT approach emphasizes that the learner's interaction with materials and activity occurs primarily in a social context of relationships. In fact, that social context is the major constituent of the activity itself. As people (adults and children) act and talk together, minds are under constant construction, particularly for the novice and the young. The social processes by which minds are formed must be understood as the very stuff of education. In teaching/learning interactions, development and learning proceed best when assistance is provided that permits a learner to perform at a level higher than would be possible alone. Vygotsky described this condition as a zone of proximal development, which is the 'distance between the actual developmental level as determined by individual problem solving and the level of potential development as determined through problem solving under adult guidance or in collaboration with more capable peers'. The proximal zone, then, is different from the 'developmental level' at which individual, unassisted performance is possible. Focusing on this proximal zone makes teaching and learning visible. 'We can therefore derive this general definition of teaching: Teaching consists of assisting performance through the [Zone of Proximal Development

(ZPD)]. Teaching can be said to occur when assistance is offered at points in the [zone] at which performance requires assistance' (Tharp and Gallimore, 1988).

There is a large body of research that, in our view, offers support and amplification of the CHAT perspective. Though sometimes couched in different terms, study, in particular of students who are at risk of educational failure, suggests that the social organization of classrooms is significantly implicated in their level of achievement. And the findings of this research turn out to be as relevant to the vast majority of students as they are to those on the educational margins. In our review of that literature, five main principles or 'standards' emerge, and these are key for quality teaching that activates dormant social contexts of classrooms for the benefit of all students' academic learning. The purpose of this chapter is to describe the five standards for effective pedagogy and provide examples of their implementation. Developed both empirically and from a CHAT perspective, these standards express criteria and crucial elements for the transformation of classrooms from the 'receptacle–recitation' model to that of the socially productive, actively engaged, dialogically based CHAT model. They focus on the teachers and students, their activities, language, beliefs, values and the ways these are applied in the learning situation to encourage students' knowledge generation within the community of learners (Boaler, 1999; Tharp, et al., 2000).

There is a remarkable consensus around these five statements, whether the original research that has produced them was guided by cognitive science, by critical theory, by atheoretical practical observations or by exemplary professional practice. We express the consensus findings in the language of CHAT, partly because that theoretical orientation has guided the majority of the research and development itself, but also because it offers an integrated and powerful explanation of the findings. In education it has often been assumed that knowledge stored in cultural artifacts can be grasped through reading and memory but, in a sociocultural view, the acquisition of cultural knowledge is more a matter of participation with others in activities that use knowledge and guidance from more expert others during learning (Wells, 1999). The constructs of CHAT are ideally suited for explaining and producing heuristics needed for the design and reform of pedagogy.

The five standards which we have identified are:

1   Joint Productive Activity (JPA): teachers and students producing together.
2   Developing Language and Literacy Across the Curriculum (LLD).
3   Making Meaning: connecting school to students' lives (MM).
4   Teaching Complex Thinking: Cognitive Challenge (CC).
5   Teaching Through Instructional Conversation (IC).

These five standards for effective pedagogy, their indicators, and illustrative examples of each are presented in the following sections of this chapter. The indicators guide implementation, provide a classroom observation format and encourage reflection on the effects of practice. The indicators are drawn from extensive observations in a variety of classrooms serving diverse and at-risk students. All of the indicators represent features reported by teachers who have used the standards to guide their teaching. While the indicators describe what we have observed teachers doing to enact the standards, their presence does not ensure that any particular standard is fully in place.

Standard 1: Joint Productive Activity (JPA): Teachers and Students Producing Together

Indicators for Standard 1 are that the teacher

1 designs instructional activities requiring student collaboration to accomplish a joint product;
2 matches the demands of the joint productive activity to the time available for accomplishing them;
3 arranges classroom seating to accommodate students' individual and group needs to communicate and work jointly;
4 participates with students in joint productive activity;
5 organizes students in a variety of groupings such as by friendship, mixed academic ability, language, project, interests, etc., to promote interaction.
6 plans with students how to work in groups and move from one activity to another, such as from large-group introduction to small-group activity, for clean-up, dismissal, and the like;
7 manages student and teacher access to materials and technology to facilitate joint productive activity;
8 monitors and supports student collaboration in positive ways.

When experts and novices work together for a common product or goal and have opportunities to converse about the activity, learning is a likely outcome (Moll, 1990; Rogoff, 1991; Tharp and Gallimore, 1988; Wertsch, 1985). The common motivation provided by a joint goal inclines all participants to offer and receive assistance, since it is in everyone's best interest that the goal is reached. Because providing assistance is the basic act of teaching, joint productive activity creates the conditions in which development will occur. The use of joint productive activity increases exponentially the amount of communication and assisted performance available in the classroom, making the teacher one source among thirty or so peer resources. Research evidence also clearly supports the role of the constructive, productive activity itself; while assistance is vital, the critical feature is applying that knowledge in productive action with others (Boaler, 1999; Webb, Troper and Fall, 1995; Tharp and Gallimore, 1988; Vygotsky, 1978).

In conventional classrooms, joint products with a common goal are relatively rare, as most tasks have an individual focus. However, when joint products are called for, their impact on learners' motivation and understanding is often observable. For example, one Chicago elementary school featured a hands-on, cooperative approach in a classroom where students jointly researched the composition of an ocean coral reef. They worked together to discover and design reef features of which most, if not all, students had no direct experience. Then they constructed a model ocean coral reef in the hallway outside their classroom, where they had room to work together to display their research findings about coral reefs creatively. Questions about shared habitats, territoriality and food-chain issues were engaged and resolved by the students in the process of constructing the most accurate display (Murphy, 1997). This vignette gives evidence of indicators 1, 3 and 5.

Indicators 1, 2, 3, 4, 5, 6, 7 and 8 are present in another example, that of a Zuni (New Mexico) middle school 8th-grade literacy class, in which students collaborate throughout the year on the production of a monthly school news-paper. Virtually every activity setting in that classroom involves joint product-ive activity, because every column, advertising segment, editorial or news story must be coordinated with other individuals or groups working on the same overarching product, the newspaper. The teacher participates as a member of the work team and does every task with the students, as needed, to ensure the publication of the paper on time. Teacher and students interact in authentic ways, just as in a 'real' newsroom: the newspaper is extremely popular and so is the class (Tharp and Dalton, 1994).

Although whole-group instruction is the major or default format in today's classrooms in the USA, it is ill-suited to accommodate activities and social organization that produce the engagement and interaction of JPA. When joint productive activities are the basis for classroom organization, a variety of concurrent activity settings is present: cooperative, individual and group work, teams working with peers and with the teacher. Teachers may arrange the classroom in more complex ways for logistical, hygienic and other pur-poses, and have concurrent activities set in separate areas of the classroom. For example, a triad might work on the computer, a small group listen to a story read by a peer, a third group finish a collaborative story draft, a fourth collect data on classroom science projects, and another group construct a bulletin board displaying some content area concept. Typically, the teacher circulates among the students, observing their progress and providing assist-ance as needed. From our point of view, students and teachers must share a significant portion of classroom activities. Only if the teacher is also present and engaged in the activities sufficiently to share the experiences will there be the sustained, intensive discourse that maximizes development and creates intersubjectivity among all participants. This is especially important when the teacher and the students are not of the same cultures. To progress from simple, large-group activities at the start of the year to more complex classroom arrangements, teachers and students jointly plan, negotiate and establish clear understandings about what will occur. Teachers themselves offer additional examples of how joint productive activities are developed and used on the web and in publications (Wells, 2001).

Standard 2: Developing Language and Literacy Across the Curriculum (LD)

Indicators for Standard 2 are that the teacher

1   listens to student talk about familiar topics such as home and community;
2   responds to student talk and questions, making 'in-flight' changes during conversation that directly relate to student comments;
3   assists language development through modelling, eliciting, probing, restating, clarifying, questioning, praising, etc., as appropriate, in purposeful conversation;
4   interacts with students in ways that respect student preferences for speaking that may be different from the teacher's, such as wait-time, eye contact, turn-taking and spotlighting;
5   makes explicit connections between student language and literacy and academic content;
6   encourages students to use content vocabulary to express their understanding;
7   provides frequent opportunity for students to interact with each other and the teacher during instructional activities;
8   encourages student use of first and second languages in instructional activities.

Language proficiency in speaking, reading and writing is key to academic achievement. The teacher's interaction with every student is critical in a view of learning that assumes that participation in social contexts influences knowledge generation and academic achievement. From the start, teachers attend to students' informal talk in general activities to assess students' language proficiency and learn about families' prior experiences in and out of school.

Students need opportunities to speak and write, to practise language use, and to receive the natural feedback of conversation from teacher and peers. Joint productive activity provides an ideal opportunity for development of the language of the activity's subject matter. Language development, both oral and written, is fostered through strategies such as restating, modelling, offering alternative phrasing, and questioning. Everyday language and concepts are the foundation teachers will build on to develop academic understanding and discourse. Teachers implementing this standard provide students with multiple opportunities to use varieties of language in appropriate forms with them and their peers.

Teachers create rich activities to stimulate language use at every grade level. A kindergarten teacher and students developed an integrated content activity on biodegradability by planting leaves, apples and other food, plastic bags and aluminum cans in soil in a glass aquarium. They kept records of the degrading process by drawing pictures, labeling them with new new vocabulary, and compiling their observations into books which they read and discussed. After the project was completed they placed the books in the classroom library to read with peers (Dalton, 1997). This example involves indicators 1, 3, 5 and 7. This project, similar to later experiments in content courses of upper grades, is applicable at any level to develop complex content lexicon and concepts.

Prevalent classroom discourse patterns (ways of asking and answering questions, challenging claims and using representations) are frequently unfamiliar to English Language Learners (ELLs) and other students placed at risk of educational failure. When teachers draw on the real-life experiences of their students, the explicit connections between students' experience and language, literacy and academic knowledge are made clear. Topics that students have an interest in discussing often include those drawn from television, the internet or other media. Conversely, given the increasing diversity of Western classrooms, students' ways of talking may be unfamiliar to their teachers. Inviting students to use their linguistic preferences within ongoing classroom activities respects students' traditions, and provides opportunities to practise culturally based ways of interacting. For Hawaiian-American students, for example, preferences for conversation include overlapping and simultaneous speech, reflecting their oral tradition of co-narration or 'talk story'. Teachers can adapt classroom participation to allow students' familiar forms of conversation, dropping unfamiliar forms such as hand-raising.

Of course, the purpose of schooling is not to further develop local-community informal speech. But teacher awareness of community-based language patterns allows them to anticipate and respond in ways that further students' academic language development. When interactive occasions are frequent in a classroom, teachers can assist students by scaffolding their language performance for academic dialogue (Tharp and Gallimore, 1988). Enacting the Language Development Standard regularly means providing students with the interactive experience needed to master academic discourse, and to understand that being a student means learning that language.

Standard 3: Making Meaning: Connecting School to Students' Lives (MM)

Indicators for Standard 3 are that the teacher

1   begins activities based on what students already know from home, community and school;

2   designs instructional activities that are meaningful to students in terms of local community norms and knowledge;
3   acquires knowledge of local norms and knowledge by talking to students, parents, community members, and by reading pertinent documents;
4   assists students to connect and apply their learning to home and community;
5   plans jointly with students to design community-based learning activities;
6   provides opportunities for parents to participate in classroom instructional activities;
7   varies activities according to students' preferences, from collective and cooperative to individual and competitive;
8   varies styles of conversation and participation to include students' cultural preferences, such as co-narration, call-and-response, choral, among others.

A wide range of social contexts and circumstances beyond classroom and school are reported to influence academic accomplishment for all students (August and Hakuta, 1997). For students placed at risk by language and culture, ethnographic studies find students' learning is highly situated within the contexts of the social environments in which they participate (August and Hakuta, 1997; Phillips, 1983; Swisher and Deyhle, 1992). Certainly, multi-ethnic and multi-racial themes, activities and materials have positive effects on the ethnic, racial and empathic attitudes of students, especially if included in ongoing, daily events of the classroom. Nevertheless, the reality of students' lives is anchored in contexts outside school (August and Hakuta, 1997; Moll, et al., 1992; Vogt, Jordan and Tharp, 1992). The Making Meaning Standard therefore encourages teachers to use a variety of direct and indirect approaches to draw on students' familiar, local contexts of experience.

Three levels of contextualization are discussed in the culture and education literature. At the first, or pedagogical level, is the necessity to invoke students' existing schema as they relate to material being instructed (Au, 1980). That is, the content of instruction should be drawn from, or carefully related to, students' own environments and experiences (Garcia, 1991; Tharp and Gallimore, 1988).

At the second, or curriculum level, there is uniform advocacy for instructional use of cultural artifacts as the media in which goals of literacy, numeracy and science are contextualized. Drawing on personal, community-based experiences affords students opportunities to apply skills acquired in home and school contexts (Garcia, 1991), and use them as the foundation for developing school skills (e.g. Wyatt, 1978/1979). The work of Gonzalez and Moll in studying the 'funds of knowledge' in students' families and communities, and using those funds as curricular bases for mathematics instruction, is an excellent example of making instruction meaningful (Gonzalez, et al., 1993; Moll, et al., 1992).

At the third, or policy level, there are advocates for contextualization of the school itself. School learning is a social process that affects and is affected by the entire community. 'More long-lasting progress has been achieved with children whose learning has been explored, modified and shaped in collaboration with their parents and communities' (John-Steiner and Smith, 1978, p. 26). Readers can find excellent examples of this level of contextualization in McIntyre, et al. (in press), Andrade, et al. (1999) and Lipka (1994, 1986).

When the sixth grade in the middle school in Zuni designed a unit on the delicious piñon nut, teachers used a traditional activity as a context for their students to think about familiar activities in entirely new ways. At the grade-level team meeting the mathematics teacher came in and proposed a project with piñons, a bumper crop for that year. He said, 'I just figured that the piñons are here, and we can't ignore them since all the students are eating them all the time. Why not study them?' The team responded enthusiastically, and came up with the following interdisciplinary unit on 'Discovery of the Community', which integrated piñon picking with academic lesson plans in the following ways:

1   In Mathematics class, students will figure out how many piñons an 'average' 6th grader picks per hour. They will weigh the piñons, practice metric conversion, study percentages and learn how these concepts are used in marketing to figure out costs and profit.
2   In Social Studies, general principles of economics will assist students' marketing strategies for selling the nuts. Students will actually sell the piñons. Any profit generated will go into the 6th grade fund.
3   In Science, students will learn about the pinion tree, agriculture and the environment.
4   In Language Arts, students will discuss and write about this experience, and design labels for the piñon packaging.
5   Family Life will stress cooperation, social skills, community and family involvement. (L. Yamauchi, field notes, 1992)

The adventure of the piñon unit provided opportunities for teachers to jointly plan, teach, learn about the community and its traditions, and debrief. In numerous ways the unit involved the contexts, external to school, where student learning is situated, such as cultural tradition, staple crop harvesting and preparation, and marketing a cash crop. Parents were included on the field trips and in other activities as well. For the students, learning was collaborative, hands-on and supported by the community. From the beginning, the tasks of the unit required considerable group cooperation, interdependence and student choice for how to participate, challenging teachers to grant independence and students to accept responsibility. The meaningful activities promoted full inclusion and the focus on tasks increased students' interaction about the topic in their home language and in the language of instruction. Student understanding builds on what they bring to learning, but they will struggle with unfamiliar language and notions about abstract material in science, mathematics and other content areas when they are motivated by compelling activities they value (Tharp, 1997; Dalton, et al., 1997; Cazden, 1986; Au, 1980; Vygotsky, 1978).

The Meaning Making Standard does not assert that 'the known' is the goal and object of instruction, nor that learning should be confined to the languages, knowledge and conventions of home, family and culture. Far from it: the known is the bridge over which students cross to gain the new (Lee, 1995). Scaffolding students from their prior knowledge into new understandings is not a simple association between the known and the new. It is an emergent process in which students and teachers relate to accomplish the tasks leading to the goals for learning.

Standard 4: Teaching Complex Thinking: Cognitive Challenge (CC)

Indicators for Standard 4 are that the teacher

1   ensures that students, for each instructional topic, see the whole picture as the basis for understanding the parts;
2   presents challenging standards for student performance;
3   designs instructional tasks that advance student understanding to more complex levels;
4   assists students to accomplish more complex understanding by relating to their real-life experience;
5   gives clear, direct feedback about how student performance compares with the challenging standard.

Standard 4 reflects research evidence that the teaching of complex thinking, by involving students in challenging tasks, is a universal principle for effective instruction. This emphasis shifts the goals of instruction from ensuring that students have command of facts and basic skills to accomplishing complex understandings that support practical problem solving in content domains. The Cognitive Challenge Standard emphasizes that students learn what they are taught, and that cognitive complexity will be learned if it is taught. Of course, neither a challenge too low nor one too high will assist development. Through the activity and language-based interaction of the CHAT approach to pedagogy, 'challenge' can be appropriately levelled. And in CHAT terminology, it is in the zone of proximal development (the ZPD) that the appropriate level of cognitive challenge is to be found. Of course, practice is useful; of course, struggling with an impossible problem can be inspirational. But for development to occur, challenge must constantly be set at the point at which assistance is necessary. Most often, we think of the teacher as the principal assistant, but to the extent that peers provide appropriate assistance, learning and development will also occur.

An example which clearly shows indicators 1 and 4 comes from a middle-school mathematics project emphasizing assessment methods, in which students were challenged to do survey research. The teacher read aloud a news story about a 10-year-old who surveyed her classmates about the amount of their allowances. The survey showed that girls received less than boys, even when they did more chores. The students developed, administered and reported on a survey of their own classmates to see whether such discrepancies existed. This project provided students with experience and data for applying their mathematics skills and critical perspectives. Students are motivated to learn skills that help them see through and into their world. In fact, the students found that girls in their class were also given less allowance than boys (Rutledge, 1997, p. 72).

We know that all students need to be challenged to stretch, to learn language and content, and to think in complex ways beyond their current capacities (see Carr, and Stetsenko and Arievitch, this volume). Teachers who teach for understanding, guiding students through their zones of proximal development by including activities and interaction in the community, know that this approach takes and warrants more time than cursory coverage designed for memorization of facts. For example, Bruer (1993) describes the successful pedagogy of a high school physics teacher who spends over a week developing Newton's laws – in contrast to the one or two days given to the topic by most traditional courses. Teachers who practise the Pedagogy Standards also stretch their own capacities to understand what their students bring to learning and how they can assist them through their individual zones of proximal development by using social influences on learning. Guidance from the standards enables them to arrange interaction about activity in community that will develop the more complex thinking that students need in today's world.

Standard 5: Teaching Through Instructional Conversation (IC)

Indicators for Standard 5 are that the teacher

1   arranges the classroom to accommodate conversation between the teacher and small groups of students on a regular and frequent schedule;
2   ensures that a clear academic goal guides conversation;
3   ensures that student talk occurs at higher rates than teacher talk;
4   guides conversation to include students' views, judgements and rationales, based on text evidence and other substantive support;
5   ensures that all students are included in the conversation;
6   listens carefully to assess levels of student understanding;
7   assists student learning throughout the conversation by questioning, restating, praising, encouraging, etc.;

8   guides the students to prepare a product that indicates that the instruc-
    tional conversation's goal was achieved.

Even kindergartners can engage in Instructional Conversation (IC) about
their learning activities, as they did in the biodegradable project example
described earlier. When they had observed the process of degrading, acquired
a selected scientific lexicon to describe it, and learned the concept, they were
competent to discourse on this scientific topic in small groups. IC teaches
students to engage in thoughtful and accountable conversation about text,
activities and cultural artifacts, ideally in small groups of three to seven. In
IC, teachers urge students to question and challenge, use content lexicon, find
alternative and deep problem solutions, rationalize and justify, and continually
seek information in order to produce more complex and higher-order thinking
habits (Resnick, 1998). Unfortunately, typical classrooms provide infre-
quent occasions for sustained conversation, and rarely arrange for it to occur
on a regular schedule. There are consequences for such a lack of cognitive
engagement. Research reports describe how students' mastery of language,
conversational conventions and academic content are effectively postponed
due to minimal classroom interaction and language production occasions
(Au, 1980; Erickson and Mohatt, 1982; Rosebery, Warren and Conant, 1992).
By middle school, such restricted opportunities result in language minority
students' limited academic success and low self-confidence in their ability to
learn (Padron, 1992; Dalton and Youpa, 1998).

Research reports that good teaching is characterized by the use of meaningful content presented in life-like situations (Allington, 1990; Chalmot, 1992;
Means and Knapp, 1991). The particular advantage of IC to the teacher of
at-risk students is the opportunity to explore and learn about students' worlds
of experience and knowledge to affirm their value and relevance to learning.
Quality IC builds on and incorporates students' funds of knowledge, their
familial and community experiences, to increase connections between students' prior knowledge and the unknown, abstract and academic content of
instruction (Dalton and Sison, 1994).

Ordinarily, IC takes place in small groups, though a teacher may have
instructional conversations with larger groups or individuals. For example,
teachers may work on a unit or thematic topic with the whole class, followed
by small-group ICs that focus on researching and analysing selected aspects
of the large-group topic. While any good conversation requires some latitude
and drift in the topic, the teacher's leadership is used to focus on the instructional goal. While the teacher holds the goal firmly in mind, the route to the
goal is responsive to student participation and developing understanding. As
students experience IC, their conversational fluency increases. For students
who have little experience of a conversation for using language or expressing
ideas, teachers must intensify their efforts to elicit their participation through
strategies like restating, interpreting, affirming and sensitive questioning.

In the following transcript of an IC from an eighth-grade class of Native-American (Zuni) English learners, notice how the teacher, Stacey, focuses and refocuses the topic to elicit her students' rationalizations. In the conversation, she reflects and restates their ideas while urging them towards more complex understandings of the IC topic.

Teacher Stacey: Girls, what's one freedom that you'd want to have?
Student 1:   No school.
Stacey: No school. The freedom not to go to school. OK, write that down. What could be ... Jessica, what's one good thing about if you didn't have to go to school? What's good about it? Why do you want it?
Student 2:   You can wake up whenever you want.
Stacey: OK, you can wake up whenever you want. So, you have your own schedule, right? It gives you more power. OK, what else does it give you?
Student 3:   You can have fun all day.
Stacey: You have fun all day. So you can hang out and do whatever you want all day.
Student 1:   Don't have to worry about tests.
Stacey: Don't have to worry about tests, OK, so, what's one bad thing about it?
Student 1:   You don't learn anything.
Stacey: OK, so what if you don't learn anything? What's the big deal about that?
Student 4:   You won't, you won't ... uh ... you won't know how to read.
Stacey: You won't know how to read. What does reading do? What does reading do for you?
Student 4:   Helps you get a job.
Stacey: It helps you get a job. OK, why do you want a job?
All students: Make money.
Stacey: OK, what else does reading do for you?
Student 1:   Learn.
Stacey: You learn new stuff.
Student 1:   You read about other cultures, new stuff.
Stacey: Why is it good to read about new stuff? I mean, doesn't Zuni have enough to offer? Why would you want to read about somewhere else?
Student 2:   To learn about their country.
Student 1:   So we know what's happening around the world.
Stacey: So you know what's happening around the world. Why would you want to know that?
Student 2:   To see if they're different from us.
Stacey: To see if they're different. That's interesting. Do you think it's a basic human desire to know about other people and other cultures? It just sorta feels like you're drawn to it, doesn't it? That's cool. OK, go ahead and write that down, you guys.

Summary

Taken together, the pedagogy standards guide teaching that reflects the social and cultural origins of learning, and focuses on the ways students' capacities and attributes develop in interaction with others. As we have seen, each standard impacts and interacts with the others. For example, the Joint Productive Activity (JPA) standard influences classroom organization and task design, which is foundational for the four other standards. An increase in the variety and richness of JPA provides more Meaning Making (MM) opportunities, because smaller groups increase opportunities for teachers to learn about their students' experiences in and out of school. JPA also makes Language and Literacy Development (LD) more likely, because students are willing to express themselves more fluently in the course of activities that have real-world value. JPA makes students' Complex Thinking (CT) more likely, because a teacher who knows students through interaction and joint activity can individualize instructional levels more sensitively and activate peer resources when there are alternatives to large-group instructional settings. JPA makes Instructional Conversation (IC) more likely, because the teacher can dialogue on academic topics with a selected group of students while the others participate independently in various joint productive activities.

The standards are not invariant templates to be imposed on all situations. On the contrary, they represent ideals that strive to fit local circumstances and respect unique features of individuals, schools and communities (Goldenberg and Gallimore, 1996). Students today enter schools with ethnicities, languages, cultures and individual needs more disparate than ever before. Community localization, and individual responsiveness to these variations, is critical to ensuring all students' participation and academic engagement. The standards encourage classrooms to become communities of learners in which increased joint activity, innovative social organizational arrangements, meaningful problem solving, and dialogue on academic topics are emphasized. Standard 3, Meaning Making, explicitly requires localization, and in general such contextualization is a fundamental quality of the standards themselves.

Basically, the pedagogy standards describe what teachers do to arrange and assist student learning in the same way that content standards describe what instruction must address; performance standards describe concrete examples and specific definitions of student proficiency; and opportunity-to-learn standards describe capacity to ensure equal access to education (McLaughlin and Shepard, 1995). Specifically, they articulate a CHAT view of learning, where knowledge emerges through social and cultural activity during community participation for the purpose of guiding teachers' enactments of the vision. Teachers' competence in pedagogy is key to quality. When distinguished teaching means every student is regularly engaged in compelling activities that encourage interaction among teacher and peers and understandings that increase in complexity, the focus of teaching and learning shifts from individuals' attributes to an emphasis on the ways in which students' attributes play out in interaction and activity with others. The pedagogy standards and their indicators present guidance for producing such teaching that is socially productive, actively engaged, dialogically based and knowledge generative.

Part III
Post-Compulsory, Adult and Professional Learning

15

Inquiry as an Orientation for Learning, Teaching and Teacher Education

Gordon Wells

Some years ago, as a participant-researcher in a multicultural inner-city class of 8- and 9-year-olds, I undertook to contribute to the exploration of the theme of time in which they were engaged by making a functioning water-clock out of 'found' materials: pieces of wood left over from renovation, a plastic spoon, a yogurt carton and bits and pieces of wire and string. When I had succeeded in getting the 'clock' to work at home, I set it up in the class-room. The teacher then asked some of the children who had been watching me to demonstrate how it worked to the rest of the class. Unfortunately, it failed to operate as expected. However, suggestions for fixing it were not slow in coming and soon an animated discussion was in full swing, as com-peting proposals were put forward, justified and evaluated. By the end of the day, with the help of various 'others', some of the most enthusiastic engineers had succeeded in making it work. Over the following days, working in groups, the children in this class constructed a variety of other ways of measuring time, using simple materials such as sand, marbles, metal washers and string.

At about the same time, in another multicultural classroom, I was present when a problem of a very different kind arose. In the course of their ongoing study of the development of a brood of caterpillars into painted lady butter-flies, the grade six students in this class, working in groups, were formulating questions about how the caterpillars turned into chrysalises: how did the chrysalises survive without food? What exactly happened inside the cocoon?

Nir and the members of his group had explored this question in discussion with me and he concluded that the best way to discover would be to dissect a chrysalis every two days to see what changes had occurred inside. Since this would involve sacrificing other students' chrysalises, the teacher called a class meeting to consider his proposal, at which the majority argued strongly against it, mainly on ethical grounds. However, Nir was not ready to abandon his plan completely. After listening to the arguments of his peers, he came up with a compromise: one of the chrysalises had fallen from its anchorage and had been lying for some time, unmoving, on the bottom of its jar. This chrysalis had obviously died, he argued; surely, therefore, it would be acceptable to carry out a dissection on a dead chrysalis. After further discussion, it was decided that if the chrysalis did indeed continue to show no signs of life, it would be deemed to be dead and an autopsy could go ahead.

The next morning, after further observation and tests to establish that the chrysalis was really dead, Nir and a group of friends prepared to carry out the operation. As the teacher had insisted, they approached the task in the spirit of scientific investigation. While Nir donned surgical gloves, Alicia held the chrysalis firmly with a pair of forceps. Another student prepared to draw what was revealed, while another took written notes on the proceedings. Finally, the video camera was trained on the operating table in order to record the investigation for the benefit of those who could not get close enough to see.

Taking a scalpel, Nir delicately made an incision along the length of the outer case. Immediately, one end of the previously inert chrysalis began to vibrate violently. The operation was halted forthwith, amid excited reactions from spectators and conflicting views on what to do next. Another class meeting was immediately convened in order to consider the implications of the changed status of the chrysalis. Was it really alive, or was this just the nerves reacting although it was actually dead? Most believed it was still alive, and the question for them was could it still recover if it were treated with care, or would it be more humane to put it out of its misery by killing it immediately? The discussion that followed was both coherent and intense. Finally, a substantial majority voted to abandon the dissection and to resecure the chrysalis in its hanging position in the hope that only minor damage had been done and that it would continue its invisible process of metamorphosis in the normal way. Nir, it should be recorded, agreed with the majority view. Some days later, a butterfly emerged from the rescued chrysalis. Unfortunately, one wing was damaged and it was unable to fly away with the others.

Neither of these events was preplanned; indeed both of them took the adults involved by surprise. But perhaps because they were spontaneous and student-initiated they made a strong impression on me. As I later reviewed the videotaped observations and reflected on their broader implications, I recognized in these events some of the key features of effective learning-and-teaching, as this has come to be understood from the perspective of Cultural Historical Activity Theory (CHAT). Over the succeeding years, in collaborative investigations with teacher colleagues, involving an ongoing interplay between practice and theory, we have attempted to find ways of creating settings in which such events are the norm rather than the exception.[1]

Knowing, Acting and Understanding

The problems tackled by the students in the preceding vignettes are certainly not typical of most contemporary classrooms. Most often, the 'problems' that are posed there have only one correct or acceptable solution, and that is already known by the teacher. In fact, the real problem for the students is more likely to be whether they can come up with the solution that is 'in the teacher's mind' or, putting it more generously, whether they can reproduce the solution that is culturally accepted.

In the preceding examples, by contrast, the problems arose in the course of ongoing activities in which the students were both affectively and intellectually engaged and they had as their focus actions to be performed or already performed. These problems had no single correct answer, and there was no all-knowing authority; nevertheless, a solution had to be constructed in order for the participants to be able to continue to act effectively and responsibly. To increase their understanding and solve the problem, they engaged in dialogue together and, in the case of the water clock, with the absent others who had created the books that they consulted. In the process, the students presented alternative solutions and argued for and against them using explanations and analogies based on causal relationships; they tried to persuade each other of the rightness of their positions, seeking to achieve a consensus on the action to be taken; and they spontaneously responded to each other without waiting to be nominated by the teacher. In other words, their discussion constituted a seriously undertaken collective attempt to solve a problem on the basis of informed consideration of the alternative options.

In these ways the two examples of problem solving were much more like what one might observe outside the classroom. There, most problems do not come neatly formulated. In fact, the first and often more difficult problem is to discover and define the problem that needs to be solved. Second, 'real' problems very rarely have single 'right' solutions. Not only are there often alternative ways of proceeding, but the choice among them is dependent on value judgements related to the larger situation in which the problem has arisen. Third, as is implied by the second objection, 'real' problems are rarely solved by individuals in isolation; on the contrary, they are typically addressed by a group that, although sharing a common goal, has varying kinds and degrees of expertise as well as diverse values, motives, interests and preferred strategies for working together. Finally, outside the classroom, whether a solution is acceptable or not is rarely decided by a single powerful arbiter but by consensus among the participants as to whether the proposed solution allows them to advance towards the goal of the activity in which the problem arose.

The question my colleagues and I have been addressing, therefore, is how to select and organize the classroom activities through which the curriculum is enacted in such a way that they not only provide systematic opportunities for learning what are referred to as 'basic knowledge and skills', but also develop the dispositions that will enable today's students to participate responsibly and effectively in solving the problems that they will encounter as citizens in the years ahead. An equally important question is how to ensure that these activities value and build on the diverse funds of knowledge that students bring to school from their diverse backgrounds (Moll and Greenberg, 1990). In other words, how can students' learning in the classroom not only equip them with the necessary knowledgeable skills to function effectively in the world of work beyond school but also, as Vygotsky urged with respect to learning to write, 'be incorporated into a task that is necessary and relevant for life' (Vygotsky, 1978, p. 118) – as they envisage it?

Building Communities of Inquiry

Two metaphors have proved generative in our thinking. The first is that of 'the improvable object'. In earlier periods of human history the impetus for the advancement of understanding was very frequently a problem arising in a practical situation, and the solution took the form of an object that was constructed by the group through their collaborative action and dialogue. This created artifact was both a tool that could be used to transform the situation and also the material embodiment of the group's knowing together (Engeström, 1987). In the twenty-first century the object on which a group works together is more likely to emphasize the ideal dimension, for example a theory of polymer bonding, or a master plan for a city's transport. But in order to be worked on and improved, it must also have a material embodiment, for example on a computer screen or a drawing board, with which participants can engage with their bodily senses; the improved version must also be materially embodied in their dialogue, whether spoken, written or represented in some other material medium (Cole, 1996; Lektorsky, 1999).

In the classroom we have found it is possible to create comparable objects, on which students work together in an attempt to improve them. In a grade-two class, for example, one such type of object was elastic-powered vehicles that the children constructed, which required them to solve practical problems that had more theoretical implications (Galbraith, Van Tassell and Wells, 1999). In a grade-seven class, the object was an explanation of why, at the time of the Black Death, doctors treating people who had caught the plague wore a cloak and mask that made them look like a bird, and why wearing this was effective in protecting them from the disease (Haneda and Wells, 2000). In this second case, the object was embodied in a sequence of Post-it notes in which students developed the explanation on the 'Knowledge Wall' (Hume, 2001). In both cases, in order to improve the objects on which they were working, the students needed to obtain additional information, to interpret it in the light of their problem, and to act on the objects in appropriate ways – all of which involved them in collaborative dialogue.

The second generative metaphor is that of 'the spiral of knowing'. This is, itself, an improvable object – a tool for thinking about the roles that speaking, writing and other semiotic modes of interaction can play in the ways of

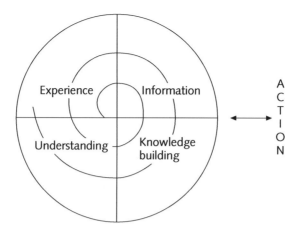

Figure 15.1   The spiral of knowing (adapted from Wells, 1999).

enacting curriculum that we wish to promote. In its material representation, it currently takes the form shown in figure 15.1.

Briefly, the diagram represents a complex spiral, in which each cycle starts with the understanding of individual past experiences that participants bring to the problem situation; to this is then added new information that is either searched for or made available by teacher, text or the situation and activity in which they are engaged. However, for this new information to lead to en-hanced understanding, it must be individually appropriated and transformed; this, we propose, occurs through collaborative knowledge building, that is to say, through action on the object that is the focus of the joint activity and through the dialogue in which the participants make sense of and evaluate new information, relate it to what they currently believe, and use it to guide action and enhance understanding of the matter at issue.

Combining these two tools for thinking – the improvable object and the spiral of knowing – we have come to conceptualize the organization of class-room activities in terms of 'inquiry'. Rather than seeing the teacher's role as that of delivering a preformulated, centrally organized curriculum of 'basic knowledge and skills', and testing to ensure that this content has been acquired, we endeavour to plan overarching themes that, while congruent with the mandated curricular topics, open up possibilities for students to select their own 'objects' for inquiry and to take responsibility for determining how to proceed. At the same time, individual investigations are also embedded within a collaborative framework of joint activity and the dialogue of knowledge building within the community as a whole.

Central to this approach is the building of a 'community of inquiry', in which students frequently work together in groups on the same or related inquiries, and in which a critically important activity is whole-class meetings

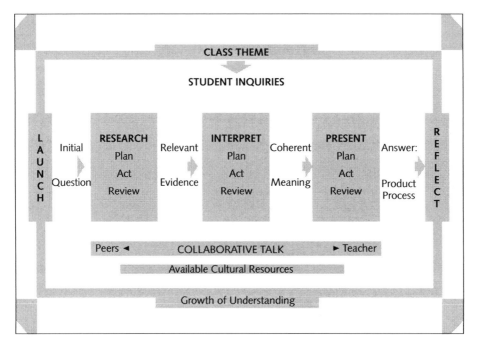

Figure 15.2 Model of an inquiry-oriented curriculum.

for review and reflection on what is planned, in progress or has been achieved. It is in these meetings, in particular, that the dialogue of knowledge building occurs most deliberately and systematically, as the relationships among the individual or group inquiries are explored in relation to the common theme, alternative suggestions and perspectives are considered and evaluated, and a serious attempt made to ensure that the knowledge building is 'progressive in the sense that understandings are being generated that are new to the local participants and that the participants recognize as superior to their previous understandings' (Bereiter, 1994, p. 9). These meetings also provide an occasion for taking a 'meta' stance with respect to the processes in which students are engaging, for describing strategies that seem to be effective, and for recognizing and valuing the diversity of ideas that are contributed to the forging of a common understanding.

We have tried to capture the key elements of this way of working in a model of an inquiry-oriented approach to curriculum (figure 15.2).[2] Of course, the model is not to be taken as a flow-diagram to be implemented in a strict linear sequence. Rather, it is a tool for thinking with, as teachers select and plan activities and negotiate the detail of the way in which the curriculum is enacted with the students as co-inquirers.

What distinguishes this approach is that, as far as possible, activities are driven by 'real' questions, to which those who pose them attempt to make answers that advance their own and others' understanding. In the process, of course, they also learn new procedures and strategies that are necessary to pursue their inquiries effectively; they also search out additional information from various sources and evaluate its relevance for the 'object' on which they are working. In this way, the 'content' of the curriculum, rather than being an end in itself, is treated as a set of resources that mediate their investigations. A further important feature of this approach is the built-in expectation that work in progress and the finished product will be presented to the rest of the class, both to provide opportunities for feedback and to contribute to the class's collective meaning making with respect to the theme under investigation. As we have repeatedly found, this attempt to represent one's understanding of the object at issue so that it is clear and convincing for others, and then to respond to their questions, suggestions or objections in a spirit of collaboration as well as competition, is a particularly powerful mode of knowledge building that advances the understanding of both the individual participants and the class as a whole (Wells, 1999).

Organized in this way, with the students taking considerable responsibility for the actions through which they meet the challenges inherent in their inquiries, the teacher is able to be a 'participant observer', using the opportunity to note how they are proceeding for purposes of assessment (Drummond, 1997; Gipps, this volume) and in order to provide assistance of various kinds when it is required (Gallimore and Tharp, 1990; Wells, 1996a).

Teachers as Inquirers

The inquiry approach to curriculum just described is by no means unique and has a history dating back at least as far as Dewey (1956). However, most classrooms deliberately organized as communities of inquiry have been pioneered by university-based educators (e.g. Brown and Campione, 1994; Hedegaard, 1996; Palincsar, et al., 1998; Scardamalia, Bereiter and Lamon, 1994). By contrast, what makes the 'Developing Inquiring Communities in Education Project' (DICEP) communities significantly different is the role of the teachers in their initiation. In each case, it was the teacher who made the decision to move to an inquiry-oriented approach and it is she or he who continues to be responsible for the way in which the curriculum is enacted (within the constraints imposed by the school and district administration). There is no outside organizer making key decisions, no university 'experts' dispensing advice on how to proceed. Instead, what enables the teachers to take this agentive stance is their understanding of the particular classroom communities for which they are responsible and this, in turn, is derived in large part from their own inquiries, both through reading and through action research in collaboration with other members of the group (Wells, 2001).

The benefits teachers gain by taking on the role of 'teacher researcher' have been variously propounded in an increasing number of publications in the last two decades (e.g. Carr and Kemmis, 1983; Elliott, 1991; Hollingsworth, 1997; Newman, 1998; Noffke, 1997; Schön, 1987). But in some, the case made is rather narrowly instrumental, based on premises of technical rationality (Cochran-Smith and Lytle, 1999). In our view, however, the arguments for this stance are as much moral as pragmatic. Essentially, to be the leader of a community of inquiry, one must be an inquirer oneself.

Since the goals of schooling are – or should be – as much concerned with the dispositions that students develop and the identities they form as with the 'content' of the curriculum that they are required to master, it is clear that the activities in which they engage cannot be focused simply on the acquisition of basic skills and knowledge. In other words, if our intention is to foster the development of students who are critical and creative thinkers and problem-solvers, who not only think about what needs to be done, why and how, but who also have the determination to carry through with knowing in action, both individually and in collaboration with others, these qualities must be emphasized throughout the course of their education, in all the activities that they undertake. Schools must therefore be places in which students are apprenticed into a way of living – of thinking, feeling and acting – that is informed by the values just described. And for this to happen, these same values must equally be practised by the adult members of the school community.

Once this is accepted, it follows that those who are to be responsible for our students' education must themselves be educated according to the same principles. For we can hardly expect teachers to create the conditions in their classrooms for students to develop these dispositions if the teachers themselves do not have similar formative experiences. Nor can students be expected to develop confidence in their own knowledge and judgement, while recognizing the benefits that are to be gained from collaborating with others, if those who teach them are trained unquestioningly to implement the decisions of distant and authoritative 'experts' and are given no encouragement to assume an agentive role in taking situationally appropriate initiatives in collaboration with their colleagues.

We are convinced, therefore, that if we wish schools to become places in which students acquire the dispositions as well as the knowledge that will enable them to play a part in transforming the societies of which they are members, we must also change the conditions under which their teachers' education and professional development take place. This includes giving teachers the opportunity to develop their own expertise in planning and enacting the curriculum through critical inquiry into their own practice that is conducted in collaboration with their colleagues and, ideally, in conjunction with parents and other community members.

These, then, are the beliefs on which the work of our collaborative action research group is based. They have been articulated and developed to a considerable extent through our use of the writings of Vygotsky and other cultural–historical activity theorists and practitioners as 'thinking devices'

(Lotman, 1988) in order to generate new ideas relevant to our own situations. In our own work, we have focused, in particular, on the central role of semiotic mediation in learning-and-teaching, using videotaped observations of interaction in classrooms in conjunction with our reading of this literature in order to understand the key features of our practice and to use this understanding to make changes that we believe will bring our practice into greater conformity with our vision. Indeed, it was in this process that we came to recognize – in practice as well as in theory – the critically important role of dialogic knowledge building in fostering the dispositions of caring, collaboration and critical inquiry that are at the heart of our vision of education.

We also recognize how important our own community of teacher researchers has been in sustaining the motivation to continue and in providing assistance and constructive criticism with respect to our individual inquiries (McGlynn-Stewart, 2001). As members note, participation in this community has also had substantial benefits for the students we teach. Being a member of DICEP has 'affected my classroom community', writes Davis (2001). 'I have felt the strongest connection with my students when I am engaged in action research in my classroom. The process of simply discussing with them my questions, what I am learning, and sharing my writing with them, has drawn them into the process' (ibid., p. 199).

From the situated perspectives of our own classrooms, we believe, we have also been able to contribute to the discourse of the larger educational community. As Kowal explains:

> At first action research was a means of taking the theory I had been reading and applying it to my practice, a means of making theory useful. But it also quickly became a means of allowing me to see how the theory needed changing in my individual context. I also think that it then gave me the confidence to refute aspects of the research I was reading about and to thereby contribute to the theory base and develop it further. . . . It helped me to stop looking for a single 'right' way to do things and to recognize the many variables and factors that influence the teaching/learning context. (Kowal, 2001, pp. 199–200)

Going Beyond the Classroom

Communities of teacher researchers such as the one I have described can certainly make a difference in their immediate environments and, through publication, they can also reach a wider audience.[3] Most importantly, by showing what can be done to improve the quality of education along the lines suggested by CHAT, they can motivate other teachers to take a more agentive stance in their own classrooms. However, it can reasonably be argued that, in themselves, such local initiatives will never lead to the changes that are necessary on an international or even a state or school-district level.

It might seem, on the face of it, therefore, that what is required is stronger direction from 'above'. Nevertheless, this is no solution either. As has been conclusively demonstrated, changes of the kind that we are recommending can never be achieved by top-down imposition (Fullan, 1992), since they are only possible through the creative agency of teachers who have a commitment to the underlying principles. Moreover, even if the majority of teachers could be persuaded to adopt a CHAT perspective, there would still be almost insuperable difficulties in bringing about a general transformation of classroom practice. Two problems, in particular, are reported to be insurmountable in practice. These are the commodification of knowledge and intolerance of diversity.

For reasons that I have spelled out elsewhere (Wells, 1999), there is a serious and widespread failure to distinguish between knowledge and knowing – at least among educational policy-makers in the English-speaking world. Because the outcome of the activity of knowing – that is, building knowledge together to solve a problem or to create a new artifact – is frequently a representation of what has come to be known by those involved, it is often convenient to speak as if the knowing was captured in the representational product. From this, it is a simple step to speak as if the knowing could be transferred to another person simply by giving them the 'knowledge object'. Nevertheless, these ways of speaking would probably not have proved so pernicious if so many other aspects of contemporary life were not subsumed within the ideology of production, consumption, profit and 'bottom-line' accountability. Within such a pervasive ideology, however, it is not surprising that the management of education should have come to be conceptualized in terms of knowledge transmission and accumulation and of product quality management.

From such a perspective, the purpose of schooling is viewed primarily as that of ensuring that students acquire the 'basic knowledge and skills' that they will need for daily life and employment after school and, for the college bound, the knowledge of the various subject disciplines that provides a basis for tertiary education. To guarantee that all students (except those who are marginalized because of their presumed inherent inadequacy) achieve these outcomes, it is argued, their learning must be organized through the delivery of a mandated, centrally designed curriculum and evaluated through assessments of their performance on standardized tasks and tests.

In other words, acquiring knowledge is largely separated from the situations in which, through knowing in action, knowledge is constructed and used. Graduates at each level 'know' a lot, but they are often neither able nor disposed to bring what they have learned to bear in the effective and responsible solving of real problems. Knowledge is treated like a commodity, to be amassed and banked (Freire, 1970), and occasionally displayed for show or as credentials when competing for further opportunities for capital acquisition. Where grades and test scores are what matter, it is difficult indeed to encourage a spirit of inquiry and a quest for genuine understanding. For both teachers and students, in this sort of knowledge economy, it is hard to find a persuasive answer when asked, 'What's in it for me?'

The second major problem is unwillingness to accept the diversity of students and of their learning trajectories. This can be understood in two different ways, although ultimately they are closely related. First, diversity of origin. Age-based classes of students have never been homogeneous; but, in the latter part of the twentieth century, the diversity found in many schools and classrooms had become markedly more pronounced. In part, this is the result of large-scale population movements, as families in poorer countries emigrate to the more affluent countries, where they hope to achieve a better standard of living. In part it is also due to the increasing gap between rich and poor, even in those most affluent countries. And, as far as teachers are concerned, perhaps the most difficult form of diversity is that associated with the 'mainstreaming' of students who were previously segregated in classes and schools on account of the 'special' difficulties they experienced in 'regular' classrooms.

As Tharp and Gallimore (1988) cogently argue, it is these various kinds of 'diverse' students who are those most disenfranchised by the conception of education as 'one-model-fits-all' transmission and accreditation. However, as they and others have demonstrated, it is students who are most different from the notional norm who benefit most from the educational practices described in this chapter (Englert, 1992; McIntyre and Stone, 1999; see also Dalton and Tharp, this volume).

However, just as important as diversity in terms of entry characteristics is diversity in terms of individual developmental trajectories. The transmission model, with its prespecified outcomes, aims to produce graduates of the system who are, essentially, interchangeable in terms of their employability and willingness to retrain, when necessary, in order to adapt to the changes in the global market-place. This may be good business policy in the short term, but it fails to honour the second major responsibility of education, which is to enable individuals to achieve their unique potential. It also ignores the necessity to encourage diversity of individual learning trajectories, which are the source of innovation and potential improvement in society as a whole.

When teachers are judged in terms of their ability to get all students successfully to jump through the same hoops, they are naturally unwilling to encourage diverse individual developmental trajectories or to give time to exploratory dialogue in which the voicing of alternative perspectives is a prerequisite for the collaborative knowledge building that leads to the enhancement of understanding. In the long term, however, with its dislike of diversity and restriction of individual initiative and creativity, the current emphasis on homogeneity of educational outcomes can only be self-defeating.

Faced with these impediments to more effective practice, then, how might we proceed?

Looking to the Future

At the level of individual classrooms, it is clear that courageous and dedicated teachers are showing that practices based on CHAT conceptions of learning and teaching can be beneficial for all students, whatever their ethnicity, class or gender. This is particularly the case when their attempts to create communities of inquiry in their classrooms are reinforced by their own commitment to teacher research, undertaken in collaboration with colleagues. By carrying out inquiries into the conditions that enable the particular students in their charge to appropriate the cultural resources of knowledge, skills and strategies necessary to become productive and responsible citizens, while at the same time developing their own unique potential to contribute to the transformation of the larger society as well as to the realization of their own objectives, these teachers both model the values that they hope their students will emulate and they also blaze a trail for other teachers to follow. By disseminating the results of their inquiries, they also challenge other teachers to look critically at their own practices and at the assumptions on which they are based.

The reforms taking place in teacher preparation at a number of universities in countries around the world also give grounds for hope. To an increasing extent, prospective teachers are being introduced to constructivist and socio-cultural theories of learning and development and are often required to undertake an action research investigation during their practicum. The intention is that this will allow them to discover how taking an inquiring stance as a teacher can enable them to recognize and respond to the diversity in their classrooms and school communities and be more effective in working with their students in their zones of proximal development. Similar developments are also taking place in further professional development courses; here too, course members' inquiries in their own classrooms enable them to make connections between their practice and the theory to which they are being introduced.

At the same time, it has to be recognized that new teachers only rarely find that the schools in which they take up their first teaching positions provide support for the practices that they have been taught. Experienced teachers, too, having been enthused by the additional courses they have taken, often find little encouragement to sustain the changes they have started to make. Clearly, therefore, there is a great need for teachers to find support in groups of the kind described above in order to fill this gap.

Partnerships between universities and teacher groups can play a significant role in this respect. These are increasing in number and many are having a powerful, if geographically limited, effect. With the increase in internet connectivity, however, it is becoming increasingly feasible to create communities of school and university teacher inquirers who, although widely dispersed, are able to meet in virtual space.

But most important, in the longer term, is the creation of democratic, self-sustaining communities of inquiry within individual schools and school districts. In the first instance, it may be necessary for an external facilitator to get things under way, but it is crucial that the teachers themselves take 'ownership' of the issues and problems to be addressed, otherwise the setting up of 'teams' can produce nothing more than 'contrived collegiality' (Hargreaves, 1991). Ideally, of course, the agenda should be a responsibility shared between teachers and school or district administration. In the light of the earlier discussion, it also seems important that there be an 'improvable object' that provides a focus for the group's activities; for example, the creation of a mode of performance-based authentic assessment as an alternative to externally imposed high-stake standardized tests, or the working out of a way of organizing effective team-teaching. As with the examples of action research reported above, such 'objects' call not just for decisions about actions to be taken, but for ongoing knowledge building where the aim is to achieve greater individual and collective understanding of the grounds on which the decisions should be taken and for evaluating evidence collected of the consequences of those decisions.

Nevertheless, it has to be recognized that these initiatives will not, in themselves, be sufficient to transform the institution of education as a whole, for that will require a change in values at every level of society and on a scale commensurate with the expanding global market-place. However, by contributing positively to the formation of the identities and dispositions of the citizens of tomorrow, today's teachers, working collaboratively with their colleagues, can certainly play their part in creating a society in which it is knowing and understanding that are aimed for rather than the mere amassing of information, and in which the value of diversity is recognized and explored, both in terms of equity of opportunity and of the unique contribution that each individual can make.

On the larger scale, moreover, there are indications that the present disregard for the ecological environment we all share will, sooner rather than later, force a general re-evaluation of current practices and values. As citizens of the 'global village', therefore, as well as in our roles as educators, our responsibility is to practise as well as to foster a stance of critical inquiry that leads to enhanced understanding as a basis for responsible action.

Notes

1   The preceding examples as well as those that follow are taken from the classrooms of teacher members of the 'Developing Inquiring Communities in Education Project'. DICEP is a democratic, self-organizing group of classroom teachers, university teacher educators and a number of graduate students. Between 1991 and 1998 the project was supported by grants from the Spencer Foundation to

the Ontario Institute for Studies in Education to investigate 'Learning through Talk'.

2   See Wells (1995) for a more detailed exposition of the model.

3   Several traditional journals now exist to publish teacher research, e.g. *Educational Action Research* (Triangle Journals Ltd, PO Box 65, Wallingford OX10 0YG, U.K.) and *Teacher Research: The Journal of Classroom Inquiry* (Johnson Press, 49 Sheridan Ave., Albany NY 12210, USA). In addition, a number of online journals have recently been started, such as Networks (http://www.oise.utoronto.ca/~ctd/networks/), which includes links to other related sites.

16

Can a School Community Learn to Master Its Own Future? An Activity-Theoretical Study of Expansive Learning Among Middle School Teachers

Yrjö Engeström, Ritva Engeström and Arja Suntio

In educational research, cultural–historical activity theory has mainly been used to study individuals and classrooms. However, we see activity theory as, above all, a framework for understanding transformations in collective practices and organizations. In this chapter, we use activity theory to examine the possibility of school change, focusing our analysis on the entire teaching faculty of a school.

There are deep constraints and built-in obstacles to collaborative self-organizing and expansive learning in schools. One is the socio-spatial structure based on autonomous classrooms, teachers working as isolated individual practitioners, and the school functioning as an encapsulated unit (Hargreaves, 1994; Huberman, 1993). Another is the temporal structure of discrete lessons and relatively short standardized time sequences of work punctuated by tests, exams and grading (Engeström, 1998). A third is motivational and ethical – the use of grades and measured success as the dominant motive of school work – which practically always leads to the classification of students into categories such as 'weak' and 'competent', or 'passive' and 'active' (Henry, 1963). One of the effects of these constraints is to make it very difficult for school communities to collectively analyse and redesign their practice.

This chapter is an analysis of such a process at a school in Finland. In the autumn of 1998 we conducted an eleven-week Change Laboratory intervention with the teachers of a middle school located in a disadvantaged area of

Helsinki heavily populated by students from immigrant families. In weekly two-hour sessions, with the help of conceptual tools from activity theory, the teachers discussed and analysed their daily practice. On this basis, the teachers constructed a vision for the school's future and designed six sets of immediate practical changes. These were implemented during the winter and spring of 1999, and continued throughout the school year 1999/2000. We videotaped all the Change Laboratory sessions as well as some classroom lessons, and interviewed teachers, students and parents. We continued to follow and document the implementation efforts for over 18 months.

The immediate changes planned by the teachers contained challenges to the constraining structures mentioned above. In this chapter, we will focus on one of the six change efforts, namely the design and implementation of the 'final project' for ninth-grade students about to finish their middle school. We will be particularly concerned with the impact of this innovation on the motivational and ethical structural constraint mentioned above. What is at issue here is the teachers' way of constructing students.

The Setting, the Intervention and the Innovation

The setting of our study is Jakomäki middle school (Junior High School) in the city of Helsinki. Jakomäki is a socially and economically disadvantaged area in Helsinki. In 1997 the unemployment rate was 25 per cent, compared to 15 per cent in the city as a whole. Only 5 per cent of the adult population of Jakomäki had higher education, compared to 21 per cent in Helsinki as a whole. In 1998 Jakomäki school had about 280 students. About 30 per cent of them were recent immigrants and refugees, mainly from Russia and Somalia. The faculty consisted of 27 full-time teachers, including the principal. All these teachers participated regularly in the Change Laboratory sessions and in the different change efforts it generated.

In Jakomäki, we researchers thought that our field data indicated three major problem areas, which we formulated as follows:

1   Teachers' weak knowledge of the students' homes and backgrounds hampers the utilization of resources for learning and succeeding.
2   Teachers' weak knowledge of the students' careers after graduation and students' weak knowledge of the entrance requirements of further education hamper the utilization of resources.
3   The poverty of the school as a physical working environment for the students hampers the utilization of resources.

However, when we asked the teachers to formulate for themselves what they saw as the key problems, they came up with a very different set:

1 War against apathy – joy of work.
2 Peaceful time for planning and preparing together.
3 Change in students' manners and use of language.

While we researchers tried to focus on sources of trouble, the teachers' problems were already formulated as goals or calls for change. The notion of student apathy as a pervasive problem was central to the teachers' discourse at this point. The two sets of problems remained as complementary sounding boards for the rest of the Change Laboratory process. The teachers didn't seem to worry about their divergence, so we decided that neither should we.

The Change Laboratory process then traced the historical roots of current troubles and moved on to modelling current activity and its inner contradictions. The final step involved envisioning future activity and selecting concrete changes and innovations to be implemented. We asked each of the teachers to use a general model of an activity system (Engeström, 1987, p. 78) to describe their vision of how the school should function in the year 2003. On the basis of their contents, we sorted the 27 visions into three groups: short-term visions, middle-range visions and long-term visions. The teachers agreed that instead of being competing or mutually exclusive, the three groups were complementary. The short-term visions focused on increasing and improving the existing means of school work. The middle-range visions introduced the notions of 'learning to learn', 'projects', 'self-confidence' and an 'open learning environment'. The long-term visions talked about merging existing school subjects, connecting instruction to the world of work, teaching outside the school, and using outside experts and networks. The three complementary visions were debated by the teachers. The three-phase vision might be summarized as a progression.

Present resources increased and improved → Learning-centred pedagogy implemented in the school → The school networked and allied with the outside world

In the seventh session of the Change Laboratory the teachers selected six concrete areas for their immediate change efforts. A taskforce group of interested teachers took responsibility for each area. The areas were (1) shared traditions and improvement of students' manners, (2) final project and integration of instruction across subjects, (3) the physical environment of the school, (4) self-confidence and individualization of instruction, (5) collaboration between the middle school and the local elementary school, (6) tandem teaching in selected subjects. In the following, we will analyse only the 'final project', an initiative which involved practically all the teachers and came to challenge the structural constraints discussed in the introduction to this chapter. It was also enthusiastically accepted by an assembly of student representatives.

The idea of the final project is simple. The graduating ninth-grade students used to leave the school with only a report card and grades in their pocket. The teachers felt that the students should leave with something more tangible, with an achievement of which they could be proud. The final project is a cross-subject project on any relevant topic chosen by the student. It is to be completed during the winter/spring semester of the last school year, and a number of school hours are set aside exclusively for work on it. A teacher is assigned to guide and supervise each final project; the supervising teacher may or may not be responsible for teaching the particular school subject closest to the topic of the project. In addition, if students wish they may ask that the final project be evaluated as grounds for raising their final grades in a school subject. The outcomes of the final projects are displayed in an exhibition at the end of the school year.

In the spring of 1999, 71 per cent of the ninth graders completed their final projects. Of those, 54 per cent used their final projects successfully to raise some of their grades. In 2000, 91 per cent of the ninth graders completed their final projects, and 65 per cent of them successfully used the project to raise their grades. The topics of the projects ranged from Einstein's theory of relativity and Picasso's Cubism to Michael Jackson, a four-channel amplifier, graffiti, and a child's pyjamas.

Activity–Theoretical Conceptualization

A few key concepts of activity theory (CHAT) are particularly relevant for our analysis of the final project case. These include 'activity system', 'contradiction', 'object/motive' and 'expansive learning' (for discussions of key concepts of activity theory, see Engeström, 1999a; 2001). We will briefly discuss each of them, relating them to the final project process.

We see the object-oriented, artifact-mediated activity system as the foundational unit of analysis in activity–theoretical research. The key to understanding activity systems is their object-orientedness, or 'objectiveness'.

> The main thing that distinguishes one activity from another is the difference of their objects. It is exactly the object of an activity that gives it a determined direction. According to the terminology I have proposed, the object of an activity is its true motive. It is understood that the motive may be either material or ideal, either present in perception or existing only in imagination or in thought. (Leont'ev, 1978, p. 62)

Leont'ev's point is that the object of an activity should not be confused with either things out there in the environment or with goals. A thing out there in the environment can only become the object of an activity when it meets the need of the actors and is invested with meaning and motivating power. The object is a cultural and collective construct which has a long historical half-life and is typically difficult to articulate by individual participants of the activity system. The object determines the horizon of possible goals and actions which have finite and relatively short half-lives.

The general object of teachers' work is students – or more accurately, the relationship between students and the knowledge they are supposed to acquire. The students are for teachers never merely raw material to be moulded. They are the reason for coming to work, for agonizing about it and for enjoying it. Any serious attempt to reconceptualize the students is therefore consequential for the identity of teachers. Such a reconceptualization of the object also opens up an expanded repertoire of possible actions and goals. Paradoxically, a reconceptualization of the object can itself only happen through engagement in novel actions.

As noted above, in Jakomäki it was not easy to formulate a convincing working hypothesis of the contradictions of the teachers' activity system. It was only after the first round of implementation that we were ready to return to the modelling of the contradictions. It seems to us that the contradictions of the teachers' activity system were in a latent state in 1999. In other words, we could not observe aggravated tensions between the components of the activity system, such as practically disturbing mismatches between a new object and old tools or rules. The teachers did talk about change in the object – the students – in terms of increased apathy. They even saw a contradiction between the two faces of the same students.

Change Laboratory session 8
Teacher 7:   What is strange is that when I teach them here in the daytime, nobody is interested and nobody cares. But when they come voluntarily in the evening, everything is fine and everyone cares. Yet the same faces are there. There is a huge contradiction there.

But they did not seem to experience this as an issue that would force them to rethink their tools. As shown in figure 16.1, according to our interpretation, the inner contradictions of the work of Jakomäki teachers appeared only in latent forms, as dilemmas within components of the activity system, not yet as aggravated contradictions between components causing constant manifest troubles or 'double bind' situations in everyday practice.

The two lightning-shaped arrows in figure 16.1 represent the latent contradictions we found salient in the teachers' activity system. The first one (within the object) was manifested in the teachers' repeated talk about students as apathetic – and in occasional utterances where they would contradict their very assessment. The second latent contradiction (within the instruments) was manifested in the teachers' repeated talk about the need to control the students' conduct – and in occasional statements suggesting that the students should be trusted.

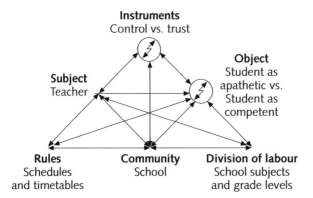

Figure 16.1   The activity system of the Jakomäki teachers and its inner contradictions.

While systemic contradictions are faced and overcome time and again in everyday practice, they keep coming back, and in more aggravated forms. They cannot be eliminated or fixed by means of isolated technical solutions. They can be resolved and transcended only by means of systemic transformations – processes we call expansive learning. Expansive learning is learning what is not yet there by means of the actions of questioning, modelling and experimentation (Engeström, 1987; 2001). Its core is the collaborative creation of new artifacts and patterns of practice.

In his important analysis of cultural learning, Michael Tomasello uses the metaphor of the 'ratchet effect'. There are two dialectically intertwined basic processes in cultural learning, imitation and innovation. After often lengthy periods of imitation, humans engage in intense moments of creation. For the creation to be sustained rather than evaporate with the demise of the particular individuals, it must be faithfully imitated by other members of the community and objectified in an artifactual form.

> The metaphor of the ratchet in this context is meant to capture the fact that imitative learning (with or without active instruction) enables the kind of faithful transmission that is necessary to hold the novel variant in place in the group so as to provide a platform for further innovations – with the innovations themselves varying in degree to which they are individual or social/cooperative. (Tomasello, 1999, p. 39)

Tomasello (ibid., p. 41) states that the typical situation of sociogenesis is 'when a small group of people attempt collaboratively to modify an artifact or practice they have inherited from others in order to meet new exigencies'. He goes on to point out that 'these group-level processes are not well understood' (ibid., p. 42; see also pp. 209–10).

We think that we can see the ratchet effect operating, at least partially, in the formation of the final project in Jakomäki.

Design and Implementation of the 'Final Project': Transforming the Teachers' Construction of Students

The idea of the final project began to emerge in November 1998, in the seventh session of the Change Laboratory. We recorded discussions in which the design and implementation were discussed. These discussions took place in three formats: (1) Change Laboratory sessions and evaluation meetings with all the teachers present – we recorded five such discussions; (2) meetings of the taskforce group of six teachers to whom the final project was assigned – we recorded four such meetings; (3) individual and group interviews with teachers in the final phase of implementation and after its completion in 1999 – we recorded two such sets of interviews (the first set consisted of nine individual interviews, the second of a group interview with the taskforce group). The interviews were conducted in a very open-ended manner, largely letting the teacher(s) take the discussion in the directions they preferred.

Bearing in mind the differences between the formats of the discussions, we decided to treat all the eleven discussions as a single longitudinal corpus of data, covering the 11-month time span from November 1998 to October 1999. The discourse was transcribed and divided into a total of 256 topical sequences.

We identified seven phases in the 1998–9 round of design and implementation:

1   Discussing alternative ideas
2   Specifying the object and idea
3   Planning the details of the 'final project'
4   Planning while starting the implementation
5   Implementing and assessing the implementation individually
6   Evaluating the idea and its implementation after the semester
7   Drawing implications for planning for the next year

In more general terms, the first three phases may be characterized as planning, phases four and five as implementation, and phases six and seven as evaluation.

A detailed analysis of the discourse corpus (Suntio, 2000) revealed that there were three dominant themes running through the data. These themes were (1) the pedagogical principles of the innovation, (2) organization of the teachers' guidance work in the final project, and (3) students and their characteristics. While the pedagogical principles were debated, the organization of teachers' guidance work was discussed in a dilemmatic fashion. Interestingly enough, the discussion about students changed its character during the course of the events. We may characterize this change as the emergence of an insight. The three dominant themes and the corresponding characteristics of discussion are summarized in Table 16.1.

Table 16.1 Dominant themes and processes in the teachers' discourse.

Dominant theme	Character of discussion
1 Pedagogical principles	Debate: integration and guidance vs. free choice; long project vs. short project
2 Organization of guidance work	Dilemma: how do we arrange the guidance of cross-subject projects within our subject-specific individual schedules?
3 Students	Insight: from students as incompetent and apathetic to students as competent and energetic

Figure 16.2 shows percentages of thematic sequences devoted to the three dominant themes in different phases of the process. The discussion of pedagogical principles follows a nice U-shaped curve: in the beginning, pedagogical principles dominate, then it fades away in the middle only to return strongly at the end. Discussion of the organization of teachers' guidance work shows a saw-like shape, from zero to over 20 per cent and back again, not surprisingly dominating at the beginning of the implementation. Discussion of students follows an overall rising pattern, becoming dominant in the last three phases.

Discussion of students is discussion about the object of teachers' work. From an activity–theoretical point of view the qualitative shift in this discussion is highly interesting. In analysing the teachers' statements concerning the students we found it surprisingly easy to categorize them either as predominantly negative or predominantly positive. Here is an example of both kinds of talk.

Change Laboratory session 8
Researcher: Well, any comments from others? What do you think of this idea [the final project]?
Teacher 8:   I'd like to ask what we'll do with the half of the students who won't do any final project on any topic. How do we check that and what will we give them?
Researcher: Well?
Teacher 8:   Half of the students will be like that, they'll skip the whole idea. I have an oral presentation assignment at the moment, one student has held a presentation, others have skipped it. This is what they will always do.

From individual teacher interviews at the end of the implementation:

Teacher 9:   Well, I thought about someone, for example in my class, that she or he at least will definitely not do it. And then there have been these positive surprises, the person has actually produced a project, and a good one, too. Students who have otherwise been doing

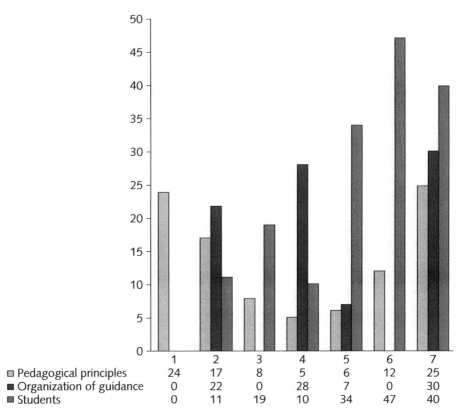

	1	2	3	4	5	6	7
▣ Pedagogical principles	24	17	8	5	6	12	25
■ Organization of guidance	0	22	0	28	7	0	30
▨ Students	0	11	19	10	34	47	40

Figure 16.2 Percentages of topical sequences of teachers' talk representing the three dominant themes in the seven phases of the final project (total number of all topical sequences in a given phase is 100 per cent).

pretty poorly, and have been absent a lot and so on, they have actually shaped up really well, like among the girls of my class, for instance. It's been nice to be able to give a good grade. A few got a 9 [on a scale from 4 to 10] in their report cards, and otherwise they've been doing pretty badly, and that's nice. And surely for them, one really notices, when I've given them feedback, one notices that they are really glowing, they know that they've worked, and then they get a good grade for it.

The shift from predominantly negative to predominantly positive talk about students is graphically shown in figure 16.3. The shift did not happen abruptly. It took place in the gradual emergence and increase of positive talk, equaling the level of negative talk in phase five, reaching its high point in phase six, and remaining strong in phase seven. Importantly, negative talk did not disappear. It did not even decrease: in phase three, 15 per cent of the topical sequences were negative, in phase seven the percentage was exactly the same. In other words, the emergence of positive talk about students was truly an

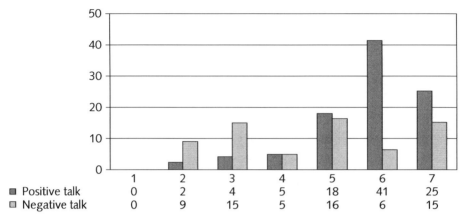

	1	2	3	4	5	6	7
▓ Positive talk	0	2	4	5	18	41	25
▢ Negative talk	0	9	15	5	16	6	15

Figure 16.3 Percentages of predominantly positive and predominantly negative topical sequences of teachers' talk about students in the seven phases of the final project process (total number of all topical sequences in a given phase is 100 per cent).

expansion and enriching of the repertoire; it did not emerge at the cost of previous ways of talking.

We examined this phenomenon of 'expansion as enrichment' by looking in detail at the contents of sub-themes of teachers' talk about students in the planning and evaluation phases of the process. In the planning phases, teachers' talk about the sub-themes 'students' participation', 'students' choice of final project topic' and 'student resources' was limited to a range of seven substantively different topics; in the evaluation phases the same sub-themes manifested themselves in sixteen substantively different topics. Again, the early topics typically did not disappear, but the range was radically widened.

We must not separate the findings about the shift in teachers' talk about students from the rest of the formation of the final project innovation. The shift was not an isolated phenomenon. At the beginning of this chapter we introduced three types of deep constraints and built-in obstacles to collaborative self-organizing and expansive learning in schools: the socio-spatial structure of encapsulation, the temporal structure of punctuation, and the motivational and ethical structure of success-as-grades. The final project violates and attempts to reach beyond all three constraints. It allows the students and forces the teachers to operate beyond and across encapsulated school subjects. It allows the students and forces the teachers to work on a longer-term basis, preparing final projects over a whole semester, thus going beyond the temporal punctuation of lessons and tests.

Perhaps most importantly, the final project opens a new angle on motivation and grades. It introduces work motivated by the pride of achieving something beyond the obligatory demands of the curriculum. But instead of dichotomously separating this opportunity from grades, the final project offers the students a chance to take their work-of-pride and use it to enhance their grades as well. In this sense, the final project cracks open and problematizes the predetermined, given-from-above nature of grades, both for students and the teachers.

From this point of view, the final project may be seen as a small but potentially expansive change capsule, or 'Trojan horse', forcing an entry into the large bastion of school-work-as-it-is. Each year it is implemented, the final project requires actions that make visible and problematic the deep constraining structures of the activity systems of teachers and students, simultaneously offering a chance to move above and beyond those constraints. It is not an accident that the teachers' positive talk about students gained momentum only during the practical implementation of the final project. In other words, while expansive learning in this case is manifested in, and possibly carried forward through, teachers' words and speech genres redefining their object (the students) as competent and energetic, it is initiated by and grounded in the practical actions and material artifacts of the final project. Without this material and practical anchoring, the ratchet effect would not be achieved.

Of course the sustainability and diffusion of the final project innovation is still an unfinished story. It remains to be seen whether the positive redefinition of students will be objectified in corresponding new concepts, and whether such new concepts will in turn open up new possibilities of innovative practice. Thus, we continue working with the school community in Jakomäki.

The Power of Multi-voicedness

In similar intervention studies we have conducted in other organizations (e.g. Engeström, 1999b), the practitioners' involvement in serious and sustained change efforts has typically been explained by aggravated contradictions in the activity system. Such aggravated contradictions generate disturbances and double bind situations in everyday work, making it evident that something must be done.

In Jakomäki this explanation works poorly. As we have already indicated, the teachers did not experience the kind of urgent pressure or pending crisis that would make expansive transformation a deeply felt necessity. Yet the teachers were very willing to design and try out new forms of practice. This was nicely expressed in the teachers' interpretation of the key problems discussed earlier in this chapter. Instead of dwelling on problems and their causes, they formulated calls for change. This is in stark contrast to our experiences in many similar projects, where the practitioners have interpreted the absence of crisis as a licence to protect the status quo.

Figure 16.4 shows the place of the final project in the effort to re-mediate the teachers' activity system. The final project is only a limited tool among many others. It would be very unrealistic to proclaim that this tool in itself is

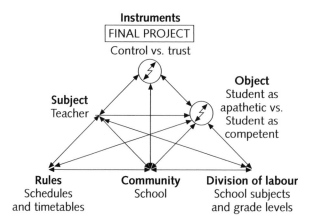

Figure 16.4 The place of the final project in re-mediating the teachers' activity system.

going to resolve the still largely latent deep-seated contradictions between student as apathetic and student as competent on the one hand, and between control and trust on the other. Certainly, it may work as a springboard or 'Trojan horse'. But why would teachers invest serious energy and time in it? Why did the Jakomäki teachers risk their peace and engage in adventurous efforts such as the final project?

We think that the answer may lie in the power of multi-voicedness inherent in the teachers' activity system. In Jakomäki new voices, different from traditional professional teacher discourse, were brought in by the teachers of immigrant students (on the concept of voice, see R. Engeström, 1995).

In Finland, multicultural and multi-ethnic education is a relatively new phenomenon. Teachers are used to teaching a quite monocultural student body. In Jakomäki the percentage of immigrant students is exceptionally high. Both Somali and Russian immigrant students have backgrounds and life worlds so different from the Finnish students that their teachers have to break down barriers between school subjects to create meaningful instructional units. They also go out into the homes of their students and often establish counselling-like relationships with students, sometimes also with their family members.

The teachers of immigrant students in Jakomäki thus operated as a microcosm that in practice and in discourse anticipated the changes subsequently put into words in the teachers' visions and implemented in the concrete change efforts. The advanced practices gave these teachers a new perspective, which they repeatedly voiced in the Change Laboratory discussions and follow-up meetings. A good example is the contribution of Teacher 10 in the following excerpt. In the last Change Laboratory session, the teachers presented their change plans to a representative of the Helsinki School Board. As the final project was being presented, this official asked whether the plan would include immigrant students. As the speaker of the taskforce (Teacher 3) started to explain that this would not be the case, a teacher of immigrant students (Teacher 10), not a member of the taskforce, took the initiative.

> *Change Laboratory session 11*
> *School Board official*: I would still like to ask, I came to think about the immigrant students. Is it the idea that they, too, will do this final project?
> *Researcher*: Has the taskforce thought about this?
> *Teacher 3*: No. This is for ninth graders.
> *Teacher 10*: Personally I thought that at least my class will do this. In one way or another. One can use the students' special competencies in this work. There are skills which may not be so academic, but there are many such areas of competence that are terribly important.

The immigrant teachers actually went ahead and implemented the final project in their classes with great success.

Conclusion

In a recent paper, David Hargreaves (1999) suggests that schools need to become knowledge-creating organizations, much in the vein advocated by Nonaka and Takeuchi (1995) for corporations. Hargreaves (1999, p. 126) recommends that 'professional knowledge creation [be] not seen as a random, undirected activity of the minority of the individual teachers with a creative talent, but as a whole-school process that has to be managed – with the allocation of material and temporal resources, coordination of people and activities, regular monitoring and support' as well as 'provision of regular opportunities for reflection, dialogue, enquiry and networking in relation to professional knowledge and practice'.

These conditions are well understood by the teachers and the principal in Jakomäki. However, there is a curious gap in Hargreaves's recommendations. He does not say a word about the students, the central object of the reflection, dialogue, inquiry and networking he is calling for. Among researchers and educational administrators there is widespread agreement about the need to move from transmission and acquisition of fixed knowledge to the construction of knowledge understood as a productive and collaborative process (as is emphasized in other chapters in this volume). However, this historical shift in educational discourse loses much of its promise when we take a closer look at how students are conceptualized within its key texts. In the influential monograph *How People Learn* (Bransford, Brown and Cocking, 1999) one looks in vain for a substantive discussion of students' lives and motives. The statement 'school failure may be partly explained by the mismatch between what students have learned in their home cultures and what is required of them in school' (p. 60) pretty much covers what the book has to offer in this respect. The more we move toward the design of learning environments, the more completely the students' lives disappear. Symptomatically, the book does not even mention the important work of Patricia Phelan and her associates on students' multiple life worlds and the boundaries between them (Phelan, Davidson and Yu, 1998). Yet, as Andy Hargreaves points out, there is much more at stake than correcting a 'mismatch'.

> Increased poverty creates hungry children who cannot learn and tired ones who cannot concentrate. Fractured, blended and lone-parent families fill teachers' classes with children who are often troubled; they present teachers with parents' nights of labyrinthine complexity, and leave them with outdated curriculum materials where families with two parents and their own children are presented as the cultural norm.
>
> For teachers, what's 'out there' beyond their school is not an academic abstraction or a futuristic projection. It stares back at them everyday through the eyes of the children they teach. What matters is not whether teachers connect with what's 'out there' beyond their school, but how effectively they do so. (A. Hargreaves, 1997, p. 6)

As we see it, the strength of the Jakomäki school community is in this very 'staring back' which has cultivated an insistence on the object: the students, their lives and possibilities. Students may be talked about in negative, nostalgic and frustrated terms. But they are not deleted or covered up with the help of fashionable jargon.

The lesson we have learned from this work is that a collective reconceptualization of the object of the teachers' activity system is possible. Our findings indicate that this may be an indirect process, mediated by two complementary factors. On the one hand, the reconceptualization of the object in Jakomäki was mediated by the design and implementation of concrete novel tools and associated actions which, while small in themselves, have the expansive potential to function as a 'Trojan horse'. On the other hand, the reconceptualization of the object was mediated by new voices among teachers, stemming from the marginal but innovative pedagogical practices of the teachers of immigrant students.

17

Cultural Historical Activity Theory and the Expansion of Opportunities for Learning After School

Katherine Brown and Michael Cole

This chapter addresses the issue of how Cultural Historical Activity Theory (CHAT) can help in the design and sustaining of after-school educational activity systems. We begin by summarizing why after-school education is a topic worthy of study. We then describe efforts to implement sustainable after-school systems and the relevance of CHAT to these efforts.

The topic of after-school educational activity has burgeoned into a major educational issue in the US in recent years (Belle, 1999). Several factors seem to have given rise to this new-found interest. First, there is an ongoing concern with declines in educational achievement across grade levels. Second, welfare reform has removed many parents from the home and into job training programmes, while programmes and organizations providing care for their children are struggling to meet the consequent increased demand for child care. Third, the last few years of the 1990s saw a turn away from 'social promotion' in K-12 education. The result is that local schools, with heavy funding from the state, are asked to begin taking responsibility for improving educational achievement for their poorly achieving students during the after-school hours or to accept the economic, social and psychological consequences of holding children back. In these circumstances, teachers and after-school care staff need effective models to work with.

To these three social factors evoking interest in after-school education, we add a fourth issue: the current reform efforts of colleges and universities to provide undergraduates with service learning opportunities, increasing student proficiency in working with new information technologies, and increasing the number of courses that expose students to rigorous research.

Confronting the Problems with a CHAT Toolkit in Hand

For the past decade we have been using CHAT to guide the design and implementation of an after-school activity system that responds to the social, political, economic and educational pressures we have identified above. During this time we have used CHAT both as an object of research and as a guide to practice.

We have found this activity to be rewarding in several ways. First, we have found it possible to create after-school programmes that children voluntarily attend and which enhance their opportunity to practise and extend academic and social abilities. Second, we have provided social science undergraduates with college and university courses that place them in community settings where they play and learn with children, assist adult staff members by enriching the ratio of attentive adults and fostering educationally beneficial interactions. Undergraduates respond with an increase in subject-matter knowledge, familiarity with ethnographic and psychological research methods, and benefit from the experience of finding theories learned at the university of practical use in an activity they value. Third, as researchers, we have been provided with facilities that enable us productively to test and expand our understanding of human development and its institutional foundations.

The Fifth Dimension: UCSD's Normative Model

An essential tool in our work is the use of a hybrid activity system we refer to as the 'Fifth Dimension'. As we shall see, an essential feature of the Fifth Dimension is its adaptability to specific local conditions such that it produces a plethora of 'offspring', not all of which can be considered close copies of a proposed 'original'. Nonetheless, there are similarities across implementations which make it useful to provide a provisional description for purposes of later exposition. When asked to describe a Fifth Dimension briefly to potential collaborators or in articles, we produce a normative description, such as the following.

The Fifth Dimension is an educational activity system that offers school-aged children a specially designed environment in which to explore a variety of off-the-shelf computer games and game-like educational activities during the after-school hours. The computer games are part of a make-believe play world that includes non-computer games like origami, chess and boggle and a variety of other artifacts. 'Task cards' or 'adventure guides' written by project staff members for each game are designed to help participants (both children and undergraduate students) orient to the game, to form goals and to chart progress toward becoming an expert. The task cards provide a variety of requirements to externalize, reflect upon and criticize information, to write to someone, to look up information in an encyclopedia, and to teach someone else what one has learned, in addition to the intellectual tasks written into the software or game activity itself.

As a means of distributing the children's and undergraduates' use of the various games, the Fifth Dimension contains a table-top or wall-chart maze consisting of some twenty rooms. Each room provides access to two or more games, and the children may choose which games to play as they enter each room. There is an electronic entity (a wizard/wizardess) who is said to live in the internet. The entity writes to (and sometimes chats with) the children and undergraduates via the internet. In the mythology of the Fifth Dimension, the wizard/ess acts as the participants' patron, provider of games, mediator of disputes, and the source of computer glitches and other misfortunes.

Because it is located in a community institution, the Fifth Dimension activities require the presence of a local 'site coordinator' who greets the participants as they arrive and supervises the flow of activity in the room. The site coordinator is trained to recognize and support the pedagogical ideals and curricular practices that mark the Fifth Dimension as 'different' – a different way for kids to use computers, a different way of playing with other children, as well as a different way for adults to interact with children.

The presence of university and college students is a major draw for the children. The participating college students are enrolled in a course focused on fieldwork in a community setting. The undergraduates write papers about the development of individual children, the educative value of different games, differences in the ways that boys and girls participate in the play world, variations in language use and site culture, and other topics that bring regular course work and field observations together.

In short, considered in its community context, the Fifth Dimension is organized to create an institutionalized version of the form of interaction that Vygotsky (1978) referred to as a zone of proximal development for participants. From time to time there is creative confusion about who the more capable peers might be (when novice undergraduates encounter children highly skilled in playing educational computer games about which the former know nothing). But the general culture of collaborative learning that is created serves the development of all.

Before moving on, we want to call attention to two important features of this description in the present context. First, because it is a normative description, it is written ahistorically: it describes a 'once and future' idealized reality. In practice, every Fifth Dimension is a reflection of its time and place, coming to fruition in diverse concrete circumstances. Second, and closely related, the description is abstract: it does not reveal the complexity involved in dealing with the ever-shifting resources on both the community and university side of the partnership that are needed to support the activity. The concrete reality gives vivid life to the notion that change is the only constant: undergraduates change every academic quarter, community personnel come and go frequently, children's participation varies enormously, from a single visit to repeated weekly visits that, in some cases, last for years. The actual games played by the children change along with the hardware at a pace we could not imagine or anticipate when these activities began two decades ago.

Some Useful CHAT Tools for Creating and Running a Fifth Dimension

There have been a number of useful presentations of the general principles of cultural–historical activity theory which we have drawn on to guide us in our work (Cole, 1996; Engeström, 1987; Vygotsky, 1978.) In this section we select some of the principles that have played an especially important role in our attempts to use CHAT as a tool for building and maintaining after-school educational activities.

The centrality of context and activity

As noted in earlier publications, the notions of context and activity are used in a variety of ways by contemporary social scientists (Cole, 1996). In some cases we have found it useful to use a 'social-ecological' concept of context, typically represented as a set of concentric circles or nested dolls, in which the focal activities are at or near the centre, constituted by and constituting the levels above and below them (Bronfenbrenner and Morris, 1998). In using a 'concentric circles' notion of context we are especially mindful of the fact that causal influences flow between largest and smallest circles in both directions. Used in this manner, the image of concentric circles captures the embeddedness of joint mediated activity: an undergraduate, child and computer in a corner of a larger club; the club as part of a neighbourhood ecology; a school district which channels children into after-school clubs on and off campus; a community whose families the school district serves, etc.

At other times it appears most useful to interpret context as 'that which weaves together', emphasizing the co-constitution of the phenomena of interest – in the current case, the ways that ideologies, artifacts, institutions and individuals interact such that a particular pattern of after-school activity emerges. The context-as-weaving metaphor also helps us to keep in mind that there is a temporal dimension essential to context, in addition to a spatial one. It is by tracing changes between the activity and its contexts, considered in both their temporal and spatial dimensions, that we are able to gain some purchase on the problem of understanding the dynamics of change.

As noted by Cole and Engeström (1993), there is a close affinity between contemporary notions of context and the notion of activity as developed in Russian and German psychology. A special virtue of the use of activity as an adjunct to, or substitute for, the concept of context is that it both forces attention to the historical dimension of the context/activity in question and allows a means of identifying crucial constituents of the phenomenon being investigated, as they relate to each other.

An example of a contextual element that is more or less constant across implementations of the Fifth Dimension is that the programme runs after school. In the life of the community, after school is a time for young people to play and to 'hang out'. Lessons in dance, music, seasonal sports leagues or scouting are standard fare for those communities/families with the resources (Zarabatany, et al., 1990). For many children, on the other hand, it is a time to attend one of a variety of loosely structured after-school care programmes which are generally designed to keep children active and amused until their parents can pick them up (Belle, 1999).

The importance of goal formation

Each adaptation of the model initiated 20 years ago is intended to be a cooperative effort between people affiliated with universities and people affiliated with community institutions. Such collaborations require what Olga Vasquez (Vasquez, et al., 1994) refers to as 'dynamic relations of exchange'. Consequently, we begin by seeking to establish common goals. At the highest level this is generally easy; community institutions want enriched educational experiences for their children; creating enriched after-school activities was the common object of the programme of the institutions with which we and our colleagues worked. But when it came to the specific goals necessary for achieving the joint activity, something like 'joint goal formation' was necessary for creating sufficiently coordinated actions among such a distributed group of participants.

Whether the point of view considered is that of a child, an undergraduate, a parent, a club staff programming director, a university administrator or research associate, we have found that each participant has to have sufficient motivation to commit time and resources to the activity. Each has to experience their involvement and its attendant benefits as preferable to existing alternatives.

The notion of leading activity

The issue of the Fifth Dimension's location 'between' home and school points to a variety of sources of goals for participation: play, peer interaction and learning are prominent candidates for children. These goals, although with somewhat different proportion and content, also apply to the undergraduates who receive course credit. For researchers, a leading activity (the activity that provided the fundamental motivation for their participation) is work, producing such goals as testing the efficacy of designed play worlds, understanding the institutional-level changes needed to sustain them, and educating students in the process (both the children and their undergraduate mentors). For the staff of the host institutions the leading activity is also work, including the work of providing children a safe haven and raising money to sustain themselves in their community contexts. Finding the right mesh of joint actions to enable joint satisfaction of all these goals is a major challenge in creating and maintaining any Fifth Dimension.

The role of dis-coordination in change

The ongoing process of modification each system undergoes over time means that dis-coordination and conflict will inevitably occur, both within and between systems (Engeström, 1987). For example, the education/play mix of the Fifth Dimension places somewhat 'formal' demands for regular staffing, upkeep of equipment, and a different way for children and adults to interact (non-hierarchical, non-directive) upon a harried community organization's administration. The staffing support for after-school activities is generally quite modest, owing to marginal institutional budgets. As a result of always-fragile funding, the wages paid to staff are generally quite low, which means high levels of turnover of personnel and hence dis-coordinations within the system. When we consider that each Fifth Dimension is itself part of a university–community partnership, the sources of dis-coordination multiply.

When we focus on dis-coordinations between community and university partners, we need look no further than the fact that the university quarter or semester system does not run on the same schedule as those of the community institutions. How is the activity to be conducted during winter holidays, for example, when Boys and Girls Clubs may remain open, while universities and schools are closed? What happens when the university closes for Easter a week before the local school?

These dis-coordinations are experienced negatively by participants, who always wish to see the system 'running smoothly', *ad infinitum* and free of conflict. But change is the only constant in a system and the processes of social change inevitably produce dis-coordination and resulting conflicts.

The centrality of communicative practices and mediational means

Vygotsky (1978) places communication at the centre of his theory of language and thought by arguing that 'the thought is completed in the word'. Therefore, in designing activities, we paid central attention to how communicative arrangements were organized. With respect to activities within the Fifth Dimension, we emphasize arranging interactions where adult and child participants have to pause to comment on their problem-solving efforts in oral or written reflections. For example, we design 'task cards' or 'game guides' as instructions for playing the games within the Fifth Dimension that require that learners pause, reflect and codify their strategies for problem solving as demonstrations of mastery (as hints for a collective repository of local game-playing knowledge, in the form of letters written to other children or the wizard).

Mediation by tools and signs is accorded great attention at every level in the system. Examples of different forms of mediation in the Fifth Dimension sessions themselves (through computers, game cards, letter writing, conversation, etc.) are described briefly in the normative description of a model Fifth Dimension. We also place a heavy emphasis on mediational means in organizing the work of the researchers and instruction at the university. At a local level, ensuring internet access at the local sites – for participating adult sponsors and university students alike – as well as conducting ongoing discussions on a common list-server are considered matters of practical necessity. More globally, computer-mediated communication has been essential to interaction among experimental enactmens of the Fifth Dimension systems located in geographically distributed regions.

Applying the principles

The list of CHAT principles invoked above could be expanded and several research projects implementing these principles could be cited (Cole, Engeström and Vasquez, 1998, for example). However, we want to use this chapter to show how we have applied this intellectual toolkit to enhance our goal of understanding how to expand opportunities for after-school learning. In order to avoid repeating ourselves by writing about one of the original systems, we will describe the origins, development and fate of two Fifth Dimension systems over the course of three years (1995–7). We will call the sites Big State University and Small Private College. They are of interest because each of the systems took as its starting point the initial Fifth Dimension, initiated at UC San Diego in 1986–7, and implemented their adaptation of it in a different way, according to the demands of their local institutional circumstances.

In applying CHAT ideas to these two 'alien' sites we rely on a combination of reports, notes posted to the Consortium list-server, and responses to specific queries from the authors (whose role in the project was to provide a description of the overall development of the Consortium activities as a whole). As an organizing device, we will describe each system in terms of the small set of conceptual tools discussed above.

Big State University

At Big State University the Fifth Dimension was formed as a collaboration between the College of Education and several schools in the local area. The Big State Fifth Dimension opened in three elementary schools. The university also runs one on-campus site to which children are bussed. The programmes run for 2–3 hours after school each day and the local school bus is present to take the children home at the end of their extended day from each of the sites.

The centrality of context

Big State University is located in a rural area where children are generally bussed to school. All local schools have an after-school programme for which parents pay a nominal fee. The usual programme consists of supervising children while they do their homework in the school cafeteria, supplemented by some outdoor activities. This circumstance creates a large pool of children who can regularly engage in Fifth Dimension activities, in contrast, for example, to the sporadic participation of children in sites where the activity is part of the 'come and go as you like' culture of after-school recreation centres with heavy turnover in membership and personnel.

Another important contextual factor to be considered in our analysis of the emergence of the Big State Fifth Dimension programme is that their College of Education has a major responsibility for supporting the development of technology-based instruction in local primary schools. In addition to making available existing relations of exchange between area schools and the university, this prior relationship meant that each programme had relatively new, sophisticated and plentiful computers which could be made available for after-school use. Importantly, the schools also have support for maintaining and upgrading their computer facilities, thus relieving the university partners of this responsibility.

Goal formation

In San Diego the first Fifth Dimensions opened after university researchers and community participants had spent a year discussing needs and goals and exploring various options before it was decided to use the Fifth Dimension as the common after-school activity. By comparison, at Big State the process of goal formation was accelerated and in some respects perfunctory. There was, to begin with, a history of prior implementations and accumulated materials to draw upon. Based on this history and local needs, the after-school activities suggested by the Fifth Dimension model were perceived by the key participants at local schools as natural extensions of existing arrangements for providing assistance with technology in order to enrich existing after-school programmes for the children. Teachers who participated in the programme could gain course credits and enhance their pay and professional expertise. It seemed that the goals were obvious and widely shared.

Dis-coordination and conflict

Although start-up and the early implementation of the Fifth Dimension at Big State appears from the foregoing account to have been a smooth operation, there were in fact important areas of dis-coordination and conflict that could only be encountered over time in connection with curricular changes, physical expansion, and experience of the ebb and flow of inter-institutional collaboration. For example, the new practicum course conflicted with older courses for time slots and resources; the larger curriculum changes required many faculty meetings, the writing of new curricular specifications, and heated discussions about disciplinary principles and standards. Arrangements with local teachers and principals, although set in a supportive context, nonetheless required provisions for assuring teachers that their classrooms would not be left in a state of chaos following the new after-school activities.

Of particular interest for purposes of illustrating the process of dis-coordination and conflict in the life of such a system is a situation that arose in the summer of 1999 when the Big State programme had been running for five years. Based on prior successes, the governing committee of the Big State–Public School Partnership decided to undertake an expansion of the system by adding one new school in each of seven counties.

The disruption began with failure on the part of both the school and university partners to organize their work before the summer break. Summer is a time for vacation, not intense inter-institutional work. But summer vacation also ends very early in this part of the country. The sense of urgency, time spent planning and the relative priorities of each of the partners were badly out of alignment until well into late summer of 1999. A crisis was averted only because the university side of the partnership poured 'unbudgeted' time and effort into providing the additional help on both university and community sides of the system that was needed to make sure that the programme could expand as planned in the fall.

The centrality of communicative practices and mediational means

At the level of interpersonal interactions between college students and children, the interactions in the Big State Fifth Dimension sites display many similarities to earlier implementations in the mediational means used: a maze with multiple rooms and multiple games within rooms, similar forms of computer hardware and software, a practice of talking about and corresponding with a mythical wizard-like patron/correspondent, instructional cards accompanying each game to provide scaffolding of the joint activity of undergraduates and children in the framework of the activity as a whole, and so on. The most interesting difference at this level concerns communicative practices that have a distinct regional flavour; in the Big State case, this arose from the cultural features of the rural communities from which their Fifth Dimension draws students. Big State's area of the US is heavily populated by Christian Fundamentalists, who are inclined to adopt relatively strict norms concerning adult–child interaction and to favour a 'transmission' model of education, in contrast with the relatively egalitarian and playful norms of (for example) the UCSD Fifth Dimensions. As a consequence, the communicative practices display somewhat more concern with issues of proper behaviour and control.

Small Private College

At Small Private College the Fifth Dimension was formed as a collaboration between one faculty member in the psychology department and the YMCA in a nearby town, which serves children from several elementary schools in the local area.

The centrality of context

For Small Private College, teaching is the primary mission. Undergraduate liberal arts education and community service overshadow opportunities for research or for exploring the uses of computer technology. Students were easily motivated to go into community settings to acquire work experience or to volunteer in community service. However, research and fieldwork associated with their college work were not important motives for them. Furthermore, the principal investigator's teaching load and the departmental norms made it very difficult for the course to function during the entire academic year, as a result requiring significant modifications of the educational practices associated with the original practicum in child development, as well as with the organization of the Fifth Dimension activities at the YMCA.

In the small town where the implementer opened her Fifth Dimension, many of the parents whose children attend the after-care programmes at the YMCA work in textile mills and biomedical light industry. The Fifth Dimension ran two days a week. In the fall it was part of the activities of a regularly scheduled class of university students, but in the spring it ran primarily with volunteer students who remained after the fall course, supplemented by two paid assistants from the same group.

Goal formation

As with Big State University the process of goal formation was truncated in the case of Small College because it coincided with the arrival there of the principal investigator as a new faculty member just as the school year was starting. The consortium of which Small College was a part was involved in an intensive effort to carry out a comparative evaluation of the different systems, creating pressure on the principal investigator to get the activities up and going so that data could be collected as part of the consortium effort.

The local YMCA staff welcomed the idea of a computer-based activity starting up at their institution. The principal investigator initiated a series of workshops so that the staff of the Y would be able to act as site coordinators, which meant learning how to use the hardware, software and artifacts important in the Fifth Dimension play world, as well as the 'principles of cooperative learning' which the principal investigator brought with her. However, this effort was not successful. The Y staff approved of having the activity at their site, but they did not exhibit significant interest in sharing responsibility for running it.

When the effort to involve Y staff failed, two students who had been in the professor's college course were hired to run the Fifth Dimension. They were encouraged to continue trying to involve the local staff because the principal investigator understood from prior experience that success hinged on local staff commitment to being trained and on obtaining financial resources to enable this to happen.

A part of the YMCA staff's reluctance to embrace the activity derived from the same contextual/cultural factors that were present at Big State University approximately 100 miles away. The local adults in the surrounding communities, including the YMCA staff, were used to the YMCA as a recreation/ daycare environment. For them, mixing play and education was an unusual idea. Moreover, in so far as the playful aspects of the Fifth Dimension induced children to be imaginative and often rambunctious, adults actively disapproved of the resulting behaviour. Hence, while play could be said to be the leading activity for the children, it was viewed with suspicion by local adults. At one point the principal investigator reported that the Fifth Dimension was 'seen by the club as a babysitter; that it was not easy to get YMCA staff to see computers and games as friendly and worthwhile'.

Leading activities

The faculty implementer of this site had interpreted her appointment in the Psychology programme as an opportunity to introduce new theories and methods for use in community settings to the students and faculty at the college. At the same time, she saw it as an opportunity to cultivate independence, ownership and responsibility for the activities on the part of the YMCA. She assumed that the college's orientation to local service would serve her well. However, the faculty of her college did not find mixing education and service an important goal. They allowed her to undertake the effort as a sideline or hobby, since teaching research methods was not a priority for the department.

For their part, the YMCA staff welcomed the help of the college students, but were not very curious about the programme or the opportunities it might open up for them or for the children. Neither college nor club staff saw their interests coinciding with those of the principal investigator. In addition, the need to depend on volunteer and paid undergraduate labour for half the year created ongoing difficulties. While the undergraduates were content to play with the children and get credit for their community service, they had little incentive to learn how to write fieldnotes or to do community-based research. Community service, which was a genuine motive for them, was treated by most as a well-bounded, short-term commitment.

Communicative practices and mediational means

As in the case of Big State University, the traditional mediational means of computer games, a maze, task cards, a corresponding mythical entity and so on, were successfully introduced into the Small Private College Fifth Dimension. However, the practices which emerged in this context diverged from the initial model considerably more than at Big State sites. Focused as they were on children's compliant behaviour, the YMCA staff discouraged playfulness. As a means to increase control, they initiated a division of children's access to the Fifth Dimension, separating boys and girls, and they monitored the activities with this goal in mind. The skewing of the activities toward transmission education and control was particularly noticeable during the spring semester when only a few undergraduate students were present. The markedly increased ratio of children to adults would have made implementation of a culture of collaborative learning difficult to implement in any context. In the YMCA authority structure, collaborative engagement was especially difficult to achieve. Fifth Dimension practices privileging collaboration over control seemed to have no chance to take hold. During the second year at this site, the principal investigator commented that while the presence of computers and computer games had gained acceptance at the YMCA, she was reluctant to call the activity a Fifth Dimension.

Symptomatically, the lack of enthusiasm for getting involved with computers on the part of the YMCA staff meant that, among other things, they did not make use of the telecommunications facilities that were available to them for making contact with the principle investigator or other Fifth Dimension implementers.

Dis-coordinations

From the foregoing description it should come as no surprise that the Small College Fifth Dimension was rife with contradictions. The principal investigator's expectations, based on her prior experience in running a Fifth Dimension in the deep South and from participating in the original Fifth Dimension at LCHC, and her identification with Vygotskian theory, did not stand her in good stead. In this case the dis-coordinations eventually overwhelmed the system, leading the principal investigator to comment:

> Near the end of her effort, the principal investigator warned her Consortium colleagues about the dangers of assuming readiness and need in target community settings for a particular philosophy of education. She directly cautioned

others not to discount a 'competing philosophy of education (or competing ideas about how best to interact with children) at work in these community settings'.

Reflections on Using the CHAT Toolkit

As we noted in our introduction, our goal is to design systems of effective educational activities that can be sustained as normal, expectable practices. Despite variations among them, these activities shared a common set of theoretical ideas and were embodied as Fifth Dimensions in after-school settings linked to corresponding university courses.

At this juncture we feel confident that it is possible, more or less routinely, to use the Fifth Dimension model to create educationally effective activities for both children and university students. Such successes have been reported for a wide variety of combinations of university and community partners (Blanton, et al., 1997; Mayer, et al., 1997). The CHAT toolkit does a good job of directing the design of such systems. However, the issue of sustainability is less clear. A few systems have been running for a decade and several, like Big State, have been in operation for five years or more. But clearly, as the case of Small College illustrates, creating sustainable after-school activity systems using the Fifth Dimension model is not guaranteed of success. Nor is it possible to point to any one factor that can guarantee success or failure. We have only sketched the history of two of some thirty efforts to implement this programme. Some in small colleges, like Small College, have prospered and show promise of great longevity. Others, similar in structure to that at Big State, have failed. So it is not size alone that counts.

The many variations we have observed among systems emphasizes the need for attention to be given to the context of the after-school activity system, as well as to the organization of the activities themselves. This context includes, minimally, the community institution within which the after-school activity is housed, the university or college with which it is linked, and also the larger community of which both are a part. We have also learned that it is impossible to overestimate the importance of a serious and extended goal-formation process that extends beyond initial discussions to include continuing joint assessment of the programme by partners on both sides of the 'university–community' divide. Development requires time, and it is only in the process of actually conducting the joint activity over time that the complex of motives energizing both sides can be revealed and realigned where necessary. Finding a system that satisfies them all is difficult at best, but is most likely to prove successful if educators enter into the process aware of the heterogeneity of motives involved at all levels of the system.

The course of development is punctuated by discontinuities and conflict no less in the case of activity systems than in the case of individual children's development. In the case of activity systems, conflict and dis-coordination are to be viewed as symptoms of underlying contradictions that must be resolved if the activity system is to continue. When the parties to the required partnership realize that the experience of dis-coordination and conflict is more than an unpleasant nuisance, and instead take such experiences as an invitation to change and grow, the likelihood of sustainability is thereby significantly increased.

Finally, when participants keep in mind the importance of communicative practices and processes of mediation, they are able to focus directly on the processes that underpin continued collaboration. When properly used, such practices and the mediational means through which they are implemented should materially help in maintaining ongoing relations of exchange between partners, thereby maximizing the possibility of continued, joint goal formation and sustainability of the systems that participants labour so hard to create.

18

Building a Community of Educators versus Effecting Conceptual Change in Individual Students: Multicultural Education for Pre-service Teachers

Eugene Matusov and Renée Hayes

In this chapter we will first develop a critique of traditional education using an example of a multicultural college course. This traditional multicultural model of education for pre-service teachers assumes that the goal of their education is to purify the students of their cultural misconceptions, biases and racism. We will then provide an alternative model of education stemming from a sociocultural approach to learning, according to which, learning for pre-service teachers involves building a learning community of educators. We will illustrate our model with the programme called La Red Mágica ('Magic Web' in Spanish) aimed at preparing pre-service teachers for working with minority children.

Dissatisfaction with a Traditional Concept of Multicultural Pre-service Education

We argue that traditional education is based mainly on the transmission of knowledge. The essence of this model is in moulding students according to a set of skills and attitudes, and a body of knowledge, pre-established by the instructor. Students are often viewed as inept, deficient and biased. In the case of multicultural education, students' presumed deficiencies often include negative stereotyping of minority children, racial prejudices, insensitive guidance

This is a short version of the paper that will be prepared for a journal publication. Parts of the paper were presented at AERA meetings, New Orleans, LA, 2000.

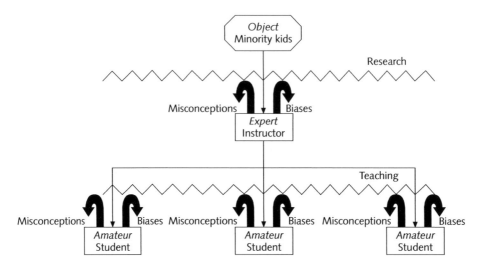

Figure 18.1   Transmission of knowledge model of multicultural education (adapted from Palmer, 1998).

and ways of talking, lack of knowledge of diverse cultural communicative styles, and discriminatory practices (e.g. tracking). Multicultural courses are considered to be remedies for such student deficiencies. Figure 18.1 presents this educational model.

Palmer (1998) calls this model 'the objectivist myth' and defines four major elements:

- Objects of knowledge that reside 'out there' somewhere, pristine in physical or conceptual space, as described by the 'facts' in a given field.
- Experts, people trained to know these objects in their pristine form without allowing their own subjectivity to spill over onto the purity of the objects themselves. This training transpires in a far-off place called graduate school, whose purpose is so thoroughly to obliterate one's sense of self that one becomes a secular priest, a safe bearer of the pure objects of knowledge.
- Amateurs, people without training and full of bias, who depend on the experts for objective or pure knowledge of the pristine objects in question.
- Baffles at every point of transmission – between objects and experts, between experts and amateurs – that allow objective knowledge to flow downstream while preventing subjectivity from flowing back up. (Palmer, 1998, pp. 100–1)

Let us illustrate how this model is often applied to multicultural college education for pre-service teachers. Researchers (experts) have found that minority children may have different patterns of communication (objects) from those that middle-class white teachers (amateurs) expect in their classrooms.

For example, some Native-American children lower their eyes before the teacher as a sign of respect to the elderly, while white middle-class teachers expect all students to look at the teacher when she or he is talking directly to them. Looking away from the teacher in the classroom is often seen as a sign of disrespect (misconception) (Philips, 1983). One textbook on cultural diversity for pre-service teachers (expert) (Nieto, 1996) reports these findings to students (amateurs) and suggests that students should examine their own assumptions about ways of communicating with future students (baffles). According to the model, teaching 'the objective truth' can follow different pedagogical methods, including constructivist ones, as soon as all students (amateurs) arrive at views specified by experts.

The prevalence of the transmission of knowledge model in US educational institutions is well documented in the educational literature (Cuban, 1993; Tyack and Cuban, 1995; Cuban, 1999). From the standpoint of multicultural education for pre-service teachers, the transmission of knowledge leads to an unavoidable conflict of interests. On the one hand, multicultural education aims to prevent culturally biased teaching by focusing teachers on how to avoid imposing the mainstream ways of communication and learning on minority children and treating these children as culturally deficient (known as the 'deficit approach' (Rogoff, 1990)). On the other hand, the transmission of knowledge educational model promotes exactly the same relations between the instructor of a multicultural course and his or her pre-service students. Like 'culturally biased' schoolteachers, instructors of multicultural courses that are based on transmission of knowledge believe that their views are superior, truer and more advanced than those of their students.

Another problem we encounter in a traditional approach to the multicultural education of pre-service teachers is that cultural sensitivity is often seen as rooted in pedagogical actions. The teacher is supposed to successfully infer from their background and past experience what kind of instruction should be used with each student. The teacher's failure to guess the appropriate actions correctly is considered to be due to the teacher's insensitivity. However, the very notion of sensitivity is a relational concept. Instructional sensitivity is an interactive process of seeking teacher–student mutuality regarding guidance, learning and what their joint activity is about. This mutuality is itself a dynamic process rather than a state. Thus, instructional sensitivity is a special way (or ways) of dealing with temporarily broken teacher–student mutuality. Educational sensitivity is rooted in teacher–student interaction rather in the teacher's action itself. Depending on this interaction, any specific action of the teacher may be sensitive or insensitive. It is never enough to simply change the teacher's action to reach pedagogical sensitivity without changing the teacher–student interaction and relations.

In addition, traditional models of multicultural education promote a split between the class curricula and 'real life'. In multicultural education, this phenomenon of splitting between 'school' and 'real' worlds that run in parallel, never overlapping, is especially troublesome because it demoralizes pre-service teachers.

In a traditional classroom, real life (consisting of students' concerns, dilemmas and experiences) is often excluded from the practices of the classroom. When a living, authentic practice bursts into the classroom, it is often expelled, suppressed or severely narrowed (castrated) because it disrupts students' focus on the instructor-defined course curriculum. Even when a teaching practicum is associated with the course, the instructor is often concerned that hot issues emerging in the practicum might distract the students from the instructor's agenda. For example, Bonk and his colleagues express their concern that their students in an educational psychology course often bring topics from their teaching practicum to class web discussions that may not be seen by the instructor as part of the course curriculum:

> A unique topic that emerged from the [practicum] cases was the 'hot topic' category. This category did not necessarily reflect any particular topic or concept from the field of educational psychology. Instead, this category encompassed global and controversial topics in education, which were of concern. Some examples of hot topics included: teacher burnout, parent–teacher relations, corporal punishment, drugs and alcohol, adolescent issues, teen suicide, violence in schools, and differences between home and school. The controversy and recency of these topics tended to generate a great deal of discussion among a wide variety of students. This area was so popular, in fact, that by the start of the second semester, a notation had to be made to use only as a last resort. (Bonk et al., 1999)

In sum, the deficit approach to the relationship between the instructor and the students of multicultural teacher education courses is a hidden curriculum, based on the transmission of knowledge model, that contradicts the goals of the multicultural course.

A Sociocultural Model of Learning as Building a Community of Practice

The traditional notion of learning focuses on a desired change in an individual student as defined and guided by the instructor. An alternative approach to learning focuses on students' changing participation in a community of practice. According to this (socio-cultural) approach, what, for example, makes a person a scientist is not a unique way of thinking (as a traditional approach implies) but the person's participation in a scientific community (recognized as such by other members of the community and by people outside the community) (Latour, 1987). Brown, Collins and Duguid (1989) argue that, in the case of learning in school, the most relevant community for the students is that of the school itself. The learning curriculum for the students – what students learn (Lave and Wenger, 1991) – is school practice itself. Thus, learning is defined by what the students do in and for the class, what concerns them, how they relate to each other and to the instructor, and the nature of their class-related communication. Making the multicultural teaching curriculum match the learning curriculum, i.e. school practice, leads to building a classroom community of the targeted practice.

Lave (1992) insists that learning is inherent to any activity. Learning occurs even despite the expectations and intentions of the more experienced members of the community; it is not a matter of whether students learn in school but of what they learn. The students might actually learn what they were not expected to learn instead of what was expected for them to learn (Eckert, 1989). Lave and Wenger (1991) further argue that learning is a communal process, situated in a community of practice. Learning is always a question about membership in the community and participation in the community practices. A novice is not simply a person who lacks some entities, called 'skills', but rather a newcomer who needs to negotiate her or his participation in the community practices (Wenger, 1998).

A view of learning as a communal process embedded in communal practices has inspired many educational practitioners and researchers to explore and define new forms of guidance that can be used in schools, such as instructional conversations (Tharp and Gallimore, 1988), reciprocal teaching (Brown and Palincsar, 1987), cognitive apprenticeship (Rogoff, 1990), community of learners (Brown and Campione, 1994; Rogoff et al., 1996), practice and problem-based learning (Wilkerson and Gijselaers, 1996) and dialogic inquiry (Wells, 1999). This family of instructional and conceptual approaches (including CHAT) shares at least the following important principles: learning is a communal process; learning is embedded in the activities and practices in which it occurs; learning involves development and negotiation of new communal identities; students require guided initiation into the discourse – defining problems and goals is crucial to their becoming active members of a community of practice; ownership of guidance and learning should be shared among students and between the students and the teacher; a community is based on practice and communication.

La Red Mágica: Building a Community of Educators

La Red Mágica is a university–community partnership started in September 1998. The partnership is designed to build an after-school programme based on voluntary, collaborative and informal learning, linking inner-city minority elementary school children at the Latin-American Community Center (LACC) in Wilmington with teacher education students at the University of Delaware (Newark, DE) as a part of their teaching practicum. The LACC children are mainly from low-income Puerto Rican and African-American families, but also recent immigrant families from Mexico, Dominican Republic and Guatemala. The class was conducted by a Russian–Jewish male immigrant in his late thirties (instructor, the first author) and by a female graduate student from Panama (teaching assistant).

During the ten-week practicum, undergraduate students, mainly young, white, middle-class females, help children who are engaged in educational activities (e.g. computer activities, telecommunication, readings, crafts, sport and board games). The programme is open four days a week at LACC for one and a half hours per day. Each undergraduate student is expected to come twice a week to work with the children. So far, the only course associated with the La Red Mágica project has been a section of 'Cultural Diversity in Teaching and Schooling', offered as the core (mandatory) class for freshmen and sophomores in the teacher education programme. The class enrolment often varies between 15 and 20 students. Besides practicum requirements and classroom meetings, students are expected to participate in the class internet discussions ('web talks'), weekly mini-projects involving students' work with the LACC children (e.g. interviews, focused field notes) and reading assigned literature.

This initiative is based on about fifteen years of research and teaching experience of the Laboratory of Comparative Human Cognition (LCHC) at UC San Diego (see Brown and Cole, this volume). Researchers at LCHC designed a programme called the Fifth Dimension that successfully capitalized on computer-based activities during the after-school hours to promote reading acquisition among minority students who were failing to read in school (cf. Brown and Cole, this volume). Like the Fifth Dimension programmes, the La Red Mágica project is based on the idea of children's voluntary participation in an after-school programme and on undergraduate students helping children as part of their teaching practicum. However, there are also important differences between the Fifth Dimension programmes and the La Red Mágica project. In the latter, there is a strong emphasis on undergraduate students' shared ownership of the running of the programme. In the Fifth Dimension, the site structure, such as task cards for children's activities, a wizard who solves problems at the site, maze organizing and limiting children's choices of the available activities, and so on (Cole, 1996), is predefined by the project leaders. In the La Red Mágica project the structure is intentionally open for students' designing (Matusov et al., in press). Designing a learning environment in practice at LACC is the curriculum for pre-service teachers.

A Community of Educators in Action

To illustrate how a class develops as a community of educators, we have selected a dramatic episode from the fall semester 1999 class, when one of the students was disrespected by one of the LACC pre-adolescent boys (not part of the LA Red Mágica programme) who used sexually exploitative language in Spanish. We selected this case because of the three following reasons.

First, it emerged as a key issue. Each semester, there are a few main issues that, for some reason, recursively surface in the class and come to constitute the class's major foci and emerging learning curricula. In the fall 1999 semester one of the major issues concerned the rough and sexually loaded language that 5–8 LACC boys sometimes used. Despite a LACC policy prohibiting cursing, they sometimes openly cursed, especially in situations when something did not go right in their activities. Many of our students were very uncomfortable and upset with children for using foul language. Their initial reaction was to demonize the boys. They did not know how to react or how to stop them.

Second, it exemplifies a broader multicultural issue. Minority children tend to be either demonized or romanticized in educational books and movies. The example we selected shows students' hard work and the complexity of our students' learning how to work with minority children without using the heroes–villains mythology.

Third, the case is messy and demonstrates our work in progress open for critique (that we welcome) rather than 'how things ideally should be'. We believe that community life can be better captured in its 'becoming' a community rather than in stable functioning. We believe that community is built through critical events. Bakhtin (1986), Altman and Rogoff (1987) and Pepper (1967) argue that an event is a social and holistic process. Bakhtin reminded us that the Russian word *sobytie* (i.e. event) literally means 'collective being'. He insisted that an event is a dramatic dialogic intersection and, sometimes, even a collision of somewhat incompatible voices, ideologies and actors. We want to add to Bakhtin's notion that an event also involves a collective situation when the participants cannot talk, act, participate, relate, or be in a way that they are used to. In an event, personal and communal identities have become changed (Lave and Wenger, 1991). The old, familiar ways of talking, acting, participating, relating, knowing, thinking and being become impossible in the collision. Critical events involve the shake-up of the entire community when old ways of practising and relating become impossible.

The prototypical case below shows how a private issue that a student initially struggled with on her own became a public issue and the focus of class discussion; how other students contributed to the communal process of meaning making; how the instructor mediated this process; what professional tools he offered to the community for tackling the problem; how the resolution of the public discussion led to students' experimentation in their practice; and how reflection on students' experimentation became a recursive process. Because of lack of space, we cannot describe all the details of the event; instead, we shall focus mainly on one class discussion, based on in-class notes made by the TA and reflective notes made by the instructor.

The Instructor's Account of the Event

I was ready to go to my Friday 50-minute class, when I decided to check the class web to see students' recent discussion. One discussion thread captured my attention by its unusual subject:

> Subject: 'Kiss my balls'
> From: NG
> Today I was greatly disrespected at the LACC. One boy in the art room, about 11 years old, said to me in Spanish that he wanted his balls in my mouth. Too shocked to respond, I gave him a dirty look and he smiled and walked away. He obviously knew what he was saying. K., Ch. [classmates] and I had a long discussion about this and I felt very uncomfortable in this situation. I go to the LACC, like everyone else, to help those kids. But the experience that I had today made the time I spend there horrible. I wanted to leave early just to get out of the situation. Cursing and sexual jokes should not be allowed in the LACC. I think we should make rules about this. I don't want to deal with the same thing again and I don't think anyone else should either. Please tell me what you guys think should be done!!!

> From: ChH (reply to NG)
> I was with N. in the art room and I heard what the kids were saying and I felt very uncomfortable in that situation, just as uncomfortable as I had felt when the comments were directed at me in the past. I really felt bad for N., b/c she was so surprised and shocked by what they said. We did not know what to do. We did not want to shut down the art room b/c there were children in there that were working nicely. So we told the boys that they needed to stop that way of talking or they would have to leave. The younger boy said back 'It's just a joke', to which we replied that it was not funny, and we would have to ask they stop it or leave. I don't know what was exactly the correct thing to do in this situation. What do you all think?

I was very surprised to read these postings, for two reasons. First, I did not know about this disturbing event, even though I had been with my students at LACC that evening. I probably was in the computer room with other students when the incident happened. The students did not mention the incident on our way back, even though we discussed our experiences as usual. I wondered whether it might have taken NG some time before she could publicly discuss what happened to her. Second, I was surprised that NG, being a rather quiet and withdrawn person, felt comfortable in bringing this painful topic to the entire class.

For this class meeting I had planned to discuss the Japanese educational system and culture. However, I felt that I could not ignore the incident at LACC. It seemed to me that it was a critical moment for NG and probably for many other students. Either we would together try to find an approach to address the situation or they might develop an antipathy toward working with some minority children.

Class Meeting (Notes by the Teaching Assistant)

After 15 minutes of discussion about Japanese culture, the instructor announced his interest in addressing the issue of foul language brought up that week on the class discussion web. The instructor distributed a copy of NG's web posting. The students talked about the chaos in the art room that day. The instructor mentioned that that day there had been a visit from the state governor and all the personnel were stressed out. However, despite this, the computer room was calm, very cooperative and engaged. In the art room there was a lot of complexity, deterioration of the ecology.

Many students expressed their opinions about the event and suggested reasons for it. The instructor summarized the discussion by referring to the table on the blackboard that he made during the students' discussion (table 18.1).

In the follow-up discussion the instructor noticed that they developed 'a big list of PROs and a short list of CONs'. He praised the students for not trying to demonize the children. However, he suggested that they are in a 'pendulum swing' of trying to be nice with the children at the expense of their own well-being. He said:

Table 18.1 Summary of discussion of possible actions.

Issue: Do we want all the kids to stay in and not kick anybody out?	
Pros	**Cons**
We care about all the kids	We're not helping kids who disrespect students by letting them stay in
Everybody should be able to come in	We feel prisoners in the art room
The programme is open	We are not used to it
Volunteer participation for the kids	
Kids' choice of activities and place to be at LACC	
Sensitivity to troubled kids	
Sensitivity to kids' culture	
Talking dirty is normal for pre-adolescent boys	
They might not understand what they said	
We should serve especially those kids who demonstrate troubled behaviour	

Teaching dilemma: How can we access and help all the kids without collapsing ourselves?

For how long can we be 'nice' to all kids before quitting, before becoming mean, before becoming burnt out? Is being always 'nice' helpful for the kids? Can slaves of kids teach the kids how to be free people?!

Teaching is very relational. We teach relations. If we are uncomfortable going to the art room, we won't be able to create a safe learning environment that promotes freedom and creativity in the kids. If we're collapsing and emotionally overwhelmed, we can't do quality teaching, and we will become useless for the kids. The only thing we will teach is how to be victims. Remember flight attendant's safety instruction, 'In case of emergency, help yourself first and then dependent others'. We should help ourselves first. We should prioritize our well-being.

He suggested that the students might want to share their emotions with the children. 'Talk with the kids about how upset you are. Share your emotions. Cry if it helps you and you feel comfortable. Share your pain. The kids will understand. They're very compassionate. They like us.' He said that, in his view, it would have been appropriate to close the art room to avoid the feeling of being trapped by the children. 'Move to the computer room and recoup by having a good teaching experience with kids. Restore yourself emotionally. Regain your willingness to come back to LACC. Have fun with kids.'

Students kept discussing the issues that the instructor defined as sexism at LACC. The instructor suggested inviting the LACC youth director who, like the students, is a young, white, middle-class female and a graduate of the University of Delaware, to the class to talk about how she deals with sexism at LACC. He also suggested asking the TA, who is a female from Panama and has had experience working at LACC. The instructor acknowledged that as a white male there were limitations as to how much insight and guidance he could provide on this important issue. He promised to check academic and educational literature on this topic for next class meeting.

Afterwards: Instructor's Account of the Event (Continued)

After the class, NG told me that she again felt excited about going to LACC because she wanted to try some new ideas about how to be more assertive. We continued looking for practical solutions to this problem. In another class meeting we had a dramatic play of simulating a situation when two children, played by our students, cursed while playing a computer game. The students split into small groups and devised a strategy for stopping the 'children's' cursing because they found cursing unpleasant. The students playing 'children' were from other groups and did not know the strategy that the 'teacher' used. The groups tried different approaches from being 'nice' with the 'children' to trying to be adversarial. After each demonstration and the following discussion by the whole class, the next group tried to take into account the consequences of the previous groups' strategies. The most successful group was the last one; they tried to be 'honest' with 'children' by communicating their discomfort with 'the children's' cursing and by providing them with alternative language to express their frustration with the game. The students continued trying new ideas to deal with the issue. For example, on the class discussion web, one of the students suggested using teasing to stop cursing at LACC. This idea stemmed from a video the class had recently watched of a Japanese classroom in which the teacher teases a small boy who steals a toy.

During our discussions, we often tried to provide alternative views, foresee desirable and undesirable consequences, and make an evaluation of suggested pedagogical actions. This student's suggestion to use teasing as a pedagogical tool sparked quite a bit of discussion on the class web, including supportive and negative responses. The instructor did not support this proposal, and warned the students to be careful in their experimenting with teasing, worrying that some children and students might be hurt. He wrote on the web:

> In my view, we should be very careful about borrowing cultural strategies because they may be supported by other elements of cultural practices. What do you think?

Despite the instructor's warning, some students tried the strategy and reported the results to the class via the discussion web:

> On our way home Wednesday night [on a van], we were talking a lot about the idea of teasing as part of Latin American culture. Eugene [the instructor] brought up a very good point. He pointed out that K., the LACC worker that is usually near the front desk, has a really strong and positive relationship with the kids. He is constantly teasing them, often about things that our culture would usually find over the limit, such as weight or calling someone ugly, but at the same time, he can silence the entire group of kids in two seconds when he needs to. Because they love and respect him, he is their friend and their disciplinarian. Inspired by this, I decided to see if I could successfully make myself part of that group of rowdier boys (Jose, Pablo, etc. [names are pseudonyms]). When we were waiting in the TV room on Thursday night before everything got started, I walked over to where they were sitting. As I approached them, Jose said to me, 'You can't sit near me!' I quickly responded, by walking around him to a seat on the other side of the group and saying, 'Why would I want to sit next to you?! You smell!' All the boys thought this was hysterical. They even brought one of the older teenage boys in to tell him how I 'dissed' Jose. Jose was a little put out at first, but he bounced right back. I know that these kids get teased a lot worse than that all of the time. He was a really good sport about it. The boys were even more surprised when I understood some of their conversations and joking in Spanish right after. So, I was successful. 'Una gringa' made it into their group! (even if it was only for a second!)

Model of Multicultural Learning Through Building a Community of Educators

Here, we abstract the model of multicultural learning through building a community of educators from our La Red Mágica project illustrated with the examples above (see figure 18.2).

It is important to note that at any given moment during the class, there were many hot issues in the foreground and background of the class's focus at different phases of their development. Thus, there should be many circles (see figure 18.2) simultaneously 'rotating' with different 'speeds' and phases.

In order to learn through building a professional community, the students have to have an opportunity to be involved in this professional activity. In

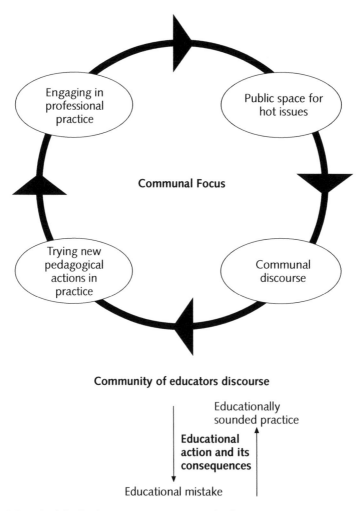

Figure 18.2 Model of a learning community of educators.

the case of a class that is focused on pre-service teachers learning how to provide sensitive guidance to culturally diverse classrooms, engagement with minority children is crucial. This engagement has to be safe for the participants in the sense that pre-service teachers' professional mistakes should not lead to irreversible deterioration of relations between them and the children. The structure of the engagement should be sufficiently open to provide shared ownership and creative input by the students.

Another layer of ecological safety in a learning community of educators is a public space for recognizing, discussing and addressing hot issues as they emerge from the students' participation in the professional practice and for sharing their experiences. By publicizing personal discomfort, concerns, dilemmas and issues, the class provides opportunities for students to reflect on their actions and to think critically about their practice. It helps to develop a professional language to talk about the practice, since this creates possibilities to recursively consider and polish learning activities and pedagogical strategies (e.g. why and how to react pedagogically to children's foul language). In sum, it creates a teaching culture (Stigler and Hiebert, 1998). Communication with and about LACC children was constantly moved from private or semi-public spaces to the formal public space of web and class discussions (see examples in the web postings cited above). Oscillation and cross-fertilization of the private, informal public, and formal public spaces of communication constituted a multi-faceted community with a central focus on how to provide culturally sensitive assistance for all children.

Conclusion

The approach and pedagogical design of this class, based on building a community of educators, allows us to avoid a trap of traditional classes on multicultural education, where instruction is based on a deficit model and the transmission/induction of the 'correct' (often liberal) values defined by the instructor, while the content of the class curriculum focuses on criticizing deficit models and the transmission of knowledge that teachers use in traditional schools. By focusing on emerging issues and the concerns of students working with LACC children as the primary classroom curriculum, there is unity between the content and the method of the class and between the classroom curriculum and studied practice. The legacy of this multicultural education is in the students' experiences and nostalgia about a professional educational community working with minority children. Students learn how to manage their relations with culturally diverse children in order to promote sensitive guidance as a part of building and living in a professional community of educators rather than accumulating 'silver bullet' teacher tricks. The worlds of school and targeted practice are united.

19

Organizing Excursions Into Specialist Discourse Communities: A Sociocultural Account of University Teaching

Andy Northedge

Whereas there are obvious grounds for viewing learning within schools as a social and cultural process, at university level the case is far less clear. School pupils spend their days within the social mêlée of classrooms, surrounded by an all too familiar peer group and taught by familiar teachers. At university, by contrast, students are expected to undertake substantial amounts of their learning alone, as they grapple with difficult texts, write lengthy assignments or solve complex problems. Moreover, even when learning in group settings such as lectures or seminars, interactions may be quite restricted and formal, and the lecturer and fellow students relative strangers, so that any social/communal component is far from obvious. In general, the higher the level, the more students are expected to become 'independent learners', capable of deciding their own needs and goals and pursuing their own inquiries. Yet, although studying becomes increasingly a solitary, inner-directed enterprise, the twin processes of learning and teaching retain their fundamentally sociocultural character, as I try to show in this chapter by taking the extreme case of students studying entirely in their own homes, as in my own institution, the UK Open University (OU).

My approach reflects the 'sociocultural' and 'activity' orientation elsewhere in this volume, in that it treats knowledge as a product of participation with others in the construction of communal meaning (Bronckart, 1995; Bruner, 1996). In particular, I take higher-level knowledge to be constituted by the discourse exchanged within communities of specialists, and the acquisition of higher-level knowledge to be a matter of becoming a functioning participant within a specialist discourse community (Resnick, Pontecorvo and Säljö, 1997; Wells, 1999). Thus usage of a specialist discourse and membership of a specialist discourse community are, within this account, a student's key goals.

There are close parallels here with Lave and Wenger's (1991) conception of 'apprenticeship to a community of practice'. However, academic communities constitute a special case in that they are spatially and temporally dispersed, with core practices enacted largely in writing within textual 'fora' such as journals. My discourse-centred account assigns to teachers the role of 'discourse guide' (Mercer, 1995) or, as in my title, 'organizer of excursions into the discourse community'. This puts the teacher's emphasis firstly on the strategic planning of journeys made by students, rather than on personally leading the way, and secondly on the 'peopled' nature of discourse, rather than just its language. As I shall show, the insights and skills required for this 'excursion organizer' role are as much social and cultural as intellectual.

The UK Open University

At the OU it is possible to study an entire degree programme without any social interaction beyond the comments that tutors write on assignments. Courses are delivered to students in their own homes, using specially designed teaching texts, audio-visual materials, CD-ROMs and websites. There are occasional opportunities for 'live' interaction at tutorials and residential schools, or by telephone, but these are optional and many choose not to participate. Most students study part-time, while continuing in employment, taking six years or more to graduate. Entry is open to anyone over 18, regardless of prior academic qualifications, and a modular degree structure allows students to take virtually any combination of courses. Two thirds of students are between 25 and 45, but ages range to 80 years and more. Thus, the population of any course will encompass a wide range of interests, motivation and background knowledge. The OU launched its first courses in 1971 and now has 185,000 students, 10,000 full-time academic staff, who develop the courses, and 7,300 part-time tutors, who mark assignments.

In this chapter I focus on a specific OU course, K100: Understanding Health and Social Care (K100 hereafter). It is a one-year course (a sixth of a BA degree), aimed at a broad range of care professionals and also a general audience. Its annual intake is over 5,000 students. Traditionally 'care' courses have been directed at specific sectors, such as nurses or social workers, and have included a large *in situ* practical component. To design a course which straddles established specialist boundaries and is studied in the student's own home presents a substantial challenge, particularly with students who range from newcomers to the care field to experienced professionals. What in such circumstances should one aim to teach, and how?

Gaining Access to Specialist Knowledge

Consider a potential student, Leila, toying with the idea of changing career from retail management to the care field. Since residential care for older people is a growth area, she thinks she might eventually run a residential home. A friend already studying K100 lends her a book of readings on care policy and practice. Leila is surprised to see that one chapter is about abuse of older care receivers. Curious, she turns to it and starts to read. Here are the opening sentences:

> *Elder abuse and the policing of community care*
> Few social gerontologists could have failed to notice the growth in literature on elder abuse that has taken place in the UK since 1992. . . . Some commentators have suspected an 'ageing enterprise' at work. . . . This phrase, first coined by Carol Estes (1979), draws attention to the manipulation of newly recognized social problems affecting older people and the possibility of their being hijacked by professional agendas of various sorts. Her work raises questions about the genesis of issues, especially where policy seems to have relied exclusively on professional/political discourse. (Biggs, 1998, p. 258)

Leila struggles through these sentences with difficulty. Little seems to lodge in her mind. What is it about? What are social gerontologists and where would you find them? Who are these 'commentators'? Is Carol Estes an important person? Is an 'ageing enterprise' a declining institution? Does 'at work' mean 'at your workplace'? Is this about old people in employment? How and why would you 'manipulate' social problems? What might be 'hijacked', and by whom? What on earth is the last sentence about? And what has all this to do with abuse of older people? It almost seems a foreign language. Another few sentences and Leila is beaten. The apparently compelling topic of abuse has turned out to be dull and impenetrable. But why? This fragment of text is not, of course, meaningless. It opens up a thought-provoking line of argument for those who regularly read such texts. Yet to Leila it presents nothing.

It is not, primarily, a problem of unknown words. A few, such as 'gerontologist', 'genesis' and 'discourse', are not common in everyday talk, but Leila feels no need to look them up in her dictionary. The problem lies in the unfamiliarity of the thoughts the words express. To read one has to be able to project meaning onto the words on the page. Unless one already has the capability to generate something like the meaning intended by the author, the words remain lifeless. Reading is a collaborative activity. It is a process which involves writer and reader sharing together in the generating of meaning. Leila's problem with this text is that, although she shares the English language with its author, she shares nothing of the ideas the author is attempting to convey.

What of those who might read this text with ease? They will tend to be academic researchers, senior care managers and policy makers who regularly participate in debates about care policy and practice. In effect they constitute a discourse community (Swales, 1990) whose members share much background knowledge of the care field and the long-running debates within it.

- They will know who social gerontologists are, and be familiar with the term 'elder abuse'.
- They will understand that 'commentators' refers back to social gerontologists, or to other active participants within the discourse community.
- They will recognize from the context that 'ageing enterprise' refers to a kind of empire-building around service provision for older people, and that 'at work' is used here as a verb.
- They will recognize that this chapter introduction is setting up an argument which questions whether policy on elder abuse is really aimed at achieving what it claims, or whether other 'agendas' are being pursued.

This chapter derives from an established discourse about the politics of care provision, within which delivering care services is not viewed simply as a pragmatic issue of identifying needs, setting priorities and allocating resources. Instead it is seen as a struggle between vested interests: professions, commercial enterprises and government departments. Policy decisions and public statements are not taken at face value, but interpreted as signs of particular interests striving for ascendancy. Conceptions such as 'professional agendas' and 'manipulation of social problems' provide the analytic tools for conducting this debate. They are elements within the 'semiotic toolkit' of a discourse which sets out to construct a layer of meaning above the policy battlefield, from which it is possible to look down on and predict the course of events at ground level.

If she proceeds with her projected studies and career switch, Leila will find it valuable to be able to engage with such debates, both in print and in practice. This will add to her intellectual powers, by helping her to analyse and interpret policy developments. Equally she will gain social power through becoming 'an insider' to the care-provider discourse community, able to present her own positions in debates at managerial and policy levels. To become a competent and recognized member of this discourse community is, in effect, the ultimate goal of any studies Leila undertakes. In reaching this goal she will need to master the use of various facts, concepts and theories. But, though she will need to know something about, for example, key pieces of legislation on care provision, or about the principles underlying accountability structures, she will not need such depth of knowledge as to be able to trade ideas within legal discourse communities. Similarly, she will need some knowledge of the sociology and psychology of 'institutionalization' as experienced by residents in homes, but she will not need to be able to pass herself off as a sociologist or psychologist. What determines the level and form of knowledge she needs is the current trade in ideas within the care-provider discourse community. She requires not so much an enormous body of theory, or information, as access to the ongoing flow of knowledge produced within her specialist discourse community, together with legitimacy as a participant within that community.

The Challenge of Engaging with a Specialist Discourse

As we have seen, however, Leila cannot begin to engage with the specialist discourse of care-providers because she cannot make their texts 'make sense'. How, then, do members of the discourse community do it? In starting to read a text they will quickly sense the 'frame of reference' within which the opening words are intended to be understood. The title gives important clues. The word 'policing' signals a line of analysis arising from such writers as Michel Foucault. However, Leila knows nothing of this work. Her repertoire does not yet extend to constructing the frame of reference required by these opening sentences. Ironically, the most obvious means of access to such frames is to read texts of the kind whose sentences she cannot understand. This is a classic dilemma for students new to a field of discourse; they find themselves 'locked out' – unable to make sense of utterances they encounter because they cannot place them within the necessary frames of reference – but equally unable to make progress in internalizing the frames of reference because they cannot engage with those utterances through which the frames are made manifest. Helping students break into this 'hermeneutic circle' is one of the key roles teachers play. They 'lend' students the capacity to frame meanings which they are, as yet, unable to frame for themselves.

University teachers often misunderstand this role through not appreciating the sociocultural groundings of meaning. Their thoughts are so deeply rooted in specialist discourse that they are unaware that meanings that they take for granted are simply not construable from outside the discourse. A common response to the challenge of helping someone read a text like that above is to start defining the meanings of specialist words and phrases, such as 'social problems' and 'professional/political discourse'. However, such terms cannot satisfactorily be understood without grasping the discursive context in which they are used. Until then, explanations and definitions tend to be as opaque as the original terms. Here is a typical example taken from the early pages of an anthropology text:

> Culture is the totality of learned, socially transmitted behaviour. It includes the ideas, values and customs of a group of people. (Ember and Ember, 1996, p. 32)

'Totality of learned, socially transmitted behaviour' is even more meaningless, outside anthropological discourse, than the term 'culture'. And terms such as 'ideas, values and customs' will not carry the richness of meaning that they do for the anthropological community. To try to teach through definitions is to mistake the way we acquire the meaning of words. We encounter them embedded within discourse, and come to apprehend their meaning in the process of participating in the discourse which generates them. Before attempting to pin down a term like culture, one needs a sense of how it is used to say worthwhile and meaningful things, within the relevant discourse.

Teachers make an equivalent mistake when they exhort students to begin essays with definitions of key concepts. Defining terms is a high-order task, even for a competent discourse speaker. For a newcomer, it is almost impossible, given their weak grip on contextual framing. They usually resort to 'off-the-shelf' definitions, which 'express' nothing for them and serve only to alienate them from their own writing. The precision of the act of defining terms marks an end-point in learning, not a beginning.

In any case, Leila's difficulties lay not in the 'words' *per se*, but in the 'thoughts' they express. She was expecting to find out what elder abuse consists of and how it arises. Instead she found herself grappling with the kind of abstract propositions typically found in academic discourse. Meaning in the 'propositional' mode is removed from the context of the experienced world and depends instead on 'the rules of the symbolic, syntactic, and conceptual systems that we use in achieving decontextualized meanings' (Bruner, 1996b, p. 98; see also Hasan, this volume). This mode of meaning making is intrinsically demanding, but is rendered particularly difficult for students in that the 'symbolic, syntactic and conceptual systems' on which it depends are precisely what they are struggling to acquire. Leila will need to learn a lot more about care practice and policy before being able to make sense of propositions as abstract as in the above extract. Receiving well-formulated explanations is not, as teachers tend to imagine, the core of the learning process. It is participating with a teacher (and other students) in the making of meanings which are a little further into the specialist discourse than those the students can currently sustain on their own. The teacher may feel the urge to 'help' by clearing away messy half-truths and approximations, leaving only the pure essence of argument, but initially a student lacks the conceptual framing to invest pure argument with meaning, or to support its logical structure. To formulate tentative, fuzzy-edged meanings within the specialist discourse is the initial goal. Explanation comes later. By the time students can understand the teacher's explanation they have, in effect, reached the point of being able to participate in the process of explaining to themselves. The teacher's first priority is to engage students in collaborative meaning making.

Sharing Meaning with Students

Since propositional meanings are very difficult for the newcomer, if teachers are to share meaning with their students, they must seek other modes of meaning making. Bruner identifies three 'primitive' modes, which arise spontaneously within the situations of daily life.

- The first arises out of the phenomenon of 'intersubjectivity', our innate inclination to fall into 'dialogue' with other people and thereby produce meaning together. Without being aware of it, in such acts of 'joint meaning' we make wide-ranging assumptions about the surrounding world and thereby project meaning out onto it.
- The second, 'actional' mode arises out of our ' "natural" grasp of how action is organised' (Bruner, 1996b, p. 96); our urge to project meaning onto 'events', in terms of who did what, why and how.
- The third, 'normative' mode involves our sense of what is 'normal', and in particular our urge to construct meanings around the 'abnormal', to bring it back under the control of our sense-making processes.

These three 'primitive' modes of meaning making can play a significant role in learning, providing a foundation of shared meaning upon which propositional meanings can be built. This is why case studies, for example, are a key device in teaching.

> Stories are the vehicles *par excellence* for entrenching the first three modes of meaning-making into a more structured whole. (Bruner, 1996b, p. 97)

Here are extracts from a 'story' early in a K100 block addressing the topic of abuse.

> Marie is a young white woman who has recently started work at a residential unit for young people with physical and learning disabilities run by a local charity. She trained as an NNEB nurse at her local FE college after leaving school. She has been going out with her boyfriend Barry for two years and is saving up to get engaged. . . . The second day . . . Marie was to get Richard up. . . . She had been told that he could move from the bed to his wheelchair but would otherwise need help with dressing and toiletting. . . . When Marie went to help Richard get up it was obvious that he had an erection. She didn't know what to do: she didn't want to embarrass him but she couldn't help herself from blushing. She wondered if she should go out of the room, or go to find Joan. . . . She decided to stay and just turn away for a bit: eventually she took Richard down to the bathroom. By this stage she was confused as well as embarrassed. She . . . saw the urinal bottles on the shelf. Since he could not use his hands she had to put his penis into the bottle and keep it there while he peed. . . . Marie had never seen a man's penis before: although she was going steady with Barry, they had decided to wait until they were married before they had sex, which was in keeping with their religious beliefs. She felt upset that she had not realized this would be involved in the job and when she got home she thought it best not to say anything in case Barry or her parents misunderstood. (K100 Course Team, 1998)

Clearly Leila will not struggle to understand this text. Meaning is developed entirely through Bruner's three primitive sociocultural modes.

- Actional: the detail about the action Marie was involved in – what happened, what happened next, and so on – produces compelling insight into her motives, the dilemmas she faced and her reasons for acting in particular ways.
- Normative: the norm-breaking encounters with an erection and penis-holding make us vividly aware of Marie's shock and confusion and her need for training and support.
- Intersubjective: the details of Marie's background, her family and her impending marriage help us to enter into her world and understand the complexities and ambiguities of her experience. We apprehend a bundle of interconnected issues, capable of subsequent unravelling and analysis in propositional mode.

A key theme of this K100 block is that relationships between carer and cared-for are fraught with ambiguities, particularly in situations of intimate care. Care work routinely breaches the boundaries of normal social interactions, raising questions of power, ethics and accountability. This is the context in which issues of abuse arise; but these complex and subtle matters are difficult for new students to engage with in purely 'propositional' terms. However, having internalized the complexity of Marie's experiences through the three primitive modes, students can then continue thinking about the implications at whatever level of sophistication they can muster. This is how students with very different background knowledge and experience can learn effectively from the same materials. All internalize the 'primitive' meanings, but they then develop these into propositional meanings according to their own capabilities. Since our minds retain the basic elements of a story relatively easily, students will be able to recall Marie's experience in weeks to come and read new meanings into it.

> One of the properties of the narrative mode is that objects . . . slip easily into the mind. . . . The mind is more resistant to objects based on the paradigmatic mode. . . . [These] need elaborate cultural assistance to allow them to enter the mind. (Oatley, 1996, p. 123)

Constructing Pathways into the Specialist Discourse

Marie's story uses everyday concepts such as 'embarrassment' and 'confusion'. However, her situation is then discussed in the teaching text and gradually reframed in terms of the specialist discourse. Three pages later, one of a list of 'key points' states that:

• Intimate care is not 'ordinary'. It presents a very unusual set of dilemmas for both the carer and the person cared for.

This marks a first move from specific, concrete experience to decontextualized 'propositional' meaning. Five pages later, we see:

• Care workers are constantly crossing and rebuilding boundaries: hence the tension between closeness and distance in their relationships with service users.

This is a considerably more complex generalization, incorporating such ideas as 'crossing and rebuilding boundaries', 'closeness and distance' and 'tensions within care relationships'. These are significant constructs within care discourse.

This sequence illustrates a key teaching manoeuvre:

1   Dialogue is launched within familiar discourse, thereby framing a set of issues in readily understood terms.
2   Then, while maintaining a flow of meaning, the teacher gradually shifts the framing by introducing analytical tools from the specialist discourse.
3   Eventually the issues are being discussed within the terms of the specialist discourse.

At this third stage students become able to share the experience of making meaning within the specialist discourse. They begin to sense what kind of meaning it is, the kinds of issue that are addressed, the kinds of evidence and mode of arguing that are in play. All this provides a model for subsequent efforts at producing meanings through reading and writing. In effect, an 'excursion' has been organized by the teacher, setting out from a familiar discursive context to visit a selected site within a specialist discourse. Meanings generated within the known context are carried along and modified to support the framing of meanings within the specialist discourse.

When students are making excursions into new discursive terrain it helps to approach from a variety of directions, enabling 'triangulation' in mapping out new meanings. The opening unit of K100 begins with a poem by a receiver of care, followed by an introductory discussion interspersed with montages of photographs. Then there is a dramatized audio-cassette case study, followed by a debate interspersed with newspaper headlines, research findings, first-hand accounts from carers and cared for, tables of statistics and more. As students move between items, the crossing trails gradually enable a makeshift mapping of meaning. Against this sketched background, such framing structures as 'core questions' and central arguments begin to take shape. Gradually students construct a temporary work-space within which they can practise using the basic tools for meaning making within the new discourse.

A diversity of sources also helps students establish their own relationship to the discourse. Rather than a single, continuous, authoritative voice, presenting a seamless argument, they 'hear' short passages of discourse at a variety of levels, ranging from domestic and media discourses, through the task-oriented discourses of care practice, to the discourses of research and theory. They acquire a sense of a bustling community of many voices and different kinds of truth; a community one might envisage joining as a participant, whereas a lone novice can only be daunted by the challenge of joining in a community peopled solely by confident experts. The author need not be the only person the student is in dialogue with. Teaching texts can be constructed as discursive spaces in which a variety of voices speak.

But, of course, mixing together many elements risks incoherence, undermining students' efforts at constructing meaning. It is vital that the elements be embedded within a carefully plotted teaching narrative. A teaching text can usefully be likened to a stage play. The audience arrives with various concerns of the day in mind, so the job of the opening scene is to capture their attention and invite curiosity as to what is going on. As incidents occur and new characters enter, various interconnected themes emerge, all of which are brought to some sort of resolution by the end. The play as a whole delivers a complex of meanings, which each member of the audience will have construed differently, according to their prior experience and understanding of the issues. Similarly, a distance educator can think of a teaching text as a sequence of 'incidents', in the form of cases, photographs, activities and so on. The words they write are what is necessary to set the incidents up and link them together as a coherent teaching narrative. Rather than think of the text as an extended written 'explanation' of the key teaching points, the incidents can be seen as doing the teaching, while the teacher manages the development of the plot.

In much educational material, intellectual thoroughness and precision are given priority over plot. Academic discourse typically makes complex cross-connections, implicitly addressing alternative theoretical accounts in passing. For the specialist reader the various strands make interconnected sense within wider frames of reference. However, newcomers to the discourse lack these wider frames, so that at every shift of focus the immediate frame evaporates and meaning making collapses. Since meaning is always effortful for the discourse newcomer, continually reconstituting it from a standing start is terribly tiring and dispiriting. The art of developing and maintaining a 'storyline' is consequently a key skill for all teachers.

Supporting Students in Becoming Speakers of the Specialist Discourse

A teacher must, however, do more than construct a compelling plot. Students fully internalize the way a discourse works only through using it to produce

meanings of their own (Lemke, 1990). And they become effective participants within the discourse community only when they can produce utterances
accepted as valid by community members. From the earliest stages in a course,
students need regular opportunities to speak or write in the presence of a
competent discourse speaker, who can guide their framing of meaning towards accepted usage. In practice, given the text-based character of academic
discourse, emphasizing literal meanings and logic (Olson, 1996), it is the
written assignment which provides the primary context for this guidance.

The teacher's insights as a speaker of the specialist discourse are called on
in two ways. First, in setting appropriate assignments: judging what kinds of
meaning students are ready to make, using elements of the discourse recently
encountered, and framing a task which positions students so that they can
generate authentic meanings. That is, the task must be pitched within the
students' 'zone of proximal development' (Vygotsky, 1986) and must be
designed to scaffold the students' participation in it. All too often, assignments are too demanding of discourse competence, or offer students too little
support in thinking their way into the issues. This leaves little choice but to
cobble together a paraphrased account.

The second call on the teacher's insights into the discourse lies in reading
the student's writing responsively, participating in the meaning they have
projected and guiding them in the practices of the discourse. Here is an
extract from guidance provided to K100 tutors:

> Your role is to enable, sustain and guide your students' efforts at speaking
> purposefully in writing. You are the absent 'audience' when your student is
> sitting writing, so you have to try to 'listen' to what they say. Don't just look
> for what you want to see. As you write comments you are providing the other
> side of a 'dialogue' – enabling the student to discover where they have and have
> not communicated successfully with you. Thus even informal markings on the
> script – 'I'm not sure what you mean', or 'aha' – carry very valuable meaning.
> They help the student to read back through their work, taking on the role of
> audience instead of speaker. But of course, you are, at the same time, the
> 'expert' who knows the content and the form of the academic discourse, so you
> have a second role in guiding the student in the ways of speaking this discourse.
> Consequently you have to perform a balancing act between encouraging the
> student's writing 'voice' to emerge and helping them to internalize the rules of
> the discourse. (K100 Course Team, 2000)

The development of the student's writing voice is critical. To become a speaker
of a discourse is to acquire a new identity as a member of that discourse
community. A central struggle throughout studenthood is to establish a voice
and an identity as a legitimate speaker/writer within the specialist community.

This approach to assignment writing sits uncomfortably with contemporary
calls for tightly specified course outcomes and detailed performance criteria.
Nevertheless, it enables profound learning and highly meaningful assessment,

because it reflects the ambiguities and indeterminacy in what is fundamentally a sociocultural process of negotiating meaning.

Conclusion

Let me conclude by revisiting my metaphor of teaching as 'organizing excursions into specialist discourse communities'. The underlying proposition is that higher knowledge is constituted in the discourse exchanged within communities of specialists and that the purpose of studying is to gain working mastery of that discourse. In this way students gain access to the intellectual power of the semiotic structures and sub-cultural know-how embedded in the specialist discourse, and also to the social power of membership of a significant community.

However, as we saw with the textbook extract, engaging with an unfamiliar discourse is a formidable challenge. Picking up meaning is fundamentally problematic, because it depends on 'frames of reference' which community members take for granted and which can only be apprehended and internalized through use. Hence the teacher's first key role is to 'lend' students the capacity to frame meanings within the specialist discourse. To achieve this, a teacher must be able to 'step outside' the specialist discourse and engage in dialogue with students within the terms of a familiar discourse. Then, having initiated a flow of meaning, the teacher guides the students on an excursion into the target discourse arena, gradually shifting the frame of reference until it corresponds well enough to allow sense to be made within the specialist discourse.

The teacher's second key role is to plan the route the excursion will take, so that students will encounter debates, issues and voices that help them develop a sense of the character of the discourse community, its participants, their core purposes and values, their customary preoccupations, how they speak and how they argue. As students establish such sociocultural bearings, they will begin to be able to anticipate and thereby participate in the meanings offered by specialist texts. They will also begin to apprehend, through participation, the force of the theoretical analysis embedded in the discourse. This is a radical inversion of conventional teaching practice, which prioritizes definitions and theoretical exposition, presuming that these need to be understood before applying them discursively. Instead, priority is given to engaging students in a flow of shared meaning, within which a discursive context is constructed, which then enables the higher activities of defining and theorizing.

The 'vehicle' for the excursion is a flow of meaning structured as a plot, initiated by the teacher but then mutually produced between teacher and students. To prevent this vehicle breaking down repeatedly, the teacher must maintain a strong, continuous framing (or storyline). This includes the use of such devices as stories and case material, which enable 'primitive' meaning making, upon which the more 'artificial' propositional meanings of academic discourse can be built. Instead of the customary academic preoccupation with precision and neat categories, the 'fuzziness' of first efforts at meaning is acknowledged and supported. A strong current, bubbling with rich meanings, carries a diverse group of students along with it.

The third key role of the teacher is to coach the student in 'speaking with the locals' within the discourse community; setting tasks which draw students into using the discourse to make their own meanings; interpreting their efforts at using unfamiliar words and ideas and joining in to elaborate on and help reformulate what they say. In particular, the teacher models the 'voice' in which the discourse is spoken, thereby helping students construct appropriate 'identities' as participants within the community.

Taken together, these three roles provide the elements of an understanding of university teaching which differs radically from that which informs most current practice. Yet it is one which offers both depth of insight and a practical working methodology sufficient to the subtle and complex challenges of teaching within a distance education institution. Ironically, it is in this extreme setting, where 'live' social and cultural interchange is pared down to a minimum, that the significance of the sociocultural nature of education is revealed most clearly, because it has to be deliberately designed in. Yet if a sociocultural model of learning and teaching works within distance education, it has even more relevance in the dynamic social milieu of conventional face-to-face university teaching. Teachers and students in all universities should work together as bands of travellers on excursions to participate in the discourse of communities of specialists. It is within such participation that new knowledge and understanding lie.

20
Afterword

Luis C. Moll

I appreciate the opportunity to offer comments on the outstanding collection of essays assembled in this volume. By way of an afterword, especially because the book offers much more than I can grasp in a few pages, I have opted to discuss a single but seminal topic: what these essays contribute to addressing issues of diversity in education. I also want to consider diversity both as a challenge to the precepts of a (Vygotskian) socio-cultural approach and as a resource for its development.

In a sense, Vygotsky's theory was built on the study of diversity. Recall his study with Luria of historical and cultural variations among the Uzbekis in the then Soviet Central Asia. But perhaps more to the point is their applied work in 'defectology', which preceded the better-known research in Uzbekistan, by the way, and provided the bases for much of the formulation of a cultural–historical approach. For example, in this early work we already find the application of a mediated approach to rehabilitation, in the sense of building on a person's strengths and of creating alternative paths to higher mental functions. Thus, the 'defect' itself (e.g. deafness) was not the focus of compensation, but the influence of the condition on the person's social communication and interactions, and the new means that could be provided for creating social (semiotic) life and, hence, expanded opportunities for psychological development.

Much has changed since Vygotsky's time, however, especially in terms of the transnational movement of people. As I write these words, newspapers are replete with articles about the changing demographics in the United States, owing to immigration and to the high birth rates of select ('minority') groups. In California, which seems to be the tail that wags the nation on these issues, the changes have been most dramatic. Suffice to say that 'whites' are no longer the numerical majority in the state, or in its major cities. Similar shifts are well underway elsewhere in the country.

But it is in the public schools, especially in the major cities, that these demographic changes have been most noticeable and most profound. In the

Los Angeles Unified School District in California, for instance, the second largest district in the country, with over 600,000 students, Latino children, enormously diverse in their own right, and mostly from low-income families, comprise over 70 per cent of the student body.[1] Middle-class whites seemed to have virtually disappeared from the system, and schools that were predominantly African American, representing hard-earned 'enclaves' within the system for African-American teachers and administrators, are now teaching 'other people's children', predominantly Latinos; a change that occurred, at least so it seems to outsiders, almost overnight.

These changing demographics, and the cultural, linguistic and class diversity it has produced, have provided fertile soil for the exercise of power, especially the power to organize and orchestrate classroom settings themselves, and control the nature and direction of pedagogical actions. Policy makers and voters (in the United States) have responded with a series of myopic and restrictive measures. These measures include the prohibition and dismantling of bilingual education, against the will of the great majority of those families and teachers affected by this policy; highly reductionist and prescriptive phonics reading programmes, legislatively imposed and mandated in several states; and, 'high-stakes' testing, making passing these arbitrary tests the sole criterion for school success, graduation, grade advancement, or even teachers' salary adjustments. I see all these as desperate efforts to impose uniformity on diversity.

The scenario depicted above represents, I believe, the 'receiving' context for the ideas presented in this volume.[2] It is not a pretty picture. These are all policies that effectively eliminate the students' lived experiences and funds of knowledge from the teaching and learning process, and severely curtail teachers' abilities to exercise autonomy over their work to make activities meaningful for learners. As such, these policies deliberately constrain teachers and students from developing the sorts of collaborative 'discourse communities' proposed in this volume, that attempt to 'make sense of and make use of every part of our communities', to borrow a phrase from Lemke, as resources for living and for expanding forms of learning. It behooves us, then, to keep in mind, as Wolf (2001) reminds us, that culture works in and through power relations, and power works through the diverse social processes and cultural practices of society.

However, power never goes unchallenged, it always produces friction, resistance and contestation; and schools are not fixed or immutable entities, they are built environments, socially produced and recreated through the actions of the human beings who participate in and mediate their realities, even when those realities include significant constraints. In this regard, the great virtue of a Vygotskian approach is that it offers a theory of possibilities. It is not necessarily that it provides specific remedies for practice, or even that it offers a foundation for that practice, but that education, in all its forms, serves as a foundation for the theory. What this approach offers, then, is a theoretical orientation to cultural mediation, to how human beings use social relations and cultural practices, including symbol systems and other artifacts, to constitute and develop their thinking.

Consequently, cultural practices, such as those found in schools and classrooms, which are generated historically, could always be otherwise, re-mediated through different arrangements of the social relations and cultural resources for thinking. These possibilities for agency, for recovering meaningful activities in education, as del Río and Álvarez propose, or for developing a dynamic 'epistemic milieu', as Claxton suggests, within which students develop their identities and 'dispositions' as learners, to borrow from Carr, are cause for optimism and very good news for teachers. It is not only the case that the essential tools for thinking are found in the nature of our social relations and in our uses of cultural (semiotic) artifacts, but that the teaching and learning process itself, as Stetsenko and Arievitch write, 'is the very pathway through which cognitive, social, and affective development takes place'. The importance of teachers, then, and the social relationships they form with students, has never been more evident.

Let me turn, therefore, to the possibilities offered by the present collection of essays in terms of issues of diversity. All of the essays, as one would expect, recognize that learning is embedded in social relations and that those relations help constitute, generate, broader cultural practices or routines of instruction. Much of the attention of these essays, then, is aimed precisely at those discursive encounters that form part of the social relations of classroom practice or of other everyday activities (e.g. Wells; Mercer; Pontecorvo and Sterponi). Discourse processes, therefore, carry a heavy theoretical load in these essays, in particular because the authors credit discourse with great powers in the formation of children's (and adults') intellectual abilities.

But it is perhaps Hasan who expresses most forcefully the power of semiotic mediation by means of language, by means of discourse, in ways that are quite reminiscent of Bernstein's differentiation of 'elaborated' and 'restricted' codes. 'The most important thing language does in discourse', she writes, 'is to enable speaking subjects to internalize the world they experience in the living of their life'. And they experience this world through specific and differential forms of discourse within what she labels 'quotidian activities', with certain forms of discourse creating particular mental dispositions, habits of mind or orientations to meaning, that shape in children a sense of what things are worthwhile doing in their communities and how these can be accomplished (or not) with language. In essence, the claim is that extensive experience with these different types of everyday discourses, especially those that are more 'epistemic' than others, makes for different types of minds, all with differential consequences for schooling.

To be sure, in all these chapters there is a concern with providing powerful modes of schooling for all children, regardless of (or, perhaps, because of) their history of learning, or their history of discourse, as in the terms put forth by Hasan. There is, however, little specification of just who are these children they are writing about, of the ethnographic details, one could say, that would situate them concretely as real children in real circumstances of life, in all their diversity. There is also little recognition, in general, of just how intractable school systems will be to implementing any of the suggestions put forth for more engaging and discursive pedagogies, especially ones that may help poor children master the 'epistemic dialect' (Hasan's term) that would make them competitive with wealthy children for the resources of schooling.

There are, however, important directions in these chapters for those interested in engaging diversity in education. I was particularly taken by Wells's programme of theoretically inspired collaborative research, the central role of teachers in this intellectual endeavour, and the experimentation with teaching and learning that it entails. I also second his call for changing radically teachers' working conditions to include, as an essential aspect of their profession, the necessary time and dialogic space to think with others and to develop inquiries into their pedagogies. Along similar lines, there are Mercer's suggestions for dialogues to help children recognize and understand the relevance of their past experiences and common knowledge as part of the 'cultural' discourse properties of classrooms. Northedge, in turn, unpackages ways of using familiar narratives to allow novices to enter and become adept with the 'specialist' discourses that characterize higher education. And there is Pontecorvo and Sterponi's point of the cognitive importance of social familiarity between teachers and students, as well as among students. It is not only that such familiarity grows through the practices of social interaction and dialogue, as they suggest, which themselves become resources for thinking, but that it leads to the identification of intellectual strengths that may otherwise not be recognized within the relatively impersonal didactic practices of schooling.

There is also a group of essays that address, not so much the discourse properties of interactions as such, but the broader nature of social practices. Dalton and Tharp, for instance, describe the essential elements, 'consensus findings' as they call them, translated into standards and indicators, for the transformation of classrooms into 'activity settings' that explicitly challenge the dominant 'recitation' model of schooling. Cobb and McClain, in turn, provide an example of a 'design experiment' in the teaching of mathematics, in this instance, of statistics to seventh-graders. They highlight how new uses of computer-based 'mini-tools' for data analysis, which provide great flexibility in exploring trends in data sets and in representing findings, helped redesign the interplay between instructional tasks, activity structures and classroom discourse in reconstituting the nature and purpose of mathematical learning and reasoning in this classroom. This re-mediation of activities, I should add, was done with an eye on public policy issues of significance, and the congruence of classroom learning situations and out-of-school experiences, especially in terms of providing socially significant content for mathematical analysis.

In terms of addressing diversity through changes in practices, however, I found the chapter by Chaiklin most intriguing. Although several other chapters address the development of students' identities, and of facilitating emotional engagements, through their participation in socially meaningful activities, Chaiklin underscores the primacy in schooling of the development of 'personality', in this instance through the students' engagement with subject-matter content (see also Stetsenko and Arievitch). This orientation to personality places the emphasis on the concrete subject, on his or her individual subjectivity, not as a fixed or independent entity, but as fluid and constituted through the nature of his or her social relations. This is what Vygotsky referred to as the 'historical' child, grounded in the socio-historical and relational particulars of life's settings (see also Engeström, et al.).

The importance of this concept of personality, in my view, is that it leads one to address the cultural particulars of children and their lives, something that is absent in most of the present essays. Children form their subjectivities, who they are as people, as human beings, and reconstitute them, using the social processes and cultural resources available to them. These subjectivities, we could say, are simultaneously 'deeply singular', for no two children have identical social histories, and 'deeply social', for they are always embedded in the dynamics of particular systems of social interaction (González Rey, 1999; see also Mahn and John-Steiner, this volume).

In this respect, one must consider that children (and adults) actively create themselves, building their own social, semiotic and ideological 'versions', but not necessarily within environments of their own choosing, especially in relation to schooling experiences. The concept of personality, therefore, may help bring, beyond the current emphasis on discursive and social practices, and on the design of learning environments, the particulars of diversity and of children's subjectivities and heterogeneity much more sharply into theoretical and pedagogical focus than what is presently the case (see also Engeström, et al.) .

Finally, I want to comment on chapters that have the ambitious agenda of creating fundamentally new activity systems, or of changing the objectives of such systems. The Brown and Cole and the Matusov and Hayes chapters summarize theoretically based efforts at creating after-school educational settings for children of varying ages. There is much here that could be discussed in relation to addressing diversity in education, and much that differs from schooling as usually delivered. What I want to highlight, however, is how universities can become 'mediating structures' for the development of not only new educational practices or innovations, but for the development of new educational relationships around issues of diversity. I think of these relationships as ways of expanding students' educational ecology. That is, these activity settings can be created practically anywhere; they involve an intergenerational (and multicultural) mix of participants, easy access to activities, a commitment to sustainability, and they feature multiple mediators, ranging from computers to interpersonal relations, and documentation of change in activity (see also Gipps). Furthermore, the knowledge generated at these settings is 'distributed', in that what is learned at one setting is communicated to other settings dispersed internationally. So that all learning may be local, but the knowledge and resources that address diversity in one place, may be communicated widely to others situated elsewhere.

The chapter by Engeström, Engeström and Suntio also addresses this issue of creating new educational relationships, in this instance, to facilitate structural changes in a school. It is revealing how a participatory stance, and a respectful, collegial relationship among teachers and researchers, can create several openings for getting to know students, rethinking teachers, their identities and their teaching, and for creating new artifacts and patterns of practice. In this case, and of significance, it was the voices of teachers who work with immigrant students, their multicultural experiences, that served as an important catalyst for innovation and change.

I am impressed by how such activity systems, both in and out of school, can accomplish, with a lot of hard work and lots of collaboration, no doubt, and with the mediated assistance of Vygotskian theoretical tools, what schools have such a terrible time creating: 'additive' conditions for learning for poor and minority students. I am using the term 'additive' here not only in the linguistic sense, important as that may be, especially in the development of new discourses, as emphasized in much of this volume, but in a broader emotional sense that reflects creating conditions that are caring or nurturing and that fully accept the children and their identities. These additive conditions not only appropriate the children's language and culture as resources for learning, but also afford the children an 'unmarked' identity, without any of the school designations, labels and practices that serve to mark certain children as deficient or incapable of learning.

Notes

1   'Latinos' is a catch-all term to refer to all people from Latin America or of such descent; as with all generic terms, it belies the great diversity that exists among Latinos, in the US or elsewhere.
2   In fact, the increase of diversity in schools may have led to the positive response to Vygotsky's ideas in the 1980s, which also coincided with a focus on issues of contextual variation in psychology, and ethnographic approaches to educational research (see Moll, in press).

Bibliography

Aidarova, L. (1982). *Child development and education* (trans. L. Lezhneva). Moscow: Progress. (Original work published 1982)

Aikenhead, C. (1997). 'A framework for reflecting on assessment and evaluation.' In *Globalization of science education: Papers for the Seoul International Conference* (pp. 195–9). Seoul: Korean Educational Development Institute.

Allington, R. (1990). 'Children who find learning to read difficult: School responses to diversity.' In E. H. Hiebert (ed.), *Literacy for a diverse society: Perspectives, programs, and policies* (pp. 237–52). Bristol, PA: Palmer Press.

Altman, I. and Rogoff, B. (1987). 'World views in psychology: Trait, interactional, organismic, and transactional perspectives.' In D. Stokols and I. Altman (eds), *Handbook of environmental psychology* (pp. 7–40). New York: Wiley.

Álvarez, A. (1990). 'Diseño cultural: Una aproximación ecológica a la educación desde el paradigma histórico-cultural.' *Infancia y Aprendizaje* (51–52), 41–77.

Álvarez, A. (1994). 'Child's everyday life: An ecological approach to the study of activity systems.' In A. Álvarez and P. del Río (eds), *Explorations in sociocultural studies, Vol. 4: Education as cultural Construction* (pp. 23–38). Madrid: Fundación Infancia y Aprendizaje.

Álvarez, A. (1996). *Los marcos culturales de actividad y el desarrollo de las funciones psicológicas*. Unpublished doctoral dissertation. Madrid: Universidad Autónoma.

Álvarez, A. (1997). 'El drama es que no hay drama. Algunas claves vygotskianas para interpretar los efectos de la televisión.' *Cultura y Educación*, 5: 69–81.

Álvarez, A. (2000a). *Situated narratives: Voices from Castilian cultural and personal identities*. Paper presented at the Third Conference for Sociocultural Research, Campinas, Brazil.

Álvarez, A. (2000b). 'Hacia un enfoque sociocultural de la Educación Abierta. Una lección multimedia sobre identidad cultural en el proyecto europeo inter-universitario Pegasus.' *Cultura y Educación*, 20: 81–101.

Ames, C. (1992). 'Classrooms: goals, structures and student motivation.' *Journal of Educational Psychology*, 84 (3): 261–71.

Andrade, R., Callanan, M. A., Cervantes, C. A., Guardino, G., Hilberg, R., Kyle, D., McIntyre, E., Rivera, H., Tharp, R. G. and Rueda, R. (1999). *Parents as intellectuals, parents as experts*. Symposium a the annual meeting of the American Educational Research Association, Montreal.

Arievitch, I. M. and Stetsenko, A. (2000). 'Development through learning: Galperin's contribution.' *Human Development*, 43: 69–93.

Atkinson, J. M. and Heritage, J. (eds) (1984). *Structures of social action*. Cambridge: Cambridge University Press.

Au, K. (1980). 'Participation structures in a reading lesson with Hawaiian children: Analysis of a culturally appropriate instructional event.' *Anthropology and Education Quarterly*, 11 (2): 91–115.

August, D. and Hakuta, K. (1997). *Improving schooling for language-minority children: A research agenda*. Washington, DC: National Academy Press.

Baird, J. R. and Northfield, J. R. (1992). *Learning from the PEEL experience*. Melbourne: Monash University Press.

Baker, E. and O'Neil, H. (1995). 'Diversity, assessment, and equity in edcational reform.' In M. Nettles and A. Nettles (eds), *Equity and excellence in educational testing and assessment* (pp. 69–87). Boston: Kluwer.

Bakhtin, M. (1981). 'Discourse in the novel.' In M. Holquist, (ed.), *The dialogic imagination* (pp. 259–422). Austin: University of Texas Press.

Bakhtin, M. (1981). *The dialogic imagination*. Austin: University of Texas Press. (First published 1935)

Bakhtin, M. (1986). *Speech genres and other late essays*, 1st edn, ed. M. Holquist and C. Emerson. Austin: University of Texas Press.

Baldwin, J. (1976). *The devil finds work*. New York: Dial.

Ball, D. (1993). 'With an eye on the mathematical horizon: Dilemmas of teaching elementary school mathematics.' *Elementary School Journal*, 93: 373–397.

Banks, C. (1995). 'Equity pedagogy: An essential component of multicultural education.' *Theory into Practice*, 34: 152–8.

Barnes, D. and Todd, F. (1995). *Communication and learning revisited*. Portsmouth, NH: Heinemann.

Beck, U. (1992). *Risk society* (trans. M. Ritter). London: Sage.

Bekendtgørelsen om folkeskolen (2000). http://www.uvm.dk/lov/lbk/2000/0000730.htm# Kapitel 1 (accessed 30 October 2000).

Belle, D. (1999). *The after school lives of children: Alone and with others while their parents work*. Hillsdale, NJ: Lawrence Erlbaum.

Bennett, N. and Cass, A. (1989). 'The effects of group composition on group interactive processes and pupil understanding.' *British Educational Research Journal*, 15: 119–32.

Bereiter, C. (1994). 'Implications of postmodernism for science, or, science as progressive discourse.' *Educational Psychologist*, 29 (1): 3–12.

Berger, J. (1965). *The success and failure of Picasso*. Harmondsworth: Penguin Books.

Berger, P. (1963). *Invitation to sociology*. Harmondsworth: Penguin Books.

Berger, P. and Luckman, T. (1966). *The social construction of reality: A treatise on the sociology of knowledge*. New York: Doubleday.

Bernstein, B. (1971). *Class, codes and control, Vol. 1: Theoretical studies toward a sociology of language*. London: Routledge and Kegan Paul.

Bernstein, B. (1982). 'Codes, modalities and the process of cultural reproduction: A model.' In M. Apple (ed.), *Cultural and economic reproduction in education*. London: Routledge and Kegan Paul.

Bernstein, B. (1990). *The structuring of pedagogic discourse, Vol. 4: Class, codes and control*. London: Routledge.

Bernstein, B. (1996). *Pedagogy, symbolic control, and identity: Theory, research, practice*. London: Taylor and Francis.

Bernstein, N. A. (1967). *The coordination and regulation of movements*. London: Pergamon.

Berry, D. C. and Dienes, Z. P. (eds) (1993). *Implicit learning: Theoretical and empirical issues*. Hove, UK: Lawrence Erlbaum.

Biehler, R. and Steinbring, H. (1991). 'Entdeckende statistik, stenget-und Blatter, Boxplots: Konzepte, Begrundungen and Enfahrungen eines Unterrichtsversuch es' ['Explorations in statistics, stem-and-leaf, boxplots: Concepts, justifications and experience in a teaching experiment']. *Der Mathematikunterricht*, 37 (6): 5–32.

Biggs, S. (1998). 'Elder abuse and the policing of community care.' In M. Allott and M. Robb (eds), *Understanding health and social care*. London: Sage.

Black, P. and William, D. (1998). 'Assessment and classroom learning.' *Assessment in Education*, 5 (1): 7–44

Blanton, W. E., Moorman, G. B., Hayes, B. A. and Warner, M. L. (1997). 'Effects of participation in the Fifth Dimension on far transfer.' *Journal of Educational Computing Research*, 16 (4): 371–96

Boaler, J. (1999). 'Participation, knowledge, and beliefs: A community perspective on mathematics learning.' *Educational studies in Math*, 40: 259–81.

Boli, J. and Ramirez, F. O. (1992). 'Compulsory schooling in the western cultural context.' In R. Arnove, P. G. Altbach and G. P. Kelly (eds), *Emergent issues in education: Comparative perspectives* (pp. 25–38). Albany: State University of New York Press.

Bonk, C. J., Daytner, K., et al. (1999). *Online mentoring of preservice teachers with web-based cases, conversations, and collaborations: Two years in review*. American Educational Research Annual Meetings, Montreal, Canada.

Bourdieu, P. (1990). *The logic of practice* (trans. R. Nice). London: Polity Press.

Bransford, J. D., Brown, A. L. and Cocking, R. R. (eds) (1999). *How people learn: Brain, mind, experience, and school*. Washington, DC: National Academy Press.

Broadfoot, P. (1996). *Education, assessment and society*. Buckingham, UK: Open University Press.

Broadfoot, P., James, M., McMeeking, S., Nuttall, D. and Stierer, S. (1988). *Records of achievement: Report of the national evaluation of pilot schemes (PRAISE)*. London: HMSO.

Broberg, A. G., Wessels, H., Lamb, M. E. and Hwang, C. P. (1997). 'Effects of day care on the development of cognitive abilities in 8-year-olds: A longitudinal study.' *Developmental Psychology*, 33 (1): 62–69.

Bronckart, J. P. (1995). 'Theories of action, speech, natural language, and discourse.' In J. V. Wertsch, P. del Río and A. Álvarez (eds), *Sociocultural studies of mind*. Cambridge: Cambridge University Press.

Bronfenbrenner, U. (1979). *The ecology of human development*. Cambridge, MA: Harvard University Press.

Bronfenbrenner, U. (1989). *Who cares for children?* (Report no. 188). UNESCO.

Bronfenbrenner, U. and Morris, P. A. (1998). 'The ecology of developmental processes.' In R. Lerner (ed.), *Handbook of child psychology*, 5th edn (pp. 993–1028). New York: Wiley.

Brothers, L. (1997). *Friday's footsteps: How society shapes the human mind*. New York: Oxford University Press.

Brown, A. L. and Campione, J. C. (1994). 'Guided discovery in a community of learners.' In K. McGilly (ed.), *Integrating cognitive theory and classroom practice: Classroom lessons* (pp. 229–70). Cambridge, MA: MIT Press/Bradford Books.

Brown, A. L. and Campione, J. C. (1996). 'Psychological theory and the design of innovative learning environments: On procedures, principles and systems.' In L. Schauble and R. Glaser (eds), *Innovations in learning: New environments for education* (pp. 289–325). Mahwah, NJ: Lawrence Erlbaum.

Brown, A. L., Campione, J. C., Webber, L. and McGilly, K. (1992). 'Interactive learning environments: A new look at assessment and instruction.' In B. Gifford and M. O'Connor (eds), *Changing Assessments: Alternative views of aptitude, achievement and instruction*. Boston: Kluwer.

Brown, A. L. and Palincsar, A. S. (1987). 'Reciprocal teaching of comprehension strategies: A natural history of one program for enhancing learning.' *Intelligence and exceptionality: New directions for theory, assessment, and instructional practices* (pp. 81–132). Norwood, NJ: Ablex Publishing.

Brown, A. L. and Palincsar, A. S. (1989). 'Guided, co-operative learning and individual knowledge acquisition.' In L. Resnick (ed.), *Knowing, learning and instruction*. New York: Lawrence Erlbaum.

Brown, J. S., Collins, A., et al. (1989). 'Situated cognition and the culture of learning.' *Educational Researcher*, 18: 32–42.

Bruer, J. T. (1993). *Schools for thought: A science of learning in the classroom*. Cambridge, MA: MIT Press.

Bruner, J. S. (1960). *The process of education*. Cambridge, MA: Harvard University Press.

Bruner, J. S. (1971). *The relevance of education*. New York: W. W. Norton.

Bruner, J. S. (1972). 'Nature and uses of immaturity.' *American Psychologist*, 27 (8): 1–22.

Bruner, J. S. (1978). 'The role of dialogue in language acquisition.' In A. Sinclair, R. Jarvella and W. Levelt (eds), *The child's conception of language*. New York: Springer-Verlag.

Bruner, J. S. (1986). *Actual minds, possible worlds*. Cambridge, MA: Harvard University Press.

Bruner, J. S. (1990a). *Acts of meaning*. Cambridge, MA: Harvard University Press.

Bruner, J. S. (1990b). 'Culture and human development: A new look.' *Human Development*, 33 (6): 344–55.

Bruner, J. S. (1991). 'The narrative construction of reality.' *Critical Inquiry*, 18: 1–21.

Bruner, J. S. (1996a). *The culture of education*. Cambridge, MA: Harvard University Press.

Bruner, J. S. (1996b). 'Frames for thinking: ways of making meaning.' In D. Olson and N. Torrance (eds), *Modes of thought: Explorations in culture and cognition*. Cambridge: Cambridge University Press.

Carpay, J. A. M. (1974). 'Foreign-language teaching and meaningful learning: A Soviet Russian point of view.' *Review of Applied Linguistics*, 25: 161–87.

Carr, M. (1999). 'Being a learner: Five learning dispositions for early childhood.' *Early Childhood Practice*, 1 (1): 81–99.

Carr, M. (2000a). 'Technological affordance, social practice and learning narratives in an early childhood setting.' *International Journal of Technology and Design Education*, 10: 61–79.

Carr, M. (2000b). 'Seeking children's perspectives about their learning.' In A. B. Smith and N. J. Taylor (eds), *Children's voice: Research, policy and practice*. Auckland: Addison Wesley Longman.

Carr, M., and May, H. (1993). 'Choosing a model: Reflecting on the development process of Te Wāriki national early childhood curriculum guidelines in New Zealand.' *International Journal of Early Years Education*, 1 (3): 7–21.

Carr, M. and May, H. (1994). 'Weaving patterns: Developing national early childhood curriculum guidelines in Aotearoa–New Zealand. *Australian Journal of Early Childhood*, 19 (1): 25–33.

Carr, W. and Kemmis, S. (1983). *Becoming critical: Knowing through action research*. Geelong, Vic.: Deakin University Press.

Cazden, C. (1986). 'Classroom discourse.' M. S. Wittrock (ed.), *Handbook of research on teaching*, 3rd edn. New York: Macmillan.

Ceci, S. (1991). 'How much does schooling influence general intelligence and its cognitive components? A reassessment of the evidence.' *Developmental Psychology*, 27: 703–22.

Chaiklin, S. (1999). 'Developmental teaching in the upper-secondary school.' In M. Hedegaard and J. Lompscher (eds), *Learning activity and development* (pp. 187–210). Aarhus, Denmark: Aarhus University Press.

Chaiklin, S. (2001). 'The category of personality in cultural–historical psychology.' In S. Chaiklin (ed.), *The theory and practice of cultural–historical psychology* (pp. 238–59). Aarhus, Denmark: Aarhus University Press.

Chalmot, A. U. (1992). 'Learning and problem-solving strategies of ESL students.' *Bilingual Research Journal*, 16 (3 and 4), Summer/Fall: 3–27.

Clark, A. (1997). *Being there: Putting brain, body and world together again*. Cambridge, MA: Bradford/MIT Press.

Claxton, G. L. (1990). *Teaching to learn*. London: Cassell.

Claxton, G. L. (1991). *Educating the inquiring mind: The challenge for school science*.

Claxton, G. L. (1997). *Hare brain, tortoise mind: Why intelligence increases when you think less*. London: Fourth Estate; Hopewell, NJ: Ecco Press.

Claxton, G. L. (1999). *Wise up: The challenge of lifelong learning*. New York and London: Bloomsbury:

Cloran, C. (1994). *Rhetorical units and decontextualization: An enquiry into some relations of context, meaning and grammar*. Monographs in Systemic Linguistics, 6. Nottingham University: School of English Studies.

Cloran, C. (1995). 'Defining and relating text segments: Subject and theme in discourse.' In R. Hasan and P. H. Fries (eds), *On subject and theme: A discourse functional perspective*. Amsterdam: John Benjamins.

Cloran, C. (1999). 'Contexts for learning.' In F. Christie (ed.), *Pedagogy and the shaping of consciousness*. London: Cassell.

Cobb, G. W. (1997). 'More literacy is not enough.' In L. A. Steen (ed.), *Why numbers count: Quantitative literacy for tomorrow's America* (pp. 75–90). New York: College Entrance Examination Board.

Cobb, G. W. and Moore, D. S. (1997). 'Mathematics, statistics, and teaching.' *American Mathematical Monthly*, 104: 801–23.

Cobb, P. (1994). 'Where is the mind?' *Educational Researcher*, 23 (7): 13–20.

Cobb, P. (1998). 'Learning from distributed theories of intelligence.' *Mind, Culture, and Activity*, 5: 187–204.

Cobb, P. (1999). 'Individual and collective mathematical learning: The case of statistical data analysis.' *Mathematical Thinking and Learning*, 1: 5–44.

Cobb, P. and Bowers, J. (1999). 'Cognitive and situated learning: Perspectives in theory and practice.' *Educational Researcher*, March: 4–15.

Cobb, P., McClain, K. and Gravemeijer, K. (2000). *Learning about statistical covariation*. Paper presented at the annual meeting of the American Educational Research Association, New Orleans.

Cochran-Smith, M. and Lytle, S. L. (1999). 'The teacher research movement: A decade later.' *Educational Researcher*, 28 (7): 15–25.

Cole, M. (1996). *Cultural psychology: A once and future discipline*. Cambridge, MA: The Bellknap Press of Harvard University Press.

Cole, M. (1999). 'Cultural psychology: Some general principles and a concrete example.' In Y. Engestrom, R. Meittinen and R.-L. Punamaki (eds), *Perspectives on activity theory* (pp. 87–106). Cambridge, MA: Cambridge University Press.

Cole, M. and Engeström, Y. (1993). 'A cultural historical approach to distributed cognition.' In G. Salomon (ed.), *Distributed cognitions* (pp. 1–46). Cambridge: Cambridge University Press.

Cole, M. and Engeström, Y. (1995). 'Commentary.' *Human Development*, 38 (1): 9–24.

Cole, M., Engeström, Y. and Vasquez, O. (eds) (1997). *Mind, culture, and activity: Seminal papers from the Laboratory of Comparative Human Cognition*. Cambridge and New York: Cambridge University Press.

Cooper, B. and Dunne, M. (1998). 'Anyone for tennis? Social class differences in children's responses to national curriculum mathematics testing.' *The Sociological Review*, 46 (1): 115–48.

Coy, M. W. (ed.) (1989). *Apprenticeship: From theory to method and back again*. Albany: State University of New York Press.

Cuban, L. (1993). *How teachers taught: Constancy and change in American classrooms, 1890–1990*. New York: Teachers College Press.

Cuban, L. (1999). *How scholars trumped teachers: Change without reform in university curriculum, teaching, and research, 1890–1990*. New York: Teachers College Press.

Dalton, S.S. (1998). *Pedagogy matters*. Research Report No. 4, Center for Research on Education, Diversity and Excellence (CREDE), University of California, Santa Cruz, CA.

Dalton, S. S. and Sison, J. (1994). *Enacting instructional conversation in math with Spanish speaking language minority students* (Research report no. 12). National Research Center on Cultural Diversity and Second Language Learning. Washington DC: Center for Applied Linguistics.

Dalton, S. S. and Youpa, D. G. (1998). 'Standards-based teaching reform in Zuni Pueblo Middle and High Schools.' *Equity and Excellence in Education*, 31 (1): 55–68.

Dalton, S. S., Stoddart, T. and Tharp, R. G. (1997). 'Teaching alive! [CD-ROM] *Principles of culturally responsive instruction for diverse students*. California Center for Teacher Development (CCTD), Center for Research on Education, Diversity, and Excellence (CREDE), University of California, Santa Cruz.

Damasio, A. (1999). *The feeling of what happens: Body and emotion in the making of consciousness*. New York: Harcourt Brace.

Darling-Hammond, L. (1996). *What matters most: Teaching for America's future*. Report of the National Commission on Teaching and America's Future. New York: Teachers College, Columbia University.

Darling-Hammond, L. (1997). *Doing what matters most: Investing in quality teaching*. Report of the National Commission on Teaching and America's Future (NCTAF). New York: Teachers College, Columbia University.

Davies, B. (1989). *Frogs and snails and feminist tales: Preschool children and gender*. Sydney: Allen and Unwin.

Davis, G. (2001). 'A comparison of student-led discussions: Class meetings and novel discussions.' In G. Wells (ed.), *Talk, text and inquiry* (pp. 60–77). New York: Teachers College Press.

Davydov, V. V. (1972). *Formy obschenija v obuchenii*. Moscow: Pedagogika.

Davydov, V. V. (1975a). 'Logical and psychological problems of elementary mathematics as an academic subject' (trans. A. Bigelow). In L. Steffe (ed.), *Soviet studies in the psychology of learning and teaching mathematics, Vol. 5: Children's capacity for learning mathematics* (pp. 55–107). Stanford, CA: School Mathematics Study Group. (Original work published 1966)

Davydov, V. V. (1975b). 'The psychological characteristics of the "prenumerical" period of mathematics instruction' (trans. A. Bigelow). In L. Steffe (ed.), *Soviet studies in the psychology of learning and teaching mathematics, Vol. 5: Children's capacity for learning mathematics* (pp. 109–205). Stanford, CA: School Mathematics Study Group. (Original work published 1966)

Davydov, V. V. (1988a). 'Problems of developmental teaching.' *Soviet Education*, 30 (9): 3–83.

Davydov, V. V. (1988b). 'The concept of theoretical generalization and problems of educational psychology.' *Studies in Soviet Thought*, 36 (3): 169–202.

Davydov, V. V. (1990). 'Types of generalization in instruction: Logical and psychological problems in the structuring of school curricula.' *Soviet studies in mathematics education, Vol. 2* (ed. J. Kilpatrick, trans. J. Teller). Reston, VA: National Council of Teachers of Mathematics. (Original work published 1972)

Dawes, L. (1997). 'Teaching talking.' In R. Wegerif and P. Scrimshaw (eds), *Computers and talk in the primary classroom*. Clevedon: Multilingual Matters.

Dawes, L. (1998). 'Developing exploratory talk.' In L. Grugeon, L. Hubbard, C. Smith and L. Dawes (eds), *Teaching speaking and listening in the primary school*. London: David Fulton Press.

Dawes, L., Mercer, N. and Wegerif, R. (2000). *Thinking together: Activities for teachers and children at Key Stage 2*. Birmingham: Questions Publishing.

de Beauvoir, S. (1984). *Adieux: A farewell to Sartre*. New York: Pantheon Books.

de Haan, M. (1999). *Learning as cultural practice: How children learn in a Mexican Mazahua community*. Amsterdam: Thela Thesis.

del Río, P. (1987). *El desarrollo de las competencias espaciales: el proceso de construcción de los instrumentos mentales*. Unpublished doctoral dissertation. Madrid: Universidad Complutense.

del Río, P. (1993). 'Marco sociocultural e identidad. El papel de los contextos de actividad en la construcción de la conciencia de género.' In F. Ortega, C. Fagoaga, M. A. García de León and P. del Río (eds), *La flotante identidad sexual. La construcción del género en la vida cotidiana de la juventud* [The floating sexual identity: Gender construction in youth's everyday life] (pp. 1929–2146). Madrid: Universidad Complutense and Instituto de la Mujer.

del Río, P. (1995). 'Some effects of media on representation: A line of research.' In P. Wintterhoff-Spurk (ed.), *Psychology of media in Europe* (pp. 177–86). Hopladen: Westedeuscher Verlag.

del Río, P. (1996a). 'Building identities in a mass communication world: Commentary on Stevens Miles.' *Culture and Psychology*, 2 (2): 159–72.

del Río, P. (1996b). *Psicología de los medios de comunicación*. Madrid: Síntesis.

del Río, P. (1998). 'De la discapacidad como problema a la discapacidad como solución: el largo camino del pensamiento defectológico desde L. S. Vygotski.' *Cultura y Educación*, 11–12: 35–58.

del Río, P. (2000). 'No me chilles, que no te veo. Atención y fragmentación audiovisual.' *Cultura y Educación*, 20: 51–80.

del Río, P. and Álvarez, A. (1992a). *Sistemas de actividad y tiempo libre del niño en España*. Madrid: Centro de Estudios del Menor.

del Río, P. and Álvarez, A. (1992b). 'Tres pies al gato: Significado, sentido y cultura cotidiana en la educación.' *Infancia y Aprendizaje* (59–60), 43–62.

del Río, P. and Álvarez, A. (1993). *Programas infantiles de televisión: Análisis de líneas actuales y diseño estratégico de alternativas*. Mimeo, Centro de Investigación para el Desarrollo Humano y la Educación de la Fundación Infancia y Aprendizaje y Dirección de Estudios de Contenido de Televisión Española.

del Río, P. and Álvarez, A. (1995). 'Directivity: The cultural and educational construction of morality and agency. Some questions arising form the legacy of L. S. Vygotski.' *Anthropology and Educational Quarterly*, 26 (4): 384–409.

Delpit, L. (1988). 'The silenced dialogue: Power and pedagogy in educating other people's children.' *Harvard Educational Review*, 58: 280–98.

Dewey, J. (1938). *Experience and education*. New York: Collier Macmillan.

Dewey, J. (1956). *The school and society*. Chicago: University of Chicago Press. (First published 1900)

Doyle, W. (1988). 'Work in mathematics classes: The context of students' thinking during instruction.' *Educational Psychologist*, 23 (2): 167–80.

Drummond, M. J. (1997). *Learning to see*. Maine: Stenhouse Publishers.

Dweck, C. S. (1986) 'Motivational processes affecting learning.' *American Psychologist*, 41: 1040–8.

Dweck, C. S. (1999). *Self-theories: Their role in motivation, personality and development*. Philadelphia, PA and Hove, UK: Psychology Press.

Eckert, P. (1989). *Jocks and burnouts: Social categories and identity in the high school*. New York: Teachers College Press.

Edelman, G. (1992). *Bright air, brilliant fire*. New York: Basic Books.

Edwards, A. D. and Westgate, D. P. G. (1994). *Investigating classroom talk*, 2nd revd edn. London: Falmer Press.

Edwards, D. (1991). 'Categories are for talking.' *Theory and Psychology*, 1 (4): 515–42.

Edwards, D. (1997). *Discourse and cognition*. London: Sage.

Edwards, D. and Mercer, N. (1987). *Common knowledge: The development of understanding in the classroom*. London: Methuen.

Egan, K. (1997). *The educated mind*. Chicago: University of Chicago Press.

Elbers, E. (1994). 'Sociogenesis and children's pretend play: A variation on Vygotskian themes.' In W. de Graaf and R. Maier (eds), *Sociogenesis re-examined*. New York: Springer.

Elkonin, D. B. (1987). 'Sobre el problema de la periodización del desarrollo psíquico en la infancia.' In V. Davydov and M. Shuare (eds), *La psicología evolutiva y pedagógica en la URSS* (pp. 104–24). Moscow: Progress.

Elliott, J. (1991). *Action research for educational change*. Milton Keynes: Open University Press.

Ember, C. and Ember, M. (1996). *Cultural anthropology*. Englewood Cliffs, NJ: Prentice Hall.

Engeström, R. (1995). 'Voice as communicative action.' *Mind, Culture, and Activity*, 2: 192–215.

Engeström, Y. (1987). *Learning by expanding: An activity–theoretical approach to developmental research*. Helsinki: Orienta-Konsultit.

Engeström, Y. (1990). *Learning, working, imagining: Twelve studies in activity theory*. Helsinki: Orienta-Konsultit.

Engeström, Y. (1991). 'Non scolae sed vitae discimus: Toward overcoming the encapsulation of school learning.' *Learning and Instruction*, 1: 243–59.

Engeström, Y. (1998). 'Reorganizing the motivational sphere of classroom culture: An activity–theoretical analysis of planning in a teacher team.' In F. Seeger, J. Voigt and U. Waschescio (eds), *The culture of the mathematics classroom: Analyses and changes* (pp. 76–103).Cambridge: Cambridge University Press.

Engeström. Y. (1999a). 'Activity theory and individual and social transformation.' In Y. Engeström, R. Miettinen and R.-L. Punamäki (eds), *Perspectives on activity theory* (pp. 19–38). Cambridge: Cambridge University Press.

Engeström, Y. (1999b). 'Expansive visibilization of work: An activity–theoretical perspective.' *Computer Supported Cooperative Work*, 8: 63–93.

Engeström, Y. (2000). *Activity theory as a framework for analysing and redesigning work*. Ergonomics, 43: 960–974.

Engeström, Y. (2001). 'Expansive learning at work: Toward an activity–theoretical reconceptualization.' *Journal of Education and Work*, 14 (1): 133–56.

Engeström, Y., Virkkunen, J., Helle, M., Pihlaja, J. and Poikela, R. (1996). 'Change laboratory as a tool for transforming work.' *Lifelong Learning in Europe*, 1 (2): 10–17.

Englert, C. S. (1992). 'Writing instruction from a sociocultural perspective: The holistic, dialogic, and social enterprise of writing.' *Journal of Learning Disabilities*, 25 (3): 153–72.

Entwistle, N. (1992). *The impact of teaching in learning ourcomes in higher education*. Sheffield: CVCP Staff Development Unit.

Erikson, E. (1968). *Identity: Youth and crisis*. New York: Norton.

Erickson, F. and J. Mohatt (1982). Cultural organization of participant structure in two classrooms of Indian students. In G.D. Spindler (ed.), *Doing the ethnography of schooling: Educational anthropology in action*, pp. 132–175. New York: Holt, Rinehart and Winston.

Fensham, P. J. and Marton, F. (1992). 'What has happened to intuition in science education?' *Research in Science Education*, 22: 114–22.

Fernie, D. E., Davies, B., Kantor, R. and McMurray, P. (1993). 'Becoming a person in the preschool: Creating integrated gender, school culture, and peer culture positionings.' *International Journal of Qualitative Studies in Education*, 6 (2): 95–110.

Franke, M. L., Carpenter, T. P., Levi, L. and Fennema, E. (1998). 'Capturing teachers' generative change: A follow-up study of teachers' professional development in mathematics.' Paper presented at the annual meeting of the American Educational Research Association, San Diego.

Frankl, V. E. (1976). *Man in search of meaning*. Waco, Texas: Word.

Frankl, V. E., Fairchild, R. W., et al. (1986). *Logotherapy*. Berkeley, CA.

Freinet, C. (1969). *Pour l'école du peuple: guide pratique pour l'organisation matérielle, technique et pédagogique de l'école populaire*. Paris: Maspero.

Freire, P. (1970). *Pedagogy of the oppressed*. New York: Herder and Herder.

Fukuyama, F. (2000). *The great disruption. Human nature and the reconstitution of social order*. Touchstone Books.

Fullan, M. (1991). *The new meaning of educational change*. London: Cassell.

Fullan, M. (1992). *Successful school improvement: The implementation perspective and beyond*. Toronto: OISE Press.

Galbraith, B., Van Tassell, M. A. and Wells, G. (1999). 'On learning with and from our students.' In G. Wells (ed.), *Dialogic inquiry: Towards a sociocultural practice and theory of education* (pp. 293–312). Cambridge: Cambridge University Press.

Gallimore, R. and Tharp, R. (1990). 'Teaching mind in society: Teaching, schooling and literate discourse.' In L. C. Moll (ed.), *Vygotsky and education: Instructional implications and applications of sociohistorical psychology* (pp. 175–205). New York: Cambridge University Press.

Gal'perin, P. I. (1989a). 'Mental actions as basis for the formation of thoughts and images.' *Soviet Psychology*, 27 (3): 45–65.

Gal'perin, P. I. (1989b). 'Organization of mental activity and the effectiveness of learning.' *Soviet Psychology*, 27 (3): 65–82.

Gal'perin, P. I. (1989c). 'Study of the intellectual development of the child.' *Soviet Psychology*, 27 (3): 26–44.

Gal'perin, P. I. and Georgiev, L. S. (1960). *Psikhologicheskijanaliz sovremennoj metodiki obuchenija nachalnim matematicheskim ponjatijam* [Psychological analysis of modern methods of teaching concepts in elementary mathematics]. Moscow: Doklady APN RSFSR, 1, 3, 4, 5, 6.

Garcia, E. E. (1991). *Education of linguistically and culturally diverse students: Effective instructional practices* (Educational practice report no. 1). Washington, DC and Santa Cruz, CA: National Center for Research on Cultural Diversity and Second Language Learning.

Garcia, G. and Pearson, P. (1991). 'The role of assessment in a diverse society.' In E. Herbert (ed.), *Literacy for a diverse society* (pp. 253–78). New York: Teachers College Press.

Garfinkel, H. (1967). *Studies in ethnomethodology*. Englewood Cliffs, NJ: Prentice-Hall.

Gauvain, M. (1995). 'Thinking in niches: sociocultural influences on cognitive development.' *Human Development*, 38: 25–45.

Gee, J. P. (1992). *The social mind*. New York: Bergin and Garvey.

Gergen, K. J. (1991), *The saturated self*. New York: Basic Books.

Gibbons. P. (in press). 'Learning a new register in a second language.' In C. Candlin and N. Mercer (eds), *English teaching in social context*. London and Milton Keynes: Routledge with the Open University.

Gibson, J. J. (1979). *The ecological approach to visual perception*. Boston: Houghton Mifflin.

Gilbert, G. N. and Mulkay, M. (1982). 'Warranting scientific belief.' *Social Studies of Science*, 12: 227–36.

Gilot, F. and Lake, C. (1964). *Life with Picasso*. New York: McGraw-Hill.

Gipps, C. (1992). 'Equal opportunities and the SATs for seven year olds.' *The Curriculum Journal*, 3: 171–83.

Gipps, C. (1994a). *Beyond testing: Towards a theory of educational assessment*. London: Falmer Press.

Gipps, C. (1994b). 'Developments in educational assessment or What makes a good test?' *Assessment in Education*, 1 (3): 283–291.

Gipps, C. (1999). 'Sociocultural aspects of assessment.' *Review of Research in Education*, 24: 355–92.

Gipps, C. and Murphy, P. (1994). *A fair test? Assessment, achievement and equity*. Buckingham, UK: Open University Press.

Glaser, R. and Silver, E. (1994). 'Assessment, testing and instruction: Retrospect and prospect.' *Review of Research in Education*, 20: 393–421.

Goldenberg, C. and Gallimore, R. (1996). 'Accommodating cultural differences and commonalities in educational practice.' *Multicultural Education*, September, 16–18.

González, N., Moll, L. C., Floyd-Tenery, M., Rivera, A., Rendon, P., Gonzales, R. and Amanti, C. (1993). *Teacher research on funds of knowledge: Learning from households*. (Educational practice report no. 6.) Santa Cruz, CA: National Center for Research on Cultural Diversity and Second Language Learning.

González Rey, F. (1999). 'Personality, subject and human development: The subjective character of human activity.' In S. Chaiklin, M. Hedegaard and U. J. Jensen (eds), *Activity theory and social practice: Cultural–historical approaches* (pp. 253–75). Aarhus, Denmark: Aarhus University Press.

Goodwin, C. (1981). *Conversational organization: Interaction between speakers and hearers*. New York: Academic Press.

Goodwin, C. (1984). 'Notes on story structure and the organization of participation.' In J. M. Atkinson and J. Heritage (eds), *Structures of social action*. Cambridge: Cambridge University Press.

Goodwin, C. (1994). 'Professional vision.' *American Anthropologist*, 96 (3): 606–33.

Green, A. (1990). *Education and state formation: The rise of education systems in England, France and the USA*. London: Macmillan.

Greenleaf, C. and Freedman, S. W. (1993). 'Linking classroom discourse and classroom content: Following the trail of intellectual work in a writing lesson.' *Discourse Processes*, 16: 465–505.

Gymnasiebekendtgørelsen (1999, May). Bilag 14, Fysik. (http://www.uvm.dk/lov/bek/1999/0000411.htm accessed 30 October 2000).

Haenen, J. (1996). *Piotr Gal'perin: Psychologist in Vygotsky's footsteps*. Commack, NY: Nova Science Publishers.

Hall, E. T. (1959). *The silent language*. Greenwich, CT: Premier Books.

Hall, E. T. (1984). *The dance of life*. New York: Anchor/Doubleday.

Halliday, M. A. K. (1993). 'Towards a language-based theory of learning.' *Linguistics and Education*, 5: 93–116.

Halliday, M. A. K. (1994). *An Introduction to Functional Grammar*. London: Edward Arnold.

Halliday, M. A. K. and Martin, J. R. (1993). *Writing science*. London: Falmer Press. (US edn: University of Pittsburgh Press)

Haneda, M. and Wells, G. (2000). 'Writing in knowledge-building communities.' *Research in the Teaching of English*, 34 (3): 430–57.

Hargreaves, A. (1991). 'Contrived collegiality: A micropolitical analysis.' In J. Blase (ed.), *The politics of life in schools*. New York: Sage.

Hargreaves, A. (1993). 'Individualism and individuality: Reinterpreting the teacher culture.' In J. Little and M. McLaughlin (eds), *Teachers' work: Individuals, colleagues, and context*. New York: Teachers College Press.

Hargreaves, A, (1994). *Changing teachers, changing times: Teachers' work and culture in the postmodern age*. London: Cassell.

Hargreaves, A. (1997). 'Rethinking educational change.' In M. Fullan (ed.), *The challenge of school change: A collection of articles*. Arlington Heights: IRI/Sky Light.

Hargreaves, D. (1995). 'School culture, school effectiveness and school improvement.' *School Effectiveness and School Improvement*, 6 (1): 23–46.

Hargreaves, D. (1999). 'The knowledge-creating school.' *British Journal of Educational Studies*, 47: 122–44.

Hasan, R. (1989). 'Semantic variation and sociolinguistics.' *Australian Journal of Linguistics*, 9 (2): 221–76.

Hasan, R. (1992). 'Rationality in everyday talk: From process to system.' In J. Svartvik (ed.), *Corpus linguistics: Proceedings of Nobel symposium 82, Stockholm 4–8 August 1991*. Berlin: Mouton de Gruyter.

Hasan, R. (1993). 'Contexts for meaning.' In J. E. Alatis (ed.), *Georgetown round table on language, communication, and social meaning 1992*. Washington, DC: Georgetown University Press.

Hasan, R. (1996). 'Literacy, everyday talk and society.' In R. Hasan and G. Williams (eds), *Literacy in Society*. London: Longmans.

Hasan, R. (1999). 'Speaking with reference to context.' In M. Ghadessy (ed.), *Text and context in functional linguistics* (pp. 219–328). Amsterdam: John Benjamins.

Hasan, R. (2000). 'The uses of talk.' In S. Sarangi and M. Coulthard (eds), *Discourse and social life*. London: Longman.

Hasan, R. and Cloran, C. (1990). 'A sociolinguistic interpretation of mother–child talk.' In M. A. K. Halliday, J. Gibbons and H. Nicholas (eds), *Learning, keeping and using language: Selected papers from the 8th World Congress of Applied Linguistics*. Amsterdam: John Benjamins.

Heath, S. B. (1983). *Ways with words: Language, life, and work in communities and classrooms*. New York: Cambridge University Press.

Hedegaard, M. (1988). *Skolebørns personlighedsudvikling set gennem orientingsfagene* [Schoolchildren's personality development seen through social studies]. Aarhus, Denmark: Aarhus University Press.

Hedegaard, M. (1990). 'The zone of proximal development as basis for instruction.' In L. C. Moll (ed.), *Vygotsky and education: Instructional implications and applications of sociohistorical psychology* (pp. 349–71). Cambridge: Cambridge University Press.

Hedegaard, M. (1996). 'How instruction influences children's concepts of evolution.' *Mind, Culture, and Activity*, 3: 11–24.

Hedegaard, M. and Sigersted, G. (1995). *Undervisning i samfundshistorie* [Teaching in social studies]. Aarhus, Denmark: Aarhus University Press.

Hedegaard, M., Chaiklin, S. and Pedraza, P. (in press). In M. Hedegaard (ed.), *Culturally sensitive teaching in a Vygotskian perspective: Learning in classrooms.* Aarhus, Denmark: Aarhus University Press.

Henry, J. (1963). *Culture against man.* New York: Random House.

Herman, J., Klein, D. and Wakai, S. (1997). 'American students' perspectives on alternative assessment: Do they know it's defferent?' *Assessment in Education*, 4 (3): 339–52.

Heyman, G. D. and Dweck C. S. (1998). 'Children's thinking about traits: Implications for judgements of the self and others.' *Child Development*, 64 (2): 391–403.

Hollingsworth, S. (ed.) (1997). *International action research: A casebook for educational reform.* Washington, DC: Falmer Press.

Huberman, M. (1993). 'The model of the independent artisan in teachers' professional relations.' In J. Little and M. McLaughlin (eds), *Teachers' work: Individuals, colleagues, and context.* New York: Teachers College Press.

Human Development (1995). 'Learning and Development.' *Human Development Special Issue*, 38 (6).

Hume, K. (2001). 'Co-researching with students: Exploring the value of class discussions.' In G. Wells (ed.), *Talk, text and inquiry* (pp. 150–67). New York: Teachers College Press.

Hutton, W. (1995). *The state we're in.* London: Cape.

Hymes, D. (1972). 'Models of the interaction of language and social life.' In J. J. Gumperz and D. Hymes (eds), *Directions in sociolinguistics: The ethnography of communication* (pp. 35–71). New York: Holt, Rinehart and Winston.

Ilyenkov, E. V. (1977). *Dialectical logic: Essays on its history and theory* (trans. H. C. Creighton). Moscow: Progress. (Original work published 1974)

Jefferson, G. (1978). 'Sequential aspects of storytelling in conversation.' In J. Schenkein (ed.), *Studies in the organization of conversational interaction.* New York: Academic Press.

John-Steiner, V. (2000). *Creative collaborations.* New York: Oxford University Press.

John-Steiner, V. and Mahn, H. (1996). 'Sociocultural approaches to learning and development: A Vygotskian framework.' *Educational Psychologist*, 31 (3/4): 191–206.

John-Steiner, V. and Smith, L. (1978). *The educational promise of cultural pluralism: What do we know about teaching and learning in urban schools?* Vol. 8. Paper read at the Urban Education Program, CEMREL, Inc.'s National Conference on Urban Education, 10–24 July, St Louis, MO.

K100 Course Team (1998). Block 6: 'When care goes wrong.' *K100: Understanding health and social care.* Milton Keynes: Open University Press.

K100 Course Team (2000). *K100 Tutor Guide: 2000.* Milton Keynes: Open University Press.

Kabanova, O. Y. (1976). *Osnovnye voprosy metodiki obuchenya inostrannomu yaziku na osnove kontseptsii upravleniya usvoeniem* [Methodology of teaching foreign language based on the concept of guided knowledge acquisition]. Moscow: Izdatel'stvo MGU.

Kagan, J. (1994). *Galen's prophecy: Temperament in human nature.* New York: Westview Press.

Kantor, R., Elgas, P. and Fernie, D. (1992). 'Diverse paths to literacy in a preschool classroom: A sociocultural perspective.' *Reading Research Quarterly*, 27 (3): 185–201.

Karpov, Y. V. and Bransford, J. D. (1995). 'L. S. Vygotsky and the doctrine of empirical and theoretical learning.' *Educational Psychologist*, 30 (2): 61–6.

Karpov, Y. V. and Haywood, H. C. (1998). 'Two ways to elaborate Vygotsky's concept of mediation: Implications for instruction.' *American Psychologist*, 53: 27–36.

Katz, L. G. (1988). 'What should young children be doing?' *American Educator* (Summer): 29–45.

Katz, L. G. (1993). 'Dispositions: Definitions and implications for early childhood practices.' *Perspectives from ERIC/ECCE: A monograph series.* Urbana, IL: ERIC Clearinghouse on ECCE.

Katz, L. G. (1999). 'Another look at what young children should be learning.' *ERIC Clearinghouse on Elementary and Early Childhood Education Digest*, June: 1–2.

Kegan, R. (1994) *In over our heads: The mental demands of modern life.* Cambridge, MA: Harvard University Press.

Konold, C., Pollatsek, A., Well, A. and Gagnon, A. (1996). *Students analysing data: Research of critical barriers.* Paper presented at the Roundtable Conference of the International Association for Statistics Education, Granada, Spain.

Koretz, D., McCaffrey, D., Klein, S., Bell, R. and Stecher, B. (1993). *The reliability of scores from the Vermont portfolio assessment program* (CSE technical report 355). CRESST, UCLA.

Kowal, M. (2001). 'Knowledge building: Learning about native issues outside in and inside out.' In G. Wells (ed.), *Talk, text and inquiry* (pp. 118–33). New York: Teachers College Press.

Kreisberg, S. (1992). *Transforming power: Domination, empowerment and education.* New York: State University of New York Press.

Krugman, H. E. (1965). 'The impact of television advertising: Learning without involvement.' *Public Opinion Quarterly*, 29 (Fall): 349–56.

Labov, W. (1972). *Language in the inner city: Studies in the Black English vernacular.* Philadelphia: University of Pennsylvania Press.

Lampert, M. (1990). 'When the problem is not the question and the solution is not the answer: Mathematical knowing and teaching.' *American Educational Research Journal*, 27 (1): 29–63.

Langer, E. J. (1989). *Mindfulness.* Reading MA: Addison-Wesley.

Langer, E. J. (1997). *The power of mindful learning.* Reading MA: Addison-Wesley.

Latour, B. (1987). *Science in action: How to follow scientists and engineers through society.* Cambridge, MA: Harvard University Press.

Latour, B. and Woolgar, S. (1979). *Laboratory life: The social construction of scientific facts.* London and Beverly Hills: Sage.

Lave, J. (1988). *Cognition in practice.* Cambridge: Cambridge University Press.

Lave, J. (1992). *Learning as participation in communities of practice.* San Francisco: American Educational Research Association.

Lave, J. and Wenger, E. (1991). *Situated learning: Legitimate peripheral participation*. Cambridge: Cambridge University Press.

Lebesgue, H. (1958). *Notice d'histoire des mathematiques* [Notes on the history of mathematics]. Geneva: L'Enseignement mathematique.

Lee, C. D. (1995). 'A culturally based cognitive apprenticeship: Teaching African American high school students skills in literary interpretation.' *Reading Research Quarterly*, 30 (4): 608–30.

Lehrer, R. and Romberg, T. (1996). 'Exploring children's data modeling.' *Cognition and Instruction*, 14: 69–108.

Lektorsky, V. A. (1999). 'Activity theory in a new era.' In Y. Engeström, R. Miettinen, and R.-L. Punamaki (eds), *Perspectives on activity theory* (pp. 65–9). Cambridge: Cambridge University Press.

Lemke, J. (1990). *Talking science: language, learning and values*. Norwood, NJ: Ablex.

Leont'ev, A. N. (1978). *Activity, consciousness, and personality*. Englewood Cliffs, NJ: Prentice-Hall. (First published 1975)

Lewicki, P., Cyzyweska, M. and Hill, T. (1997). 'Nonconscious information processing and personality.' In D. C. Berry (ed.), *How implicit is implicit learning?* New York: Oxford University Press.

Linder-Scholer, B. (1996). 'Industry's role in standards-based systemic reform, for K-12 mathematics, science and technology education.' *A Look at Industry and Community Commitment to Educational Systemic Reform, A Handbook*. College Park, MD: Triangle Coalition for Science and Technology Education.

Linn, R. L. (1993). 'Educational assessment: expanded expectations and challenges.' *Educational Evaluation and Policy Analysis*, 15: 1–16.

Linn, R. L., Baker, E. and Dunbar, S. (1991). 'Complex, performance-based assessment: Expectations and validation criteria.' *Educational Researcher*, 20 (8): 15–2.

Lipka, J. (1986). School-community partnerships in rural Alaska. *Rural Educator* 7 (3): 11–14.

Lipka, J. (1994). 'Culturally negotiated schooling: Toward a Yup'ik mathematics.' *Journal of American Indian Education* (Spring): 14–30.

Lipman, M. (1970). *Philosophy for children*. Montclair, NJ: Institute for the Advancement of Philosophy for Children.

Littleton, K. and Light, P. (eds) (1999). *Learning with computers: Analysing productive interaction*. London: Routledge.

Lompscher, J. (1984). 'Problems and results of experimental research on the formation of theoretical thinking through instruction.' In M. Hedegaard, P. Hakkarainen and Y. Engeström (eds), *Learning and teaching on a scientific basis: Methodological and epistemological aspects of the activity theory of learning and teaching* (pp. 293–357). Aarhus, Denmark: Aarhus University, Psykologisk Institut.

Lompscher, J. (1999). 'Learning activity and its formation: Ascending from the abstract to the concrete.' In M. Hedegaard and J. Lompscher (eds), *Learning activity and development* (pp. 139–66). Aarhus, Denmark: Aarhus University Press.

Lotman, Y. M. (1988). 'Text within a text.' *Soviet Psychology*, 26 (3): 32–51.

Lucariello, J. and Nelson, K. (1987). 'Remembering and planning talk between mothers and children.' *Discourse Processes*, 10 (3): 219–35.

Lunt, I. (1994). 'The practice of assessment.' In H. Daniels (ed.), *Charting the agenda*. London: Routledge.

Luria, A. R. (1979). *The making of mind*. Cambridge, MA: Harvard University Press.

Luria, A. R. (1983). 'La organización funcional del cerebro' ['Functional organization of brain']. In A. A. Smirnov, A. R. Luria and V. D. Nebylitzin (eds), *Fundamentos de Psicofisiología* (pp. 113–157). Madrid: Siglo XXI (O. V. Estestviennonauchnie osnobi psijologii. Moscow: Pedagogika).

Luria, A. R. (1987). 'Afterword.' In R. W. Rieber and A. S. Carton (eds), *The collected works of L. S. Vygotsky, Vol. 1: Problems of general psychology*. New York: Plenum.

Lyle, S. (1993). 'An investigation in which children talk themselves into meaning.' *Language and Education*, 7 (3): 181–96.

McClain, K., Cobb, P. and Gravemeijer, K. (in press). 'Supporting students' ways of reasoning abut data.' In M. Burke (ed.), *Learning mathematics for a new century (2001 Yearbook of the National Council of Teachers of Mathematics)*. Reston, VA: NCTM.

McClelland, D. C. (1961). *The achieving society*. Princeton, NJ: Van Nostrand.

McGatha, M., Cobb, P. and McClain, D. (1999). *An analysis of students' initial statistical understandings*. Paper presented at the annual meeting of the American Educational Research Association, Montreal, Canada.

McGlynn-Stewart, M. (2001). 'Look how we've grown.' In G. Wells (ed.), *Action, talk, and text: Learning and teaching through inquiry* (pp. 195–200). New York: Teachers College Press.

McIntyre, E. and Stone, N. J. (1999). 'Culturally contextualized instruction in Appalachian and African American classrooms.' In T. Shanahan and R. Rodriguez-Brown (eds), *National Reading Council Yearbook*.

McIntyre, E., Rosebery, A. and Gonzalez, N. (eds) (in press). *Classroom diversity*. Portsmouth, NH: Heinemann.

McLaughlin, M. W. and Shepard, L. A. (1995). *Improving education through standards-based reform*. A report by the National Academy of Education Panel on Standards-Based Education Reform. Palo Alto, CA: Stanford University Press.

McLeod, J. M., Kosicki, G. M. and McLeod, D. M. (1994). 'The expanding boundaries of political communication effects.' In J. Bryant and D. Zillmann (eds), *Media effects* (pp. 123–62). Hillsdale, NJ: Lawrence Erlbaum.

McTighe, J. and Lyman, F. T. (1988). 'Cueing thinking in the classroom: The promise of theory embedded tools.' *Educational Leadership*, 45 (7): 18–24.

Mahn, H. (1997). *Dialogue journals: Perspectives of second language learners in a Vygotskian theoretical framework*. Unpublished doctoral dissertation. Albuquerque: University of New Mexico.

Mann, C. (1999). *The effectiveness of meditation in schools*. Ph.D. thesis, University of Bristol Graduate School of Education.

Markova, A. K. (1979). *The teaching and mastery of language* (trans. M. Vale). White Plains, NY: M. E. Sharpe. (First published 1974)

Marshall, S. P. (1995). *Schemas in problem solving*. New York: Cambridge University Press.

Marton, F. and Saljo, R. (1984) Approaches to learning, in Marton, F., Hounsell, D. and Entwistle, N. (eds) *The Experience of Learning*, Scottish Academic Press, Edinburgh.

Matusov, E., Pease-Alvarez, C., et al. (in press). 'Critical dialoguing as a way to negotiate meaning beyond wizard's walls.' *The service of diversity: Educational partnerships, technology, and innovative learning environments*. Cambridge: Cambridge University Press.

Maybin, J., Mercer, N. and Stierer, B. (1992) 'Scaffolding' learning in the classroom. In Norman, K. (ed.), Thinking Voices. London: Hodder and Stoughton.

Mayer, R. E., Quilici, J., Moreno, R., Duran, R., Woodbridge, S., Simon, R., Sanchez, D. and Lavezzo, A. (1997). 'Cognitive consequences of participation in a "Fifth Dimension" after school computer club.' Journal of Educational Computing Research, 16 (4): 353–70.

Marton, F. and Saljo, R. (1984) 'Approaches to learning.' In F. Marton, D. Hounsell and N. Entwistle (des), The experience of learning. Edinburgh: Scottish Academic Press.

Means, B. and Knapp, M. S. (1991). Models for teaching advanced skills to educationally disadvantaged children: Teaching advanced skills to educationally disadvantaged children. Washington, DC: US Department of Education, Office of Planning.

Mehan, H. (1979). Learning lessons: Social organization in the classroom. Cambridge, MA: Harvard University Press.

Mercer, N. (1995). The guided construction of knowledge: Talk amongst teachers and learners. Clevedon, UK: Multilingual Matters.

Mercer, N. (1998). 'Development through dialogue: A sociocultural perspective on the process of being educated.' In A. C. Quelhas and F. Pereira (eds), Cognition and context. Lisbon: Instituto Superior de Psicología Aplicada.

Mercer, N. (2000). Words and minds: How we use language to think together. London: Routledge.

Mercer, N., Wegerif, R. and Dawes, L. (1999). 'Children's talk and the development of reasoning in the classroom.' British Educational Research Journal, 25 (1): 95–111.

Mintz, E. and Yun, J. T. (1999). The complex world of teaching: Perspectives from theory and practice. Cambridge, MA: Harvard Educational Review.

Mitchell, A. A. (1993). Advertising exposure, memory and choice. Hillsdale, NJ: Lawrence Erlbaum.

Moll, L. C. (ed.) (1990). Vygotsky and education: Instructional implications and applications of sociohistorical psychology. New York: Cambridge University Press.

Moll, L. C. (in press). 'Through the mediation of others: Vygotskian research on teaching.' In V. Richardson (ed.), Handbook of research on teaching, 4th edn. Washington, DC: American Educational Research Association.

Moll, L. C. and Greenberg, J. B. (1990). 'Creating zones of possibilities: Combining social contexts for instruction.' In L. C. Moll (ed.), Vygotsky and education: Instructional implications and applications of sociohistorical psychology (pp. 319–48). Cambridge: Cambridge University Press.

Moll, L. C. and Whitmore, K. F. (1993). 'Vygotsky in classroom practice: Moving from individual transmission to social transaction.' In E. A. Forman, N. Minick and C. A. Stone (eds), Contexts for learning: Sociocultural dynamics in children's development (pp. 19–42). New York: Oxford University Press.

Moll, L. C., Amanti, C., Neff, D. and Gonzalez, N. (1992). 'Funds of knowledge for teaching: Using a qualitative approach to connect homes and classrooms.' Theory into Practice, 31 (2): 32–141.

Moore, D. S. (1996). 'New pedagogy and new content: The case of statistics.' In B. Phillips (ed.), Papers on statistics education. Hawthern, Australia: Swinburne.

Murphy, S. (1997). 'Hands-on learning helps North Chicago scores soar.' Chicago Tribune, 25 March, section 2, p. 5.

Nassaji, H. and Wells, G. (2000). 'What's the use of triadic dialogue?: An investigation of teacher–student interaction.' *Applied Linguistics*, 21 (3): 376–406.

National Research Council (1999). *How people learn: Brain, mind, experience, and school*. Washington, DC: National Academy Press.

Neill, M. (1995). 'Some prerequisites for the establishment of equitable, inclusive, multicultural assessment systems.' In M. Nettles and A. Nettles (eds), *Equity and excellence in educational testing and assessment* (pp. 115–57). Boston: Kluwer.

Nespor, J. (1997). *Tangled up in school: Politics, space, bodies, and signs in the educational process*. Mahwah: Lawrence Erlbaum.

New, R. S. (1994). 'Meeting the challenge of Reggio Emilia in realizing the potentials of all children: Keynote address.' Paper presented at The Challenge of Reggio Emilia: Realizing the potential of children, Melbourne.

New Zealand Ministry of Education (1996). *Te Whāriki. He Whāriki Mtauranga mā Mokopuna o Aotearoa: Early childhood curriculum*. Wellington: Learning Media.

Newman, D., Griffin, P. and Cole, M. (1989). *The construction zone: Working for cognitive change in school*. Cambridge: Cambridge University Press.

Newman, J. M. (ed.) (1998). *Tensions of teaching: Beyond tips to critical reflection*. New York: Teachers College Press.

Nicolopolou, A. and Cole, M. (1993). 'The Fifth Dimension, its playworld and its institutional context: The generation and transmission of shared knowledge in the culture of collaborative learning.' In E. A. Foreman, N. Minnick and C. A. Stone (eds), *Contexts for learning: Sociocultural dynamics in children's development* (pp. 283–314). New York: Oxford University Press.

Nieto, S. (1996). *Affirming diversity: The sociopolitical context of multicultural education*. White Plains, NY, Longman Publishers.

Noddings, N. (1997). 'Thinking about standards.' *Phi Delta Kappan*, 79 (3): November.

Noffke, S. (1997). 'Professional, personal, and political dimensions of action research.' In M. Apple (ed.), *Review of research in education* (pp. 305–43). Washington, DC: American Educational Research Association.

Nonaka, I. and Takeuchi, H. (1995). *The knowledge-creating company*. Oxford: Oxford University Press.

Norman, D. (1988). *The psychology of everyday things*. New York: Basic Books.

Norman, D. (1993). *Things that make us smart: Defending human attributes in the age of the machine*. Reading, MA: Addison-Wesley.

Nuttall, D. (1987). 'The validity of assessments.' *European Journal of Psychology of Education*, 11 (2): 108–18.

Nystrand, M. (1997). *Opening dialogue: Understanding the dynamics of language and learning in the English classroom*. New York: Teachers College Press.

Oatley, K. (1996). 'Inference in narrative and science.' In D. Olson and N. Torrance (eds), *Modes of thought: Explorations in culture and cognition*. Cambridge: Cambridge University Press.

Ochs, E. (1997). 'Narrative.' In T. van Dijk (ed.), *Discourse. A multidisciplinary approach*. London: Sage.

Ochs, E. and Capps, L. (1996). 'Narrating the self.' *Annual Review of Anthropology*, 25: 19–43.

Ochs, E. and Capps, L. (in press). *Living narrative*. Cambridge: Harvard University Press.

Ochs, E. and Taylor, C. (1992). 'Family narrative as political activity.' *Discourse and Society*, 3 (3): 301–40.

Ochs, E. and Taylor, C. (1995). 'Science at dinner.' In C. Kransen and S. McConnell-Ginet (eds), *Text and context: Cross-disciplinary perspectives on language study*. Lexington, MA: D. C. Heath.

Ochs, E., Taylor, C., Rudolph, D. and Smith, R. (1992). 'Story-telling as a theory-building activity.' *Discourse Processes*, 15 (1): 37–72.

Olson, D. (1996). 'Literate mentalities: Literacy, consciousness of language, and modes of thought.' In D. Olson and N. Torrance (eds), *Modes of thought: Explorations in culture and cognition* (pp. 141–51). Cambridge: Cambridge University Press.

Orsolini, M. and Pontecorvo, C. (1992). 'Children's talk in classroom discussion.' *Cognition and Instruction*, 9 (2): 113–36.

Padron, Y. N. (1992). 'The effect of strategy instruction on bilingual students' cognitive strategy use in reading.' *Bilingual Research Journal*, 16 (Summer/Fall, 3 and 4): 35–51.

Palincsar, A. S., Magnusson, S. J., Marano, N., Ford, D. and Brown, N. (1998). 'Designing a community of practice: Principles and practices of the GIsML community.' *Teaching and Teacher Education*, 14 (1): 5–20.

Palmer, P. J. (1998). *The courage to teach: Exploring the inner landscape of a teacher's life*. San Francisco: Jossey-Bass.

Penuel, W. and Wertsch, J. (1995). 'Vygotsky and identity formation: A sociocultural approach.' *Educational Psychologist*, 30 (2): 83–92.

Pepper, S. C. (1967). *Concept and quality: A world hypothesis*. La Salle, IL: Open Court.

Perkins, D. N. (1993). 'Person plus: A distributed view of thinking and learning.' In G. Salomon (ed.), *Distributed cognitions*. Cambridge: Cambridge University Press.

Perkins, D. N. (1995). *Outsmarting IQ: The emerging science of learnable intelligence*. New York: Free Press.

Perkins, D. N., Jay, E. and Tishman, S. (1993). 'Beyond abilities: A dispositional theory of thinking. *Merrill-Palmer Quarterly*, 39 (1): 1–21.

Perrenoud, P. (1991). 'Towards a pragmatic approach to formative evaluation.' In P. Weston (ed.), *Assessment of pupils' achievement: Motivation and school success* (pp. 77–101). Amsterdam: Swets and Zeitlinger.

Petrick-Steward, E. (1995). *Beginning writers in the zone of proximal development*. Mahwah, NJ: Lawrence Erlbaum.

Petty, R. E. and Cacioppo, J. T. (1986). 'The elaboration likelihood model of persuasion.' In L. Berkowitz (ed.), *Advances in experimental social psychology*. New York: Academic Press.

Phelan, P., Davidson, A. L. and Yu, H. C. (1998). *Adolescents' worlds: Negotiating family, peers, and school*. New York: Teachers College Press.

Philips, S. U. (1983). *The invisible culture: Communication in classroom and community on the Warm Springs Indian Reservation*. New York: Longman.

Pollard, A. (1985). *The social world of the primary school*. London: Rinehart and Winston.

Pontecorvo, C. and Fasulo, A. (1997). 'Learning to argue in family dinner conversation: The reconstruction of past events.' In L. Resnick, R. Saljo and C. Pontecorvo (eds), *Discourse, tools and reasoning*. Berlin: Springer Verlag.

Pontecorvo, C., Amendola, S. and Fasulo, A. (1994). 'Storiein famiglia. La narrazione come prodotto collettivo.' *Età evolutiva*, 47: 14–29.

Pontecorvo, C., Fasulo, A. and Sterponi, L. (in press). 'Mutual apprentices: The making of parenthood and childhood in family dinner conversations.' *Human Development*.

Popper, K. R. (1979). *Objective knowledge: An evolutionary approach*, revd edn. Oxford: Clarendon Press.

Prawat, R. S. (2000). 'Social constructivism and the process–content distinction as viewed by Vygotsky and the pragmatists.' *Mind, Culture, and Activity*, 6 (4): 255–73.

Raven, J., Court, J. and Raven, J. C. (1995). *Manual for Raven's progressive matrices and vocabulary scales*. Oxford: Oxford Psychologists Press.

Reich, L. R. (1993). 'Circle time in pre-school – an analysis of educational praxis.' Paper presented at the European Conference on Practice-orientated Research related to the Quality of Early Childhood Education, Athens.

Reich, R. B. (1991). *The work of nations*. New York: Knopf.

Resnick, L. B., Pontecorvo, C. and Säljö, R. (1997). 'Discourse, tools, and reasoning.' In L. B. Resnick, R. Säljö, C. Pontecorvo and B. Burge (eds), *Discourse, tools and reasoning*. Berlin: Springer-Verlag.

Resnick, L. B., Levine, J. M. and Teasley, S. (eds) (1991). *Perspectives on socially shared cognition*. Washington, DC: American Psychological Association.

Resnick, L. G. and Klopfer, L. E. (1989). 'Toward the thinking curriculum: An overview.' In L. G. Resnick and L. E. Klopfer (eds), *Toward the thinking curriculum: Current cognitive research* (pp. 1–18). Alexandria, VA: American Society for Curriculum and Development.

Resnick, R. B. and Hall, M. W. (1998). 'Learning organizations for sustainable education reform.' *Daedalus*, 127: 89–118.

Rogers, C. R. (1951). *Client-centered therapy*. Boston: Houghton Mifflin.

Rogoff, B. (1990). *Apprenticeship in thinking: Cognitive development in social context*. New York: Oxford University Press.

Rogoff, B. (1991). 'Social interaction as apprenticeship in thinking: Guidance and participation in spatial planning.' In L. B. Resnick, J. M. Levine, and S. Teasley (eds), *Perspectives on socially shared cognition*. Washington: American Psychological Association.

Rogoff, B. (1995). 'Observing sociocultural activity on three planes: Participatory appropriation, guided participation and apprenticeship.' In J. W. Wertsch, P. del Río and A. Álvarez (eds), *Sociocultural studies of mind*. Cambridge: Cambridge University Press.

Rogoff, B. (1998). 'Cognition as a collaborative process.' In W. Damon (ed.) and D. Kuhn and R. S. Siegler (vol. eds), *Handbook of Child Psychology, Vol. 2: Cognition, Perception and Language*, 5th edn (pp. 679–744). New York: John Wiley.

Rogoff, B. and Chavajay, P. (1995). 'What's become of research on the cultural basis of cognitive development?' *American Psychologist*, 50: 859–77.

Rogoff, B., Matusov, E. and White, C. (1996). 'Models of teaching and learning: Participation in a community of learners.' In D. R. Olson and N. Torrance (eds), *The handbook of education and human development: New models of learning, teaching and schooling* (pp. 388–414). Oxford: Blackwell Publishers.

Rojas-Drummond, S. (in press). 'Guided participation, discourse and the construction of knowledge in Mexican classrooms.' In H. Cowie and D. van der Aalsvoort (eds), *Social interaction in learning and instruction: The meaning of discourse for the construction of knowledge*. Oxford: Elsevier.

Rojas-Drummond, S., Mercer, N. and Dabrowski, E. (2001) 'Collaboration, scaffolding and the promotion of problem solving strategies in Mexican pre-school students.' *European Journal of Psychology of Education*, 15 (3).

Rojas-Drummond, S., Hernandez, G., Velez, M. and Villagran, G. (1998). 'Co-operative learning and the appropriation of procedural knowledge by primary school children.' *Learning and Instruction*, 8 (1): 37–62.

Romig, J. (1999). *Cogito: The cognitive paradigm*. http://www.educ.drake.edu/romig/cogito.html

Roseberry, A., Warren, B. and Conant, F. (1992) 'Appropriating scientific discourse: Findings from language minority classrooms.' *The Journal of the Learning Sciences*, 2, 61–94.

Roth, W.-M. (1997). 'Where is the context in contextual word problems? Mathematical practices and products in grade 8 students' answers to story problems.' *Cognition and Instruction*, 14: 487–527.

Roth, W.-M., Woszczyna, C. and Smith, G. (1996). 'Affordances and constraints of computers in science education.' *Journal of Research in Science Teaching*, 33 (9): 995–1017.

Roth, W.-M., (1998). *Designing communities*. Dordrecht, Netherlands: Kluwer Academic Publishing.

Runeson, S. (1977). 'On the possibility of 'smart' perceptual mechanisms.' *Scandinavian Journal of Psychology*, 18: 172–9.

Russell, D. (1997). 'Rethinking genre in school and society: An activity theory analysis.' *Written Communication*, 14 (4): 504–54.

Rutledge, M. (1997). 'Reading the subtext on gender.' *Educational Leadership*, 7, April.

Sacks, H. (1992). *Lectures on conversation*. Oxford: Blackwell Publishers.

Sacks, H., Schegloff, E. and Jefferson, G. (1974). 'A simplest systematics for the organization of turn-taking in conversation.' *Language*, 50: 696–735.

Sadler, R. (1989). 'Formative assessment and the design of instructional systems.' *Instructional Science*, 18: 119–44.

Salomon, G. (ed.) (1993). *Distributed cognitions*. Cambridge: Cambridge University Press.

Salomon, G. (1997). 'Of mind and media: how culture's symbolic forms are affecting learning and thinking'. *Phi Delta Kappan*, January: 375–80.

Scardamalia, M. and Bereiter, C. (1985). 'Fostering the development of self-regulation in children's knowledge processing.' In S. F. Chipman, J. W. Segal and R. Glaser (eds), *Thinking and learning skills, Vol. 2: Research and open questions* (pp. 563–77).

Scardamalia, M., Bereiter, C. and Lamon, M. (1994). 'The CSILE project: Trying to bring the classroom into World 3.' In K. McGilley (ed.), *Classroom lessons: Integrating cognitive theory and classroom practice* (pp. 201–28). Cambridge, MA: MIT Press.

Scarr, S. and McCartney, K. (1983). 'How people make their own environments: A theory of genotype–environment effects.' *Child Development*, 54: 424–35.

Schoenfield, A. (1985). *Mathematical problem-solving*. New York: Academic Press.

Schön, D. (1987). *Educating the reflective practitioner*. San Francisco: Jossey-Bass

Schweinhart, L. J. and Weikart, D. P. (1993). *A summary of significant benefits: The High Scope Perry pre-school study through age 27.* Ypsilanti, MI: High Scope.

Scribner, S. and Cole, M. (1981). *The psychology of literacy.* Cambridge, MA: Harvard University Press.

SEAC (1991). *National Curriculum Assessment at Key Stage 3: A review of the 1991 pilots with implications for 1992.* London: EMU: SEAC.

Simon, M. A. (1995). 'Reconstructing mathematics pedagogy from a constructivist perspective.' *Journal for Research in Mathematics Education,* 26: 114–45.

Sinclair, J. M. and Coulthard, R. M. (1975). *Towards an analysis of discourse.* Oxford: Oxford University Press.

Siraj-Blatchford, I. (1994). *The early years: Laying the foundations for racial equality.* Stoke-on-Trent: Trentham.

Smiley, P. A. and Dweck, C. S. (1994). 'Individual differences in achievement goals among young children.' *Child Development,* 65: 1723–43.

Stanton, J., Shuy, R., Peyton, J. K. and Reed, L. (1988). *Dialogue journal communication: Classroom, linguistic, social, and cognitive views.* Norwood, NJ: Ablex.

Stein, N. and Glenn, C. G. (1979). 'An analysis of story comprehension in elementary school children.' In R. O. Freedle (ed.), *New directions in discourse processing.* Norwood, NJ: Ablex.

Steiner, G. (1998). *Errata: An examined life.* Cambridge, MA: Yale University Press.

Stern, D. (1985). *The interpersonal world of the infant: A view from psychoanalysis and developmental psychology.* New York: Basic Books.

Stetsenko, A. (1999). 'Social interaction, cultural tools, and the zone of proximal development: In search of a synthesis.' In M. Hedegaard, S. Chaiklin, S. Boedker and U. J. Jensen (eds), *Activity theory and social practice.* Proceedings of the ISCRAT 1998: Keynote speeches and panels (pp. 235–53). Aarhus, Denmark: Aarhus University Press.

Stevenson, H. (1983). 'How children learn? The quest for a theory.' In P. H. Mussen (ed.), *Handbook of child psychology, Vol. 1: History, theory, and methods,* 4th edn (pp. 213–37). New York: John Wiley.

Stigler, J. W. and Hiebert, J. (1998). 'Teaching is a cultural activity.' *American Educator,* Winter, 4–11.

Stigler, J. W. and Hiebert, J. (1999). *The teaching gap.* New York: Free Press.

Strauss, S. (1998). 'Cognitive development and science education: Toward a middle level model.' In I. E. Sigel and K. A. Renninger (eds), *Handbook of child psychology: Vol. 4: Child psychology in practice,* 5th edn (pp. 357–400). New York: John Wiley.

Suntio, A. (2000). *The object is expanded and enriched: Teachers as developers of teaching activity.* Unpublished Master's thesis. Department of Education, University of Helsinki (in Finnish).

Swales, J. M. (1990). *Genre analysis: English in academic and research settings.* Cambridge: Cambridge University Press.

Swisher, K. and Deyhle, D. (1992). 'Adapting instruction to culture.' In J. Reyhner (ed.), *Teaching American Indian students* (pp. 81–95). Norman: University of Oklahoma Press.

Taylor, P., Fraser, B. and Fisher, D. (1997). 'Monitoring constructivist classroom learning environments.' *International Journal of Educational Research,* 27 (4): 293–301.

Teasley, S. (1997). 'Talking about reasoning: How important is the peer group in peer collaboration?' In L. Resnick, R. Säljö, C. Pontecorvo and B. Burge (eds), *Discourses, tools and reasoning: Essays on situated cognition*. Berlin: Springer Verlag.

Tharp, R. G. (1997). *From at-risk to excellence: Research, theory and principles for practice*. Santa Cruz: Center for Research on Education, Diversity and Excellence, University of California.

Tharp, R. G. and Gallimore, R. (1988). *Rousing minds to life: Teaching, learning, and schooling in social context*. Cambridge: Cambridge University Press.

Tharp, R. G., Estrada, P., Dalton, S. S. and Yamauchi, L. (2000). *Teaching transformed: Achieving excellence, fairness, inclusion, harmony*. Denver, CO: Westview Press.

Tittle, C. (1989). 'Validity: Whose construction is it in the teaching and learning context?' *Educational Measurement: Issues and Practice*, 8 (1), Spring: 5–13.

Tittle, C. (1994). 'Toward an educational-psychology of assessment for teaching and learning – theories, contexts, and validation arguments. *Educational Psychologist*, 29 (3): 149–62.

Tolman, C. (1981). 'The metaphysics of relations in Klaus Riegel's "dialectics" of human development.' *Human Development*, 24: 33–51.

Tomasello, M. (1999). *The cultural origins of human cognition*. Cambridge, MA: Harvard University Press.

Torrance, H. (1993). 'Formative assessment: Some theoretical problems and empirical questions.' *Cambridge Journal of Education*, 23: 333–43.

Torrance, H. and Pryor, J. (1998). *Investigating formative assessment: Teaching, learning and assessment in the classroom*. Buckingham, UK: Open University Press.

Tukey, J. W. (1977). *Exploratory data analysis*. Reading, MA: Addison-Wesley.

Tunstall, P. and Gipps, C. (1996). 'Teacher feedback to young children in formative assessment: A typology.' *British Educational Research Journal*, 22 (4): 389–404.

Tyack, D. B. and Cuban, L. (1995). *Tinkering toward utopia: A century of public school reform*. Cambridge, MA: Harvard University Press.

Tzou, C. (2000). 'Learning about data creation.' Paper to be presented at the annual meeting of the American Educational Research Association, New Orleans.

UNICEF (2000). *La voz de los niños, las niñas y los adolescentes en Iberoamérica*.

Van Aalsvoort, J. (2000). *Chemistry in products: A cultural–historical approach to initial chemical education*. Proefschrift, the Netherlands: University of Utrecht.

Van der Veer, R. and Valsiner, J. (eds) (1994). *The Vygotsky reader*. Cambridge, MA: Blackwell Publishers.

Vasquez, O., Pease-Alvarez, L. and Shanon, S. (1994). *Pushing boundaries: Language and culture in a Mexicano community*. Cambridge: Cambridge University Press.

Vogt, L. A., Jordan, C. and Tharp, R. G. (1992). 'Explaining school failure, producing school success: Two cases.' In E. Jacob and C. Jordan (eds), *Minority education: Anthropological perspectives* (pp. 53–66). Norwood, NJ: Ablex. (Reprinted from *Anthropology and Education Quarterly*, 18, pp. 276–86).

Vygotskaya, G. (1999). 'On Vygotsky's research and life.' In S. Chaiklin, M. Hedegaard and U. J. Jensen (eds), *Activity theory and social practice* (pp. 31–38). Aarhus, Denmark: Aarhus University Press .

Vygotsky, L. (1963) *Thought and language*. Cambridge, MA: MIT Press. (Translation of the Russian original, published 1934)

Vygotsky, L. S. (1978). *Mind in society: The development of higher psychological processes*, ed. M. Cole, V. John-Steiner, S. Scribner and E. Souberman. Cambridge, MA: Harvard University Press.

Vygotsky, L. S. (1981). 'The genesis of higher mental functions.' In J. V. Wertsch (ed.), *The concept of activity in Soviet psychology* (pp. 144–88). Armonk, NY: Sharpe.

Vygotsky, L. S. (1983). 'Istorie razvitie vyshij psijicheski functii.' In *Sobranie Sochinenie, Tom 3. Problemi razvitie psijique* (pp. 11–340). Moscow: Pedagogika.

Vygotsky, L. S. (1984). 'Orudie I znak v razvitie rebenka' ['Tool and sign in child development']. In *Sobranie Sochinenie, Vol. 6: Nachonie Nasledtsvo* (pp. 5–90). Moscow: Pedagogica.

Vygotsky, L. S. (1986). *Thought and language* (trans. Alex Kozulin). Cambridge, MA: MIT Press.

Vygotsky, L. S. (1987). 'Thinking and speech' (trans. N. Minick). In R. W. Rieber and A. S. Carton (eds), *The collected works of L. S. Vygotsky, Vol. 1: Problems of general psychology* (pp. 39–285). New York: Plenum. (Original work published 1934)

Vygotsky, L. S. (1989). 'Concrete human psychology.' *Soviet Psychology*, 27 (2): 53–77.

Vygotsky, L. S. (1994). 'The problem of the environment.' In R. van der Veer and J. Valsiner (eds), *The Vygotsky reader* (pp. 338–54). Oxford: Blackwell Publishers.

Walkerdine, V. (1997). 'Redefining the subject in situated cognition theory.' In D. Kirshner and A. Whitson (eds), *Situated cognition theory: Social, neurological, and semiotic perspectives* (pp. 57–71). Hillsdale, NJ: Erlbaum.

Walsh, D. J., Tobin, J. J. and Graue, M. E. (1993). 'The interpretive voice: Qualitative research in early childhood education.' In B. Spodek (ed.) *Handbook of research on the education of young children*. New York: Macmillan.

Wartofsky, M. (1979). *Models, representation and scientific understanding*. Boston: Reidel.

Webb, Troper, and Fall (1995). Constructive activity and learning in collaborative small groups. *Journal of Educational Psychology*, 87 (3): 406–423.

Wegerif, R. and Mercer, N. (1997). 'Using computer-based text analysis to integrate quantitative and qualitative methods in the investigation of collaborative learning.' *Language and Education*, 11 (4): 271–86.

Wegerif, R. and Scrimshaw, P. (eds) (1997). *Computers and talk in the primary classroom*. Clevedon: Multilingual Matters.

Wegerif, R., Mercer, N. and Dawes, L. (1998) 'Software design to support discussion in the primary classroom.' *Journal of Computer Assisted Learning*, 14: 199–211.

Wegerif, R., Mercer, N. and Dawes, L. (1999). 'From social interaction to individual reasoning: An empirical investigation of a possible sociocultural model of cognitive development.' *Learning and Instruction*, 9 (6).

Wegerif, R., Rojas-Drummond, S. and Mercer, N. (1999). 'Language for the social construction of knowledge: Comparing classroom talk in Mexican pre-schools.' *Language and Education*, 13 (2): 133–50.

Wells, G. (1986). *The meaning makers: Children learning language and using language to learn*. Portsmouth, NH: Heinemann.

Wells, G. (1993). 'Reevaluating the IRF sequence: A proposal for the articulation of theories of activity and discourse for the analysis of teaching and learning in the classroom.' *Linguistics and Education*, 5: 1–37.

Wells, G. (1995). 'Language and the inquiry-oriented curriculum.' *Curriculum Inquiry*, 25 (3): 233–69.

Wells, G. (1996a). 'Using the tool-kit of discourse in the activity of learning and teaching.' *Mind, Culture, and Activity*, 3 (2): 74–101.

Wells, G. (1996b). 'Profesores e investigación.' *Cultura y Educación*, 1: 25–9.

Wells, G. (1999). *Dialogic inquiry: Towards a sociocultural practice and theory of education*. Cambridge: Cambridge University Press.

Wells, G. (2000). 'Dialogic inquiry in the classroom: Building on the legacy of Vygotsky.' In C. Lee and P. Smagorinsky (eds), *Vygotskian perspectives on literacy research* (pp. 51–85). New York: Cambridge University Press.

Wells, G. (ed.) (2001). *Action, talk, and text: Learning and teaching through inquiry*. New York: Teachers College Press.

Wenger, E. (1998). *Communities of practice: Learning, meaning, and identity*. Cambridge: Cambridge University Press.

Wertsch, J. V. (1985). 'Adult–child interaction as a source of self-regualtion in children.' In S. R. Yussen (ed.), *The growth of reflection in children*. Orlando, FL: Academic Press.

Wertsch, J. V. (ed.) (1985). *Culture, communication, and cognition: Vygotskian perspectives*. Cambridge: Cambridge University Press.

Wertsch, J. V. (1991). *Voices of the mind: A sociocultural approach to mediated action*. Cambridge MA: Harvard University Press.

Wertsch, J. V. (1995). 'The need for action in sociocultural research.' In J. V. Wertsch, P. del Río and A. Álvarez (eds), *Sociocultural studies of mind*. Cambridge: Cambridge University Press.

Wertsch, J. V. (1998). *Mind as action*. Oxford: Oxford University Press.

Wertsch, J. V. and Tulviste, P. (1992). 'L. S. Vygotsky and contemporary developmental psychology.' *Developmental Psychology*, 28 (4): 548–57.

Wilkerson, L. and Gijselaers, W. H. (1996). *Bringing problem-based learning to higher education: Theory and practice*. San Francisco: Jossey-Bass.

Williams, G. (1995). 'Joint Book-reading and Literacy Pedagogy: A Socio-semantic Interpretation.' Unpublished Ph.D. dissertation, Macquarie University, NSW, Australia.

Williams, G. (1999). 'The pedagogic device and the production of pedagogic discourse: A case example in early literacy education.' In F. Christie (ed.), *Pedagogy and the Shaping of Consciousness*. London: Cassell.

Wittgenstein, L. (1958). *Philosophical investigations*. Oxford: Blackwell Publishers.

Wittrock, M. C. and Baker, E. L. (1991). *Testing and cognition*. Englewood Cliffs, NJ: Prentice-Hall.

Wolf, D. (1989). 'Portfolio assessment: Sampling student work.' *Educational Leadership*, 46 (7): 35–9.

Wolf, D., Bixby, J., Glenn, J. and Gardner, H. (1991). 'To use their minds well: Investigating new forms of student assessment.' *Review of Research in Education*, 17: 31–74.

Wolf, E. (2001). *Pathways of power*. Berkeley: University of California Press.

Wood, D., Bruner, J. and Ross, G. (1976) The role of tutoring in problem-solving. Journal of Child Psychology and Child Psychiatry, 17: 89–100.

Wood, D. and Wood, H. (1983). 'Questioning the pre-school child.' *Educational Review*, 35 (2): 149–62.

Wyatt, J. D. (1978–9). 'Native involvement in curriculum development: The native teacher as cultural broker.' *Interchange*, 9: 17–28.

Yaroshevsky, M. G. and Gurgenidze, G. S. (1997). 'Epilogue.' In R. W. Reiber and J. Wollack (eds), *The collected works of L. S. Vygotsky, Vol. 3: Problems of theory and history of psychology* (pp. 345–69). New York: Plenum.

Zaporozhets, A. V. (1970). 'The development of perception in the preschool child.' In R. Brown (ed.), *Cognitive development in children: Five monographs of the Society for Research in Child Development* (pp. 647–66). Chicago: University of Chicago Press.

Zaporozhets, A. V. (1987). *Vospratie i deitsvie* [Perception and action]. Moscow: Progress.

Zarbatany, L., Hartmann, D. P. and Rankin, D. B. (1990). 'The psychological functions of preadolescent peer activities.' *Child Development*, 61 (4): 1067–80.

Index

19627758R00178

Printed in Poland
by Amazon Fulfillment
Poland Sp. z o.o., Wrocław